Loanwords in the Chinese Language

A loanword, or *wailaici*, is a word with similar meaning and phonetic form to a word from a foreign language that has been naturalized in the recipient language. From ancient times, cultural exchanges between China and other countries has brought and integrated a myriad of loanwords to the Chinese language. Approaching the topic from a diachronic perspective, this volume is the first book-length work to chart the developmental trajectory, features, functions, and categories of loanwords into Chinese.

Beginning with a general introduction to the Chinese loanword system, the author delves deeper to explore trends and standardization in Chinese loanword studies and the research landscape of contemporary loanword studies more generally. Combining theoretical reflections with real-life examples of Chinese loanwords, the author discusses not only long-established examples from the dictionary but also a great number of significant loanwords adopted in the 21st century. The author shows how the complexity of the Chinese loanword system is intertwined with the intricacies of the Chinese character system.

This title will be an essential reference for students, scholars, and general readers who are interested in Chinese loanwords, linguistics, and language and culture.

Shi Youwei is Professor at Meikai University, Associate Professor of Minzu University of China, Guest Professor of Osaka University of Foreign Studies, and Professor of Nanchang University. His main research interests include modern Chinese grammar, loanwords in the Chinese Language, and teaching Chinese as a foreign language.

Chinese Linguistics

Chinese Linguistics series selects representative and frontier works in linguistic disciplines including lexicology, grammar, phonetics, dialectology, philology and rhetoric. Mostly published in Chinese before, the selection has had far-reaching influence on China's linguistics and offered inspiration and reference for the world's linguistics. The aim of this series is to reflect the general level and latest development of Chinese linguistics from an overall and objective view.

Titles in this series currently include:

Practical Grammar of Modern Chinese I
Overview and Notional Words
Liu Yuehua, Pan Wenyu and Gu Wei

Practical Grammar of Modern Chinese II
Function Words
Liu Yuehua, Pan Wenyu and Gu Wei

Practical Grammar of Modern Chinese III
Sentence Constituents
Liu Yuehua, Pan Wenyu and Gu Wei

Practical Grammar of Modern Chinese IV
Simple Sentence, Compound Sentence and Discourse
Liu Yuehua, Pan Wenyu and Gu Wei

Loanwords in the Chinese Language
Shi Youwei

For more information, please visit https://www.routledge.com/Chinese-Linguistics/book-series/CL

Loanwords in the Chinese Language

Shi Youwei

Taylor & Francis Group

LONDON AND NEW YORK

This book is published with financial support from the Chinese Fund for the Humanities and Social Sciences.

First published in English 2021
by Routledge
2 Park Square, Milton Park, Abingdon, Oxon, OX14 4RN

and by Routledge
52 Vanderbilt Avenue, New York, NY 10017

Routledge is an imprint of the Taylor & Francis Group, an informa business

© 2021 Shi Youwei
Translated by Hu Zhengmao

The right of Shi Youwei to be identified as author of this work has been asserted by him in accordance with sections 77 and 78 of the Copyright, Designs and Patents Act 1988.

All rights reserved. No part of this book may be reprinted or reproduced or utilised in any form or by any electronic, mechanical, or other means, now known or hereafter invented, including photocopying and recording, or in any information storage or retrieval system, without permission in writing from the publishers.

Trademark notice: Product or corporate names may be trademarks or registered trademarks, and are used only for identification and explanation without intent to infringe.

English Version by permission of The Commercial Press.

British Library Cataloguing-in-Publication Data
A catalogue record for this book is available from the British Library

Library of Congress Cataloging-in-Publication Data
A catalog record has been requested for this book

ISBN: 978-0-367-67439-7 (hbk)
ISBN: 978-1-003-13135-9 (ebk)

Typeset in Times New Roman
by codeMantra

Contents

Preface to the revised and enlarged Chinese edition and
its English version   vii
Preface to the first edition   xi
Preface to the enlarged edition   xv

1 Chinese loanwords: an external lexical influence on the native language   1

2 A historical overview of Chinese loanwords   32

3 The characteristics and functions of Chinese loanwords   106

4 Classification of Chinese loanwords   136

5 Trends in and standardization of Chinese loanwords   187

6 An overview of Chinese loanword studies   206

Appendix: a typological table of Chinese loanwords
(and their relatives)   239
Bibliography of loanword studies   243
Index   267

Preface to the revised and enlarged Chinese edition and its English version

I feel at once pleasantly surprised and uneasy that several overseas publishers have expressed interest in publishing a translated version of this book so that their local readers can get a handle on loanwords in the Chinese language. One cause for such uneasiness is its possible errors and omissions as the book deals with both theoretical reflections on and real-life examples of Chinese loanwords. Another concern is that, despite revision in the 2010s, it is still hard to reflect developments in the new century as the book was first written in the 1990s. A third concern is that the book has not caught up with the rapid development of *zimuci*, essentially borrowed initialisms, in the Chinese language in the 21st century and has thus offered little theoretical discussion about their qualification as loanwords. A fourth concern is that, as part of the Chinese language popular series by the Commercial Press (*Shangwu yinshuguan* or CP for short), this book is expected to serve general readers, but at the same time, it has attempted to construct a preliminary discourse system for loanword studies as a discipline. With detailed academically oriented investigations into quite a few topics, the book becomes something of a mix between being part of the CP popular series and an academic monograph, in terms of both content and style. One last cause for uneasiness is that occasional errors or inconsistencies can still be detected (and corrected), despite several rounds of proofreading.

Given the established body and structure of the book, a major revision, including either substantial addition or substantial deletion, does not sound realistic in such a short span of time. So, I have decided to keep the current framework as it is while doing proper revisions and expansion in order to try to present a broader or a more balanced perspective and some clues toward facilitating the translation of this current enlarged edition. Specifically, addition is made mainly in the following three areas.

The first is a general picture of Chinese loanwords and loanword studies in the early 21st century, with the correspondingly added Sections 2.7 in Chapter 2 and 6.8 in Chapter 6, along with a table of MA and PhD dissertations in China related to loanword studies in the 21st century (2000–2018) and an updated and expanded Bibliography (a selected Bibliography for the

English version, though), all aimed to reflect the latest developments during this period.

The second is the provision of theoretical discussion about borrowed initialisms or *zimuci* in Chinese, as represented in the addition of Section 1.4.2 in Chapter 1. Since there has been no general academic consensus on the linguistic identity of such words, a new approach is needed, and I think, for now, we may just classify *zimuci* among quasi-loanwords so as to de-escalate the on-going controversy and concentrate on more meaningful aspects of research.

The third is the addition of Section 6.9 in Chapter 6 as an afterword to finally reflect on the subject matter and its academic research. In addition, the opportunity has been taken to correct a number of errors and omissions in the book and to eliminate the Key to the Phonetic Symbols and Characters, which was placed right after the front cover in the previous impressions, so that phonetic symbols used in the book in the current version revert to the original phonetic symbols from the source.

I have decided that the at once popular and academic mix is related to the very purpose of this CP series, which is to provide new views and the latest developments in the subject matter. In fact, as an innovative approach in the publishing field, this new series by the CP is designed to follow the style of the late Chinese linguist Zhu Dexi in his exemplary work *Yufa dawen* (*Grammar: questions and answers*), also included in this CP series, which is not a mere popular reader for the general public but one with a perfect combination of general interest and academic depth.

When the book was begun, there was a lack of adequate resources to refer to since the loanword was a fairly new topic in the general study of the Chinese language, resulting in both insufficient data collection and theoretical buildup. So, the writing tended to oscillate between comprehensive introduction and theoretical discussion, presumably in an attempt to perform a delicate balancing act between the need for deeper exploration and the general restrictions on book length in this series. Given this challenge, no fundamental change should be expected of the current revision, which I hope readers can understand and put up with.

As the latest that the book covers can only be the present, it may become completely outdated in a few years' time due to new findings. As I said in the Preface to the first edition, I "expect to see more and better researches by others in the future to render this book obsolete so that it can end its mission sooner," and that wish holds true to this day.

By the time the revised and enlarged Chinese edition gets into print, its English version may have already been released to the public. I would like to thank Routledge, the very first overseas publisher to have expressed interest in publishing an English version of this book, and Professor Hu Zhengmao, the untiring translator, who might have had to rack his brains to figure out many of the terms or expressions in the book. No wonder the inter-lingual translator is a magic messenger for cross-cultural communication, academic or otherwise. Thanks also go to Ms. Gong Ying, the CP copyeditor of the book, for her meticulous reading, saving me from quite a few otherwise regrettable inaccuracies when finalizing this new edition. For those efforts, they certainly deserve more credit.

Shi Youwei
February 2019
Beijing, China

Preface to the first edition

Ten years ago, I promised to write a book on loanwords for the Commercial Press. However, too many distractions kept me from working on it until my teaching in Japan. The reasons for which I chose to start writing in earnest in Japan are both accidental and natural. Books on loanwords can easily be found in Japan, and the country's loanword studies are detailed, in-depth, and enlightening. Chinese scholars in Japan have also recently published a number of monographs on lexical exchange between the two countries. All has prompted me to tap into the convenient resources in fulfilling my long-cherished wish.

There are quite a few things I feel strongly about in the process of writing the book. The first concerns the accessibility, or lack thereof, of relevant resources and citation. Despite their obvious Chinese origin, some resources are counter-intuitively difficult to find in China but unbelievably easy to obtain overseas. Though perhaps made earlier in China, relevant Chinese dictionaries lag far behind their overseas counterparts for the lack of earlier documented references or, if available, the lack of the date of the first attested appearance, making it impossible to know where to find the references without going to a lot of trouble. I strongly believe that only with our academic resources well documented and referenced, and users being taken into full consideration can there be a solid foundation for rapid and sustained enhancement in Chinese scholarship.

The second concerns the apparent tension between Chinese loanwords and the purity of the language, on which divergent opinions exist. At one end of the continuum, the small size of Chinese loanwords is believed to indicate that the Chinese language is not open enough or advanced enough, as if the loanword is the only reliable yardstick by which to measure the standing, if it exists at all, of a language. At the other end, however, some simply do not acknowledge that a considerable number of words used in China originated from Japanese or that those Chinese words which did come from Japanese are loanwords at all, as if admitting to an external origin or a certain number of those borrowed words would immediately make the Chinese (language and people) lose face. Neither of the views are objective. We cannot ascertain the position of a language simply from how much it has lexically borrowed from others, nor can we decide whether it is pure or clean simply based on the uniformity or diversity of its lexical source.

Mutual influence among languages in contact with one another has been in existence since ancient times: wherever there is inter-ethnic or inter-racial contact, there may be cross-influence. Direct borrowing of a foreign lexicon is just one manifestation of cross-linguistic influence, another being translation. The ultimate choice of one over the other is determined by the intrinsic characteristics of the concerned languages themselves rather than arbitrary human will. All we can and should do is understand those linguistic properties and accommodate or facilitate such cross-linguistic influence. It should be crystal clear that, should there be one, a pure language, in the sense of the single lexical source or origin, must necessarily be an uncompetitive language because it will inevitably lead to a diminishing user community. On the other hand, the evaluation of the viability of a language boils downs to its practicality, namely, its perfectibility in signifying the things or concepts it is supposed to in the current society and in meeting the current communicative needs. On issues of language contact and cross-linguistic influence, national identity or awareness is needed, to be sure, but a global perspective is more important so that a healthy measure of tension between the two is maintained. In other words, any idea or practice in linguistic research that only considers one aspect to the total neglect of others is not only unhelpful but is doomed to be divorced from reality.

One last thing I feel strongly about is the renewed sense of mission toward loanword studies. I still recall the passionate lament in the late Chinese scholar Ji Xianlin's Foreword to my book *Yiwenhua de shizhe: wailaici* (*Messenger for foreign cultures: loanwords*, 1991; renamed in reverse order *Wailaici: yiwenhua de shizhe* in its 2004 enlarged edition), which was aimed at providing a cultural overview of Chinese loanwords by synthesizing the loanword-related etymological discoveries by previous researchers. He pointed out in the Foreword that

> in some of the developed countries there are usually a whole group of scholars dedicated to loanword studies and a good number of loanword dictionaries available. Ordinary people there can easily refer to those ready resources any time they become interested, which in turn can not only expand their specific knowledge but over time also enhance their self-culture. In sharp contrast, there are few scholars dedicated to loanword studies and even fewer monographs or dictionaries on loanwords in China, so the general public here barely has any idea of this area. This goes highly against the general culture of the country's reform and opening-up.

This forthright and incisive remark has long been etched in my heart as a constant prod to keep me moving forward. Given the general indifference and narrow-minded approaches to loanword studies, I feel a keen sense of mission and responsibility in exploring this seemingly narrow subject-matter from a theoretical and more comprehensive perspective, and calling for academic attention to it from more interested scholars. With this calling in mind, I have completed writing this book and expect to see more and better researches by others in the future to render this book obsolete so that it can end its mission sooner.

I am indebted to the Commercial Press, and its senior editor Mr. Zhang Wanqi, for their enthusiastic support; to the Japanese sinologist Mr. Kiyohide Arakawa for giving me his new book *The formation and dissemination of common academic terms in modern Japan and China* (1997, in Japanese), which adds substantive weight to the final revision of this book; to Mr. Yao Te Hwai of the Chinese Language Society of Hong Kong for mailing me the English-to-Chinese version done by Mr. Huang Heqing of *The Formation of Modern Chinese Lexicon and Its Evolution Toward a National Language* (Masini 1993), which played a particularly important role in supplementing the key chapters of my book; and to my wife Qian Yuping for her painstaking statistical assistance (thus causing her retinal detachment). Without such aid and support, I could not have completed the book. In keeping with the consistent style of this popular language series, one-fifth of the final draft has to be cut off, including the loanword-related key terms index. Finally, it is a great pity that the final copy of the book was already sent to the printer when I chanced upon *The Golden Peaches of Samarkand: A Study of T'ang Exotics*, a highly influential work related to historical loanword studies by American scholar Edward H. Schafer, so it was a bit too late to draw on his scholarship. I hereby apologize to my readers.

Shi Youwei
December 1997
Osaka, Japan

Preface to the enlarged edition

This book was initially titled *Hanyu de wailaici* (hanyu meaning "Chinese," wailaici meaning "loanword") instead of the current *Hanyu wailaici*. In comparison, the obvious addition of the little function word *de* in the initial title was intended to preclude semantic ambiguity but was ultimately dropped because, with *de*, it would indeed not have read like a typical Chinese title, though it would have unmistakably meant "loanwords in the Chinese language" rather than "loanwords of Chinese origin," as the current title might sometimes be construed. In fact, this titular dilemma due to semantic ambiguity prompted me to elaborate in a rather long paper on the grammatical differences between these two kinds of wording, arguing that the addition of *de* in this case implies the possibility for predicational explanation, while the absence of *de* does not. To avoid any further confusion, therefore, loanwords discussed in this book generally have their linguistic origin specified, such as "loanwords of English origin."

In fact, *wailaici*, the prevalent Chinese equivalent to the English "loanword(s)," is also a semantically ambiguous term. Contrary to what the Chinese term literally suggests ("word or words coming from outside": *wai* meaning "outside" or "foreign," *lai* meaning "coming," and *ci* meaning "word"), the loanword does not usually come to the borrowing language on its own initiative; instead, the borrowing language (or its speaking community) intentionally embraces it. What is more, loanwords in the Chinese context also contain some loan-blends or hybrids and Chinese words of Japanese origin, which is again drastically different from the concept of *gairaigo* 外来語, the Japanese equivalent of "loanwords." Some argue that loanwords also include borrowed phrases besides *ci* or "words," though those phrases will all be lexicalized if borrowed by means of phonemic loaning, which is much different from the predominantly semantic loaning for lexical borrowing between those major European languages. Given the proverbial significance of naming, the apparent ambiguity in the semantic extension of *wailaici*, and the obvious phonetic confusion of *jieci*—an alternative Chinese term for *wailaici*, with its Chinese homophone meaning "preposition"—I draw on the broader term *jieyu* (meaning "borrowed lexicon") created by modern Chinese linguist Zhao Yuanren and propose here to use a new term called *jieyuci* (meaning "borrowed word or phrase") as the equivalent of "loanword" so as to reflect the central concept of "borrowing" in the universally recognized English term on the one hand and incorporate the meanings of alternative Chinese terms on the other hand.

Speaking of terms or terminology, I strongly feel that Chinese scholars are overly cautious in creating conceptual terms, despite their solid research, very much like "a transmitter rather than a creative thinker" (*shuerbuzuo*), a self-deprecating comment by Confucius. A new term oftentimes reflects a new concept, and a new concept may open up a new academic realm, thus gaining the initial position to set the parameters of acceptable discourse. Of course, that initial advantageous position would immediately be lost without well-grounded follow-up research to lead the field. I believe both are urgently needed in China's academic community today.

Since the publication of this book in 2000, more than a decade ago, there have been a constant inflow of new loanwords, new discoveries concerning loanword resources, and new published researches on loanword studies, all of which have helped broaden my understanding of the field. Weighing the possible pros and cons, I decide to take the reprint of the book by the Commercial Press as an opportunity for revision and enrichment to better serve the reader. Beyond the correction of inaccuracies and omissions, nearly every page has been updated in one way or another. Major paragraph-level revisions or additions include: Section 1.1.3 in Chapter 1 on defining "loanword"; Section 1.3 in Chapter 1 on some loanword-related terms; Section 2.2.1 in Chapter 2 on the origin of the loanword of Sanskrit origin, *Zhina* (China); Section 2.4.4.2 in Chapter 2 to supplement the historical role of the Western missionaries and scholars in the Ming and Qing dynasties; Section 2.6.5 in Chapter 2 to analyze graphic loaning from Japanese in the late 20th century; Section 4.1.3 in Chapter 4 on Chinese self-made words from foreign lexical elements; Section 4.2.1.1 in Chapter 4 on the trichotomy of use-oriented assimilation of loanwords (original, extended, and figurative); Section 4.4.3 in Chapter 4 on my proposed lexical trichotomy (terminology, daily-life lexicon, and proper nouns) and a new interpretation of terminology; Section 5.2.2.1 in Chapter 5 on the discrepancy between graphic transcription and phonetic readjustment; Section 6.1 in Chapter 6 for additional areas of loanword studies; Sections 6.2, 6.4, and 6.5 in Chapter 6 on the history and developments of loanword studies; and, finally, the addition of a typological table of loanwords at the end of the book. I have also added what I can access as regards the latest loanword research to the bibliography. Given various terms discussed in this book, a key terms index is provided this time for easier reference. For all the revision and enrichment, there must still be errors and omissions, which I hope readers can put up with.

The study of loanwords is heavily dependent on reference books, the most important of which, in my case, is the 12-volume *Hanyu da cidian* (Luo 1993), the largest unabridged Chinese dictionary on historical principles and lexicographically, comparable to the *Oxford English Dictionary*. Unfortunately, many words from the late Qing Dynasty up to the first half of the 20th century are not found in the Chinese dictionary. In most cases, it also fails to provide earlier documented references or, if they are available, the more specific date of the attested appearance, which, in turn, causes too much difficulty, for instance, in the determination of graphic loanwords from Japanese in the writing of this book. Had the dictionary been more considerate and open-minded, it would have been more helpful for loanword research. While no one knows when, exactly, the second edition of the *Hanyu da cidian* will be available, the comparable 20-volume Japanese dictionary *Nihon kokugo daijiten* by Shogakukan, a private publisher already published its second edition in 2002, following the first edition in 1976. More important than a mere expansion of entry words, the Japanese dictionary not only provides earlier documentary evidence of usage but also indicates the year and month of the first attestation for most entries in its second edition. So, for good reason, we look forward to that direly needed information from the revised second edition of the *Hanyu da cidian*. Interestingly, the inadequacies in the Chinese dictionary have already been partially remedied, not through institutional efforts but by an individual practically single-handedly: namely, the *Jin xiandai hanyu xinci ciyuan cidian* (2001) and the *Jin xiandai ciyuan* (2010) by Huang Heqing on the etymology of modern Chinese neologisms, including loanwords with documented first attestations of usage. Given these thought-provoking contrasts, we sincerely hope to see improvement in the greatly anticipated revised edition of the *Hanyu da cidian* soon.

One probable cause for the lack of documented lexical evidence of usage in the *Hanyu da cidian* is that, while lexical resources from the late Qing dynasty up to the first half of the 20th century may touch upon something that is, for whatever reason, considered sensitive, so much of the lexicon and its evidence of usage might lie beyond the self-imposed scope. However, from a broader perspective, it is exactly words and documentary evidence of their usage that are needed for works of reference to present an objective and historical record. After all, restrictions, however inadvertent, imposed on others will ultimately constrain oneself and hinder the progress of scientific enquiry. As truth seeking is the highest academic pursuit, we should be more open-minded in order to free ourselves from the psychological, intellectual, institutional, or bibliographical bondage for the best possible resource collection and collation. Only in this way can our lexical research be better grounded and our academic works of reference be truly comparable to those of the best in the world.

As my main research is on grammar, I am just a latecomer and part-timer to loanword studies. Ten years ago, with a strongly felt sense of mission because of the public's tepid interest in such studies in China, I wrote this book in the hope of building a humble bridge to help more interested scholars walk across barriers into this seemingly small aspect of language. The more I wrote in the process, however, the more I found myself doing serious research into the loanword instead of merely working on a book of the

Chinese language popular series. Considering the fact that there has been little, if any, innovative book-length research dedicated to loanword studies since the publication of *Xiandai hanyu wailaici yanjiu* [*A study of loanwords in Modern Chinese*] (Gao and Liu 1958) more than half a century ago, and in keeping with the publisher's aim of this popular series, which is aimed toward a perfect mix of both general interest and academic depth, I decided to continue writing along that path. In a similar vein, this revision aims to add more research-oriented content so as to facilitate deeper inquiry for future scholars.

It is really encouraging and refreshing to have seen a constant stream of new publications on the Chinese loanword since the beginning of the 21st century by those admirable and inspiring researchers who choose a life of solitude and simplicity. In closing, I would like to quote the last two lines of a poem I wrote during the Spring Festival earlier this year as a token of respect to the researchers of common interest, with best wishes for the future: "Loneliness is best appreciated by the sedentary scholar; the outstanding are best recognized through unpretentious charm."

Shi Youwei
June 2011
Beijing, China

1 Chinese loanwords

An external lexical influence on the native language

1.1 Loanword as a concept

1.1.1 Defining the concept: the first cut

A tentative definition. A loanword (or *wailaici* 外来词 in Chinese, which literally mean "words coming from outside") is a word of foreign origin and is, in a sense, equivalent to a "borrowed word" (or *jieci* 借词 in Chinese). Generally speaking, a loanword in the Chinese language is a word which must, first and foremost, be in a direct or indirect etymological relationship in terms of meaning with a certain word of a foreign language; that is completely or partially (about 50%) borrowed from that corresponding foreign word in terms of phonetic form; and that has, to varying degrees, been naturalized in the recipient Chinese language. Strictly speaking, a word is not a loanword unless or until it has been in use in the Chinese language for a relatively long period of time or with considerable frequency. Take *jiasha* 袈裟 (the outer patchwork—usually saffron—robe worn by a Buddhist monk), for example. Though written in Chinese characters, *jiasha* comes from the Sanskrit word *kasaya* in both meaning and pronunciation. *Bingqilin* 冰淇淋, or its variant *bingjiling* 冰激凌, is another example. Borrowed from the English "ice cream" in both meaning and composition, the Chinese loanword represents the second component of the English compound (cream) in sound (*qilin* or *jiling*) and the first component (ice) in lexical meaning with an autochthonous Chinese morpheme (*bing*, meaning "ice"), thus making it a hybrid kind of loanword. *Kache* 卡车 ("car") is still another example: it only partially originates from another language in that the first component *ka* 卡 is borrowed in both meaning and pronunciation from the English "car," while the second component *che* 车 meaning "vehicle," an autochthonous Chinese morpheme, is added as semantic marker for the purpose of easier comprehension and acceptance by Chinese speakers. Having been in use in the Chinese language for a long time, words like these have all taken root and become *bona fide* members of the Chinese lexicon. In the following section, we will explore the loanword as a concept before offering a revised definition.

2 *Chinese loanwords*

Four tiers of loanwords. There are four basic tiers in what we usually refer to as loanwords despite the quasi nature for the last tier.

Tier One. Tier-one loanwords refer to total phonemic loaning, that is, the borrowing of sound, from other languages (e.g. *buding* 布丁 from the English "pudding") or those total phonemic loans added with a Chinese morpheme as semantic marker (e.g. *kache* from the English "car").

Tier Two. Tier-two loanwords refer to part phonemic and part semantic loaning, that is, the borrowing of lexical meaning, from other languages, such as *motuoche* 摩托车 (motorcycle: *motuo* as phonemic loaning from "motor" and *che* as semantic loaning from "cycle") and the above-mentioned *bingjilin* (*bing* as semantic loaning from "ice" and *jilin* as phonemic loaning from "cream").

Tier Three. Tier-three Chinese loanwords, with a broader definition than the first two tiers, refer to graphic loaning, i.e. adoption of both the writing form and meaning from other languages. There are two kinds of graphic loaning. One is direct borrowing of words formed partially or wholly out of Western alphabetic letters (fully letter-composed words are called *zimuci* in Chinese, and there will be separate and detailed discussions about them later). Because of their unmistakable foreign origin but ambiguous linguistic Chinese-ness, there is still some controversy over the status of these fully or partially letter-composed words. This book regards those words in alphabetic graphic loaning which have already taken root and settled down in the Chinese language as loanwords in general or at least as "quasi-loanwords." The other kind of graphic loaning involves the borrowing of those Japanese words which are composed of Chinese characters (called *kanji* in Japan). These words are not directly phonemic but predominantly graphic or graphemic borrowing, such as *shenjing* 神经 (meaning "nerve"), which is directly graphemically borrowed from the Japanese *shinkei* 神経 (*shinkei*: the Romanized representation based on the Japanese pronunciation system of *on-yomi*[1]) and *shouxu* 手续 ("procedure"), which comes directly from the Japanese *tetsuzuki* 手続 (*tetsuzuki*: the Romanized transcription based on the Japanese pronunciation system of *kun-yomi*). Both composed of and written in Chinese characters, these directly borrowed words are, in their origin, either created or modified in the source culture. *Tetsuzuki* belongs to a kind of Japanese word which uses Chinese characters to express autochthonous Japanese morphemes, so its corresponding Chinese *shouxu* is a typical loanword. *Shinkei* belongs to another kind of Japanese word which borrows Chinese morphemes or lexicons and infuses them with a slightly new meaning; the words are borrowed in graphic form and semantic shape but not according to the pronunciation of the borrowed language, so such Chinese words of foreign etymological origin may better be regarded as a kind of "quasi-loanwords." At the same time, seen from the perspective of the Chinese language, because they are completely naturalized in Chinese—with Chinese characters with basically the same meaning and graphic form as well as the same word formation as the Chinese language—these loosely termed loanwords may also be regarded as "quasi-indigenous Chinese words" (more on this in Section 1.4 of this chapter).

Tier Four. The tier-four Chinese loanword refers to loan-translation or calque, that is, a word which is morphemically translated from its corresponding foreign word, with the original morphemic order and lexical structure retained, such as *heiban* 黑板 (*hei* meaning "black" and *ban* meaning "board") from the English word "blackboard." Such words may be considered loanwords in the broadest sense of the term or, theoretically speaking, may at least be treated as another kind of quasi-loanwords. In general, however, words in tier four are not placed in the *bona fide* Chinese loanword category in mainland China; this book will follow that convention for now.

Words with borrowed morpheme(s). It should be noted that not all words which contain borrowed lexical elements are loanwords. Despite some borrowed phonemic elements, semantically speaking, these words do not come completely from foreign words and therefore are not generally classified as *bona fide* loanwords. Take *shafa tao* 沙发套, *lu jipu* 驴吉普, *dadi* 打的, and *pingtan* 乒坛. As their component parts, respectively, *shafa* is obviously a phonemic loan from the English word "sofa"; *jipu* comes from "jeep"; *di* is short for *dishi*, a (Cantonese) phonemic loan from "taxi"; and *ping* is short for *pingpang* 乒乓, a phonemic loan from "ping-pong" or table tennis. But, taken as a whole, these words are formed with the addition of indigenous Chinese morphemes, such as "*tao*" (meaning "cover" in English), "*lu*" (donkey), "*da*" (take), and "*tan*" (field or arena), to the above phonemically borrowed foreign components, resulting in distinctively Chinese practices or phenomena. In other words, the words are derivative of loanwords but are not *bona fide* loanwords themselves. Some other words, like *dika* 涤卡 (from Dacron + khaki) and *diba* 迪吧 (from disco + bar), originate from foreign elements but do not in their totality come directly from one single foreign word; instead, they are created in the Chinese language itself as a combination of two independently used terms (e.g. "disco" and "bar"). Their borrowed elements are merely imported morphemes that join the words as component parts (more on this in Sections 4.2.1, 4.2.3, and 4.3 in Chapter 4).

1.1.2 Types of loanword formation

There are two basic types of loanword formation: lexical borrowing and substrate influence in language assimilation.

Lexical borrowing. There are two kinds of lexical borrowing: borrowing through proximity and borrowing through culture. Borrowing through proximity occurs either under duress or when multi-ethnic groups live together, whereas borrowing through culture happens in the process of cultural diffusion. The majority of Chinese loanwords enter the language by means of the latter, but historically, there have also been cases of borrowing through proximity, either during specific periods in time or in some demographically distinct areas, such as those during the early Yuan dynasty

(1271–1368 AD), in Taiwan under Japanese rule (1895–1945), and in some ethnically populated frontier regions.

Substrate influence. Substrate influence refers to a process in which there remain some linguistic residual fragments of one's native language (called "substrate") in its adoption of (or replacement by) another language (called "superstrate") as a result of multi-ethnic integration and/or cultural integration based upon multi-ethnic contact. These linguistic traces out of this long accumulative process may contain not only phonemic and syntactic features but also lexical units of the original substrate language. For example, the Cantonese dialect of Chinese still retains some of the phonemic lexicon used by the ancient non-Han *Baiyue* 百越 (literally "Hundred *Yue*") ethnic peoples who lived in southern China between the first millennium BC and the first millennium AD, such as the Cantonese la^5 (meaning "search"), pronounced in the fifth tone (first tone in the ethnic Zhuang language 状语 and fifth tone in the ethnic Dong 侗语 and Shui 水语 languages); *tam* (meaning "tread") in the sixth tone (tam^6 in the sixth tone in Zhuang and tam^6 in the sixth tone in Dong and tom^2 in the second tone in the ethnic Li language 黎语); and kap^7 (meaning "frog") in the seventh tone (kop^7 in the seventh tone in the ethnic Zhuang, Dai 傣语, and Thai languages 泰语). Residual substrate influence is fundamentally different from situations in which some language (or speech community) borrows, of its own volition, from another language in order to enrich the borrowing language. But, as far as the end result is concerned, they are the same: seen from the standpoint of the recipient language, words arising from either type of formation come from outside and have not altered the recipient language in any meaningful way.

Therefore, loanwords can be seen as the result of either or both of two processes. One is lexical borrowing, the result of which can be called "borrowed words" (*jieci*) in the narrow sense. The other is language shift due to the above-mentioned racial/ethnic and cultural process, the resultant words of which may be called "substrate words," though they are not strictly "borrowed words," as the term is generally understood. Some can be the result of both: Chinese words such as *gege* 格格 (young daughter of a rich or noble family) and *saqima* 萨其马 (candied fritter, similar to a Rice Krispies square), which originated from the Manchu language (*gege* and *sacima*, respectively), might have been borrowed by both the Han Chinese and the Manchu linguistic fragments retained in Chinese when the Manchu people abandoned their ethnic language. So, while it is highly improbable to determine the exact types of formation for some lexical component units, it might not be a bad idea to collectively place them in the category of loanwords for easier systematic analysis. This is one major aspect where loanwords conceptually differ from borrowed words.

Direct and backflow lexical entry. Examined from the perspective of language contact involving the ties between loanwords and the interacting languages, both loanwords of the first lexical borrowing and substrate loanwords arrive in the recipient language by means of either direct entry or backflow entry. Backflow entry refers to a phenomenon in language contact in which a word in language B, which is originally borrowed from language A but has later been assimilated by and integrated into language B, flows back to language A as a loanword. This is a very obvious case of lexical backflow, and it has occurred on many occasions throughout the history of the contact between Chinese and the languages of other ethnic communities.

A classic example of Chinese loanwords via backflow entry in modern history is *boshi* 博士, borrowed graphically *verbatim* from Japanese, which was, in turn, borrowed from Old Chinese 博士. Further back in Chinese history, there were quite a few of these return loanwords, some even experiencing multiple flows back and forth. Here are some examples: *sangkun* 桑昆 (a high-ranking military title in the Yuan dynasty), which was borrowed from the Mongolian word *sanggun*, which was, in turn, first borrowed from the Chinese word *jiangjun* 将军 (incidentally, *sangkun* shared the same etymological origin with another return loanword, *wenxiang* 详稳, used in China's Liao dynasty, which lasted from 907 AD to 1125 AD); *laba* 喇叭, which came from the Mongolian *labai*, which was from the Turkic *labay*, which originated from the Chinese *luobei* 螺贝; *tuli* 秃里 (a large square banner symbolizing the status of a general in the Yuan dynasty), which was from the Mongolian *tug*, which, in turn, originated from the Chinese *dao* 纛; *shahai* 沙海 (cloth shoes), which came from the Mongolian *saxai*, which, in turn, originated from the Chinese *saxie* 靸鞋; *taiji* 台吉 (title of a duke or regional magistrate), which was borrowed from the Mongolian *taiji*, which, in turn, originated from the Chinese *taizi* 太子; *bahashi* 八哈失 or *bashi* 八石 (teacher), which came from the Mongolian *bagsi*, which, in turn, originated from *boshi* 博士; *bashi* 把势 or 把式 (a skillful master good at martial arts; skill; *wushu*), which came from the Mongolian *bagsi*, which came from the Manchu *baksi*, which, in turn, originated from the Chinese *boshi* 博士; *zhangjing* 章京 (a title of a military official in the Qing dynasty 清朝, spanning the years 1644–1911), which came from the Manchu *janggin*, which, in turn, originated from the Chinese *jiangjun* 将军; *fujin* 福晋 (an emperor-conferred title for a prince or other nobility in the Qing dynasty), which came from the Manchu *fujin*, which was, in turn, borrowed from the Chinese *furen* 夫人; and *sefu* 瑟夫 (master; teacher), which came from the Manchu *sefu*, which was originally from the Chinese *shifu* 师父.

Many Chinese loanwords of Japanese origin were originally Old Chinese words, which Japanese speakers borrowed and modified for the purpose of translating the Western lexicon and later lent back to modern Chinese, such as *jingji* 经济, *geming* 革命, *zhonghe* 中和, *roudao* 柔道, and *lishi* 理事, totaling a couple dozen, at least. These "return loans" constitute a kind of lexical backflow and are even jokingly called *ciqiao guiguo* 词侨归国, or "overseas Chinese words returning to the native country," by some.[2] Such descriptive terms as "return loans" or *ciqiao guiguo*, however, seem to have overlooked the fact that those borrowed words have already gone through some changes in phonetic or semantic shape.

In contrast to backflow type, direct entry refers to the straightforward lexical flow from the borrowed language to the recipient language. The source word may have originated from a third or even a fourth language, but it is not etymologically related to the recipient language. The majority of Chinese loanwords are the result of such direct inflow, and they are the main focus of this book.

1.1.3 Concept of loanword redefined: a revised definition

Based on the discussion so far and considering the great complexities surrounding words of foreign origin, we may now attempt to define the concept of "loanword" in both a narrow and a broad sense. Broadly speaking, loanwords refer to those words in the lexicon used in one's native language which, each in their totality, originate either phonemically, graphically, or semantically from the lexicon of another language. They include semantic loans, formed through meaning translation, and those borrowed words mixed with the indigenous lexicon. On the other hand, loanwords in the narrow sense refer to those which correspond, in their totality, to the borrowed words in the source language; which completely or partially (approximately 50%) originated either phonemically or graphically from the borrowed words; and which, at the same time, have already become *bona fide* members of the Chinese lexicon.

The key to becoming part of the Chinese lexicon is Sinicization or linguistic naturalization in writing, phonetics, internal composition, semantics, and actual usage. As the most important indicator of linguistic naturalization, graphic shape or writing in Chinese characters seems to immediately distinguish those Sinicized words from the rest. It may sometimes, however, hide their phonetic complexity as some of them maintain the pronunciation of the source words during their initial use in the recipient language. Therefore, phonetic adjustment should also be part of the naturalization process. Graphic representation in Chinese characters often also obscures the internal lexical composition of the source word or has been remodeled into a different lexical structure through phonetic/semantic approximation, making it a *bona fide* Chinese word. When introduced to the Chinese language, most of those polysemous source words only retain one sense while giving up other possible meanings; for some other source words, a completely different meaning is born when they are borrowed into Chinese. This is what semantic naturalization is about. Finally, there is the naturalization in actual use. This refers to the duration or frequency of use in order to prove whether a specific borrowed word has taken root in the Chinese language. It also refers to the changes in usage. Some source words can be used on multiple pragmatic occasions in the source language but, once in Chinese, are reduced to use on only one occasion, while others see their pragmatic situation changed once used in Chinese. All of the five aspects (writing, phonetics, internal composition, semantics, and actual usage) should be considered when we examine the Sinicization of a particular borrowed word.

Whether they are loanwords in a broad or narrow sense, however, the lines of demarcation between the two are not that straightforward. This will be dealt with in greater detail in Section 4 of Chapter 3.

1.2 A historical overview of Chinese terms for the concept of loanword

1.2.1 Evolution of the relevant Chinese terms

In pre-modern times, *yiyu* 译语, *yiming* 译名, *yici* 译词, and *waiguoyu* 外国语 were used in Chinese to refer to Chinese words of foreign origin. The following is a brief explanation of each.

First used in the Tang dynasty (618–907 AD), *yiyu* (literally meaning "translated language") refers to vocabulary that came into being through translation, as used by Tang poet Jia Dao 贾岛 (779–843) in a line of his poem titled *"Song Yu zhongcheng shi Huihe celi"* 送于中丞使回纥册立 (Seeing off senior official Yu on a mission to Huihe to deliver the imperial appointment): *Jiantong qingzhong xiangshan jin, yuda huangqing yiyuchu* 渐通青冢乡山尽, 欲达皇情译语初 ("Getting further away from home and closer to the west frontier, thinking hard how the imperial order could be conveyed through *translated words* ("*yiyu*") when first meeting the khan of Huihe"). Later, during the Yuan dynasty, *yiguan* 译馆 (imperial translation bureaus) were established, and in the Ming (1368–1644) and Qing dynasties, the same word, *yiyu*, was used as the general title for the multi-lingual vocabularies (*huayi yiyu* 华夷译语) compiled by imperial translation bureaus (the *Huitongguan* 会同馆 and the *Siyiguan* 四夷馆), such as *Monggu yiyu* 蒙古译语 (Translated Mongolian glossary), *Sulu yiyu* 苏禄译语 (Translated glossary of Sulu language), *Liuqiu yiyu* 琉球译语 (Translated glossary of Ryukyu language), and *Xiyangguan* Yiyu 西洋馆译语 (Translated glossary of Western languages) (Wen and Shi 1988). The meaning of the term *yiyu*, as used in those contexts, ranged from words and phrases to short passages rendered through translation of meaning. It also included semantic loans and a very limited number of phonemic loans. Strictly speaking, those alien words and phrases that were transcribed in Chinese were not loanwords *per se* but just alien ones with Chinese characters, used for translated meaning or as phonetic notation in order to facilitate pronunciation. This convention of *yiyu* compilation lasted all the way until the end of China's feudal dynasties in the early 20th century.

Almost concurrent with *yiyu* was the term *yiming* 译名 (literally "translated name or term"), which is still in use today. Also used as a general term, *yiming* refers to both semantic and phonemic loans. As the concept and term of *ci* 词 (word) appeared and took root in the Chinese language, the term *yici*, or "translated word," began to come into use; still, it was not treated as a technical term due to the ambiguity of its exact meaning.

A simple, colloquial expression, *waiguoyu* 外国语 (literally "foreign language") is not a formal technical term. It may refer to either words of a foreign language that have not yet become part of one's native language and loanwords in a strict sense or semantic loans, the latter of which meaning had its first attested use in writing in at least the Qing dynasty.[3]

Formal technical terms for borrowed words in modern China started with *wailaiyu* 外来语, which is an original graphic loan from Japanese with the same *kanji* or Chinese characters 外來語 (*gairaigo* in Japanese, literally "lexicon coming from outside") from the early 20th century (1902, to be exact). In Japanese, *gairaigo* refers to words which are phonologically translated by means of *katakana*, one of the two forms of Japanese syllabic writing. In general, those words originated from Western languages and do not include those which both come from Chinese and are written in Chinese characters. Until the early 1950s, *wailaiyu* had still been limited to total or partial phonemic loanwords as well as those Japanese words written with borrowed Chinese characters but read with the Japanese pronunciation scheme of *kun-yomi*, as differentiated from *on-yomi*. In 1934, for example, Chen Wangdao 陈望道 (1891–1977), a Chinese scholar, stated that *wailaiyu* were limited to total phonemic loans (e.g. *modeng* 摩登 and *motuo* 摩托) and partial phonemic loans (e.g. the previously mentioned *bingqilin*) as well as the Chinese words that were based in Japanese but pronounced via *kun-yomi* (e.g. *shouxu* 手续). The *Wailaiyu cidian* 外來语词典 (*Dictionary of words of foreign origin*), edited by Hu Xingzhi 胡行之 and published in 1936, however, included a large number of semantic loans in the category of *wailaiyu*. Hu Xingzhi's classification did not have a big impact, nor was it recognized by the academic community. Between 1942 and 1944, Lu Shuxiang 吕叔湘, a respected Chinese linguist, held the view, as stated in the "*Wailaiyu*" section of Chapter One of his monograph *Zhongguo wenfa yaolue* 中国文法要略 (*Essentials of Chinese grammar*), that *wailaiyu* should only refer to "phonemic loans" and "partially phonemic loans," and that "those words by means of translation of meaning should not be considered *wailaiyu* in a strict sense but instead should be classified as lexical compounds because they take the autochthonous words or root forms from their native language to assemble with others." This is a fair and reasonable comment.

In the mid-1950s, some Chinese scholars, such as Gao Mingkai 高名凯 and Liu Zhengtan 刘正埮, thought that the wording *wailaiyu* was not in agreement with the way in which other lexicological terms were used in the Chinese language, which usually ended with *ci* 词 rather than *yu* 语 as a suffix. The scholars started working on a revised wording and, in 1958, formally used the term *wailaici* 外来词 (literally "words coming from outside") instead. *Wailaici* included various phonemic loans and the borrowed Chinese words of Japanese origin, which, taken together, are generally used to delimit the scope of loanwords today. As it made better linguistic sense and accommodated the convention of the Chinese language, the term was used by more and more people, and in broader contexts, ultimately replacing *wailaiyu*, which had hitherto been used on most occasions, as a predominant term to this day. Adopted early, with a very special link to Japanese, however, *wailaiyu* remains an important technical term and is still being used in specific contexts or within specific scopes: for example, in the community of Japanese language teaching and research, among linguists in Taiwan, and in discussions of issues concerning the scope of loanwords.

With all due respect and in all fairness, both *wailaici* and *wailaiyu* may be open to discussion or debate. Seen from the process of language contact, words of this nature do not come to the recipient language by themselves as *wailai* (coming from foreign or the outside) suggests; instead, the recipient language borrows them based on its own initiative. From that perspective, the term *jieci* ("borrowed words") makes more conceptual or denotational sense. In order to differentiate *jieci* from its current narrow interpretation, as discussed in Section 1.1.2 of this chapter, and from its Chinese homophone *jieci* 介词 (meaning "preposition"), one may draw on the broader term *jieyu* 借语 (meaning "borrowed lexicon") proposed by Zhao Yuanren 赵元任 (Yuen Ren Chao, 1892–1982), a renowned modern Chinese linguist, and create a new term called *jieyuci* 借语词 ("borrowed word or phrase") as a hyponym of Zhao's concept of *jieyu*.

Some also suggest using *waiyuanci* 外源词 (literally "words of foreign etymological source") to replace *wailaici*. Good intentions notwithstanding, a careful analysis reveals that this term is greatly flawed. "Foreign etymological source" could indicate that all three aspects (phonetic, graphic, and semantic) of a word have originated from a foreign language. While semantic loans naturally belong in this category, the term cannot conceptually apply to those loanwords covered by *jieci* or *wailaiyu*. In fact, many scholars in the community of Japanese language teaching and research in the 21st century use Japanese "*jieci*" instead of Japanese "*wailaiyu*," presumably to avoid the existing issues confronting the term *wailaiyu*.

There is yet another class of formal terms with regard to loanwords: namely, *jieruyu* 借入语, *jieyongyu* 借用语, *jiezi* 借字, and *jieyu* 借语 (and, by extension, *wailai jieci* 外来借词 and *wailai jieyu* 外来借语), which are all believed to be real equivalents to the English "loanword." Among them, the term *jieruyu* had its first attestation in 1905, in an English-Chinese Mandarin dictionary by Karl Hemeling.[4] Originated in Japanese and first seen in China in 1914 in an influential article by Hu Yilu 胡以鲁,[5] a Japan-educated Chinese linguist, *jieyongyu* refers to words which borrow the sound and written form of foreign words as well as the graphic form of the Chinese characters used by the foreign word, here specifically referring to Japan-made Chinese words.

Luo Changpei 罗常培 (Lo Chang Pei, 1899–1958), a Chinese linguist, first used the term *jiezi* 借字 in 1950, extending its denotational coverage from various phonemic loans to loan-translations: namely, calques by means of semantic translation of morphemes, such as *yinyuan* 因缘 (cause, opportunity) from the Sanskrit *hetupratyaya* (*hetu* "cause" and *pratyaya* "condition") and *ziwo shixian* 自我实现 from the English "self-realization," and what he called *miaoxieci* 描写词 (descriptive loaning), which refers to a combination of autochthonous Chinese words and a semantic marker which serves to indicate foreignness, such as *hucong* 胡葱 (green onion), *fanqie* 番茄 (tomato), and *yanghuo* 洋火 (match which can light or ignite)—*hu*, *fan*, and *yang* here all mean "foreign"—and pure semantic loans, like *huochai* 火柴 (match which can light or ignite).

In the 1950s, with the established use of *ci* 词 (word), the term *jieci* appeared as the semantic loan from the English "loanword." Generally considered the equivalent of *wailaici* in meaning, *jieci* was listed in the then new edition of *Cihai* 辞海 (literally, "sea of words"), one of the most authoritative, encyclopedia-type dictionaries of the Chinese language. It was also used in most of the course books on modern Chinese at this time. However, it is more complicated than this may indicate. Some thought that *jieci* was limited to phonemic loans, such as the renowned Chinese linguist Wang Li 王力 (1958) and the *Zhongguo dabaike quanshu—yuyan wenzi* 中国大百科全书—语言文字 (*Encyclopedia of China | Languages*). Some other scholars, like Gao Mingkai 高名凯 and Liu Zhengtan 刘正埮 (1958), held the view that *jieci* was different from *wailaici* because the former was not yet a member of the lexicon of the native language but a foreign word, while the latter was. Their interpretation and application, however, were diametrically opposite to the German differentiation between the two corresponding terms.[6] Because of the great confusion and chaos it caused, the interpretation by Gao and Liu has received almost no response to this day.

Jieyu 借语, the technical term that Zhao Yuanren started to use in 1967, not only covered loanwords but was also intended to include the myriad forms or areas of borrowing, ranging from phoneme, morpheme, word, phrase, and usage all the way to grammar structure. Though no one has taken Zhao's proposed term very seriously, even today, *jieyu*, as a hypernym, still has practical value—*jieyuci*, a hyponym of *jieyu*, proposed in the earlier discussion of this chapter, is a case in point. Given such a great divergence of opinion and confusion, some even choose to use the term "phonemic loan" only as it is strictly defined and clear cut in meaning.

1.2.2 The term wailaiyu

As a predecessor to *wailaici*, *wailaiyu* was a very important term in the history of the Chinese language. However, we have thus far had a deplorably poor understanding of its ins and outs. If we trace it to its origin, *wailaiyu* was itself a loanword from Japanese *gairaigo* 外來語 in kanji, using the same three Chinese characters. It is believed that, as far back as the 1880s, *gairaigo* gained wide currency in Japan; before then, the term *hakuraigo* 舶來語 (literally "words imported from outside") had been used in the country. By 1884, Japanese linguist Otsuki Fumihiko (1847–1928) had written the book *Gairaigo genko* (*Notes on loanword etymologies*), and in 1904, Japan had its first dictionary of *gairaigo*. Judging from the fact that *gairaigo* was already being used in book titles in Japan, one may infer the extent of its popularity there at the time. In 1902, Zhang Taiyan 章太炎 (also known as Zhang Binglin 章炳麟, 1869–1936), a Chinese scholar, published *Wenxue shuoli* 文学说例 (*Introduction to Chinese graphemics*) in the Japan-based, Chinese biweekly journal *Sein Min Choong Bou* 新民叢報, in which he quoted, through his Chinese translation, a passage from the book *Shujigaku* (Rhetoric, 1898) by Japanese scholar Takejima Matajiro (also known as Takeshima Hagoromo, 1872–1967):

> For example, the *wailaiyu* [emphasis added] not only ruins the purity of one's native language but also hampers understanding; sometimes, however, due to the constraints by the actual situation where no other word could be used in its stead, it is then acceptable to use it.

Based on this passage, Zhang went on, after his introduction, to elaborate his views on the Chinese language. On two other occasions as well, he mentioned *wailaiyu*:

> Comment: Takejima thinks that *wailaiyu* [emphasis added] and neologisms are needed on some occasions while obsolete archaisms are dismissed by scholar-bureaucrats as worthless. Since he talks about the situation in Japan, it is quite understandable. In China, though evolution is slower, things are a lot more complicated, so it should be different from Japan...
>
> Therefore it is fair to say that, similar to our attitude to *wailaiyu* [emphasis added] and neologisms, the suspended use of archaisms should also be taken with great caution to prevent indiscriminate abuse.[7]

Zhang's views did not, however, draw much attention or response from the Chinese public at the time, presumably because it was at the end of the Qing dynasty—high time for revolution rather than academic endeavor—so *wailaiyu* and its discussion fell into neglect. It was only after the Chinese Revolution of 1911 and the May Fourth Movement in 1919 that scholars could have had the chance, interest, or time to care about the topic that Zhang had elaborated above.

In 1934—more than 30 years later—the Japan-educated scholar Chen Wangdao 陈望道 returned to the discussion of *wailaiyu*. In his *Guanyu dazhong yuwen de jianshe* 关于大众语文的建设 (*On promoting the Chinese language for the general public*), published on June 19, 1934, in *Ziyoutan* 自由谈 (*Free Talk*), one of the influential supplements to the Shanghai-based *Shun Pao* 申报 (Shanghai Journal), the longest-lasting newspaper (1872–1949) in modern China, Chen wrote,

> In the future lexicon of the Chinese language for the general public there will inevitably be the coming of *wailaiyu*, but they must be transliterated in our own characters so that everybody knows how to read them. Judging from the past experience, importing some *wailaiyu* or reinstalling some archaisms would not make the general public feel inconvenient,

as long as the words are needed by the public at the time, words like *modeng* 摩登, *motuo* 摩托, *bingqilin* 冰淇淋, *shouxu* 手续, and *yindu* 引渡.

Meanwhile, just a couple of days later, on June 26, in his *Zaijinyibu* 再进一步 (One more step forward), published in *Dongxiang* 动向 (*Trends*), a supplement to the newspaper *Zhonghua ribao* 中华日报, Long Gonggong 龙贡公 (1908–2000, also known as Ouyang Shan 欧阳山), a writer, pointed out,

> To be accurate and correct, we must reject cutting corners due to laziness, getting things easy without any result, being concise without any substance, and being fluent without any sincerity. Instead, we must be brave enough to accept some dignified style and take the trouble of creating new words and characters and taking in *wailaiyu*. To be substantive may require exhaustive details; to be serious may call for being unpolished and hard to understand.

Again, on many occasions during the wave of discussions about reforming Chinese grammar in 1940, Chen Wangdao expounded his views on *wailaiyu*. Related articles published in the decade between the 1930s and 1940s were all part of a stream of academic efforts on the topic. On the one hand, these discussions show that the introduction of the concept by Zhang Taiyan, for all intents and purposes, failed because it fell on deaf ears, but the 1930s saw a renewed effort and a highly effective one at that. On the other hand, they also tell us about the interpretation of *wailaiyu* at the time, its necessity to Chinese language and culture, and those great scholars' attitudes towards the introduction of *wailaiyu* (Shi 1995).

Incidentally, the term *guyou mingci* 固有名词 (indigenous or autochthonous words), an opposite of *wailaiyu*, also came from Japanese. Evolving into *guyouci* 固有词 in Chinese, it is used to refer to words composed of autochthonous Chinese morphemes, including obsolete, original, or even newly formed words. In terms of denotation, however, this term is not accurate. Newly formed words cannot be classified as "autochthonous" because "autochthonous" means that something has been in existence from the very beginning, not something newly created. A more appropriate term would be *ziyuanci* 自源词: namely, words that are intrinsically self-originated. When entering into the Chinese language, those graphic loanwords from Japanese *kanji* can at best be regarded as quasi-autochthonous.

1.3 Currently used English and Chinese terms for the concept of loanword

1.3.1 Related English terms and their Chinese equivalents

Since terms related to loanwords are essentially imported concepts, it is necessary to straighten out those relevant English terms and compare them with their corresponding Chinese ones so as to facilitate international academic exchange and get a handle on how the subject is approached internationally. There are quite a few English terms or expressions that correspond, or which are similar, to the concept of loanword; among the most commonly used are loan word, alien word, foreign word, and borrowing. Others include alienism, loan, loan blend, and foreignism. In addition, there is one special type of loanword called hybrids. There exist some differences between and among these in terms of what they each mean and the extent to which they apply. The following is a brief description and comparison:

Loan word. Same as loanword. A word incorporated by means of direct copy, phonetic loaning (*yinyi* 音译)[8], or loan translation from another language (or dialect). The English "loanword" is a calque from the German "Lehnwort." According to the original meaning of both "Lehnwort" and "loanword," it should be translated as "*jieci*" 借词 or "*jieyongci*" 借用词 in Chinese. Japanese still uses *gairaigo* (*wailaiyu* in Chinese) to correspond to "loanword."

Borrow/borrowing. A term in historical contrastive linguistics, this refers to a language form (word, phonetics, or grammar structure) borrowed directly from another language or dialect. It can include words which have or have not undergone phonetic changes. It is translated as "*jieyong*" 借用 (for "borrow" or "borrowing"), "*jieyongci*" 借用词, or "*jieci*" 借词 (for "borrowed word") in Chinese.

Alien word. This mainly refers to words which come directly from another language, typically excluding semantic loans or loan-translations. Since the word "alien" means "foreign," alien words are specifically associated with words that come from a foreign language; therefore, the term is translated as *waiguoci* 外国词 in Chinese.

Foreign word. This refers to words coming from a foreign language and is roughly equivalent to *waiguoyu* 外国语, which was used in pre-modern times. The Japanese "*gairaigo*" originated from a translation of the English "foreign word" but later came to correspond to "loanword." So, in the Japanese language, *gairaigo* is limited to words coming from foreign languages and, more specifically, from Western languages.

Alienism. Beside alien words, the term "alienism" also includes a way of expression which results from the influence of a foreign language and is regarded as incompatible with one's native language. This term gives the impression of a word's "coming from foreign countries and incompatible here in the native country."

Foreignism. Same as alienism but less formal.

Peregrinism. Same as alienism, with a suggestion of being exotic or outlandish.

Loan. This refers to linguistic units (words or other units) which originated from other languages or dialects and have been used in the native language. As a latecomer, it is used to encompass loanwords, hybrids, and calques. Depending on the context, it can be translated as "*jieyongyu*"

借用语 (borrowed lexicon) or *"jieyong yuyan danwe"* 借用语言单位 (borrowed linguistic unit) in Chinese.

Loan blend. This refers to words which are semantically entirely but phonetically partially borrowed from other languages or dialects and partially still presented in the native language in phonetic form. It can be translated as *"hunhe jieci"* 混合借词 or *"wailai hunheci"* 外来混合词 in Chinese.

Hybrid word. This refers to a compound word made up of components that originate from different languages. The most common type of hybrid word is a mixture of both foreign and native lexical components. It is translated as *"hunchengci"* 混成词, *"hunzhongci"* 混种词, or *"hunxueci"* 混血词 in Chinese. Specifically perceived from the origin of composition, the hybrid word distinguishes itself, in terms of classification, from all the terms mentioned above. It may include not only loan blends but also words that native speakers create by either blending a foreign component with an indigenous one or blending variously foreign components together. It contains, for example, hybrid loanwords with a semantic marker, like *kache* 卡车 and *nigu* 尼姑 (*ni* is short for *biqiuni* 比丘尼, a fully ordained female monastic above the age of 20 in Buddhism, from the Sanskrit *Bhiksuni*, combined with the semantic marker *gu*, meaning "lady or girl"), and those words which do not strictly belong to loanwords and find no direct or whole equivalence from foreign languages, such as *luohanguo* 罗汉果 (monk fruit, Siraitia grosvenorii), *payin* 琶音 (arpeggio), *suqu* 苏区 (Chinese communist rural bases called "Chinese Soviet Republics," formed in the 1930s to fight the ruling Nationalists; *su* for "Soviet" and *qu* for "area" or "region"), and *dika* 涤卡.

Loan shift. This refers to words that are semantically borrowed from a foreign language but read or pronounced according to the phonological system of the recipient language. Words of this kind are very similar to Japan-made Chinese words (*kanji*) read with the Japanese pronunciation scheme of *on-yomi* and Japan-made Chinese words read with the Japanese pronunciation scheme of *kun-yomi*. The term is so similar to the latter that the two can be considered approximately equivalent. The loan shift can be translated as *"bianyin jieci"* 变音借词 in Chinese.

Calque/loan translation. This refers to a word that is semantically translated from each of the morphemes of the borrowed foreign word. It is usually translated as *"fangyi(ci)"* 仿译(词), *"mojie(ci)"* 摹借(词), *"jieyi(ci)"* 借译(词), or *"fangzao(ci)"* 仿造(词) in Chinese.

1.3.2 Three Chinese terms: wailaici, wailaiyu, *and* jieci

Despite the various English terms which have been discussed, there are only three common terms for loanwords in the Chinese language: *wailaici* 外来词, *wailaiyu* 外来语, and *jieci* 借词. Despite the largely unfulfilled hopes by many scholars for a clear distinction among the three terms, possible differences among them can still be observed from both conceptual and pragmatic considerations.

Conceptual differences. Since the very beginning of its use, the term *jieci* has not only referred to words borrowed from foreign languages but may also refer to those from languages of ethnic groups within the country. It is also used in discussion of the relations between foreign languages and their dialects. In following their convention, it has obviously been directly influenced by the Western terminology.

Influenced by Japanese for the initial period after its introduction, *wailaiyu* only referred to words from foreign languages, mainly those phonemic loans and some kanji (Japan-made Chinese words) which are read with the Japanese pronunciation (*kun-yomi*). This is because Japan had long since enforced a policy of mandatory naturalization, preventing ethnic minorities from living in the country. Given this and the guiding ideology of Datsua Nyuo (Leave Asia, enter the West), linguistic terms, *gairaigo* included, were ideologically affected in terms of their internal content. In the late 1940s, *wailaiyu* began to extend to words borrowed not only from foreign languages alone but also from other ethnic languages in China. What's more, it not only included those total phonemic loans but also started to include those partial phonemic loans (i.e. loan blend and some hybrid words). In the late 1950s, *wailaici* started to partially take the place of *wailaiyu*, and its use was further extended, so all the words borrowed from Japanese kanji formally became members of Chinese loanwords.

In many publications, *jieci* is treated as a synonymous variation for *wailaiyu* and *wailaici*, but its use is still limited, in more normatives works, such as the *Zhongguo dabaike quanshu* 中国大百科全书 (*Encyclopedia of China*), to what the English term "loanword" means, which refers only to phonemic loans, excluding the so called "substrate words," as discussed in Section 1.1.2.

Pragmatic differences. It seems that Western-educated Chinese scholars tend to use *jieci* far more frequently than *wailaiyu*, while Japanese-educated Chinese scholars are generally more used to *wailaiyu*. Those in the field of Japanese studies choose to use the latter only. Of course, there are some exceptions to this generalization. For instance, UK-educated Chinese linguist Lu Shuxiang 吕叔湘 (1904–1998) used the term *wailaiyu* in his work *Zhongguo wenfa yaolue* 中国文法要略 (*Essentials of Chinese grammar*) in 1947, and French-educated Cen Qixiang 岑麒祥 used *wailaiyu* in 1990 in the title of his work *Hanyu wailaiyu cidian* 汉语外来语词典 (Dictionary of Chinese loanwords).[9] In some larger projects with a national impact, there may also exist a divergence of opinion, presumably due to the different academic backgrounds of those editors (or editorial institutions) involved. For instance, in the Chinese language section of the languages volume of the *Zhongguo dabaike quanshu* (1st edition), compiled by the Institute of Linguistics, Chinese Academy of Social Sciences, only *jieci* is used; *wailaiyu* is used elsewhere in the volume, referring only to those words in the German language that retain the original characteristics of the foreign language. By contrast, the encyclopedic *Cihai* by Shanghai cishu chubanshe 上海辞书出版社

(Shanghai Cishu Press or Shanghai Lexicographical Publishing House in English) lists *wailaici* as a main entry while treating *wailaiyu* and *jieci* as alternative entries. Presumably to avoid the homophony between *jieci* 借词 and *jieci* 介词 (meaning "preposition"), all textbooks on modern Chinese in China choose *wailaici* as the preferred term.

As can be seen in the discussion above, it is clear that there exists considerable confusion between the terms in both meaning and usage. For the purpose of clarity and better academic exchange, it is necessary to draw a basic distinction between them and clarify when each should be used. In line with both international practice and China's own conventions, *jieci* should correspond to loanwords in the narrow sense, referring to purely phonemic loans and phonemic loans added with a semantic marker. In terms of general linguistics, it also includes words borrowed from other dialects (in phonetic form). *Wailaici* or *wailaiyu* can have a broader scope, encompassing the above-mentioned *jieci* and loan blend as well as graphic loans (mainly words in Chinese characters which were borrowed from Japanese) but excluding words from dialects. Following from Section 1.1.2 of this chapter, *wailaici* or *wailaiyu* should also include lexical units of external origin in the substrate: namely, "*substrate loanwords*" 底层外来词. It is hoped that this clarification not only accommodates the convention which has already been established in China but also takes into consideration international practice and general linguistic theories, thus facilitating the academic endeavors of both.[10]

1.4 The status of graphic loanwords from Japanese and *zimuci:* between pure loanword and autochthonous Chinese word

1.4.1 The status of graphic loans from Japanese in the Chinese language

Historically, the status of graphic loans from Japanese in the Chinese language has been a controversial subject. For an appropriate solution to this issue, it is perhaps necessary to understand how lexical borrowing happens. There are essentially four major means by which one's native language borrows words from other languages: borrowing of both sound and meaning (i.e. phonemic loaning or *yinyi* 音译 in Chinese, which is itself borrowed from the Japanese *onyaku* 音訳); borrowing of meaning alone (i.e. semantic loaning or *yiyi* 意译 in Chinese, which is again borrowed from the Japanese *iyaku* 意訳); borrowing of graphic form and meaning (i.e. graphic loaning); and, finally, complete borrowing of graphic shape, sound, and meaning, as typically represented by alphabetic loaning. As total phonetic borrowings, phonemic loans are typical, genuine loans or borrowed words, constituting the core of all loanwords. Words of partial phonemic and partial semantic borrowing (namely, loan blend or hybrid words) are considered quasi-loanwords, which may as well deserve a place in the category of loanword, a result of redefining *wailaici* in the Chinese context. As for pure semantic loans, most scholars would not recognize them as *bona fide* loanwords. As regards pure graphic loans (Japanese-made Chinese words), there has been a consistent divergence of opinion on where they belong since this marks a very special case in the Sino-sphere, i.e. countries or regions where Chinese characters are in use.

With theoretical reflections and empirical observations over time, most scholars in the field now agree that loanwords should also include Chinese words borrowed from Japanese, that is, graphic loans of kanji (mainly on the Japanese on-yomi pronunciation scheme). The reason for this shift is that linguistic scholars come to realize that different languages are entitled to have different characteristics, and therefore, it is acceptable to have some distinctive theoretical interpretations and practical applications which are strictly based on the distinctive features of the language in question as long as the universality of the established theories concerned is upheld as much as possible. In the case of Chinese, it is written Chinese characters which are used to represent the languages that have brought about the change of attitude.

Before the existence of a written form of the language, lexical borrowing between languages was simple and straightforward: either phonemic or semantic. The invention of the written language was an earth-shattering event of biblical proportions, a watershed not just in the history of languages but in every single aspect of human civilization. It has brought about convenience and inconvenience, hitherto unimaginable.[11]

In lexical borrowing, the most convenient means involves either direct borrowing or transplanting the written forms of the borrowed language. Between many phonetic languages, semantic and phonetic loaning are the only means of inter-language borrowing for written representation because either the two languages involved use the same (alphabetic) writing system, or they use different writing systems. In the former case, since they both have the same system for writing and pronunciation, borrowing the graphemic shape of the word is the same as borrowing its corresponding phonetic form, as in borrowing between English and French. In the latter, because the writing systems of the borrowing and borrowed languages in question are diametrically different, only phonemic borrowing is possible due to the general incompatibility in graphemic shape between the two languages, as in borrowing between Chinese and English.

Lexical borrowing between Chinese and Japanese, however, is drastically different. Both languages use the ideographic Chinese characters—practically the same in both graphic form and lexical meaning, except for pronunciation or reading. Though the sound, under the Japanese *on-yomi* pronunciation scheme, of the kanji in Japanese comes from Chinese, it comes from pre-modern Chinese and, what's more, has undergone changes to accommodate the Japanese phonological system. After hundreds of years of evolution, the Old Chinese sounds for kanji under the *on-yomi* scheme have naturalized into Japanese, meaning that they are far removed from the sounds of the originating Chinese. Due to their undeniable independent status, it is impossible for the Chinese language to conveniently pronounce the borrowed Chinese characters in line with the *on-yomi* scheme while borrowing the written form from the Japanese kanji. In other words, the typical correspondence in graphic, phonetic, and semantic representation among alphabetic languages would not apply to Chinese characters in the two languages: though graphically and semantically closely matching, they are very different phonetically. Between the Chinese and Japanese languages, graphic form and lexical meaning of a word in one language can seamlessly integrate with the phonetic representation of the other language into a loanword. Therefore, the most convenient borrowing between Chinese and Japanese is the graphic one: obtaining the written forms of the Chinese words without changing their distinct pronunciation of each character, according to their respective phonetic schemes. Since the graphic form and lexical meaning of Chinese characters remain closely associated, such graphic borrowing necessarily entails semantic borrowing.

Strictly speaking, this kind of borrowing cannot be called total or typical lexical borrowing because it does not involve borrowing of phonetic shape, which is an indispensable component of the loaned word. It is exhilarating to see that, as part of a special and mainly ideographic writing system, Chinese characters can be safely grafted on to a different phonological scheme and find a new form of existence in other languages–a contribution to the world of languages. In this regard, graphic loans from Japanese used in the Chinese language deserve a special place in the family of loanwords. These borrowed words lie somewhere between the indigenous Chinese lexicon and pure loanwords. As Chinese words made in Japan, they use indigenous Chinese morphemes and word formation but are not made in the environment where the Han Chinese live or the native Chinese language is used, nor are they made for the Han Chinese or the native Chinese language. They each borrow the graphic or written, not phonetic, form of the word. So, strictly speaking, they are quasi-loanwords, if seen from the typical loanword perspective, or quasi-indigenous words, if seen from the standpoint of the pure autochthonous Chinese lexicon. In a broader sense, however, they are still classified as loanwords—graphic loanwords, to be exact.

Unlike Japan-made Chinese words pronounced on the *on-yomi* scheme, words read on the *kun-yomi* pronunciation scheme, such as Japanese *tetsuzuki* 手続, from which Chinese *shouxu* 手续 is borrowed, are generally not considered Japan-made Chinese words in the narrow sense, and there is no disagreement among scholars over their status as loanwords.

In fact, we can also choose to examine these kanji from the viewpoint of lexical sharing. Instead of paying too much attention to the differences between Chinese and Japanese, we may focus on the commonalities between the two as well as the sharing and the assimilation of those words so as to overcome the "mine versus yours" mentality. This, however, should not in any way obscure the fact of language contact and cultural exchanges between the two nations, which are what this discussion is all about (cf. Section 6.7.2 in Chapter 6).

1.4.2 The status of lettered or alphabetic words in the Chinese language

Lettered or alphabetic words, *zimuci* 字母词 in Chinese, refer to initialisms, acronyms, and letter-character or letter-numeral combinations either borrowed directly from a European language or coined by native speakers of Modern Standard Chinese. The status here refers to both their significance and their identity or qualification in the Chinese language.

Latin script appeared as early as 1868 in the symbols for chemical elements in the *Gewu rumen* 格物入门 (Introduction to natural philosophy), the first textbook of Western science published in Chinese, written by William Alexander Parsons Martin. Since the 20th century, the Latin script alphabet has become internationally accepted as part of the universal character set but their actual use in common lexicons has been very limited in most countries. For example, prior to the 1950s, perhaps only two ("X ray" and "OK") of such words which contain Latin script were in wide currency in China. With its national promulgation of the *Hanyu Pinyin Fangan* 汉语拼音方案 (Phonetic system of the Chinese language), a system of romanization for the Chinese written language based on the pronunciation of the Beijing dialect of Mandarin Chinese, in 1958, Latin script, or its alphabet, immediately became an integral part of the scheme rather than one used in foreign languages alone.

Written in Latin alphabetic letters rather than Chinese characters, *zimuci* have since evolved into two subcategories in the Chinese language. Most of those alphabetic lettered words are initialisms or acronyms from European languages, predominantly English and occasionally Latin, French, and Greek. A newly emerging, very small part of those alphabetic lettered words constitute the second kind of *zimuci*, which are abbreviated from the Chinese lexicon in Romanized pinyin. Thanks to their wide use, alphabetic lettered words from European languages are becoming more global than Western in terms of lexical or linguistic identity since users do not really care whether they are loanwords or simply foreign. The size and usage of such alphabetic lettered words continue to grow and are in the process of changing the ecology, so to speak, of the Chinese language, bringing it closer in form to other world languages, more in sync with the times, and therefore more receptive and accessible to the rest of the world. In terms of meaning or the signified, those lettered words are mostly terms associated with science, business, finance, military, linguistics, or institutional proper names, such as GPS, Wi-Fi, 5G, and WTO, all reflecting the social and cultural development of the times—hence, their value or significance.

From the perspective of the Chinese language, the exact lexical identity or qualification of Western-originated lettered words is more of a continuum: there is no diametrically defined line of demarcation between purely foreign alphabetic words and those which have taken root upon being naturalized in the Chinese language. As with any other language, the identity of alphabetic letter words in the Chinese lexicon is dynamic and flexible. With increasing frequency and scope in use, they may be incrementally perceived as Chinese-like and ultimately be assimilated into it. Given the complexities of their identity, the *Xiandai hanyu cidian* 现代汉语词典 (*The Contemporary Chinese Dictionary*) has consistently included acronyms and words beginning with Greek or Latin letters which are frequently used in contemporary Chinese at the end of the main body of the dictionary. The author of this book also includes alphabetic letter words in his *Xinhua wailaici cidian* 新华外来词词典 (*Xinhua dictionary of Chinese loanwords*, 2019) as an important supplement. Both reflect an attempt to preclude possible controversy over their delicate lexical identity.

It is generally believed that loanwords in the Chinese language should be those which have been naturalized or Sinicized. This lexical Sinicization has generally focused on graphic and phonetic naturalization. Graphically and semantically identical to their foreign source words, alphabetic letter words used in modern Chinese naturally do not possess the above markers of Sinicization, making it challenging to determine their linguistic identity; this also makes it even more necessary to delve deeper into the identity of loanwords in general.

Theoretically speaking, there are six major aspects to consider in the determination or identification of loanwords including alphabetic letter words: character type, semantic variation, phonetic affiliation, grammatical domestication, cognitive acceptance, and user diffusion.[12] Though phonetic loanwords are generally defined by whether they are transcribed in Chinese characters, the situation is more complicated than it appears. In the actual colloquial context, for example, many of those phonemic loanwords are read in their original foreign pronunciation, such as *paidui* 派对 and Shanghainese *daei* 达诶, which in Chinese are pronounced as "party" and "die"; their respective source words, then, are in English. Given the fact that these phonemic loans are not pronounced the way their Chinese characters suggest, as is the case with most Chinese words, it can be hard to determine whether they are *bona fide* Chinese loanwords. Similarly, alphabetic letter words, which are graphemically represented in Latin letters, naturally call for more careful consideration. The following is a brief discussion of phonetic affiliation, grammatical domestication, cognitive acceptance, and user diffusion, with the exception of character type and semantic variation.

Phonetic affiliation. Alphabetic letter words are usually pronounced according to the sound of each component letter, but there are two outstanding issues with the Phonetic System of the Chinese Language. Many sounds in the pronunciation of the alphabetic letters in isolation in the Chinese phonetic system do not line up with the phonetics of the Beijing dialect on which modern standard Chinese (Mandarin) is based, so those sounds are divorced from the linguistic roots of Chinese, making it difficult to put the pronunciations into practice. What is more, no serious efforts have been made toward putting the pronunciation of the alphabetic letters in isolation into practice. So, those alphabetic pronunciations have no actual use in real life. Whether something is wrong with the design for alphabetic pronunciations or how it should be revised is another matter; the obvious result is that there comes a phonetic vacuum in *zimuci* or alphabetic letter words, and this vacuum is naturally filled by the English pronunciation of the corresponding alphabetic letters. This not only applies to Western-originated letter words; Chinese-originated words also have to adopt English alphabetic pronunciation, such as HSK (initialism from *Hanyu Shuiping Kaoshi* or "Test of Chinese as a Foreign Language") and GB (initialism from *Guojia Biaozhun* or "national standard"), pronounced /eitʃ esi kei/ and / dʒi: bi:/, respectively. The pronunciation of the component letters is not a proper criterion by which to determine the linguistic or lexical identity of a letter word.

Grammatical domestication. If a foreign word entering the Chinese environment maintains its original grammatical properties without accommodating to the linguistic norms of Chinese, that word certainly remains foreign in its identity; examples include occasionally used foreign words in Chinese lyrics or whole sentences in a foreign language as these are still not naturalized. However, if an alphabetic word enters into such compact syntactic structures as resultative or directional verb complements, accepts Chinese morphological components such as post-verbal particles, joins autochthonous Chinese morpheme in forming compact phrases such as the modifier-modified structure without the usual marker of *de* 的 in between, or even evolves into a word-forming component morpheme, then this alphabetic word should be recognized as a naturalized Chinese word, such as *hold zhu* hold 住 (hold), *PK diao yixie duishou* PK掉一些对手 (Player killing or knocking out opponents in competition), *P guo jizhang zhaopian* P过几张照片 (Photoshopped some pictures), *SUV che* SUV车 (sports utility vehicle), *IT jishu* IT技术 (information technology), *CD lufangji* CD 录放机 (CD player), *4K dianshiji* 4K 电视机 (TV set with 4K resolution), *X guang* X 光 (X-ray), *K xian* K 线 (candlestick chart that shows the open, high, low, and close prices for an asset), *PC ji* PC 机 (personal computer), *POS ji* POS 机 (POS machine), and *LED deng* LED 灯 (LED lamp or bulb). As research moves on, there may be more discoveries of grammatical means by which to determine loanword identity.

Cognitive acceptance. When a loanword (in particular, an alphabetic one) belongs in the Chinese language, there must be cognitive and psychological evidence. Are its users aware, and, if so, to what extent, that it is borrowed from outside? Do the users know its full form before abbreviation: namely, are they supported by their foreign language educational background? To what extent are they psychologically receptive, or otherwise, to the loanword? Though these questions are theoretically very important, it is extremely hard to assess this level of cognitive or psychological acceptance in real life. Hopefully, a handy method for such a purpose will be developed in the foreseeable future, but for now, we have to make do.

User diffusion. As a flexible measure for the determination of alphabetic words, user diffusion refers to frequency and scope in usage. Easy to understand and measure, frequency in usage refers to how frequently the word is used in real life. Scope in usage refers to the size of user distribution, which can be roughly simplified into three types: limited, local, and broad. The change in user distribution can be assessed or verified through survey and statistical investigation. Limited distribution occurs when the word is regularly used by some individuals or occasionally used by a few, so it has not taken root in the recipient language yet; such words are still foreign words. Words of local distribution are commonly used within certain social professional classes or communities, such as *demo* (a musical recording made to demonstrate the quality of an unsigned performer) or *key* (a scale of musical notes that starts on one specific note) among vocal performers, *DJ* in entertainment, *VP* (verbal phrase) and *PP* (prepositional phrase) in grammar, *case* in business, and *offer* in job seeking and application for overseas studies. Frequently used in their respective fields, these words are already part of the Chinese lexicon within those communities. As far as the general public or the Chinese language as a whole is concerned, however, they remain foreign words. Borrowed words of broad distribution are those commonly used by the general public, such as OK, WTO, PK, and "hold" (pronounced /hōu/ and used in the above-mentioned verb complement structure of *hold zhu* only). Originally used in some specific fields in most cases, these alphabetic letter words gradually spread into popular use and therefore have been assimilated into Chinese as special members of its lexicon.

Just as a foreign matter may most probably experience its initial resistance or rejection when interacting with another body, the integration or naturalization of alphabetic letter words can only be a gradual process at best since these words are completely foreign to Chinese in every sense of the word. If one insists that Chinese characters are the only written form of the language, it is indeed difficult to grant alphabetic words a Chinese identity. Yet if one takes a long-term view of the future development, acknowledging that the Latin alphabet is also auxiliary to Chinese, then there will be more tolerance and imagination toward alphabetic words (*zimuci*). At present, if the main consideration is on grammatical naturalization and user diffusion, letter words of local and broad diffusion can be regarded as a special type of loanwords within their fields or communities—"quasi-loanwords" for lack of a better term, which are different from another kind of quasi-loanwords, namely, those borrowed Chinese words of Japanese origin, in that the former look like foreign words (most of them indeed are), while the latter look Chinese. It can be understood from the above discussion that great attention should be paid to the identity determination of letter words; this is not only an operational matter but also reflects their theoretical underpinnings.

1.5 Other external influences on the native language

1.5.1 Borrowed concepts and external influence on the lexicon

1.5.1.1 Borrowed concepts

Seen from the conceptual point of view, most of the concepts contained in the words of phonemic, graphic, and pure semantic borrowing also come from the outside. We might as well think, further, that these words are by and large words of borrowed concepts or notions. Given the fact of generalization, some even suggest that phonemic, graphic, and semantic borrowings should collectively be called "*wailai gainian ci*" 外来概念词 (meaning "conceptual loan-words" or "words of borrowed concepts").[13] This new approach may enhance our understanding of these borrowed words in terms of cultural exchange and influence and through them our understanding of language contact and cultural diffusion between different national or ethnic communities. Upon closer examination, however, we find that these loanwords, by different means of borrowing, cannot simply be lumped together as "borrowed concepts."

Some of these words are indeed borrowed from the outside and phonetically transliterated, though they cannot be said to contain borrowed concepts. Take Chinese phonemic loanword *zhan* 站 (meaning "courier station"), for example. Though *zhan* corresponds in pronunciation to the Mongolian word "*jam*" from which it is borrowed, the Chinese language used this same notion (and lexical equivalent) of "courier station" in China's second imperial dynasty of Han (206 BC–220 AD), represented by its indigenous word, *yi* 驿. Similarly, Chinese *eniang* 额娘 is phonemically borrowed from the Manchu word "*eniye*," but the concept of mother (*muqin* 母亲) has certainly long been in existence in Chinese; Chinese phonemic loanword *kaisi* 开司 is from the English "kiss," but the Chinese word *qinzhui* 亲嘴, with the same meaning and practice as "kiss," has long been in existence too. Chinese phonemic loanword *baibai* 拜拜 is from the English "bye-bye," but has *baibai* introduced any foreign concept beyond the long-existing indigenous Chinese word *zaijian* 再见? Doesn't the word *bo* 波, which is phonemically borrowed from English "ball" and which people in Guangzhou and Hong Kong prefer to use, mean the same thing as the Chinese autochthonous word "*qiu*" 球 in most cases? Has *bo* conceptually introduced any foreign element? Another commonly used word is *okai* 喔开, which obviously comes from the English "OK." During the initial period of borrowing, it could only be used as a stand-alone articulation to express agreement or approval. Before *okai*, there were a number of functionally equivalent Chinese words, such as *bucuo* 不错, *duide* 对的, *xing* 行, and *keyi* 可以. So, it is impossible to conclude, as in this case, what notion or idea the Chinese language has borrowed along with its use of *okai*; what it has adopted is just a new or alternative way of expressing the same object, idea, or quality which is already in existence in the recipient Chinese language.

Some other loanwords do not even contain concepts of their own, let alone borrowed ones. For example, *haluo* 哈罗, which comes from the English "hello," is always used as an exclamation, which does not contain any concept in the usual sense of the word. There is a near identical equivalent in both meaning and usage in the Chinese language: *wei* 喂. Obviously, such borrowing is not meant to bring in any unique concept but instead is used mostly to display a certain kind of lexical identity and usage or tone of expression which is associated with something exotic or foreign before it is widely used in society. Few in number, these words would not affect the argument made at the beginning of this section but still have some special theoretical implications. In other words, besides fulfilling the conceptual and semiotic function of introducing concepts which are lacking in the native language, loanwords may also perform the additional function of both introducing new meanings or usages to existing Chinese characters and indicating some special social or cultural symbols, such as level of education received, social status, moral values, and even the zeitgeist of the time. So, from a broad perspective, these words might more properly be described as "words based on borrowed concepts or tone of expression." It must be emphasized once again that conceptual loanwords are not totally equal to loanwords. Conceptual loanwords may include both non-proper-noun loanwords and semantic loans, which are generally excluded from the narrower category of loanwords, but do not count proper-noun loanwords because, unlike the common-noun type of loanwords, those proper nouns, such as *Shashibiya* 莎士比亚 (from the English "Shakespeare") and *Harbin* 哈尔滨 (from the Manchu "Harbin"), do not indicate any concept or idea beyond a mere personal name in the former and a place name in the latter.

1.5.1.2 Words under external influence

In terms of morphemic composition, some other words definitely do not come from the outside: they are not phonetically transliterated, graphically loaned, or of simple semantic loaning. Yet it is very clear to see that they are somewhat related to some other language, either phonetically or graphically. In other words, they directly or indirectly imitate that language one way or another.

For instance, the Chinese word *wailaici* which this book uses came into being under the influence of the Japanese word *gairaigo* (*wailaiyu* 外來語 in Japanese kanji). Though initially intended to be independent from Japanese, *wailaici* is in origin inextricably influenced by it. Similar cases abound. The Chinese *cidian* 词典 (dictionary) came into being under the influence of the Japan-made Chinese word *jiten* 辞典, which had, in turn, been created in Japan under the influence of the Chinese *zidian* 字典 (character dictionary). Early imported Chinese words like *dianhua* 电话 (telephone), *dianbao* 电报 (telegram), and *dianche* 电车 (trolley) were all from Japanese (*denwa* 電話, *denpa* 電報, and *densha* 電車, respectively), but when Japanese essentially abandoned this method of using Chinese characters for semantic loans from the West, the Chinese language was still influenced by this Japanese method of lexical borrowing when it had its own semantic loaning. *Dianshi* 电视 (television) and *dianchuan* 电传 (telefax) were two recent examples, which were based on the established prefix of *dian*, equivalent to "tele."

The two-character word *jinlun* 锦纶 represents another type of words under external influence. Influenced by both *nilun* 尼纶 (also written as *nilong* 尼龙), a phonemic loanword from English "nylon," and *dilun* 涤纶 (from English "dacron"), and also called *diqueliang* 的确良 (from English "terylene"),[14] *jinlun* is a remodeling of the former. Though the second character *lun* is an indigenous Chinese morpheme, its choice here is evidently influenced by the sounds "-lon" and "-ron" from the above English words (nylon, dacron). *Lun*, here, does not mean "cyan ribbon" or "fishing line" any more, as it originally did in the Chinese language, but extends to the material made by weaving or synthetic fiber (since 纟, the left-side component, technically called "radical," of the character *lun* 纶 means "textile"). *Lun* thus gains a new morphemic sense or meaning, and so *jinlun* as a whole is influenced by a foreign language in both phonetic and morphemic aspects.

There is still another type under external influence. Though it sounds very like the English expression "motor car," *motuoka* 摩托卡 in the Shanghai dialect is, counter-intuitively, not a phonemic loan from "motor car," which itself is an old-fashioned word for four-wheeled "car," but is instead remodeled from its Chinese synonym *motuoche* 摩托车, which is indeed a hybrid loanword from English "motorcycle," then somewhat pidginized. Such Chinese words formed through reverse pidginization may be called "Chinese-made English words." *Maxam*, the English name for *Meijiajing* 美加净, a well-known Chinese cosmetic brand, is another example. Words of this kind are not very common, but, considering what the Japanese language has experienced, their number will continue increasing as the society opens up, and international exchanges expand. It is already clear that, in an open society today, mutual influence between languages has become increasingly frequent and intense as long as science knows no national boundary, and we live in a global village. Besides loanwords and borrowed notions, the influences which have been discussed above are not uncommon at all. Whether or not there is a need to set up a new category of "*wailai yingxiang ci*" (words of foreign influence),[15] there is no denying the external lexical influence that is reflected in these words.

1.5.2 *Other external influences on the native language*

The loanword is one of many manifestations of mutual influence and diffusion between languages; the impact of this mutual assimilation or osmosis goes beyond the lexicon. Rather, it extends to phonetic, grammatical, and pragmatic aspects of the language. Zhao Yuanren (1959/1968) cites a number of cases to illustrate the sheer complexity of the influences between languages. Though his investigation also includes intra-lingual dialects, ours is limited to different languages.

1.5.2.1 External phonetic influence

Zhao points out that Chinese Cantonese long vowels have their entering tone at mid-point, and short vowels at high point, but long vowels in Cantonese loanwords from English usually have their entering tone at high point. For instance, the long vowel in the English word "court" is pronounced with high entering tone in Hong Kong, which is different from the Cantonese indigenous phonological system. We have also noticed that there are changes to the phonetic structure of some loanwords used in the Shanghai dialect, such as *sidike* 司的克 (loanword from English "stick") and "*sibiling(suo)*" 司必灵(锁) (loanword from English "spring lock"). Many Shanghainese people already pronounce the former as /stiʔk/ and the latter as /spiʔlin/. That means that there appear such compound consonants as [sd] and [sb] as well as the occlusive consonant [k] in some language user groups. Incidentally, from a broader perspective, tones in the Qinghai dialect 青海方言 are also an interesting phenomenon to note. They are pronounced very quickly in Mandarin Chinese and reduced to three tones only. Even toneless cases appear in some areas in the Qinghai dialect. All these words are likely influenced by the following factors: complex ethnic makeup, frequent interactions, and the long-term impact of the toneless Altaic languages on Chinese. In addition, the disappearance of the entering tone and "-m" in the Chinese Northern Dialects is most likely influenced by ancient non-Han ethnic languages.

Phonetic borrowing is most prominent in those words which are solely made up of alphabetic letters. For instance, HSK, an acronym for *Hanyu Shuiping Kaoshi* 汉语水平考试 (Chinese Proficiency Test), is pronounced according to the English letters. So is QQ, a popular instant messaging service in China. Another, much earlier, example is *Ah Q*, the well-known fictional character of the typical Chinese everyman, created by Lu Xun 鲁迅 (Lu Hsun, 1881–1936), one of the greatest writers in 20th-century Chinese literature. Although the author has advised his readers otherwise, people still prefer to pronounce the "Q" in the name as it is in the English language / kjuː/, a combination sound not indigenous to Chinese.

The appearance of phonetic borrowing in loanwords and even one's native language is a common phenomenon; it is a major contributor to advancing the evolution of language. But this does not go against the requirement that loanwords as a whole must be naturalized to varying degrees in the Chinese language (see Section 1.1.1 "Defining the concept"). The necessary condition for the entry of this kind of foreign phonetic elements into Chinese is that they must have been used for a relatively long period of time and broadly accepted or widely used in the Chinese language. It also presupposes that using the lexical forms of words which contain borrowed phonetic elements is both natural and necessary. Only in this way can these words transform themselves from foreign words to Chinese loanwords through an acceptable degree of Sinicization or Chinese naturalization.

1.5.2.2 External syntactic influence

Again, as Chinese linguist Zhao (1970) points out, there also exists a "structural borrowing," namely, grammatical borrowing in the Chinese language, as a result of external linguistic influence. Zhao cites the Chinese expression *Zhengbian zai Yuenan* 政变在越南 as a result of directly borrowing the English nominal syntax of "coup in Vietnam." Similar examples of the passive indicator "bei" include *beida* 被打, *beipian* 被骗, and *beifa* 被罚, all influenced by the English passive structures of "being beaten, being swindled, and being punished," respectively. Another example is *chuban yiben shu* 出版一本书, which is directly influenced by the English "publish a book."[16] Here, *chuban* is used in a "verb + object" (V+O) structure as a transitive verb followed by a direct object. Originally an intransitive verb, *chuban* can now take an object due to foreign influence.

As a contemporary example, an examination of the widely used syntactic structure in the 20th century of *zhengzai...zhong* 正在...中 or *zai...zhong* 在...中, as in *(zheng)zai jianshe zhong* (正)在建设中 (is being constructed or under construction) or *(zheng)zai yanjiu zhong* 正在研究中 (is being discussed), may probably come from Japanese. Typically, the Chinese indigenous expression for a particular attendant state of an action process, such as "*shuohuajian*" 说话间 (while talking) and "*xiantanzhong*" 闲谈中 (while chatting), can only be used as adverbial or attributive. With Japanese borrowing, however, this kind of expression branches out into a new structure of "verb + *Zhong*," such as "*yingye zhong*" 营业中, "*jianshe zhong*" 建设中, "*zuoye zhong*" 作业中, and "*yanjiu zhong*" 研究中, to express the state of some action being carried out, very similar to the progressive or continuous tense in Western languages. In other words, it can be used as a predicate or form a sentence alone. Furthermore, while the Japanese words before the suffix "*zhong*" (e.g. Japanese equivalents to *yingye*, *jianshe*, *zuoye*, and *yanjiu*) are invariably nouns, which contain the meaning of their corresponding verbs, their Chinese counterparts are mainly used as verbs. Therefore, from the three indigenous Chinese syntactic structures—"verb + *zhong*" to indicate being in the middle of doing something, "*zai* + location word + *zhong*" to indicate a specific location, and "*zhengzai* + verb" or "*zai* + verb" to indicate that some action is taking place—evolves a new mode of verbal expression indicating the progressive tense.

Here is another case of the external influence on the Chinese syntax. Until recently, the structure of *yongyuan de xiaoyuan* 永远的校园 (literally "forever campus") had been criticized as grammatically incorrect, and "*yongjiu*" 永久 (long-lasting) should have been used to replace *yongyuan* (forever). The argument was that *yongyuan* is an adverb (while *yongjiu* is an adjective) and as such should only be used to modify a verb; an adjective; a phrase; or another adverb, like *"yongyuan kuaile"* 永远快乐 (forever happy) and *"yongyuan baochi"* 永远保持 (forever maintain). However, the adjectival use of *"yongyuan de"* has been increasing, making it a new and established custom through common practice, a *fait accompli*, if you will, in such book titles as *Yongyuan de Eileen Chang* 永远的张爱玲 and *Yongyuan de meili* 永远的美丽, and in such essays titles as *"yongyuan de huannian"* 永远的怀念, *"yongyuan de senlin"* 永远的森林, and *"yongyuan de chulian"* 永远的初恋. This structure is in fact influenced by Japanese as *eien* 永遠, the Japanese equivalent of *yongyuan*, can be used as an adjective, as can the Chinese *yongjiu*, such as "永遠の祈り" (eternal prayer), "永遠の愛"(everlasting love), and "永遠の響" (eternal sound). This Japanese structure first influenced Chinese language communities in Taiwan and Hong Kong before it came to influence the Chinese mainland through artistic works from the two regions.

1.5.2.3 External influence on practical word usage

The external influence on lexical usage can easily be seen in the film industry too. Until recently, it was always the case that Chinese movies ended with the word *"wan"* 完 (the end), but now, some films depart from the established practice and end with the word *"zhong"* 終 (the end) instead, which is borrowed from the Japanese practice of displaying *shuu* 終 at the end of a movie. The Chinese word *wan*, after all, is also copied from the English "End" or the French "Fin". Another example of Japanese influence is the word *"zhan"* 展 (exhibition, show). Today, exhibitions we typically see are phrased in the format of "theme of the exhibition + *zhan*," such as *xiandai guohua zhan* 现代国画展 and *mingqing taoci yishu zhan* 明清陶瓷艺术展. Until recently, however, such events were usually phrased in the format of "theme of the exhibition + *zhanlanhui* 展览会" instead of *"zhan."* Thanks to the increasing cultural exchanges between China and Japan, the more concise expression of *"zhan"* has helped create a new lexical usage in China.

External influence on lexical usage is also reflected in the form of address. *Tongzhi* 同志 ("comrade") as a common form of address in contemporary China was not even used to address anyone in feudal China. In the early 20th century, *tongzhi'* came into use as a form of address to correspond to "comrade" in the Western languages. But until 1949, when the People's Republic was founded by the Chinese Communist Party, it was only used within a political party or its affiliated organizations, be that the Communist Party or the Kuomintang (Nationalist Party). After 1949, however, *tongzhi* was extended to all ordinary citizens; it was obviously influenced by the usage of its equivalent in foreign languages, especially the Russian "товарищ" in the former Soviet Union. As another brief example, *"nushimen xianshengmen"* 女生们、先生们 ("ladies and gentlemen"), as used at the beginning of a formal speech, obviously follows the Western custom of putting ladies before gentlemen, another instance of foreign influence on the usage of Chinese lexicon.

Although not strictly belonging to the lexicon itself, they may sometimes exert an influence on lexical forms and the broader lexical intensions or extensions, such as the syntactic evolution of the above-mentioned *yongyuan*. Therefore, it is necessary to pay attention to external influences on the native language beyond the lexicon while examining the loanword in its traditional sense.

Notes

1 *On-yomi*, literally "sound reading," is the pronunciation of a Japanese word written in Chinese characters that is roughly based on the pronunciation of those characters in the originating Chinese dialect at the time the word was introduced into Japanese, in contrast to the other Japanese pronunciation system, called "*kun-yomi*."
2 When borrowed into Japanese or other foreign languages, some of those autochthonous Chinese words or Chinese self-originated words fell into disuse for some time in their native Chinese language before returning to Chinese via Japanese or other foreign languages, with the same lexical meaning as before the borrowing. These words should be called 'returned words', not *bona fide* loanwords. The classification of such words as "return loans" by Masini (1993, 2.2.1) is not really proper. As for *ciqiao* 词侨 (overseas Chinese words), this is obviously not serious terminology but a tongue-in-cheek metaphor since it does not, for one thing, distinguish itself from 'returned words' or 'return loanwords'.
3 One of the earliest appearances of the word *waiguoyu* 外国语 was in the second of the ten volumes of *Shuying* 书影, a collection of literary essays, by Zhou Lianggong 周亮工 (1612–1672), a scholar in the Qing dynasty:

> Chen Wugong 陈无功 from Xieli complied the *Shuwu yiming shu*庶物异名疏 (*Various names of things explained*). There are 2,452 entries in total. It is erudite. In my opinion, no words in *waiguoyu* or Buddhist Scriptures are certain. What is worse, through many translations there appear many errors and mistakes. So it's better to have them cut out. Then it can be called a great work.

4 *Jieruyu*借入语 first appeared in the *English-Chinese Dictionary of the Standard Chinese Spoken Language (Chinese characters for "Mandarin")* in 1905 by Karl Hemeling.
5 *Jieyongyu*借用语 was originally a Japanese translation of the English 'loanword' and made its first appearance in China in the long essay titled *Lun yiming*论译名 (*On translating names and terms*) by Hu Yilu胡以鲁: "Transferring languages across four corners of the world is called translation, so translation has to follow the meaning of the source language. If its sound is followed instead, it is '*jieyongyu*'. So sound and translation cannot go together."
6 Gao Mingkai and Liu Zhengtan wrote in their book *Xiandai hanyu wailaici yanjiu* 现代汉语外来词研究 (*A study of loanwords in modern Chinese*) (1958:13) that *wailaici* refers to words in the native language that are of foreign origin while *jieci* refers to borrowed words of a foreign language. *Jieci* are still foreign; they are just borrowed for use only. In the process of assimilating foreign words, sometimes we borrow them first and then slowly change them to *wailaici*. Only when the borrowed foreign words have taken root in the phonetic, grammatical and lexical systems, can it be sure that they become loanwords.

Their argument here makes sense. There do indeed exist two ways of using foreign words, but the terminology used by them to tell the difference could only

cause terminological confusion. The two terms have been synonymously used in China but used opposite to each other in Germany. So, it is worth exploring whether a new interpretation of the concept of "borrowed foreign words" should be used to avoid confusion.
7 Zhang's *Wenxue shuoli* first appeared in 1902 in the 15th issue of the *Sein Min Choong Bou*, run by Chinese students studying in Japan. Its revised version was included in his self-collected anthology *Qiushu* 廑书 with a new title *Zhengming shuoli* 正名说例 (*Introduction to naming verification*).
8 *Yinyi* 音译 and *yiyi* 意译 are also from Japanese. Hu Yilu (1914) doubted the idea of *yinyi*, claiming that " '*yin*' (sound) and '*yi*' (translation) cannot go together" (cf. footnote 5). In fact, the term *yinyi* properly reflects the characteristics with which Chinese phonetically borrows foreign words. *Yi* means turn or change. So, there is no absolute phonetic borrowing, but the original sound will be changed more or less in order to adapt to the phonological system of the recipient language.
9 The first draft of Cen's work *Hanyu wailaici cidian* 汉语外来词词典, completed in the 1970s, had the same title as the work by Liu Zhengtan. So, when officially published, it was changed to the current title to avoid confusion. In 1981, when talking about his dictionary, Cen still used the term *wailaici*. Please refer to the Preface to Cen's work, published in the second issue in 1981 in a Hong Kong-based journal *Zhongguo yuwen yanjiu* 中国语文研究 (*Studies in Chinese Linguistics*) (Cen 1981).
10 *Translator's note*: Considering the canonical works by major international scholars of the field today and terms used therein, this English version of the book still chooses to stick to 'loanword'—rather than other English alternatives—to refer to *wailaici* throughout (including in the book title) for the sake of clarity and better discussion. Works that have contributed to this choice include, among others, *Borrowed Words: A History of Loanwords in English* (Oxford, 2014) by Philip Durkin, Deputy Chief Editor of the *Oxford English Dictionary*; *The Routledge Encyclopedia of the Chinese Language* (Routledge, 2016); *Loanwords in Japanese* (Benjamins, 2011); and the monumental *The Formation of Modern Chinese Lexicon and Its Evolution Toward a National Language: The Period from 1840 to 1898* (Berkeley, 1993).
11 Sōbē Arakawa, a Japanese authority on loanword studies, called the phonetic, semantic, and graphic representations the "three essential elements" that influence loanwords (1932:10–17).
12 In another discussion of loanword identity, Section 4.1.1 in Chapter 4 of this book also mentions aspects to consider as a way of borrowing (phonemic or semantic loaning), usage (for actual use or mere reference, source provision or academic inquiry), frequency in usage, user community (popular or small group), and semantics (semantic traceability to the source word) in the determination of a loanword in the Chinese language. While this applies to loanwords which are represented in writing in Chinese characters as a general rule, alphabetic letter words are more complicated and require more consideration.
13 *Ciku jianshe tongxun* 《词库建设通讯》, a now discontinued journal in Hong Kong dedicated to loanword studies, was the first to propose the name "conceptual loanword." Based on this concept, the journal organizes academic activities and publishes relevant articles. Please refer to the very first issue (in Chinese) in July 1993, accessible at http://www.huayuqiao.org/articles/cikujianshetongxun/ckjs01.pdf, for a general introduction to and discussions about creating a corpus of conceptual loanwords.
14 The association of Chinese *dilun* with the British word 'terylene,' as shown in the *Hanyu wailaici cidian* 汉语外来词词典, is highly open to question. 'Te' in

the latter is equivalent to the aspirated 'te' in Chinese so is highly unlikely to correspond to Chinese sound 'di', which is not aspirated. In contrast, 'd' in the American English word 'dacron' is a voiced consonant, which happens to be phonetically the same as 'di' in *dilun* in the Chinese dialect and equivalent to that pronounced in the Beijing dialect. As far as this author knows, when the word *dilun* was adopted, there didn't seem to be any fabric called terylene on the Chinese market. What is more, the origin of *dilun* can be learned from the variant forms of a word. The Chinese words for dacron were first 的确凉, then 的确良 or 涤确良, all three pronounced *diqueliang* in pinyin, and later shortened to 的良 or 涤良, both pronounced *diliang* in pinyin. The Chinese words for terylene were 特丽纶 *telilun*, 缇缡纶 *tililun*, 特锐烯 *teruixi*, and the shortened form 特纶 *telun*. The first sound of all these variants is 't'. Seen from another perspective, *dilun* may be a creation out of dacron and nylon.

15 '*Wailai yingxiang c*i' (words of foreign influence) was first proposed by two scholars separately in articles published in the seventh issue of *Cikun jianshe tongxun* in 1995. Huang Heqing proposed that the currently defined phonetic, semantic, and graphic loans be collectively called words of foreign influence. His proposed concept includes loanwords but is broader in scope than loanwords. Shi Youwei, on the other hand, proposed another type of words than loanwords, as discussed in Section 1.5.1.2. Please also refer to the two articles and "Wailaiyu, wailai gainian ci, wailai yingxiang ci zhi huiying" 外来语和外来概念词外来影响词之回应 [My reflections on loanwords, conceptual loanwords and words of foreign influence] (Shi 1996).

16 Some research claims that the Chinese word '*chuban*' 出版 is a graphic loanword from Japanese *shuppan* 出版, which is, in turn, a semantic loan from the English word 'publish' or 'publication'. If this holds true, then the function of *chuban* to take a direct object in the Chinese language is perhaps directly influenced by Japanese. In other words, while borrowing the Japanese word *shuppan*, *chuban* has also borrowed the function of its taking an object in the Japanese language. It is characteristic of Japanese that its verb's taking an object is not affected by the V+O structure. So, Zhao's opinion here is questionable.

2 A historical overview of Chinese loanwords

2.1 Chinese loanwords prior to 2070 BC

2.1.1 Introduction

History and culture are usually two parts of one whole; the continuation and development of a society constitute the sum total of its culture, and at the same time, its history takes shape out of them both. History requires specific vehicles for its representation and preservation. As one of those vehicles, however, language is a special kind of cultural attainment: it can be intangible and transient. Its preservation depends on word of mouth and written documentation from generation to generation. By the same token, loanwords are also composed of two parts: those recorded by written words and those which have remained oral are but yet to be documented in writing. Whether written or oral, they constitute a living epitome of the history and culture to which they relate. For about 5,000 years, since the very beginning of Chinese civilization, cultural exchanges and ethnic conflicts have not paused in or around what is often called the "Central Plain" (*Zhongyuan* 中原) in North China, an area on the lower reaches of the Yellow River, which formed the cradle of Chinese civilization. Those exchanges and conflicts necessarily contained language contact, which to some extent boiled down to loanwords. Chinese history in written records only dates back 4,000 years—at most, 5,000, if unverified legend is taken into account. Knowledge about the history prior to that can only be gleaned by means of the archeology of material culture and language. With its spoken form in existence eons before the written word, language is both a system characterized by certain order and an accumulation which is constantly being affected by historical contingencies and in which many new members or elements become part of the language over the eras. Although each era may see quite a few old members turning obsolete, it is always the case that the majority of the language is carried on from one generation to the next. Otherwise, it would not be possible for languages to have evolved into the huge system they are today. People can now explore linguistic "fossils" through archeological comparisons of different languages. Despite a lack of absolute certainty, the latest research suggests that it is quite possible that, as far as loanwords are concerned, certain traces of foreign or external influence can be uncovered. Among the traces, some are of lexical borrowing, while others belong to substrate influence. What follows is a brief discussion of them.

2.1.2 *Origin of the ancient Chinese names for the 12 years*

In the long poem *Lisao* 离骚 ("On Encountering Sorrow"), the most famous work by Qu Yuan 屈原 (Chu Yuan, c. 339–c. 278 BC), one of the greatest poets of ancient China and the earliest known by name, there already appeared such Chinese names for the year as *sheti* 摄提 and *chanyan* 单阏. By integrating the 10 celestial stems called *tiangan* 天干 (*jia* 甲, *yi* 乙, *bing* 丙, *ding* 丁, *wu* 戊, *ji* 己, *geng* 庚, *xin* 辛, *ren* 壬, and *gui* 癸) and the 12 terrestrial branches called *dizhi* 地支 (*zi* 子, *chou* 丑, *yin* 寅, *mao* 卯, *chen* 辰, *si* 巳, *wu* 午, *wei* 未, *shen* 申, *you* 酉, *xu* 戌, and *hai* 亥) into 60 units, the ancient Chinese counted the years and days with the *tiangan* and *dizhi* combinations cyclically. They knew that the orbital period of Jupiter, called *suixing* 岁星 ("the year star") in ancient China, is about 4,332 days, which is 12 times 361 days. So, the orbital period of Jupiter was divided into 12 sections, which were used to number the year. When Jupiter is moving above the *yin* 寅 terrestrial branch, that year is called the year of *yin* (*yinnian* 寅年), and its corresponding technical term by the ancient Chinese is *sheti* 摄提 or *shetige* 摄提格. There are, of course, 12 such years. By coincidence, there are also 12 imaginary constellations or signs of the zodiac in the West, first invented in ancient Babylon. According to research by the pre-eminent Chinese archeologist Guo Moruo 郭沫若 (Kuo Mo-jo, 1892–1978), there exists some interesting etymological affinity between those 12 signs and the ancient Chinese names for the 12 years, as illustrated below:

Yin 寅, technical term *sheti* 摄提 or *shetige* 摄提格, corresponds to Virgo, which is *súpa* (meaning "Arcturus") in ancient Babylonian and *svati* in Sanskrit.
Mao 卯, technical term *chanyan* 单阏 or 蝉焉 *shan'an* 擅安, corresponds to Leo, which is *sarru* or *ṣìru* in Babylonian.
Chen 辰, technical term *zhixu* 执徐, corresponds to Cancer, which is *kaksidi* or *kakzizi* in Babylonian. With the Babylonian "kak" being removed, *zhixu* probably sounds similar to the Babylonian words.
Si 巳, technical term *dahuangluo* 大荒落, corresponds to Gemini, which is *tuamurabuti* in Akkadian.
Wu 午, technical term *dunzang* 敦牂, corresponds to Taurus, which is *gùan-na* in Babylonian. Literally meaning "stout female sheep," *dunzang* seems like a semantic loan from the Babylonian.
Wei 未, technical term *xieqia* 协恰, corresponds to Aries, which is *ekue* in Babylonian.

34 *A historical overview of Chinese loanwords*

Shen 申, technical term *tuntan* 涽滩, *tunhan* 涽汉, or *ruihan* 芮汉, corresponds to Pisces, which is *nûnu* (plural *nûnê*) in Babylonian.

You 酉, technical term *zuo'e* 作噩 or *zuoluo* 作洛, corresponds to Aquarius, which is *gula* in Babylonian.

Xu 戌, technical term *yanmao* 阉茂, corresponds to Capricorn, which is *enzu* in Akkadian.

Hai 亥, technical term *dayuanxian* 大渊献, corresponds to Sagittarius, which is *pabilsag* in Babylonian.

Zi 子, technical term *kundun* 困敦, corresponds to Scorpio, which is *girtab* in Babylonian.

Chou 丑, technical term *chifenruo* 赤奋若, corresponds to Libra, which is *ziba-anna* in Sumerian and *zibanitu* in Akkadian.

As can be seen from the words in Babylonian (or its cognate languages) provided by Guo, there indeed exists a phonetic similarity between the Western 12 signs of the zodiac and the Chinese technical terms for the terrestrial branches which mark 12 years. As holds true in most cases, such correspondence must be more than merely coincidental. Moreover, those 12 Chinese technical terms do not sound like indigenous Chinese because they each represent a weird combination of Chinese characters, thus running counter to the usual morphemic monosyllabicity in Old Chinese prior to 220 AD. A very plausible explanation is that interactions between ancient Chinese and the outside world had started far before there were historical records so that astronomical knowledge, including the zodiacal signs in Babylonian, might have been introduced to China in the process since ancient astronomy had its earliest beginnings and mostly developed in Babylon.

2.1.3 Origin of the ancient Chinese names for the 12 months

Beside the terms for 12 years, the ancient Chinese also had special terms, totally different from those in current use, for the 12 months in a year: *gu* 辜 for January, *tu* 涂 for February, *zou* 陬 for March, *ru* 如 for April, *bing* 病 for May, *yu* 余 for June, *gao* 皋 for July, *ju* 且 for August, *xiang* 相 for September, *zhuang* 壮 for October, *xuan* 玄 for November, and *yang* 阳 for December.

Guo also compares the above Chinese terms to their Babylonian counterparts,[1] discovering that half of those Chinese one-character terms had similar sounds to the first syllable of their Babylonian equivalents, thus concluding that such phonetic similarity was "probably not coincidental." In fact, this possibility of lexical borrowing from Babylonian can be further proved by the following three aspects. First, those Chinese terms are purely phonetic representations, without any corresponding semantic meaning. Second, many Western nations have special terms for the months, some originating from Babylonian and others from Greek or Roman, but China has consistently used its own numerals in naming months (terms such as *heyue* 荷月 for June, *dongyue* 冬月 for November, and *layue* 腊月

for December are more recent indigenous inventions). Third, since ancient Babylon and Egypt were considered the most astronomically advanced regions in the world, such expertise must have been broadly disseminated in the long process of global interactions, in which the Chinese nation imbibed a rich variety of cultural elements, linguistic ones included. It could then be argued that those ancient Chinese terms for the months might have been introduced from the West or from Babylon into China via some intermediary languages; what is more, they might have been brought to China along with the above-mentioned ancient technical terms for the years.

2.1.4 Unraveling the mysteries of Lisao

Located in the central valley of the Yangtze River, the ancient state of Chu 楚国, Qu Yuan's home state, in which he wrote his long melancholic poem *Lisao*, was a land on which many ethnic groups lived: hence, "the land of *sanmiao*" (*san* for many, *miao* referring to non-Han ethnic groups in the South). Though it is not certain exactly those ethnic groups were, it is clear that they were many and diverse. Some scholars think that some were Turkic Tulans from the west and, with that, try to unravel the mystery of some of the words in *Lisao*. Chinese historian Cen Zhongmian 岑仲勉 (1961), for example, proves that the following words in the *Chuci* 楚辞 ("*The Songs of the South*"), an anthology which includes Qu Yuan's works, such as *Lisao*, *Jiuge* 九歌 ("Nine songs"), *Zhaohun* 招魂 ("Summoning the soul"), and others, originated from Old Turkic.

Lisao 离骚, the title of the famed melancholic poem, is believed to be an inversion of the Old Turkic *sola/sula*, originally meaning "restriction," "severance," and later "sorrow"

Quan 荃, as in *Lisao*: "**Your Majesty** does not give a good understanding of my loyalty but believes in slanders and gets angry with me." (荃不察余之情兮, 反信谗而齐怒). This can be pronounced and interpreted as *sun* 荪, which phonetically corresponds to Old Turkic *sun*, an honorific term to address a social superior.

Ling 灵, as in *Jiuge*: "The **shaman** is swirling to dance while the spirits are still in him" (灵连蜷兮既留). *Ling*, referring to *lingzi* 灵子 or shaman, phonetically corresponds to Old Turkic *ārinč(i)*, which originally meant "indeed, very similar," with an extended meaning of "divination."

Qiang 羌, as in *Lisao*: "Having made the promise for the dusk, **why** change horse in midstream?" (曰黄昏以为期兮, 羌中道而改路). This seems to phonetically correspond to Old Turkic *qaiti* (probably pronounced *kang* by means of inter-mutation between vowel and nasal finals), meaning "for what reason" or "at that time."

Suo 些, as in *Zhaohun* 招魂: "Oh come back, soul, the east is not the place to entrust it" (魂兮归来, 东方不可以托些). *Suo* is a modal auxiliary frequently used in conjuring up the spirit at the end of a sentence. It corresponds to Old Turkic *sa*, meaning "I say" or "he says."

Cen believes that 18 other words, such as *chanyuan* 婵媛 (haunting), *xibi* 犀比 (belt hook for ancient nobles and literati warriors), and *xisuai* 蟋蟀 (grasshopper), also originated from Old Turkic. Though many scholars do not agree with such a bold opinion, they cannot present any convincing evidence to prove otherwise, so their actual origin remains a mystery unresolved. It is safe to say, however, that those words were heterogeneous parts of Old Chinese, which did not have any semantic significance in the language system at the time, so most probably, they were remnants of very ancient foreign words.

2.1.5 Bulu, yu, *and* fu *for* bi *("pen")*

According to the *Shuowen Jiezi* 说文解字 ("An explication of written characters"), an early 2nd-century Chinese dictionary in the Han Dynasty 东汉, "*yu* 聿 is what to write with. It was the word used in the State of Chu. It was called *bulu* 不律 in the State of Wu, *fu* 弗 in the State of Yan, and *bi* 笔 in the State of Qin." Seen both from word formation and phonetics perspectives, all those variations were of the same origin—each probably formed out of two syllables (b- and l-) or words with compound consonants (bl). They also became increasingly simplified as they were used in more geographically southern areas; hence their presumably originating from the southern part of China at the time, where, in the States of Chu and Wu, the dominant Han people lived with non-Han southern ethnic groups, who, in turn, had close ties with people in the Austronesian language family further south. Interestingly, in the Austronesian languages, there is a word, *bulut*, meaning "fiber" or "soft fur," and in Indonesian, there is *balut*, meaning "daub," both of which are closely related to those Chinese words for "pen" in meaning and formation. So, there is a strong possibility that they were borrowed as archaic Chinese loanwords from Austronesian languages via non-Han ethnic groups in the south. To a lesser extent, some other scholars believe that those linguistic affinities may point to some kind of a kinship between Chinese and Austronesian languages (Xing Gongwan 邢公畹 1991).

2.1.6 Feilian *for* feng *("wind")*

Another historical mystery is that *feilian* 飞廉 was the word used in *Chuci* for the "deity of the wind" and also stood for "wind" (*feng* 风) itself. Though opinions over its exact origin vary, the latest research suggests that it is a remnant loanword from the language of *Dongyi* 东夷 (literally "eastern barbarians," inhabitants of eastern and northeastern China, the Korean peninsula, or Japan), who are believed by some to be the same as the Tungusic people, who are, in turn, related to old Korean. *Feilian* seems to be of the same origin as *bolan* 孛缆 (Old Korean for "wind"). As Dongyi people settled in different regions, various languages evolved, including the Austronesian and Kra-Dai languages (Yuchi Zhiping 尉迟治平 1995).

2.1.7 Gu and he

Dao 稻, the Chinese word for "rice," is also called *gu* 谷 or *he* 禾 in the southern part of China. Examining plant history and archeological discoveries, recent studies in historical and comparative linguistics have proved that the two southern alternative words for "rice" might both have originated from the Kra-Dai language family. Rice originated from the Southeast Asian region spanning China's southwestern Guangxi and southern Yun'nan provinces; northern Vietnam; Laos and Thailand; and Myanmar's Shan State, bordering China. Ancient northern Han Chinese people came down to live with non-Han indigenous people in Guangxi and Yun'nan who were Kra-Dai language speakers; learned how to grow rice from them, as shown from the grains excavated at the *Hemudu* 河姆渡 site, which reveals life at the Neolithic Age 7,000 years ago; and probably borrowed the people's terms in the process. According to Zhou Zhenhe 周振鹤 and You Rujie 游汝杰 (1986), the original term might have been **khau*, only later splintering off into two separate ones: *k'ao* and *hau*, on which Chinese *gu* and *he* were based, respectively.

2.2 Between 2070 BC and 220 AD (Qin and Han dynasties)

2.2.1 Introduction

Interactions between Han and non-Han Chinese people became incrementally frequent in this period and were carried out at both political and non-governmental levels. While people-to-people interactions, characterized by the promotion of ethnic and racial integration, had been in existence since very ancient times, interactions at the political level were explorative and proactive in nature, and dominated in the Han dynasty 汉代 (206 BC–220 AD).

Though the prior dynasties of Xia 夏, Shang 商, and Zhou 周 lasted a long time, presumably with lots of interactions with their various neighboring ethnic groups, only a few written forms of alien words are found in the Zhou dynasty.

One of them was *qinglu* 轻吕, also called *qingjian* 轻剑, a double-edged sword at the time. According to Guo Moruo's research, it was believed to be *jinglu* 径路 (from *qingrak* or *kyngrak* in Turkic), used by the Huns (also known as "*Xiongnu*" 匈奴 in Chinese), a warlike nomadic people of central Asian origin who controlled large parts of eastern and central Europe in the 5th century. Recent studies suggest that it probably came from the now-extinct Tocharian "*kare*." The *qilin* 麒麟 mentioned by Confucius in China's Spring and Autumn Period 春秋时代 (770–476 BC) was probably the African giraffe, which was called *giri* in the modern eastern Somalian dialect. By means of inter-mutation between vowel and nasal finals, the sound of *giri* corresponds to that of *qilin*. When knowledge about that African animal finally reached China via central Asia, it became a mythical or legendary creature.

2.2.2 Loanwords from Hun

The long-lasting interactions between the Huns and Chinese in the Han dynasty alternated between war and peace, constituting a thrilling saga of history. While it is not clear where other Huns later settled (possibly in Europe), some of this nomadic race was assimilated into the Han Chinese. In their exchanges, Chinese people absorbed some vocabulary from the Hun language, mostly related to royal titles and a few related to article names, such as:

Hu 胡, a self-designation for Huns themselves, originating from the Hun *ghua, ghuan,* or *ghuana.*

Chanyu/shanyu 单于/善于, king of the Huns, probably originating from the Hun *senogu/senhu* or *sanok/tsanak.*

Chengligutu 撑犁孤涂, another name for the *chanyu*, meaning "the son of Heaven." *Chengli* may have originated from the Hun *tangara/tangri,* meaning "heaven," and *gutu* 孤涂 or 孤屠 maybe originated from *kutu/toy,* meaning "son."

Yanshi/yanzhi/nianzhi 阏氏/烟支(燕支, 焉支)/撚支, queen of the Huns, official wife of *chanyu. Yanshi* may have originated from *asi/aši, hatsi/katsi,* or *hati/hatin. Yanzhi* or *nianzhi* originated from the Hun *yanci/yansi,* the name of a mountain famous for its rouge, possibly with an extended meaning of "married woman."

Tuqi/zhuqi 涂耆/诸耆, the nobility under *chanyu*, may have originated from the Hun *tuki* or *šoki/čoki.*

Xibi/xupi/shibi/sipi/xianbei 犀比(犀毗)/胥纰/师比/私纰/鲜卑, belt hook, from the name of a Hun creature, may have originated from the Hun *serbi.*

Guoluo/gouluo/kuoluo 郭落(郭洛)/钩络/廓落(廓络), girdle, originated from the Hun *qwaylag/qwayrag.*

2.2.3 Things which came from the "Western Regions"

As a historical term specified in the Chinese chronicles between the 3rd century BC to the 8th century AD, the "Western Regions" or *Xiyu* spanned a very wide area, from Yumen Pass 玉门关 in western China's Gansu province today to Congling 葱岭 (the Pamir Mountains today) in the narrow sense; more broadly speaking, it extended to the Near or Middle East, India, Arabia, and Byzantium. Following the order of the Wudi emperor 汉武帝 of the Han dynasty in 138 BC, Zhang Qian started his diplomatic journey to the west, trying to ally the Han Chinese with their neighboring ethnic states against the Huns and setting up the Protectorate of the Western Regions in 60 BC, thus establishing official administrative relations with the vast area west of Congling. As a result of his journey, more loanwords about life in the Western Regions were introduced to the Chinese language, such as:

Luotuo 骆驼 ("camel") may have originated from the Hun **dada*, with earlier forms of tuota/tuotuo 橐它(橐他)/橐佗, and later evolved toward meaning-signifying 橐驼 or 駝驼 and settled into its current form as a result of phonetic mis-transformation.

Shizi 狮子 ("lion") may have originated from old Persian *ser* or old East Iranian *se* or *si*, with earlier written forms 师/师子, and from *suan'ni* 狻猊 (or *zun'er* 尊耳), the origins of which are unknown.

Muxu 苜蓿 or 牧蓿 (alfalfa), also written as *musu* 目宿 (or 木粟), originated from the Uzbek or Elamite *buksuk/buxsux/buxsuk*.

Shiliu 石榴, also *ruoliu* 若榴, earlier form *anshiliu* 安石榴 (pomegranate), may have originated from Elamite *Arsak* (name of a country in central Asia) or from Sogdian *anaraka*.

Konghou 箜篌(空侯) or *kanhou* 坎侯, an Elamite 23-stringed pluck instrument, later also with 7, 17, 30, or other numbers of strings, may have originated from the Turkic *qobuz/qubuz*.

Pipa 琵琶, also written as 枇杷 or *pipo* 鼙婆, initially *piba* 批把 (a 4-stringed lute-like Chinese musical instrument plucked like a guitar), may have originated from the Elamite *barbat* or been related to old Greek *barbiton*.

2.2.4 Nai *as a substrate influence*

Though the Chinese indigenous word *ru* 乳 (meaning "breast") is now synonymous with *nai* 奶, the latter was written as 嬭 (妳) about 2,000 years ago in the Han dynasty, which means both "mother" and "breast." *Nai* may not have been indigenous but may have come from some non-Han ancient language. In the current Wu Chinese dialect 吴语, which is spoken in Shanghai and the southern Zhejiang and northern Fujian provinces, *nai* is still used in isolation or with a prefix to mean "mother" and "grandmother" by extension, such as $a?na^1$ (meaning "grandma") in Shanghai, a^7na^1 in Wenzhou, $noung^6ne^3$ in Fuzhou, ne^3 in Fudong, a^1ne^1 in Fuding, and nai^3 in Jian'ou and Jianyang. Research indicates that *nai* might have been a substrate word in the ancient non-Han *Baiyue* ethnic languages. Its counterparts in the Kra-Dai language family, which was related to the Baiyue languages, were $nəi^{31}$ in the ethnic Dong 侗语; ni^4 in the ethnic Gelao 仡佬语, Shui 水语, and Maonan 毛难 languages; and me^6 in the ethnic Dai 傣语, Buyi 布依语, and Zhuang 壮语 languages, all of which seem to have evolved from the same source.

The Chinese language in the period between 2070 BC and 220 AD left behind some more substrate words, which will be discussed in the next section.

2.3 From 220 to 684 AD (Wei, Jin, Northern, Southern, Sui, and Tang dynasties)

2.3.1 Introduction

For better discussion of Buddhist terms, this book puts the Eastern Han dynasty (25–220 AD) and the period of the Three Kingdoms (220–280 AD) in this section; for a similar purpose of linguistic and historical continuity, the latter period of the Tang dynasty is also included. Loanwords in this period will be explored with regards to the following four types: Buddhist terms, everyday words borrowed via the Silk Road, words out of interaction with or invasion of other ethnic groups, and substrate words due to ethnic integration. Unlike the previous period (2070 BC and 220 AD), loanwords in this period not only increased drastically in number but covered more aspects of society, making this the first major wave in the history of the inflow of Chinese loanwords. It indicates that Han Chinese interactions with non-Han Chinese or foreign peoples turned increasingly frequent, and the areas of their interchanges were no longer limited to the social titles or rare artefacts but extended to deeper and broader areas, that is, words of everyday life and belief systems.

2.3.2 Borrowed Buddhist terms

Though first introduced in the Eastern Han, Buddhism had its real boom in the Wei 魏, Jin 晋, Northern, and Southern dynasties 南北朝 when a large number of Buddhist terms were introduced to China. The Chinese translation and assimilation of those terms can be divided into three phases: from the "Western Regions" in the Eastern Han; from the Indian and central Asian Buddhist monks stationed in China; and from the large-scale systematic translation of the sacred scriptures of Buddhism from Sanskrit into Chinese after Xuanzang 玄奘 (Hsüan-tsang, 602–664), the famous Chinese monk, returned from his pilgrimage to India to study at the fountainhead of Buddhism. Since there are so many Buddhist terms in Chinese translation, only a small portion will be discussed below.

Fo/Fotuo 佛/佛陀, a title given to a person regarded as having attained full "prajna" or awakening or enlightenment. Its earliest written form was *futu* 浮屠 or 浮图 in the Eastern Han dynasty, both of which were translated from ancient Pali *Buddho*, while the currently used form, *fo*, was translated from old Tocharian *pät* or *pūd*. *Fotuo* came into use after *fo* and was translated from Sanskrit *Buddha*.

Emituo Fo 阿弥陀佛, one of the three Buddhas in Mahayana Buddhism who presides over the Western Paradise of Bliss, called *Sukhavati* ("the Pure Land"). Originating from Sanskrit *Amitabha*, the term is often prefixed with *namo* 南无, meaning "believe in" or "willingly convert myself to," originating from Pali *namo*.

Lushena Fo 卢舍那佛 originated from the Sanskrit *vairocana*. It is one of three bodies (*trikaya*) of the Buddha in Mahayana Buddhism. In China, it refers to the combined *dharmakaya* (body of essence, *pilushena* 毗卢舍那 or *darirulai* 大日如来 in Chinese) and the *sambhogakaya* (body of enjoyment, *lushena* 卢舍那 or *luzhena* 卢遮那 in Chinese). The third body is called the *nirmanakaya* (body of transformation).

Mile Fo 弥勒佛, the Buddha who will appear in the future, the successor to Tathagata or Siddhartha Gautama. *Mile Fo* originated from Sanskrit *Maitreya*, meaning "friendliness."

Luohan 罗汉, initially written as *aluohan* 阿罗汉, were close disciples of the Buddha, who were entrusted by him to remain in the world and not enter nirvana until the coming of the next Buddha in order to provide people with objects of worship. The word originated from the Sanskrit *Arhan/Arhat*.

Yanluo 阎罗, *yanmoluo* 阎摩罗, or *yanmoluoshe* 阎摩罗社, in full, god of death and lord of the underworld, originated from the Sanskrit *Yamaraja*. It is now more commonly known as *yanwang* 阎王 or *yanluowang* 阎罗王.

Mo 魔, *moluo* 魔罗 in full, the Buddhist demon, originated from the Sanskrit *Mara*.

Heshang 和尚, initially written as 和上, a Buddhist monk or teacher with high moral and spiritual cultivation. It may have originated from Central Asian *khosha*, later phonetically mis-transformed into *härši(a)ng*, which was from the Sanskrit *Upadhyaya*, once translated as *wubotuoye* 邬波驮耶.

Seng 僧 or *sengjia* 僧伽, initially the Buddhist community, later referring specifically to a male Buddhist who has given up most or all of his worldly possessions and responsibilities to commit full-time to Buddhist practice. The term originated from the Sanskrit *Samgha*.

Biqiu 比丘, a fully ordained male monastic in Buddhism above the age of 20 who has passed the upasampada ritual and is thus fully ordained, originated from the Sanskrit *Bhiksu* or Pali *Bhikkhu*.

Biqiuni 比丘尼, a fully ordained female monastic above the age of 20 in Buddhism, originated from the Sanskrit *Bhikṣuṇī*.

Shamen 沙门, an individual *seng*, probably originated from old Kuchaean *Samane*, which was from Pali *Samana*.

Shami 沙弥, a partially ordained male monastic in Buddhism between 7 and 20 years old who keeps the Ten Precepts as their code of behavior. The equivalent term for girls is *shamini* 沙弥尼. *Shami* probably originated from old Kuchaean *Samir*, and *shamini* may also have originated from Central Asian Pali *Samaneri*.

Toutuo 头陀, an ascetic, mendicant, and roving monk seeking the Buddhist truth, originated from the Sanskrit *Dhuta*.

Jialan 伽蓝 or *sengjialan* 僧伽蓝, or *sengjialanmo* 僧伽蓝摩 in full, a Buddhist temple or monastery, originated from the Sanskrit *Samgharama*.

Ta 塔, once written as *tapo* 塔婆, originated from the Sanskrit *Thuba/Thupa*. Its variant *futu* 浮屠/浮图 was probably abbreviated from *fotuozudubo* 佛陀窣堵波, from the Sanskrit "Buddha Stupa," meaning "a Buddhist burial mound."

Cha 刹, a tall vertical structure with streamers on a Buddhist mound or grave in which the relics of the deceased Buddhist (*sarira* in Sanskrit and Chinese phonemic loanword *sheli* 舍利) were hidden. It then came to refer to a stupa or pagoda, later extended to refer to a temple as its main structure evolved into the vertical shaft atop a stupa, called *sorin*, meaning "alternate rings." *Cha* is short for *lachadi* 拉刹底, from the Sanskrit *Laksata*. When referring to a temple, *cha* may also have come from *chaduoluo* 刹多罗 from the Sanskrit *Kṣetra*, meaning "field" or "land."

Fan 梵, short for *fanmo* 梵摩. Initially meaning "tranquility and absence from desires," *fan* originated from the Sanskrit *Brahma*. It also referred to a major god in Brahmanism, later one of the three realms of the cosmos in Buddhism, thus translated as *fantian* 梵天. In China, it is also used as a modifier to suggest the Buddhist nature.

Niepan 涅槃 or *niepanna* 涅槃那, freedom from the endless cycle of personal reincarnations, the passing away of a Buddha or arhat. The term originated from the Pali *Nibbana* or the Sanskrit *Nirvana*. The semantically rendered alternative is *yuanji* 圆寂.

Yulanpen 盂兰盆 or *yulanpen jie* 盂兰盆节, a Buddhist festival which falls on the 15th of July in the Chinese calendar to honor the spirits of past ancestors and strive to relieve aching souls from suffering. It originated from the Sanskrit *Ullambana* or *Ullumbana*.

Jie 偈, originally translated as *jietuo* 偈陀 from the Sanskrit *Gatha*. Also semantically rendered *jieju* 偈句, *jiesong* 偈颂, or *jieyu* 偈语, it refers to the words sung to praise the Buddha in the Buddhist scripture. Buddhists may also make their own *jieyu* to spread the Buddhist truth and enlighten their disciples.

Mantuluo 曼荼罗, *mantuoluo* 曼陀罗, or semantic loanword *lunyuan juzu* 轮圆具足, a concentric configuration of geometric shapes, representing the ten spiritual realms of life. It originated from the Sanskrit *Mandala*. It often refers to the place where religious preaching or teaching takes place. Esoteric Buddhism often had all different buddhas and bodhisattvas painted on square diagrams as secret artefacts for religious cultivation.

Puti 菩提, supreme enlightenment, wisdom attained upon supreme enlightenment, or means of attaining supreme enlightenment. It originated from the Sanskrit *Bodhi*.

Yujia 瑜伽, yoking of body and mind, a system of exercises for attaining physical and mental cultivation. It originated from the Sanskrit *yoga*.

Chan 禅, a Buddhist way of self-cultivation through sitting in meditation with legs crossed, to withdraw the mind so as to lead to a state of perfect equanimity and awareness. Initially translated as *channa* 禅那, it originated from the Sanskrit *Dhyana*.

Chan 忏, meaning *chanhui* 忏悔 in modern Chinese, or "asking for forgiveness," was initially one of the Buddhist rituals. *Chanmo* 忏摩 in full, it originated from the Sanskrit *Ksama*.

Jie 劫, a recurring, extremely long period of calamity. *Jiebo* 劫波 in full, it originated from the Sanskrit *Kalpa*.

Cha'na 刹那, an imperceptibly small amount of time in Buddhism, approximately 0.08 seconds, in which there are 900 arisings and ceasings, originated from the Sanskrit *Kṣāṇa*.

The translation of the Buddhist scriptures also brought in an alien word to China, that is, *Zhina* 支那. Also variously translated (with the same pronunciation in slightly different tones) as 脂那 and 至那, it is what ancient China was called by India in the Buddhist scriptures, as evidenced in the 25th chapter of the *Nanhai jigui neifa zhuan* 南海寄归内法传 (Account of Buddhism sent from the south seas), a personal account of the state of Buddhism practiced in India and Southeast Asia by Yijing 义净 (I-ching, I-tsing, 635–713), a well-known pilgrim and translator of Buddhism in the Tang Dynasty. *Zhina* originated from the Sanskrit *Cīna*, which became *Thin* when entering Greece and *Sinae* when entering Rome. Based on *Cīna*, *Cinisthāna* is another ancient Indian term for China, transliterated as *Zhendan* 震旦 in Chinese, as evidenced in the sixth chapter of the *Guangding jing* 灌顶经 (Consecration scripture), a translated collection in the mid-5th century of 12 semi-independent scriptures on magical spells (*Dharani*).

The Sanskrit *Cīna* used to be considered ancient India's phonemic loan from the Chinese word *Qin* 秦 (Ch'in in Wade-Giles romanization), the title of the dynasty that established the first great Chinese empire (221–206 BC), yet, according to Su Manshu 苏曼殊 (1884–1918), a Chinese writer well-versed in English, French, Japanese and Sanskrit, the word *Cīna* already appeared in *Mahabharata* ("Great Epic of the Bharata Dynasty"), one of the two Sanskrit epic poems of ancient India (the other being the Ramayana) in the period roughly equivalent to that of China's Shang dynasty (1600–1046 BC), which was well ahead of the Qin dynasty. So, phonetically at least, the *Cīna*-Ch'in association does not hold water.

Assuming its appearance in the epic poem, the search for the etymological Chinese equivalent for *Cīna* is still ongoing. One recent view takes Jin 晋, the title of China's dynasty (265–420 AD), as its etymological equivalent, but again, the Shang predates the Jin by a wide margin. Granted that slight possibility, how it reached ancient India, which was tens of thousands of miles away and separated from China by insurmountable mountains, definitely requires documentary and archaeological evidence. All things considered, a more plausible explanation is that *Cīna* is a case of the common noun-turned-proper noun: namely, from the autochthonous Sanskrit word *cina*, meaning "relic," "thinking" or "ingenuity," which seemed to have conveyed an imagination of that big legendary empire far up to the north. After all, the conversion of a common noun into a place name is an extremely common linguistic phenomenon, and this explanation is more in line with the latest evidence available.

2.3.3 Borrowed terms for physical things

This period from 220 to 684 AD also saw the introduction of a large variety of physical things into China, including plants, vegetables, fruits, minerals, and medicinal material; hence, their borrowed names.

1   Plants:
    Ganlan 橄榄, meaning olive, introduced to China in the Jin dynasty, probably originated from a certain language in the South China Sea, sounding like *k(a)lam* or *k(a)riam*.
    Pingguo 苹果, meaning apple, introduced to China in the Sui or Tang dynasty. Initially written as *pinpoluo* 频婆罗, later changed to *pinpo* 频婆, *pingluo* 频螺, and *pinguo* 频果, it originated from the Sanskrit *Vimbara* (>*Bimba*) or from *Bilva*, which corresponded to *pinluo*.
    Bocai 菠菜, initially written as *bolengcai* 波棱菜, meaning spinach, probably originated in the Tang dynasty from the name of a kingdom in Nepal called *Palinga*.
    Cile 慈勒, also known as *shiluo* 莳萝, cumin or a plant of the parsley family, used as a spice, introduced to China in the Tang dynasty, probably originated from the Sanskrit *Jīra(ka)*. Its currently used Chinese word, *ziran* 孜然, was borrowed from Uighur.
    Yeximing 耶悉茗, or *yeximi* 野悉蜜, namely, *suxing* 素馨, meaning "jasmine." Introduced to China in the Jin dynasty from the Western Regions, it originated from Old Persian or the Arabic *yasamin*.
    Doukou 豆蔻, meaning cardamom, introduced to China in the Tang dynasty, probably originated from Arabic *takur*, related to the name of the ancient port Takola.

2   Medicinal material:
    Moshizi 没食子, also written as *wushizi* 无食子 or *moshi* 没石; an abnormal growth called "gall," formed in response to the presence of insect larvae, mites, or fungi on plants and trees, containing gallic acid. Introduced from Persia to China in the Sui or Tang dynasty, it originated from the Persian *maxzak* or *muzak*.
    Awei 阿魏, also written as *yangkui* 央匮, a succulent plant, called ferula, whose medicinal gum resins helps kill worms and relieve internal heat and indigestion. First introduced in the Tang dynasty from the Western Regions, it originated from the Tocharian *ankwa*. It also entered China from India and was thus called *xingyu* 形虞 or *xingqu* 兴瞿, both of which were phonemic loanwords from the Sanskrit *hingīu*.
    Moyao 没药 or 末药, a gum resin obtained from myrrh which can be used to promote blood circulation, remove blood stasis, relieve pain, and assist digestion. Introduced to China in the Northern Dynasty, it

probably originated from the Persian *mor*, and its modern Arabic equivalent is *murr*, meaning "bitter."

3   Names of minerals or gemstones:

Sese 瑟瑟, gemstone similar to emerald or turquoise. Introduced to China in the Wei dynasty from the Western Regions, it originated from some old Middle Persian word sounding like "sirsir."

Bintie 镔铁 or 宾铁, patterned iron alloy. Introduced to China in the Tang dynasty, it was related to the Proto-Iranian *spaina* and Pamir *spin*.

Falang 珐琅, first introduced from the Western Regions to China in the Tang dynasty, was known as *falan* 法蓝 or *lan* 蓝 in the Ming dynasty and has evolved into *jingtailan* 景泰蓝 ("cloisonné") today. It originated from the Persian *farang*.

4   Names related to textile or shipping:

Gubei 古贝, also written as *jibei* 吉贝 or *jiebei* 劫贝, referring to cotton or cotton fabric. Introduced from the South China Sea to China in the Sui dynasty, it probably originated from the Bahnaric *kopaih*.

Die 叠 or *jindie* 锦叠, a type of fine cotton cloth, introduced from Persia to China in the Sui dynasty. It probably originated from the old Middle Persian *deb* or *dip*.

Qushu 氍毹, a type of wool or wool and linen mixed fabric, often used as carpet or rug for sitting on. Probably related to the Gandhari *koj'ava*, it was first introduced from the Western Regions to China in the Wei dynasty.

Bo 舶, ocean-going or large ship. Introduced to China in the Three Kingdoms period of the late Eastern Han dynasty and pronounced in Early Middle Chinese like /buak/, it originated from the Malay *boekot*, a Java ship.

2.3.4 Borrowed terms of music and dance

With its frequent interactions with the rest of the world in the Sui and Tang dynasties, China embraced various exotic musics and dances, accessible to both the imperial court and the general public. The extent and frequency of cross-boundary interactions at the time can be imagined from the court music in the Sui dynasty, which was already classified into seven or nine types according to their geographic origin, including music from India, Qiuci in the present Kucha, Xiliang in the present Gansu Province, Shule in the present Kashgar, Goryeo and Silla in the Korean peninsula, Uzbekistan, and Japan. In the process of this cultural interchange, many loanwords, such as names for musical instruments and dancing, were naturally introduced to China.

Bili 筚篥, a short pipe, also written as *beili* 悲栗/贝蠡. First introduced from the Western Regions to China in the Jin of the Eastern Han dynasty, it probably originated from the Turkic *bari* or *beri*.

Dala gu 答腊鼓, a drum from Kucha with a large drumhead and short body, sounded by being struck with the hands. First introduced to China in the Tang dynasty, it was related to the Persian *taburah*.

Zhezhi wu 柘枝舞, a Persian swaying dance with jingling bells attached to the dancer. With the word of origin yet unknown, it was first introduced to China in the Tang dynasty.

Sumuzhe 苏幕遮, an exotic dance with the dancer wearing a special Turpan hat. With the word of origin yet unknown, it was first introduced, and the dance went viral in the Tang dynasty.

Different from its five-tone scale, the seven-tone scale from Kucha was well received in ancient China, and, along with the music, the terms for those seven tones were thus introduced into the Chinese lexicon in the Sui dynasty:

Jishi 鸡识 or *qishi* 乞食, meaning "long sound." Corresponding to the *shang* 商 tone, it probably originated from the ancient Kuchan *keṣe* or the Sanskrit *kaiśika*.

Shashi 沙识 or *shazhe* 沙折, meaning "heaven and earth." Corresponding to the *jue* 角 tone, it probably originated from the ancient Kuchan *śaiṣṣe* or the Sanskrit *sadja* or *sasika*.

Shahoujialan 沙侯加滥 or *shasijialan* 沙侯加滥, meaning "echo the sound." Corresponding to the *bianzhi* 变徵 tone, it probably originated from the ancient Kuchan *sakgranth*, the vulgar Pali *sagikram*, or the Sanskrit *saha-grama/sadja-grama*.

Shala 沙腊 or *sala* 洒腊, meaning "empty string." Corresponding to the *zhi* 徵 tone, it probably originated from the Kuchan *sale* or the Sanskrit *sadava*.

Banshan 般赡 or *banshee* 般涉, meaning "five." Corresponding to the *yu* 羽 tone, it probably originated from the Kuchan *pañcam* or the Sanskrit *pannama*.

Houlisha 侯利箋 or *silisha* 俟利箋, meaning "opaque." Corresponding to the *biangong* 变宫 tone, it probably originated from the Kuchan *orkamñe* or the Sanskrit *rṣabha* or *vṛṣa(bha)*.

Suotuoli 娑陀力 or *shatuo* 沙陀 or *shatuoli* 沙陀力, meaning "soft." Corresponding to the *gong* 变宫 tone, it probably originated from the Kuchan *ṣatar* or the Sanskrit *sadharika*.

2.3.5 Words for the seven days of the week

The western seven-day week was probably introduced to China in the Tang dynasty by the Manichaean believers from the Western Regions in central Asia. This introduction of the western chronological institution turned out to be ill-timed, and its translated terms didn't fit in well with Chinese. So, it came and went without actually being adopted but still serves as memorable historical evidence for cross-cultural exchange at the time.

Mi 密 or 蜜, that is, *riyaori* 日曜日. It originated from *mir*, meaning "Sunday," in the language by ancient central Asian kingdom *Kangju* 康居 living approximately in the region of modern Toshkent, Uzbekistan and Shymkent, Kazakhstan.

Mo 莫 or *mokong* 莫空, that is, *yueyaori* 月曜日. It originated from the central Asian Kanju language *maq/mah* or from the Sogdian *makh*, meaning "Monday."

Yunhan 云汉, that is, *huoyaori* 火曜日. It originated from the Kanju language *wnqan* or from the Sogdian *wunkhan*, meaning "Tuesday."

Die 咥 or *di* 滴, that is, *shuiyaori* 水曜日. It originated from the Kanju language or from the Sogdian *ṭir*, meaning "Wednesday."

Wenmosi 温没司 or *guwusi* 鹘勿斯, that is, *muyaori* 木曜日. It originated from the Kanju language *wrmzt* or from the Sogdian *wurmazt*, meaning "Thursday."

Naxie 那颉 or 那歇, that is, *jinyaori* 金曜日. It originated from the Kanju language *naqit* or *nahid*, meaning "Friday."

Jihuan 鸡缓 or *zhihuan* 枳浣, that is, *tuyaori* 土曜日. It originated from the Kanju language or from the Sogdian *kewan*, meaning "Saturday."

2.3.6 Institutional titles from non-Han ethnic people

From 220 to 684 AD, inter-ethnic wars or integration and interactions between those ethnic ruling classes introduced to China some different institutions for governance, along with their titles. The peoples which had the most impact were the Uyghur, Turkic, and now extinct Xianbei 鲜卑 as well as Persians.

2.3.6.1 Institutional titles from the Xianbei

An ancient nomadic people that lived in the eastern Eurasian steppes, roughly what is now Mongolia, Inner Mongolia, and Northeastern China, from 156 to 234 AD, Xianbei was thriving in the east almost simultaneously with the Turkic in the west, and they were closely linked linguistically. After establishing its Northern Wei empire, Xianbei integrated itself into the Han community. However, it used some distinct institutional titles, such as

Kehan 可汗, title for Xianbei ruler. It originated from the Turkic *qaghan*, or *khan*, title for king.

Kesun 可孙 or *kezun* 恪尊, wife of khan. It originated from the Turkic *qasun*, title for queen.

Zhiqin 直勤 or 直懃, title for the sibling of the royal family. It originated from *tagin*.

Xianzhen 咸真, messenger at courier station. It probably originated from *yamčin*.

Xianbei people addressed their elder brothers and fathers as *agan* 阿干 or *abugan* 阿步干, which originated from **akan* and **abkan*, respectively. This form of address may have remained as a substrate loanword or simply been borrowed into Chinese in the process of ethnic integration, and it evolved into *ge* 哥 in the Tang dynasty, for addressing both one's elder brother and one's father.

2.3.6.2 Words for Turkic titles

The Uyghur is an ethnic group which splintered from the Turkic people and later conquered the Turkic, so the Uyghur used essentially the same institutional titles as the Turkic. The following are some Chinese loanwords from Turkic titles.

Kehedun 可贺敦 or *kedun* 可敦, title for Turkic queen. It originated from the Turkic *qaghatun* or *qatun*.

Teqin 特勤 or *diqin* 地勤, title for prince or tribe chief. It originated from the Turkic *tagin* or *tegin*.

She 设, magistrate commissioned to rule a non-Turkic tribe. It originated from the Turkic *sad*.

Yehu 叶护, magistrate commissioned to rule another tribe, similar to the above *she* post. It originated from the Turkic *yabghu* of the Hun.

Xielifa 颉利发 or *silifa* 俟利发, chief of a clan or title for an official below minister, commonly known as *fa* 发 from *bar* or *bat*. It probably originated from the Turkic *eltabar*.

Tutun 吐屯 or *tutunfa* 吐屯发, ombudsman. It probably originated from the Turkic *tudun*.

Yiduhu 亦都护, alternate title for tribe chief. It originated from the Turkic *iduq-qut*.

Tumen 土门, title for a general in command of 10,000 soldiers. It originated from the Turkic *tuman*.

2.3.7 The residual substrate loanwords in the Baiyue and Sanmiao ethnic groups

2.3.7.1 Substrate loanwords in the Fujian dialects from ancient Kra-Dai languages

The earliest settlers in today's Fujian province were Baiyue people, who were ancestors of the Kra-Dai language family. The conquest of the Baiyue's kingdom in 110 BC by the Wudi emperor of the Western Han dynasty was followed by a massive forced migration of the Baiyue people to the northern region between the Yangtze and Huaihe Rivers. Many Han Chinese people later started to settle in Fujian, reaching their first peak of migration circa 300 AD, and the trend lasted well into the Five Dynasties (907–960 AD), with the second and third waves of migration in between. Over time, the incremental integration of the Han and non-Han Baiyue saw both gradual acceptance of Han culture, integration into the Han, and use of the Han Chinese language by the latter. In the process, the Fujian dialects, collectively called Min languages, came into being out of Chinese assimilation of some elements of Baiyue language and retained quite a few substrate words, such as Fujian dialect *lia?^{7}* (meaning "lick") from the Kra-Dai *ri^2*, *lut^8* (meaning "fall off") from the Kra-Dai *lo:t^7*, *lim^6* (meaning "drink") from *dum^5* or *lim^2*, *kieu^1* (meaning "cringe") from *kot^8*, and *ka^{1}la^{28}* (meaning "cockroach") from *tu^{2}sa:p^7*.

2.3.7.2 Substrate loanwords in the Fujian dialects from ancient Hmong-Mien languages

In ancient Fujian also lived non-Han Sanmiao 三苗, the ancestors of the people of the Hmong-Mien language family. While most of the Sanmiao people settled in today's Guangxi, Sichuan, and Yunnan, some migrated to Fujian, and their integration with the Han Chinese also resulted in some substrate loanwords, such as Fujian dialect *tshu* (meaning "house") from *tse^3*, *phai* (meaning "bad") from *pa^4*, *bat* (meaning "know") from *pu^1*, *gap* (meaning "close eyes") from *qa^5*, and *to^3* (meaning "where") from *tei^6*.

Later than the Fujian dialects, the Cantonese dialect also had some substrate loanwords, which are discussed in Sections 1.1.2 in Chapter 1 and 2.4.6 in this chapter.

2.4 Between 685 and 1840 (Song, Yuan, Ming, and Qing dynasties)

2.4.1 Introduction

As a transition between the Song and early Qing dynasties, this period is characterized by China's opening-up in external exchanges, including a number of bold diplomatic explorations in expressing goodwill toward its northern and southern neighbors, frequent but sometimes tense interactions among its domestic ethnic groups, and vigorous and considerable growth in both domestic and cross-border trade. In the Song dynasty (960–1279 AD), envoys were sent to visit other countries on many occasions. With the territorial expansion under the Mongol Empire, the Yuan dynasty (1206–1368 AD) saw unprecedented contact with various peoples in the West, and the first official translation agency was established at the time. The Ming dynasty (1368–1644 AD) saw the well-known seven naval expeditions to the "Western Oceans," led by court eunuch and fleet admiral Zheng He 郑和 (Cheng Ho, original name Ma Sanbao, 1371–1433), marking China's official contact with countries in the Pacific and Indian oceans. The Ming also saw the first appearance of Western missionaries in China and the first

50 *A historical overview of Chinese loanwords*

translations of Western science and technology. The first half of the Qing dynasty (1616–1911) saw both a lot of interactions among its domestic ethnic groups and limited interactions with Western countries. As a result, Chinese loanwords during this period were fundamentally different from those that existed in the previous period in that China was, for the first time, exposed to modern science, with a gradual flow of scientific terms introduced to the country. Meanwhile, further integration of ethnic groups in China made it possible that substrate loanwords were constantly retained in the Chinese dialects from non-Han ethnic groups.

2.4.2 The impact of the ethnic Khitans, Jurchens, Mongols, and Manchus on the Chinese language

Representing the Liao, Jin, Yuan, and Qing dynasties respectively, the above four ethnic groups once ruled the whole or part of China. Though they naturally brought in some lexicon from their languages, Chinese still prevailed since Chinese culture was more developed than those of the ruling ethnic groups, so much so that the ruling class had to learn Chinese in order to better govern; some ruling ethnic groups even had to phase out their native languages and switch to Chinese. Chinese loanwords from those ethnic groups were small in number, very limited in scope, and mostly phased out along with the end of their rule.

2.4.2.1 Loanwords of Khitan origin

During the Liao dynasty in what is now Liaoning Province, from 916 to 1125 AD, the ruling Khitans set great store by Chinese culture, so most of the loanwords of Khitan origin enjoyed only fleeting currency.

Kehan 可汗, title for Khitan ruler. Borrowed from the Xianbei and Turkic peoples, it originated from the Turkic *qaghan*, or *khan*, title for king.

Yilijin 夷离堇, title for Khitan ruler when subjugated by the Turkic. It originated from the Turkic *irkin* or *erkin*.

Tiyin 惕隐, title for senior official in charge of imperial political affairs in the Liao dynasty. It originated from the Khitan *teyin*, which was from the Turkic *tagin* or *tegin*.

Woluduo 斡鲁朵 or *woerduo* 斡耳朵, the imperial guards, or an economic-cum-military institution in the Liao dynasty. It probably originated from the Turkic *ordo*.

Tama 挞马, imperial bodyguard, or corps of imperial bodyguards under the *woluduo*. It probably originated from *tama*.

Meng'an 猛安, unit of a tribe or tribal alliance. It probably originated from *mängan*.

Mouke 谋克, a Khitan organizational unit. It probably originated from *mäke*.

Jiu 乣, a widely used modifier in the Liao dynasty, meaning "alien." For example, *jiumin* 乣民 refers to aliens, and *jiujun* 乣军 refers to an army made up of such alien people. More include *jiujiang* 乣将, *jiuguan* 乣官, *jiuhu* 乣户, and *jiushou* 乣首. It was previously believed to come from the Chinese-derived branch of Khitan but actually was the vulgar form of the Chinese character *zha* 札, meaning "chicken" (there will be a more detailed discussion of this word in Section 6.2 in Chapter 6).

2.4.2.2 Loanwords of Jurchen origin

Probably the main source of the ethnic Manchus, Jurchens had their Jin dynasty from 1115 to 1234 AD, reaching the Yellow River valley in their heyday. Less developed than Chinese culture, Jurchens invented their own language largely based on Chinese characters, and their upper echelons all learned Chinese. So, their rule over Han Chinese notwithstanding, the few Chinese loanwords of Jurchen origin were usually of temporary nature. The following are some of the better known.

Meng'an 猛安, *ming'an* 明安, or *min'a* 闵阿, a Jurchen tribal unit, later an organizational unit integrating the military, production, and administration, and used as title for a general in command of 1,000 soldiers. It originated from the Jurchen *ming'an*.

Mouke 谋克 or *mukun* 穆昆, unit of a Jurchen tribal alliance, later used as the title for a general in command of 100 soldiers. It originated from the Jurchen *möke* or *mukön*. Three hundred households were then called a *mouke*, while ten *mouke*'s made one *meng'an*.

Bojilie 勃极列, the title for a tribal or clan chief, also used as a title for some officials in the early Jin dynasty. Originating from the Jurchen begile, *bojilie* is further divided into: *dubojilie* 都勃极列 (from the Jurchen *du* meaning "head") for commander-in-chief of a tribal alliance, *anbanbojilie* 谙版勃极列 (from the Jurchen *amban*, meaning "minister") for commander next to *dubojilie*, *guolunbojilie* 国论勃极列 (from the Jurchen *gurun*, meaning "national") for prime minister, and *hulubojilie* 忽鲁勃极列 or 胡鲁勃极列 (from the Jurchen *gurun*, meaning "chief") for army commander.

Bojin 勃堇 or 孛堇 chief of a small tribe. It originated from the Jurchen *begin*.

Andahai 安答海, guest. It originated from the Jurchen *antaha*.

Shanman 珊蛮 or *samo* 萨摩, shamanism or shaman. It originated from the Jurchen *saman*, meaning "wizard."

2.4.2.3 Loanwords of Mongol origin

Related to the Old Turkic people, Mongols had contact with Han Chinese for a long time. In its reign from 1206, when Temüjin (Temuchin) was proclaimed Genghis Khan through 1368 AD, the Mongol Empire conquered the Southern Song dynasty and unified China by establishing the Yuan dynasty in 1271. Despite its long-time rule over China and its great influence, Chinese loanwords from Mongol were surprisingly few. Various degrees of borrowing from Mongol words were seen in different fields in the Yuan dynasty, and there were even pidgin forms of Chinese and Mongol in the well-known *zaju* 杂剧, a four-act dramatic form, in which songs alternate with dialogue. But along with the fall of the Yuan came the vanishing of such Mongol-originated loanwords, especially political or military ones. Those that did stay were mostly of a civil nature.

Chengjisihan 成吉思汗, Genghis Khan, supreme khan. It was originated from the Mongol "*cingiz (kha)gan*," the first word from the Hun *sanok*, *tsanak*, *senogu*, *senhu*, or *snkn*, meaning "supreme," or from the Hun *tangri* or the Mongol *tegri*, meaning "heaven."

Zhaluhuachi 札鲁花赤 or *zhaluhuochi* 札鲁火赤, attorney-general. It originated from *jarguci*.

Daluhuachi 达鲁花赤 or *dalahuochi* 答剌火赤, title for a designated official in the Mongol Empire in charge of taxes and administration in a certain province. It originated from the Mongol *darugaci*.

Yekenayan 也可那颜 or *yekenayin* 也可那寅, not a title but a senior official in general. It originated from the Mongol *yeke noyan*, meaning "big official."

-chi 赤, used like a suffix following a specific field of duty, meaning an official or public servant who performs that specified duty. Examples include *bizhechi* 必者赤 from the Mongol *bicigeci*, meaning "secretary"; *qielimachi* 怯里马赤 from the Mongol *kelemurci*, meaning "translator"; *huoduchi* 火都赤 from *xotuci*, meaning "garrison command"; *huoluchi* 火鲁赤 from *xoruci*, meaning "official in charge of arrows and bows"; *wulachi* 兀剌赤 from *ulagaci*, meaning "official in charge of a courier station"; hybrid word *cangchi* 仓赤, from the Mongol *sangci*, meaning "official in charge of granaries," with *sang* from the Chinese *cang* meaning "granary"; and *kuoduanchi* 阔端赤 from *kotuci*, meaning "bodyguard" or "attendant."

Qiexue(dan) 怯薛(丹), household troops to guard the khan. It originated from the Mongol *kesig(ten)*.

Tuluhuajun 秃鲁花军, an army composed of sons of those imperial officials with the top three ranks in the nine-grade civil service hierarchy. One son from each such official was recruited so as to ensure loyalty from those officials, so the army was also called a hostage army. It originated from the Mongol *turug* or *torug*.

Tanmachi 探马赤, advance or garrison army. It originated from *tamaci*.

Aolu 奥鲁, logistic forces or institution. It originated from *oro*.

Zhasa 札撒, *zhasake* 札撒克 or 札萨克, grand code, later meaning "government organ or rule." It originated from *jasag*.

Zhanchi 站赤, *zhan* 蘸, or *yizhan* 驿站, courier station. It originated from the Turkic *yamci*, *yamcin*, or *jam* and later the Xianbei *yancin*, meaning

A historical overview of Chinese loanwords 53

"messenger in a courier station," then "message communication system" in the Yuan dynasty and later "courier station," which has been shortened to *zhan* 站 today.

Woerduo 斡耳朵 or *wuluduo* 兀鲁朵, tent for military force, imperial tent, or palace. It originated from *ordu*.

Wulusi 兀鲁思, person on the street; domain. It originated from *ulus*.

Wotuo 斡脱, merchant or caravan, originated from *ordu*; also toast proposal "cheers" originated from *otok* or *xotok*.

Anda 安达 or 按答, friend, sworn brother, originated from *anda*.

Bolanxi 孛兰奚/卜兰奚 or *bulanxi* 不兰奚, runaway slave servant, originated from *bogulcid*.

Lama 喇嘛, monk of Tibetan Buddhism (Esoteric Buddhism), lama, originated from Mongol *lama*.

Yelikewen 也里可温, a Christian believer, especially one in Nestorian Christianity. It originated from *erkegun*.

Zhuhu 术忽/主鹘 or *zhuwu* 主吾, Jew. It probably originated from *jugu* or *juxu*.

Hutong 胡同, alley, probably originated from *ottok/xuttuk* or *gudum*, all of which mean "a hole sunk into the earth to reach a supply of water."

Gebi 戈壁, desert or gobi, originated from *gobi*.

Hebisi 和必斯, a plucked four-stringed instrument, still in use in its original or adapted form in Yunnan and Shaanxi today. It originated from the Mongol *xubis*, which then originated from the Turkic instrument *qobuz/qūpūz* or *huobusi* 火不思 in Chinese.

Nashishi 纳石失, gold brocade woven by Uyghurs in the Yuan dynasty, originated from the Mongol *nacid*, which was from the Persian *nasij*.

Saohua 扫花 or *sahua* 撒花, tip or award money, originated from the Mongol *sauya*, previously thought to be originated from *sang*, which was from the ancient Chinese *sang* 赏, meaning "award."

Dai 歹, not good, probably originating from *tai*.

Haba'er 哈巴尔 or *habagou* 哈巴狗, a dwarf pug-dog of a breed originally brought from Beijing, also called a Pekingese. It originated from *xaba*.

Shili 失利, *shilisun* 失利孙, or *sheli* 猞猁, lynx or an approximately one meter-long wild animal of the cat family. It originated from *silugusu(n)* or *silegusu(n)*.

2.4.2.4 Loanwords of Manchu origin

The two-character Chinese word for the ethnic group of Manchu (满族, *Manzu* in pinyin) probably originated, similar to the English portmanteau word, from the combination of Mañjuśrī, the Buddhist bodhisattva personifying supreme wisdom, and the Juchen, their formidable ancestors. Nearly 400 years after their fall, the descendants of these Juchen again came into prominence and resumed complete control over all sections of China under the name of the Qing dynasty. Though the native language for the ancestors of the Manchu emperors, the Manchu language was in gradual decline at the time and was replaced by Chinese until it completely vanished from use. It therefore resulted in the limited entry of Manchu words into Chinese, so, with the nearly 300-year reign in the Qing, there was about the same number of Chinese loanwords of Manchu origin as there were of Mongol origin. Mainly used in ancient Beijing and, to a lesser degree, northeast China, a large portion were substrate words. With the demise of the Qing, they began to decay, with only a few exceptions that have stayed in modern Chinese. Nonetheless, currently existing Chinese loanwords of Manchu origin still considerably outnumber those of Mongol origin.

Words related to some social organizations or personal titles:

Gulun 固伦 or *guolun* 国论, nation, later referring to titles granted to the royal clan. It originated from the Manchu *gurun*.

Niulu 牛录, a production-cum-military organization in the Juchen tribal era. Later, every 300 people were called a *niulu* as the basic organization unit in the banner system, called *baqi* or *Pa-chi* 八旗, the institution combining the military, production, and administration, developed by the Manchu leader Nurhachi, who organized his warriors into companies of 300 men each, with each compay distinguished by eight banners of different colors (hence, *baqi*, literally "eight banners"). The word *niulu* originated from *niru*.

Jiala 甲喇 or *zhalan* 札栏, an organization unit equivalent to five *niulu*. It originated from *jalan*.

Gushan 固山, an organization unit equivalent to five *jiala*, also used as a noble title. It originated from *guusa*.

Duizi 堆子 or *duika* 堆卡, the residence in the urban district for the military under the banner system in the Qing dynasty. It originated from *juce*.

The following were some words for various forms of address:

Da a'ge 大阿哥, crown prince. Originating from Manchu *age*, *a'ge* was used by the Manchu in the Beijing dialect to address the young son of a rich or noble family.

Beile 贝勒, order of feudal nobility, second only to the prince or ruler of a small independent state. It originated from *beile*.

Beizi 贝子, order of feudal nobility below beile, originating from *beise*.

Gege 格格, order of feudal nobility for son or daughter of the *beile* or *beizi*. It originated from *gege*.

Efu 额驸, son-in-law of the royal or noble family, originating from the Manchu *efu*.

Heshuo 和硕, meaning "bestowed," used before the first-class prince, princess, and *efu*. It originated from *hoso*.

Angbang 昂邦 or *anban* 谙版, minister, later used to address the commander-in-chief of one of the "Eight Banners" or a minister dispatched to the frontier region. It originated from *amban*.

Fujin 福晋, title for the legal wife of a nobleman, princess, prince, or their son. It originated from *fujin*, which was, in turn, from the Chinese *furen* 夫人, meaning "wife."

Hafan 哈番, a widely used title of an official or for a nobleman, originated from *hafan*.

Bitieshi 笔帖式, clerk in charge of translation, documentation, and filing. It originated from the Manchu *bithesi*, which was, in turn, from the Mongol *bicigci*, which was from the Chinese *bi* 笔 for *pen*.

Boshihu 伯什户 or *boshiku* 拨什库, meaning *lingcui* 领催 in indigenous Chinese or a junior officer in charge of documents and salary-giving. It originated from Manchu *bosokuu*.

Anda 谙达 or 安达 friend, title for the mentor of the emperor's son, reverential address to a senior eunuch. It originated from the Manchu *anda*.

Dada 达达, head, reverential address to a senior eunuch of grandparental generation by children of royal family. It originated from *da*.

Dalami 达拉密, head, used to address the person in charge of a specific organ. It originated from *dalambi*.

Geshi 戈什 or *geshiha* 戈什哈, senior officer's bodyguard, originating from *gocika*.

Ka 卡 or *kalun* 卡伦, military scout, originating from *karun*.

Baoyi 包衣 or *baoyiaha* 包衣阿哈 or *aha* 阿哈, slave or domestic servant. It originated from *booi aha*.

Ama 阿玛, father, used by Manchu in Beijing, originating from *ama*.

E'niang 额娘, mother, used by Manchu in Beijing, also used to address the father king's concubines. It originated from *eniye*.

Momo 嬷嬷/嬤嬤 or *mo'er* 嬷儿, wet nurse used by Manchu in Beijing, usually one employed by feudal officials. It originated from *meme eniye*.

Niuniu 妞妞, little girl in Beijing dialect, probably originated from *nionio*, used to describe the loveliness of a little girl.

Words in daily life:

Saqima 萨其马 or 萨奇马 candied fritter, similar to a Rice Krispies square, originating from *sacima*.

Wenpu 温朴, a kind of food made from hawthorn and sugar fried together, originating from *umpu tepse*.

Mangshi 莽式 or 莽势, a Manchu dance, originating from *maksi*.

Hashima 哈士蚂 or 哈士蟆, a health-enhancing frog in northeast China, originating frm *hasima*.

Lalagu 喇喇蛄, mole cricket, originating from *lagulako*.

Mahuzi 妈胡子 or 麻胡子, a legendary monster with a large nose and red eyes, used by people in Beijing to scare children, probably from *mahuntu*.

Pi mahu 皮马虎, hat made of fur to fend off wind, *pi* from Chinese, meaning "fur" and *mahu* from the Manchu *mahuu*.

Gualan'er 挂懒儿, Beijing dialect for long Chinese waistcoat, from *guwalasur*.

56 *A historical overview of Chinese loanwords*

Wadan 挖单 or 哇单, Beijing dialect for double-layered clothes wrapper or cloth cover for jugglers. It originated from *wadan*.

Wula 乌拉 or 靰鞡, northeastern Chinese dialect, originally meaning "river," later used as a kind of heat-retaining weed or shoes lined with such weed. It originated from *ula*.

Halaba 哈拉巴, *haleiba* 哈肋巴, or *haliba* 哈力巴, Beijing dialect for shoulder bone or shoulder blade, also used as a disparaging term for a person or a poor person. It originated from *halba*.

Gezhi 胳肢 or 隔肢, tickle, from *gejihesembi*.

Motuozi 磨驼子, Beijing dialect for dawdle, from *modo*.

Lahu 喇忽, Beijing dialect for careless, from *lahu*.

Guli 骨力 or 骨立, Beijing dialect for "sturdy" and northeast Chinese dialect for "full in form," from *guli*.

Lete 肋贼, Beijing dialect for slovenly appearance, from *lete*.

Mahuer 妈虎儿 or 麻虎儿, Beijing dialect for making faces by stretching the corners of the eye and mouth to scare people, from *mohu*.

Zhe 嗻, a frequently used exclamation by the Manchu in Beijing for "yes," from Manchu *je*.

2.4.3 Loanwords for things introduced to China from foreign lands

China's interactions with and opening-up to its western and southern neighbors brought in many exotic things, including alien flora and fauna, resin, minerals, and precious stones.

Flora, fauna, and their derivatives:

Cula 徂蜡, *zulafa* 祖剌法, or *qilin* 麒麟: giraffe. All borrowed in the Ming dynasty, the first two were from Arabic *zurafa* or *zarafa*, while the third was from the Somalian dialect *giri* or *geri* (its equivalent in the local Arabic dialect was *girafe* or *giraffe*). Later forms in the latter part of the 19th century included *zhiliehu* 支列胡, *zhi'erlafu* 支而拉夫, *jilafu* 吉拉夫, and *zhilafei* 支拉斐, which were all from the English "giraffe." *Qilin* 麒麟 was actually an indigenous Chinese word for a mythical, hooved, one-horned chimerical creature known in Chinese and other East Asian cultures but used by Ma Huan 马欢, voyager Zheng He's translator, in his world-famous naval expeditions, to refer to the giraffe they saw for the very first time when traveling the ancient kingdom of Aden. This practice of putting "new wine in old bottles" is surprising but quite acceptable.

Huafulu 花福禄 or *fulu* 福禄: zebra. It was borrowed in the Ming dynasty from the Arabic *foro* or *fara*.

Pilile 毗梨勒: a medicinal plant. It was borrowed in the Song dynasty from the Persian *balīla* and the Sanskrit *vibhītaka*. A special wine can be made by mixing the plant together with *haritaki* (etymologically from Persian *halila*) and Indian gooseberry (etymologically from Persian *amola*).

Kulumazao 苦鲁麻枣 or *kuluma* 苦鲁麻: date palm fruits. It was borrowed in the Yuan dynasty from Persian *khurma* or *xurma* or perhaps from Javanese *kurma*. It entered China in the Han or Wei dynasty and was translated as *gumang* 鹘莽 or *kumang* 窟莽 from the middle Old Persian *gurman* or *kurman*.

Balan 巴榄/芭榄, *palan* 杷榄, or *badanxing* 巴旦杏: badam, an almond. It was borrowed in the Song dynasty from new the Persian *dadam*, with slightly different written forms in the Yuan and Ming dynasties.

Yingriguo 映日果: common fig. It was borrowed from the new Persian *anjir* or *enjir*.

Boluomi 波罗蜜: jackfruit. It was borrowed in the Ming dynasty via South China from the Sanskrit *panasa*.

Yabulu 押不芦: mandrake. It was borrowed in the Yuan dynasty from the Arabic *yabruh/abruh* or the Persian *abruh*.

Luhui 芦荟: aloe, a medicinal plant and its resin. It was borrowed in the Song dynasty from the Persian *alwa*, from the Arabic *alua/alwa*, and from the Greek *aloe*.

Huluba 胡芦巴: fenugreek, a leguminous annual plant of the pea family with aromatic seeds. It was borrowed in the Song dynasty from the Persian *hulbat* and from the Arabic *hulba/hulbah*.

Poguzhi 婆固脂, *buguzhi* 补骨脂, or *poguzhi* 破故纸: Psoralea corylifolia, commonly known as *babchi*, a leguminous annual plant of the pea family. It borrowed in the Song dynasty from the Sanskrit *vakuci*.

Zhada 鲊答 or 札答: medicinal stony secretion similar to the ox bezoar. It was from the Turkic-Mongol *jada* or *yada*.

Xunlu 薰陆: frankincense, an aromatic gum resin. It was borrowed in the Song dynasty from the Arabic *kundur*, from *kundura* or *kundu(ruka)*.

Afurong 阿芙蓉, *yapian* 鸦片, or *apian* 阿片: a drug prepared from the juice of the opium poppy. The first form was borrowed in the Ming dynasty from the Arabic *afyum*, and the second and third were borrowed in the mid-Qing dynasty from the English *opium*.

Minerals and precious stones:

Sabazhi 撒白植 or *saba'er* 撒巴尔: amber, a fossilized resin. It was borrowed in the Ming dynasty from the Persian *sabhoi* or *sabhari*.

Zhumula 助木剌 or *zumulu* 祖母绿: emerald, a valuable green gemstone. It was borrowed in the Yuan dynasty from the Persian or Arabic *zumurrud*, *zmerud*, or *zamudag*.

Gumulan 古木兰 or *kumeilan* 窟没蓝: a red blackish precious gemstone. It was borrowed in the Yuan dynasty from the Malay *kumala* or *kumula*.

Yahu 鸦鹘 or 押忽: a multi-colored gemstone. It was borrowed in the Yuan dynasty from the Arabic/Persian *yaqut* or the Turkic-Mongol *yakut*.

Sahala 撒哈剌: a Persian wool material from which cape can be made. It was borrowed in the Ming dynasty from the Persian *saqalat* or *saqallat*.

Mesi 麽斯 or *maoxilisha* 毛夕里纱: a finely woven cotton cloth. It was borrowed in the Yuan dynasty from the Arabic *mossul* or *mosul*.

Aidai 叆叇 or *aina* 矮纳: spectacles. It was borrowed in the Song dynasty from the Arabic *uwainat*.

Zong 艐: a large boat or a group of boats. It was borrowed in the Yuan dynasty probably from the Malay *jong* or *doing* and from the Javanese *jongque*.

2.4.4 Earlier borrowing of scientific terms

In its 3,000 years of history since the flourishing contention of a "Hundred Schools of Thought" (*baijia zhengming* 百家争鸣) in the Warring States period (475–221 BC), China has created a brilliant civilization that witnessed a great number of scientific or technological inventions and discoveries, many of which were made earlier than the Western world made them. However, it must be realized that what those ancient Chinese people did and the approaches they adopted in the process were not systematic in that there existed a general lack of scientific or empirical evidence, hence low replicability, making it difficult to theorize their achievements and thus evolve into science in the modern sense of the word. Just as China did in its Yuan dynasty, when a nation becomes well aware of the necessity of borrowing and learning from others under such circumstances and turns less prejudiced against other cultures, it will be more open to absorbing foreign material or conceptual achievements in such fields as science and technology.

2.4.4.1 Introduction of weapons and astronomical instruments in the Yuan dynasty

Military expansion and cultural backwardness, as reflected in the Mongolian ethnic group in the Yuan dynasty, accidentally brought in something positive in transcending the rigid custom-observing conservatism characteristic of the previous Han rulers. Since they welcomed exotic wizardry with open arms, some of the talents and technologies from Arabia and Persia came to China, promoting its scientific development. Jamal al-Din ibn Muhammad al-Najjari (Chinese name Zhamaluding 札马鲁丁) was representative of that era. A Persian astronomer and scholar in the ancient Islamic calendar in the Ilkhanate, one of the four khanates within the Mongol Empire, in the mid-13th century, Jamal al-Din brought Arab astronomy and the Greek 12 signs of the zodiac to China. The year 1267 marked two *tours de force* of his for the imperial court: the compilation of an astronomical almanac and the delivery of seven Arab astronomical instruments, including a Persian astrolabe, a globe, and an armillary sphere, which, in turn, pushed forward China's astronomical observation. Here are some of the borrowed terms used in the Yuan and later Ming dynasties.

Zantushuobatai 咱秃朔八台: astrolabe, borrowed from the Mongol *cag odu sabatai*.
Kulaiyisama 苦来亦撒麻: armillary sphere, borrowed from the Mongol *kuriyen saba*.
Kulaiyiaerzi 苦来亦阿儿子: globe, borrowed from the Mongol *kuriyen gajar*.
Folangji 佛郎机 or *fulangji* 伏狼机: artillery or musket, introduced in the Ming dynasty from the Persian *frangi* or *farangi*, from the Arabic *efranki*, meaning "foreign" or "European in the Latin family," which was related to the word "*farang*." People in the Yuan dynasty translated it as *falang* 发郎 or *fulang* 拂郎/富浪 to refer to Western Europe.

2.4.4.2 Translation of scientific terminology in the Ming and Qing dynasties

Serious and systematic introduction of modern science and technology into China did not occur until the Ming dynasty and was attributable to both the Western missionaries and the development of translation itself. Despite the ultimate failure of the westward expansion in the Yuan dynasty and the controversy that the *Travels of Marco Polo* has aroused today regarding its historical truth, both events did reverberate through the West. As a result, Jesuit missionaries flocked to China in the Ming dynasty, the best-known of which were Michael Ruggieri, Matteo Ricci, Julius Aleni, and Jacobus Rho—who, all Italian, came to China in 1580, 1583, 1613, and 1624, respectively—and Francisco Furtado from Portugal, who came in 1621. Missionaries kept coming in the Qing dynasty, including Ferdinand Verbiest from Belgium, Jean Adam Schall von Bell from Germany, and Michel Bernoit from France, who arrived in China in 1659, 1662, and 1744, respectively. With 70 in total across the Ming and Qing dynasties, those well-learned missionaries propagated the faith and translated religious books; some also translated European books on science and culture, totaling 120, while others compiled well-known dictionaries, such as the three-volume *Dictionary of the Chinese Language* (1815–1823), the very first Chinese-English and English-Chinese dictionary, compiled by Robert Morrison; *An English and Chinese Dictionary* (1866); and *A Chinese and English Dictionary* (1871) by William Lobscheid. Missionaries with professional expertise translated or wrote books on specific fields of knowledge, the best known of whom was Benjamin Hobson, a British Protestant medical missionary who published *Quanti xinlun* 全体新论 (*Treatise on Physiology*, 1851), *Buowu xinbian* 博物新编 (*Treatise of Natural Philosophy*, 1855), *Xiyi luelun* 西医略伦 (*First Lines on the Practice of Surgery in the West*, 1857), *Neike xinshuo* 内科新说 (*Practice of Medicine and Materia Medica*, 1858), and *Fuying xinshuo* 妇婴新说 (*Treatise on Midwifery and Diseases of Children*, 1858), all in Chinese. The most highly acclaimed of the five, the *Treatise on Physiology* was instrumental in introducing Western anatomical knowledge to China and Japan.

At the same time, home-grown scholars who were good at foreign languages, such as Xu Guangqi 徐光启, Li Zhizao 李之藻, Wang Zheng 王徵, and Li Jingtian 李经天 in the late Ming dynasty, also translated, either on their own or in collaboration with their foreign counterparts, a large number of books on modern science. The predominant *modus operandi* in translation at the time was oral interpretation plus transcription: oral interpretation by foreign collaborators first, then transcription by the Chinese to integrate, revise, and polish. The difficulty in such a mode of translation varied greatly, depending on how much expertise both sides had or how much they could match (Wang Yangzong 2003). Terms in their translated works were mostly rendered semantically and sometimes combined with phonemic transliterations corresponding to the original. The work most associated with loanwords was the ten-volume *Minglitan* 名理探 (*A study of logic*), translated from Latin by Francois Furtado, a Portuguese Jesuit missionary, and Li Zhizao between 1623 and 1630. The transliterated words in *Minglitan*, however, were generally not in actual use but used for footnote-like purposes, except for the phonemic loanword of *jihe* 几何 or *jihexue* 几何学, from *Jihe yuanben* 几何原本, the Chinese translation of *Euclid's Elements of Geometry* by Mateo Ricci and Xu Guangqi 徐光启. Here are some of the translated terms in *Minglitan* in both its phonetically rendered temporary versions and its semantically rendered permanent versions (more discussion in Section 2.5.2 of this chapter):

Feilusuofeiya 斐录琐费亚 (phonetic) and *aizhixue* 爱知学 (semantic): philosophy, from the Latin *philosophia*.
Egenuomijia 额各诺靡加 (phonetic) and *zhijia* 治家 (semantic): economics, from the Latin *oeconomica*.
Bolidijia 薄利第加 (phonetic) and *zhishi* 治世 (semantic): politics, from the Latin *politica*.
Elemadijia 额勒玛第加 (phonetic) and *tanyi* 谈艺 (semantic): grammar, from the Latin *grammatica*.
Ledulijia 额读理加 (phonetic) and *wenyi* 文艺 (semantic): rhetoric, from the Latin *rhetorica*. Its modern Chinese version *xiucixue* 修辞学 was from Japanese.
Luorijia 络日伽 (phonetic) and *bianyi* 辨艺 (semantic): logic, from the Latin *logica*.
Feixijia 斐西加 (phonetic) and *xingxingxue* 形性学 (semantic): physics, from *physica*.
Modafeixijia 默达费西加 (phonetic) and *chaoyouxingzhixingzhixue* 超有形之性之学 (semantic): metaphysics, from the Latin *metaphysica*.
Yalimodijia 亚利默第加 (phonetic) and *suanfa* 算法 (semantic): arithmetic, from the Latin *arithmetica*.
Muxijia 慕细加 (phonetic) and *yueyi* 乐艺 (semantic): music, from the Latin *musica*.
Yasiduoluoriya 亚斯多落日亚 (phonetic) and *xingyi* 星艺 (semantic): astrology, from the Latin *astrologia*.

2.4.5 The development of Islam in China

Islam had its initial contact with China as early as 651 AD in the Tang dynasty and grew gradually during the Song dynasty, with the frontier regions enjoying even faster dissemination. The establishment of the Qarakhanid dynasty in Central Asia by the ancient Uighurs to the north and south of Tianshan (Tien Shan) Mountains in the 10th century coincided with its intense conversion from Buddhism to Islam, which was completed roughly by the mid-Ming dynasty. It was during the Yuan dynasty that Islam's impact was felt in earnest in the north-central part (*Zhongyuan*)—the heart—of imperial China as it saw a sharp increase in the arrival of mostly Arab merchants as well as some politicians and religious figures. Here are some of the Chinese loanwords related to Islam in or around that period:

Musuluman 木速鲁蛮 or *musuman* 木速蛮: Islamic believer, borrowed in the Yuan dynasty from the Arabic *mussulman*.
Bie'anbaer 别谙拔尔 or *piyanbaer* 癖颜八儿: prophet in Islam, borrowed in the Yuan and Ming from the Persian *paighambar*.
Kaba 喀巴 or *kai'abai* 恺阿白: Kaaba, a Muslim shrine in Mecca toward which the faithful turn to pray, borrowed from the Arabic *ka'ba*.
Dashiman 答失蛮, *dasuman* 答速蛮, *dashima* 大石马, or *dashimi* 达实密: Islamic preacher, scholar, borrowed in the Yuan from the Persian *danishmend*.
Suolutan 锁鲁檀, *suanduan* 算端, *sutan* 速檀/苏檀: sultan, the title given to a Muslim sovereign, borrowed in the Yuan and Ming from the Arabic *sultan*.
Huozhe 火者 or *hezhuo* 和卓: khoja, a reverential title to the noted descendants or other Islamic scholars, borrowed in the Ming and Qing from the Persian *khwaja*.

2.4.6 Substrate loanwords in Cantonese dialect from Baiyue people

The loosely termed *Lingnan* area 岭南, roughly the provinces of Guangdong, Guangxi, and Hainan today, had been primarily inhabited by the ancient ethnic Baiyue people. Massive numbers of troops were sent and stationed here in the Qin dynasty, but, just as the Qin was being defeated by the Han in 206 BC, Zhao Tuo 赵陀, a Qin general in Lingnan, united Baiyue chiefs and established the independent kingdom of Nanyue. After it was taken back by the Han in 111 BC, people continued settling in Lingnan as frontier soldiers, exiles, businessmen, or wartime refugees. Prior to 220 AD, the use of ethnic Baiyue languages had been predominant. From 220 AD to 684 AD, there were still more Baiyue than Han people, with Chinese and Baiyue languages both in use. During the northern Song dynasty, the population of Han nearly reached that of Baiyue. From the Yuan onwards, ethnic integration began to gather momentum, and by late the Ming, Baiyue descendants in today's Guangdong were all Sinicized. Though words retained in Cantonese dialect under the substrate influence of ethnic Baiyue languages had already appeared prior to 684 AD, they were in full swing between 685 and 1840 AD. Some examples have been given in Section 1.1.2 in this book. Here are some more:

Cantonse luk^7puk^7 (meaning "grapefruit"), from the Kra-Dai luk^8puk^8
Cantonese $na{:}m^2$ (meaning "python"), from the Kra-Dai $nu{:}m^1$
Cantonese jap^7 (meaning "blink"), from the Kra-Dai jap^7
Cantonese kap, hap^7 (meaning "bite" and "bully," respectively), from the Kra-Dai hap^8
Cantonese na^3 (meaning "female"), from the Kra-Dai na^4
Cantonese ma^1 (meaning "twin"), from the Kra-Dai wa^1
Cantonese nam^2 (meaning "soft"), from the Kra-Dai $no{:}m^2$
Cantonese ni^1 (meaning "this"), from the Kra-Dai nei^4
Cantonese mou^4 (meaning "no" or "not"), from the Kra-Dai bou^3
Cantonese mi^4 (meaning "don't"), from the Kra-Dai mi^6

2.5 Between 1840 and 1948

2.5.1 Introduction

The Opium War in 1840 marked a new political era in China. The language had already evolved into modern Chinese in the mid-Qing dynasty, when the empire was beginning to fall into decay while the patriotic and newly emerging classes started to walk onto the historical stage. Pushed by external forces, especially invasions with powerful weapons, technology, and ideologies of Western imperialism and colonialism, China was trudging, first passively, then on its own initiative, toward modern society. The same external forces also helped bring about a historically rare transformation of the Chinese language in vocabulary, grammar, and usage which lasted from 1840 to the 1940s. Part of this linguistic change was represented by a massive increase in loanwords, which can be divided into two drastically different types.

2.5.2 Translation of Western science works

As the usual follow-up to the introduction of foreign things, translation is also a necessary precondition for their actual assimilation. Since the practice by Western missionaries prior to 1840, translation as an independent activity had rapid growth in the late Qing. With the support of government-run translation agencies and the institutional training of foreign languages, translation of Western science works flourished.

The most well-known advocates and contributors during that period include Yi Xin 奕䜣, Lin Zexu 林则徐, Xu Shou 徐寿 and his son Xu Jianyin 徐建寅, Li Shanlan 李善兰, Hua Hengfang 华蘅芳, Wang Tao 王韬, Zhu Zhixin 朱执信, Li Hongzhang 李鸿章, Wei Yuan 魏源, Xu Jishe 徐继畬, Sheng Xuanhuai 盛宣怀, Zuo Zongtang 左宗棠, Kang Youwei 康有为, Liang Qichao 梁启超, Ma Jianzhong 马建忠, and Yan Fu 严复. Building on what Lin Zexu had done, the 60-volume *Haiguo tuzhi* 海国图志 (Illustrated gazetteer of the countries overseas) by Wei Yuan on the geography and material conditions of foreign nations served as an encyclopedia of the time, including many newly borrowed terms, such as *gongsi* 公司 (company), *bang* 磅 (pound), *xinwen* 新闻 (news), *guohui* 国会 (parliament), *maoyi* 贸易 (trade), *chukou* 出口 (export), *tielu* 铁路 (railroad), *falu* 法律 (law), *zhengzhi* 政治 (politics), and *wenxue* 文学 (literature).

During that period, in 1862, the *Tongwenguan* academy 同文馆 was set up in Beijing, dedicated to the study of Western civilization and translation, to which William Alexander Parsons Martin made the greatest contribution. At about the same time, the translation department of the famous *Jiangnan Arsenal* 江南制造局, founded in 1865 in Shanghai, also attracted many foreign and Chinese scholars, and there the Englishman John Fryer made the greatest contribution. He created the *Gezhi huibian* 格致汇编 (The Chinese Scientific and Industrial Magazine), China's first popular science magazine, which was published from 1876 to 1892. He translated more than ten science books on topography, geology, electricity, acoustics, heat, plants, chemistry, and math.

Among the Chinese translators at the time, Yan Fu 严复 was the most influential with the greatest achievements. In addition to his widely known translation principle of *xindaya* 信达雅 ("faithfulness, expressiveness, and elegance"), he also translated more than ten books.

As far as loanwords were concerned, the flourishing of translated works and bilingual dictionaries, and the introduction of modern science to popular education constituted the two non-political determining factors in the growth of loanwords in this period.

2.5.2.1 Loanwords in Yan's translations

Yan's well-known translated works were *Tianyan lun* 天演论 (1898) from Thomas H. Huxley's *Evolution and Ethics*, *Yuanfu* 原富 (1902) from Adam Smith's *The Wealth of Nations*, *Qunxue yiyan* 群学肄言 (1903) from Spencer's *The Study of Sociology*, *Qunji quanjie lun* 群己权界论 (1903) from John Stuart Mill's *On Liberty*, *Shehui tongquan* 社会通诠 (1904) from Edward Jenks's *A History of Politics*, *Mengdesijiu fayi* 孟德斯鸠法意 (1904–1909) from Montesquieu's *The Spirit of the Laws*, *Mule mingxue* 穆勒名学 (1905) from John Stuart Mill's *A System of Logic*, and *Mingxue qianxue* 名学浅学 (1909) from William Stanley Jevons's *Elementary Lessons in Logic*. Though most of the transliterated terms in Yan's works have already been replaced with new

64 *A historical overview of Chinese loanwords*

phonemic or semantic loanwords, they played great historical roles. Some of the better-known words from his translations include:

Wutuobang 乌托邦, from the English *utopia*
Feiluosufei 斐洛苏菲, now *zhexue* 哲学, from *philosophy*
Niepu 涅菩 or *niepulasi* 涅菩剌斯, now *xingyun* 星云, from *nebula* (nebulas in plural)
Yituo 伊脱, now *yitai* 以太, from *ether*
Zhibula 芝不拉, now *banma* 斑马, from *zebra*
Gelila 戈栗拉, now *daxingxing* 大猩猩, from *gorilla*
Qingmingzi 清明子, now *heixingxing* 黑猩猩, from *chimpanzee*
Luoji 逻辑, from *logic*
Luogesi 逻各斯, from *logos*
Feiji 斐辑, now *wulixue* 物理学, from *physics*
Sha 沙, from *tsar*
Linfei 林肥, now *linba* 淋巴, from *lymph*
Tuteng 图腾, from *totem*
Banke 板克, now *yinhang* 银行, from *bank*
Bolixi 伯理玺 or *bolixitiande* 伯理玺天德, now *zongtong* 总统, from *president*
Jiabidan 甲必丹, now *chuanzhang* 船长, *shouling* 首领, from *captain*
Sidanshui 斯旦税, now *yinhuashui* 印花税, from *stamp duty*
Bixie 毕协, now *zhujiao* 主教, from *bishop*
Pubo 朴柏, now *jiaohuang* 教皇, from *pope*
Pi'er 啤儿, now *pijiu* 啤酒, from *beer*
Jiafei 加非, now *kafei* 咖啡, from *coffee*
Shaokeli 勺克力, now *qiaokeli* 巧克力, from *chocolate*
Wali 䞐䞕, *shadaishu* 沙袋鼠, from *wallaby*

As shown in the last item above, Yan's inclination to ignore pre-existing translated terms by making up new terms and even characters, and the impact of the local Fujian dialect on his transliteration and word choice contributed to the general unpopularity of his transliterated terms. So many of them were later phased out, but some few remain in use today or enjoyed a long lifecycle, such as *luoji, wutuobang, tuteng, yamoniya*, and *ge* 镅 (now *nie* 镍, from nickel). Some other terms of his served as prototypes on which versions in current usage were developed, such as *pi'er* (now *pijiu*) and *shaokeli* (now *qiaokeli*). It is fair to say that the translated terms by Yan Fu made a great contribution to satisfying the immediate and eager needs at the time for understanding Western science and technology.

2.5.2.2 *Loanwords coming by other means*

With imperial China being forced open by invading guns and warships, Western technology and other cultural elements were beginning to make massive inroads from the time of the May Fourth Movement in 1919 to the first half of the century. Besides various means of entry, Chinese loanwords in this period also represent different types, including full phonemic loans, like *oumu* 欧姆, from "ohm," and *leida* 雷达, from "radar"; phonemic borrowing combined with an autochthonous Chinese morpheme as a semantic marker, like *jiuba* 酒吧, from "bar," and *kabinqiang* 卡宾枪, from "carbine"; half-phonemic, half-semantic hybrids, like *shawenzhuyi* 沙文主义, from the French "chauvinisme"; abbreviated phonemic loans, like *beng* 泵, from "pump," and *lu* 铝, from "aluminum"; abbreviated phonemic borrowing combined with an autochthonous Chinese morpheme as semantic marker, like *Masheng* 麻省, from "Massachusetts," and *Feicheng* 费城, from "Philadelphia"; and *verbatim* borrowing of words which are made up solely of alphabetic letters, like *OK*. These loanwords can be classified into the following four semantic categories according to what they refer to.

1. Political, economic, or military terms:
   Demokelaxi 德谟克拉西 or *dexiansheng* 德先生 (literally "Mr. De," with *de* standing for "democracy"), from *democracy*. *Dexiansheng* was one of the most frequently used words during the May Fourth Movement.
   Buerqiaoya 布尔乔亚, from the French or English *bourgeois*
   Puluolietaliya 普罗列塔利亚 or *puluo* 普罗, from the French *proletariat*
   Aidimeidunshu 哀的美敦书, from *ultimatum*
   Buershiweike 布尔什维克, from Russian большевик
   Suwei'ai 苏维埃, from Russian Советская
   Shawenzhuyi 沙文主义, from French *chauvinisme*
   Kudieda 苦迭打, from French *coup d'etat*
   Nacui 纳粹 from German *Nazi*, abbreviated from *Nationalsozialist*
   Faxisi(zhuyi) 法西斯(主义), from Italian *fascismo* and from Latin *fascis*
   Bei'ge 杯葛, from *boycott*
   Tuolasi 托拉斯, from *trust*
   Qike 乞克, from *check*
   Tanke 坦克, from *tank*
   Jianongpao 加农炮, from *cannon*
   Laifuqiang 来复枪, from *rifle*
2. Scientific or mechanical terms:
   Anpei 安培, from French *ampere*
   Shengna 声呐, from *sonar*
   Delufeng 德律风, from *telephone*
   Maikefeng 麦克风, from *microphone*
   Jipu(che) 吉普(车), from *jeep*
   Mada 马达, from *motor*
   Bangpu 帮浦 or *beng* 泵, from *pump*
   Kaluli 卡路里, from *calory*
   Weitaming 维他命, from *vitamin*
   He'ermeng 荷尔蒙, from *hormone*
   Asipilin 阿司匹林, from *aspirin*

Kuining 奎宁, from *quinine*
Peinixilin 配尼西林, from *penicillin*

3. Cultural, artistic, or sport terms:
   Gelangma 葛朗玛, from *grammar*
   Aofuhebian 奥伏赫变, from German *aufheben*
   Yinde 引得, from *index*
   Katong 卡通, from *cartoon*
   Mengtaiqi 蒙太奇, from French *montage*
   Kaimaila 开麦拉, from *camera*
   Jita 吉他 (pronounced *gêta* in Shanghai dialect), from *guitar*
   Basong(guan) 巴松(管), from French *basson*
   Tan'ge(wu) 探戈舞, from *tango*
   Hua'erzi(wu) 华尔兹(舞), from *waltz*
   Sangba(wu) 桑巴(舞), from *samba*
   Puke(pai) 扑克(牌), from *poker*
   Malasong 马拉松, from *marathon*
   Gao'erfu(qiu) 高尔夫(球), from *golf*
   Aolinpike 奥林匹克 or *Aolinpike yundonghui* 奥林匹克运动会, from *Olympic Games*
   Fei'epolai 费尔泼赖, from *fair play*

4. Words used in daily life:
   Jiake 夹克, from *jacket*
   Kaisimi 开司米, from *cashmere* or *casimire* and from the place of origin *Kashmir*
   Kaqi 卡其 or *kaji* 咔叽, from *khaki*
   Falanrong 法兰绒, from *flannel*
   Jiuba 酒吧, from *bar*
   Xiangbinjiu 香槟酒, from French *champagne*
   Bailandi 白兰地 or *bolandi* 勃兰地, from *brandy*
   Buding 布丁, from *pudding*
   Tusi 吐司, from *toast*
   Baituo(you) 白脱(油), from *butter*
   Shala 沙拉 or *sela* 色拉, from *salad*
   Shuiting 水汀, referring to "steam heating," from *steam*
   Pasi 派司 referring to "a permit, ticket, or authorization to come and go at will," from *pass*
   Youmo 幽默, from *humour*
   Modeng 摩登, from *modern*
   Kaisi 开司, from *kiss*
   Misituo 密司脱, from *mister*
   Misi 蜜丝, from *miss*, as a courtesy title before the name of an unmarried woman or girl
   Daling 达令/大令, from *darling*
   OK or *wokai* 喔开, from *OK*

2.5.3 Graphic loans from Japanese[2]

In the Chinese context, discussion of modern scientific terms is inextricably intertwined with graphic loaning from Japanese, which, as discussed at the beginning of this book, is an indisputable fact of life in the development of Modern Chinese, despite divided opinion over its identity. Cultural exchange between China and Japan enjoyed a long history, though it was mostly one way, with the latter as the destination. Japan started its Westernization and modernization with the Meiji Restoration in 1868. With the Opium War in 1840 and Japan's growing threat, the Qing government started to pay serious attention to this island nation by sending officials there; they then reported back with written observations about its culture and society. There appeared quite a few graphic loanwords from Japanese in their written works, though mostly out of mere curiosity rather than an earnest need to borrow for permanent use. It was only after the First Sino-Japanese War in 1895 that China was rudely awakened to the necessity of learning from its Asian rival in order to absorb modern science from the West. This coincided with *Yangwu yundong* 洋务运动 (or the Self-Strengthening Movement) featuring "Chinese learning as substance and Western learning for application," and the wave of going to study in Japan. Since then, Chinese-character expressions in the Japanese language have continued to enter the Chinese lexicon and began to balance (and even reverse) the hitherto predominantly one-way exchange. Meanwhile, thanks to its official government support, multitudes of products, objects, and ideas from the West have flocked to Japan since the Meiji Restoration in 1868. Japanese translated words for those Western things and ideas had therefore been in use for years. Some of those translations directly borrowed words which had already existed in earlier Chinese works, while others invented words using a new combination of Chinese characters. Compared with most of the translated terms by Yan Fu, Japanese translations using Chinese characters were naturally easier to accept for the general public. So, the Chinese lexicon between the late 19th century and the early 1930s tended to abound, with both original graphic loanwords from Japanese and return loans (terms which had already existed in earlier Chinese texts with the meaning unchanged), while words directly transliterated or phonemically borrowed from Western languages were surprisingly few. Though the trend began to change slightly after the 1940s, the proportion of graphic loans from Japanese in the Chinese loanwords remains high today. In the *Xiandai hanyu cidian* 现代汉语词典 (*The Contemporary Chinese Dictionary*, 1996, third edition), there are 768 graphic loanwords from Japanese, original and return included, as compared to 721 transliterations from the Western languages. So, it should be fair to say that graphic loanwords from Japanese made great contributions to China's entry into modernity and its integration with the rest of the world.

2.5.3.1 Earlier introduction of graphic loans from Japanese

Beyond the introduction of Chinese-character expressions in the Japanese language into the Japan-based, Chinese-language, biweekly journal *Sein Min Choong Bou* 新民叢報 (1902–1907), more noticeable were the early works by those Chinese who had been to Japan, such as *Riben Riji* 日本日记 (*Diary in Japan*, 1854) by Luo Sen 罗森; *Shidong shulue bing zayong* 使东述略并杂咏 (*Short account of the mission to Japan and miscellaneous poems*, 1877) by He Ruzhang 何如璋; *Shidong shilu* 使东诗录 (*Poems during the mission to Japan*, 1893) by Zhang Sigui 张斯桂; *Fusang youji* 扶桑游记 (*Travel notes in Japan*, 1879) by Wang Tao 王韬; *Riben jiyou* 日本记游 (*A travelogue in Japan*, 1880) by Li Xiaopu 李筱圃; *Youli riben tujing yuji* 游历日本图经馀记 (*Supplement to maps and treatises of a journey to Japan*, 1887–1889) by Fu Yunlong 傅云龙; *Ce'ao zazhi* 策鳌杂摭 (*My miscellaneous studies on Japan*, 1889) by Ye Qingyi 叶庆颐; *Dongyou riji* 东游日记 (*Diary of a journey to Japan*, 1894) by Huang Qingcheng 黄庆澄; *Riben zashishi* 日本杂事诗 (*Poems on various aspects of Japan*, 1879) and *Riben guozhi* 日本国志 (*A history of Japan*, 1890) by Huang Zunxian 黄遵宪; and the weekly *Shiwubao* 时务报 (1896–1898) founded by Liang Qichao, who also introduced a lot about new things in Japan in his essay collection *Yinbingshi heji* 饮冰室合集 (1896–1929). Here are some of the graphic loans mentioned in three of the above-mentioned works.

1. Loanwords from Japanese in the *Shidong shulue bing zayong* by He Ruzhang:
   Yuanlaoyuan 元老院, dazhengyuan 大政院, dashenyuan 大审院, waiwusheng 外务省 (now waijiaobu 外交部), dazangsheng 大藏省 (now caizhengbu 财政部), caipansuo 裁判所 (now fayuan 法院), jingshiting 警视厅 (now jingchating 警察厅 or gong'anbu 公安部), yiyuan 议员, chuzhangsuo 出张所 (now paichu jigou 派出机构), changbeibing 常备兵, shaozuo 少佐 (now shaoxiao 少校), shichang 市场, gongyuan 公园, shifan 师范, youzhiyuan 幼稚园, tiedao 铁道, youbian 邮便 (now youzheng 邮政 or youdi 邮递), jingfei 经费, yijiang 意匠 (now gousi 构思 or jiangxin 匠心), danbagu 淡巴菰 (now yancao 烟草), and shenshe 神社.

2. Loanwords from Japanese in the *Ce'ao zazhi* by Ye Qingyi. Most of the 130 words listed in Volume Eight of Ye's work dedicated to alternative foreign names for things were from Japanese:
   Shijishi 时计师 (watchmaker), biaojushi 裱具师 (now zhangbiaojiang 装裱匠), dagong 大工 (now mujiang 木匠), zuoguan 左官 (now niwajiang 泥瓦匠), zhipeiren 支配人 (now jingli 经理), liangtiwu 两替屋 (now huanlingqianchu 换零钱处), dawenwu 大问屋 (now pifadian 批发店), zhijia 质家 (now dangpu 当铺), xueyin 雪隐 (now cesuo 厕所), dianzhu 佃煮 (dishes that are simmered in soy, seaweed, and sugar, commonly known as *tsukudani*), hantian 寒天 (now qiongzhi 琼脂 or yangcai 洋菜), tianfuluo 天麸罗 (tempura, a type of Japanese food which consists of fish or vegetables fried in batter), hailao 海老 (now xia 虾), yundou 熨斗,

wasideng 瓦斯灯, zhengqiche 蒸汽车 (now zhengqi jiche 蒸汽机车), xiaozi 硝子 (now boli 玻璃, from Old Chinese, originally meaning "man-made crystal"), suimu 燧木 (now huochai 火柴), and die 叠 (now tatami 榻榻米, a traditional Japanese floor covering made from dried rushes).

3 Loanwords from Japanese in the *Youli riben tujing yuji* by Fu Yunlong. While 30 chapters in Fu's work were dedicated to Japan, he interpreted the Japanese language as one "with the same ideographic writing system as in China but with Japanese pronunciation," and the book served as a general survey rather than a deliberate call for assimilating those words into the Chinese lexicon.

Dashenyuan 大审院, caipansuo 裁判所, nei'ge 内阁 (Chinese origin), yinhang 银行 (Chinese origin), jinku 金库, guozhai 国债, yiyuan 议员, xiehui 协会, zhuren 主任, ganshi 干事, jishi 技师, kezhang 课长 (now chuzhang 处长), dingyuan 定员, juanyangji 卷扬机, zhongjiang 中将, dawei 大尉, dazuo 大佐 (now daxiao 大校), xianbing 宪兵, gongbing 工兵, juncao 军曹 (now zhongshi 中士), jingcha 警察, tushuguan 图书馆, youzhiyuan 幼稚园, yundonghui 运动会, ticao 体操, wuli 物理, weisheng 卫生, gongyuan 公园, xueke 学科, jiepou 解剖, tongji 统计, xiezhen 写真 (Chinese origin but with acquired different meaning), boshi 博士 (Chinese origin but with acquired different meaning), jiaoshou 教授 (Chinese origin, with the original meaning of the title of an official in charge of school performance of a prefecture or county in the Song and Yuan dynasties), jiaoyu 教谕 (now zhongxue jiaoshi 中学教师; Chinese origin, with the original meaning of the title of an official in charge of school performance of a prefecture or county in the Song and Yuan dynasties), fanshe 反射, fengqin 风琴, qingjiu 清酒 (Japanese sake; graphic loan from China with a different meaning), maijiu 麦酒 (now pijiu 啤酒), shouxisuo 手洗所 (now cesuo 厕所), huazhuang 化妆, youchuan 邮船, baoxian 保险 (Chinese origin but with acquired different meaning), diandeng 电灯, dianhuaji 电话机, renliche 人力车, caoda 曹达 (now suda 苏打), and wasi 瓦斯 (now meiqi 煤气).

While most are Japanese semantic loans (using Chinese characters) from the West, the last two represent some few Japanese phonemic loans using Chinese characters.

4 Loanwords from Japanese in the *Riben guozhi* by Huang Zunxian, in which he surveyed Japanese society following its Meiji Restoration.

Shehui 社会, guoti 国体, lixian zhengti 立宪政体, guoqi 国旗, gonghe 共和, fengjianzhi 封建制, guohui 国会, yiyuan 议院, zhengdang 政党, gonghedang 共和党, ziyoudang 自由党, minzhudang 民主党, lixiandang 立宪党, zhuyi 主义, xianfa 宪法, nei'ge 内阁, zongli 总理, yizhang 议长, yiyuan 议员, zongcai 总裁, toupiao 投票, jiefang 解放, jinbu 进步, quanxian 权限, minquan 民权, falu 法律, minfa 民法, xingfa 刑法, fating 法庭, yushen 预审, gongpan 公判, baoshi 保释, guominjun 国民军, zhongjiang 中将, changbei 常备, houbei 后备, shiguan 士官, xuexiao 学校, caolianchang 操练场, zhengbingling 征兵令, jingbu 警部, jingcha

警察, jiaofan 交番 (now jiaotonggang 交通岗), xuncha 巡查, and xiaofang 消防.

Yinhang 银行 (Chinese origin), zhengquan 政权, huishe 会社, zhizaosuo 制造所 (now gongchang 工厂), fangjisuo 纺绩所, zaobichang 造币厂, zhibi 纸币, mianzhiwu 棉织物, shichang 市场 (Chinese origin but with acquired different meaning), tongji 统计, kuaiji 会计, jianzhu 建筑, jingfei 经费, jin'e 金额, guimo 规模, yinzhi 印纸, liaoliwu 料理屋

Zhishi 知识, bowuguan 博物馆, xueke 学科, shengwuxue 生物学, zhengzhixue 政治学, yishu 艺术, xiaoshuo 小说, kemu 课目, xundao 训导, jiaoyuan 教员, gongli 公立, sili 私立, shifan xuexiao 师范学校, youzhiyuan 幼稚园, gongyuan 公园, youbianju 邮便局, yinshuaju 印刷局, jizhe 记者, yale 雅乐 (Chinese origin but with acquired different meaning), hege 和歌, sanweixian 三味线, neng 能, yuanyue 猿乐, luoyu 落语, ticao 体操, xiangpu 相扑 (Chinese origin but read with the Japanese pronunciation scheme of *kun-yomi*), and weisheng 卫生.

Yangfu 洋服, jingbing 镜饼, zazhu 杂煮, kunbu 昆布, danbagu 淡巴菰, die 叠 or tatamei 榻榻美, putuan 蒲团, xiezhen 写真, canguan 参观, diyuanji 祇园祭, daoheji 稻荷祭, zongjiao 宗教, shendao 神道 (Chinese origin), jingma 竞马, and guangchang 广场 (Chinese origin but with acquired different meaning).

2.5.3.2 *New terms collected in the* Xin Erya 新尔雅, *a dictionary of neologisms*

At the turn of the century, many of those students who studied in Japan or the revolutionaries who fled to Japan after the failed Hundred Days of Reform 戊戌变法 of 1898 were either already public figures or big names-to-be, such as Wang Rongbao 汪荣宝 and Ye Lan 叶澜, among the first group, both of whom went to Japan in 1901, and Liang Qichao and Zhang Taiyan 章太炎, among the second. A well-known language scholar, Wang served in the government as a congressman and minister resident representing China in Switzerland and later Japan. A bourgeois revolutionary, Ye assisted Chen Duxiu 陈独秀, later a co-founder of the Communist Party of China, with organizing the Tokyo Youth Society 东京青年会, a revolutionary group, and founded a voluntary corps to resist Russian aggression as well as a society for militaristic civic education in 1903 in Japan. In the same year, Wang and Ye co-wrote and published the *Xin Erya*, a brief survey of basic concepts in 14 categories, including government, law, economics, science, culture, and education, most of which they had learned in Japan. So, this reference book of new terms was also an excellent primer on new ideas, obviously an act of willing dedication to diffuse new learning and advance their home country's self-strengthening cause.

Each of the 14 chapters was divided into several sections which might be further divided into subsections of explanation around the specific key concept. Under the chapter on nomenclature, for example, new terms were introduced when it explained that the application of intellectual knowledge to reasoning and predication is called *mingxue* 名学 (i.e. logic), also known as *lunlixue* 论理学. In another passage, the book stated that, when a noun is the name, which applies to every member of a group of similar things, regardless of their individual differences, it is called *gongming* 公名 (i.e. common noun) or *putong mingci* 普通名词. The book stated in the same chapter that, when a noun denotes a topic about which a statement is made, it is called *zhuci* 主词 (i.e. subject), while the part which is affirmed or denied about the subject is called *weici* 谓词 (i.e. predicate).

The new terms in each chapter were listed with a dot placed beside (or under) each component character to be emphasized, such as the following possibly original or return graphic loanwords from Japanese.

Terms in the chapter on government: guoji 国籍, quanxian 权限, canzhengquan 参政权, and xuanjufa 选举法,

Terms in the chapter on laws: guojifa 国际法, gongfa 公法, dongchan 动产, and zhiwaifaquan 治外法权.

Terms in the chapter on accounting: gongzhai 公债, ziben 资本, caizheng 财政, and baoxian 保险.

Terms in the chapter on education: jiaocai 教材, xunyu 训育, yiyuanlun 一元论, and yuzhoulun 宇宙论.

Terms in the chapter on groups: gongchanzhuyi 共产主义, jieji 阶级, guoji 国际, and rendaozhuyi 人道主义.

Terms in the chapter on nomenclature: mingti 命题, gainian 概念, sanduanlunfa 三段论法, and zhuci 主词.

Terms in the chapter on geometry: duobianxing 多边形, qiexian 切线, yuanzhuti 圆柱体, and pingxingxian 平行线.

Terms in the chapter on the heavenly bodies: paowuxian 抛物线, guidao 轨道, taiyangxi 太阳系, haiwangxing 海王星, and tianwenxue 天文.

Terms in the chapter on earth: gaoqiya 高气压, huiguixian 回归线, gushengdai 古生代, and huochengyan 火成岩.

Terms in the chapter on physics: jiasudu 加速度, qiya 气压, yinli 引力, and dianhua 电话.

Terms in the chapter on chemistry: huahe 化合, yanji 盐基, yingshui 硬水, and dianli 电离.

Terms in the chapter on physiology: hanxian 汗腺, linbaguan 淋巴管, dongmai 动脉, and mizou shenjing 迷走神经.

Terms in the chapter on animals: shu 属 (probably Chinese origin), gang 纲 (probably Chinese origin), mu 目 (probably Chinese origin), and burulei 哺乳类.

Terms in the chapter on plants: qiujing 球茎, huaxu 花序, xibaomo 细胞膜, and hushengye 互生叶.

Among the 135 words which have been randomly sampled from the *Xin Erya*, 23 were indigenous to the Modern Chinese lexicon, 36 were graphic loans from Japanese, and some of the remaining 76 were taken from classical Chinese but might mostly have been used in Japanese with a new imposed meaning. Today, most of those new terms are used in the same or similar way they were used back then, suggesting that many original or return graphic loanwords from Japanese had indeed entered the Modern Chinese lexicon almost *en masse* by the early 20th century.

2.5.3.3 Borrowing of graphic loanwords from modern Japanese by various means

Since the 20th century, graphic loanwords from Japanese have continued to come into Chinese by various means, including their use and promotion by students returning from Japan, works translated from Japanese, and language dictionaries compiled from time to time. Take two fields of study, rhetoric and medical science, as examples.

Despite the fact that the term *xiuci* 修辞 (meaning "rhetoric"), which shifts in meaning historically, appeared in classical Chinese thousands of years ago, and as early as the Yuan dynasty saw the publication of *Xiuci jianheng* 修辞鉴衡 (*The craft of poetry and prose writing*) by Chinese scholar Wang Gou 王构 (1245–1310 AD), it was in Japanese, not Chinese that the term *xiucixue* 修辞学 was first invented as a translation of the English *rhetoric* or the German *Rhetorik*, while Chinese scholar Chen Wangdao transliterated it as *letuolieke* 勒托列克. As the very first systematic work of its kind in China, *Xiucixue fafan* 修辞学发凡 (*An introduction to rhetoric*) by Chen in 1938 drew its inspiration from Japanese scholarship in this field. As the first in Japan to offer courses on rhetoric in 1889 and having published at least three monographs on the subject by the end of the 20th century, Waseda University became the center for rhetorical studies in the country. Having studied literature in Waseda at the time, Chen was obviously inspired by Japanese scholars, despite his strenuous efforts to avoid their scholarship or terms used by them. As a newly emerging field of learning in China, *xiucixue* still had to borrow some words. The following terms, once used or still in use in Chinese rhetorical studies, were borrowed from Japan. Though some of them were taken from classical Chinese, they either take on a new imposed meaning or are used in translating Western terminology.

Change 场合, dingyi 定义, duanluo 段落, gouxiang 构想, jiaozhuoyu 胶着语, jiaoyun 脚韵, jiehe 结合, jieshiwen 解释文, jiedai 借代, jinhualun 进化论, kuohu 括弧, langman zhuyi 浪漫主义, lizheng 例证, lianxiang 联想, mudi 目的, mudilun 目的论, neirong 内容, neizai 内在, peilie 配列, peizhi 配置, rendao zhuyi 人道主义, shenmeixue 审美学, shuyu 术语, timing 题名, tuiduan 推断, wenxue geming 文学革命, xinwenhua yundong 新文化运动, xingshi 形式, xingtailun 形态论, yanwen yizhi 言文一致, yaosu 要素, yilunwen 议论文, yinyu 引语, yinyu 隐喻, yuyan 预言/豫言, yuanli 原理, zhongjie 终结, and zhuanyi 转义.

If rhetoric represented a small part of Chinese loanwords in the field of the humanities at the time, medicine may have represented a larger part in sciences. Though Japan also learned modern medical science from the

West, geographical proximity and the Chinese characters used in Japanese made it easier to go to Japan to study medicine (and other fields of modern science) systematically. Though the word *yixue* 医学, meaning "medical science," is autochthonously Chinese, most of the earlier Japanese terms for Western medicine were semantically translated in Japan, which was also heavily influenced by German medical science as well as the British or American school of the field. Many of the earliest students to go to Japan chose to study medicine, including Lu Xun and Guo Moruo. Though they turned to literature and politics, respectively, most of these Chinese students still dedicated themselves to the medical cause. As a result, medical terms introduced to Chinese at the time were far more than those listed in the current few dictionaries of Chinese loanwords. The following terms, for example, were graphic loans borrowed from Japanese.

Baixuebing 白血病 (from German Leukemia), biyi 鼻翼 (German Nasenflugel), boli 剥离 (Latin ablation), daqi wuran 大气污染 (air pollution), dangliang 当量 (German aquivalent), dongmailiu 动脉瘤 (aneurysm), daochu 导出 (German Ableitung), fushen 副肾 (German Nebenniere or Englis adrenal gland), fubi 腹壁 (abdowall), gouchong 钩虫 (German Ancylostoma), guanjieyan 关节炎 (arthritis), henggemo 横膈膜 (German Zwerchfell), jiasi 假死 (apparent death), jiejie 结节 (node), jiepouxue 解剖学 (German Anatomy), juxibao 巨细胞 (German Riesen Zelle), kangti 抗体 (antibody), kangningxuexing 抗凝血性 (anticoagulant), mazuiyao 麻醉药 (anesthetic), maiguanyan 脉管炎 (angitis), mangchang 盲肠 (German Zokum), ningji 凝集 (agglomeration), nongyang 脓疡 (abscess), qiguan 器官 (organ or organum), qianyin 牵引 (German Zug), qianxue 潜血 (occult blood), ruangao 软膏 (ointment), ruoshi 弱视 (amblyopia), semang 色盲 (achromatopia), shenjingyan 神经炎 (neuritis), shenjieshi 肾结石 (renal calculus), shidao 食道 (German osophagus), shidaoyan 食道炎 (Latin oesophagitis), shoushu 手术 (operation), tangniaobing 糖尿病 (German Zuckerharnruhr), tiaojie 调节 (accommodation), tingli 听力 (audibility), xibao 细胞 (German Zelle), xian'ai 腺癌 (adenocarcinoma), xueya 血压 (blood pressure), yichi 义齿 (German Kunstlicher Zahn), yingyang 营养 or rongyang 荣养 (nutrition), yundong shitiao 运动失调 (dynamic ataxia), zhichi 智齿 (German Weisheitszahn), and zhong'er'yan 中耳炎 (German Mittelohrentzundung).

The above are only a very small part of the medical lexicon, but they reflect the extent to which current dictionaries of Chinese loanwords have missed out on graphic borrowing from Japanese. It is quite understandable that, without well-documented evidence, it would be very risky to say with absolute certainty that a certain term originated from one language rather another. After all, with the same graphic forms and similar rules in word formation, Japanese and Chinese are very much intertwined with each other. For this reason, some seriously doubt that so many Chinese words are graphic loans from Japanese. However, it would not be rational to deny the fact that Chinese has borrowed from Japanese. What is more, linguistic borrowing, however much it is done, does not bring shame on the recipient language. On the contrary, it proves that it is a great language due to its openness, inclusiveness, and power to integrate. Take the English language. The fact that English has absorbed huge amounts from other languages, with more than four-fifths of its vocabulary borrowed, mostly from other languages in the Latin family, such as French, has actually helped raise, rather than compromise, its communicative function and social status, making it a *de facto* language of the world.[3]

Unlike English borrowing, most of the Chinese characters in Japanese strictly align with Chinese morphemes, their lexical meanings, and Chinese rules of word formation. Those homogeneities, along with the huge number of Chinese words used in Japanese, prove nothing less than the productiveness of the Chinese morpheme and word formation, and, indeed, the great advantages that the Chinese language enjoys. In fact, when someone else has invented so many valid Chinese words or terms, isn't it a nice thing to have, and shouldn't one be happy about it and go ahead and use them?

2.6 Between 1949 and 1977

2.6.1 Introduction

Chinese loanwords in the first half of the 20th century were mainly of English and Japanese origin, but in the second half of the century, their source changed drastically as a result of the tectonic shift in international relations with regard to China. With the founding of the People's Republic of China in 1949, replacing the Republic of China, the new nation suffered from the Western blockade represented by the US and the UK, with Japan following in these nations' footsteps as their ally; these countries, together with their languages, of course, stopped directly impacting the language used on the Chinese mainland. Meanwhile, China's foreign policy of "leaning to one side" (i.e. Soviet Union) for its first decade after 1949 made Russian virtually monopolize the way in which foreign ideas were introduced to China. In the 1950s through 1960s, nearly no important loanwords came from English, French, or German, let alone Japanese, since the intermediary role of the Japanese had given way to Cold War politics. What is more, since World War II, Japan had tended to borrow Western words using phonological translation via katakana and to phase out the traditional semantic loaning via Chinese characters, meaning that Japanese had no direct influence on modern Chinese in that period in the way that it had had at the turn of the century. The more cautious language normalization policy under the new government further contributed to this trend. In short, as far as linguistic interaction with the rest of the world is concerned, China's mainland entered a new phase in which independently translated loanwords were prioritized and encouraged.

In the meantime, the mainland's interactions with the rest of the world and the ties across the Taiwan Strait, if any, had to rely on Hong Kong and the assistance from many friendly countries, through which words of European and Japanese origin came to the mainland. Since the founding of the People's Republic, China had treated all other countries based on the principle of peaceful coexistence, equality, and mutual benefit, so attempts to diversify its contact, not merely linguistically, with the world were deemed necessary by the Chinese government at the time. Theoretically speaking, various foreign languages other than English or Japanese could be a source of Chinese loanwords since the 1950s.

Great changes took place in the mainland's ethnic relations too. The status of China's ethnic groups other than the majority group of the Han Chinese began to rise toward interactions on equal footing. As ethnic cultures began receiving more and more attention, many of the words of distinct ethnic origin gradually entered and thus enriched the Chinese lexicon.

2.6.2 The great rise and rapid fall of loanwords from Russian

Except for *Suwei'ai* 苏维埃, *Buershiweike* 布尔什维克, and a couple of others, loanwords of Russian origin had been very few prior to the 1950s. With the founding of the new republic and its official alliance with the Soviet Union, China regarded the latter as a mentor and example to follow. A massive number of Soviet professional experts came to help China in its development. Teachers of English had to learn or teach Russian. A constant stream of Russian books or journals were translated into Chinese. Thanks to the more cautious and independence-oriented language policy at the time, Chinese phonemic loans were mainly from Russian, and semantic loaning noticeably dominated. Despite the great number of words borrowed from Russian, they did not attract much attention because many of them were proper nouns; those in daily and permanent use were therefore quite few. They include the following:

Kangbaiyin 康拜因: combine or combine harvester, from the Russian комбайн.
Bulaji 布拉吉: now *lianyiqun* 连衣裙, female one-piece skirt, from the Russian Платы.
Kaqiusha 喀秋莎: Katyusha, a type of Russian rocket mortar, from the Russian КАТЮША.
Qika 乞卡/契卡: Cheka, early Soviet secret police agency and a forerunner of the KGB, from the Russian Чека.
Duma 杜马: duma, the Russian parliament before and since the Communist era, from the Russian Дума.
Ximingna'er 习明纳尔: seminar, from the Russian Семинар.
Tuolaji 拖拉机: tractor, from the Russian трактор.

Siputenike 斯普特尼克: man-made satellite, from the Russian *Спутник*.
Pute 普特: pood, a unit of mass equal to 16.38 kg, from the Russian *ПУД*.
Wula 乌拉: hooray, from the Russian *Ура*.
Kelikong 客里空: Krikun, a special correspondent in Russian playwright Aleksandr Korneichuk's *The Front* (1942), who is known for his fabrication of news, from the Russian *Крикун*.
Duluoke 杜洛克: fool; also a kind of card game, from the Russian *Дурак*.
Maheyan 马合烟: a strong-smelling, low-quality tobacco made in Russia, from the Russian *Махорка*.

The above loanwords were in use for quite some time, and some had even been very popular. Though some dictionaries list quite a few loanwords of Russian origin, many of them were occasionally used or just came and went, such as:

Kangbingna 康秉纳: combine, a term for industrial business groups, conglomerates, or trusts in the former socialist countries, from the Russian *комбинат*.
Naipuman 耐普曼: NEPmen, businesspeople in the early Soviet Union, who took advantage of the opportunities for private trade and small-scale manufacturing provided under the New Economic Policy (NEP, 1921–1928), from the Russian *Нэпман*.
Azhalin 阿札林: a kind of yellow pigment, from the Russian *аЗарин*.
Wanka 万卡: a rough-made horse-drawn carriage, from the Russian *Ванка*.
Ayier 阿依尔: a nomadic or semi-nomadic village among the Kyrgyz and Altai in the past, from the Russian *аил*.
Aipipeiwu 爱匹配舞: a Tartarian folk dance in Kazan, from the Russian *эпипэ*.
Aoluopeila 奥罗裴拉: an old folk song in the former Russian republic of Georgia, from the Russian *оровела*.

Loanwords from the former republics of the Soviet Union, as seen from above, were introduced to Chinese via Russian, but they were generally short-lived because they were not what China really needed at the time. The wave of lexical borrowing from Russian lasted a little more than ten years, mainly during the 1950s. The Sino-Soviet split later on led to the complete withdrawal of Soviet experts and the abrupt termination of the use of Russian, followed by political and social unrest due to the Cultural Revolution which started in the mid-1960s and China's dwindling interaction with the outside world. In short, Russian played a minimal role in introducing foreign ideas to China during this period, with the only exception in the frontier regions bordering Russia, where daily life-related loanwords from Russian remained in stable use. With the readjustment of international relations, however, interactions between the two languages became based on a more rational basis.

2.6.3 The impact of the four regions on Chinese loanwords

For historical reasons, the four Chinese regions have existed more or less separately since 1949: the mainland, Taiwan, Hong Kong, and Macao. The mainland first saw the dominance of Russian as a source of loanwords due to the alliance between China and the Soviet Union. Having initially been influenced by Japanese because of its colonization, Taiwan also had loanwords of English origin from Shanghai and later displayed the dominance of American English as the source of linguistic loans. Over the past 100 years, British English had been virtually the only source of loanwords in Hong Kong. The tenuous connection via Hong Kong made it possible for the mainland and Taiwan to exchange some of their respective loanwords. Small in both size and population, Macao mainly followed Hong Kong linguistically (thus, it is roughly subsumed here under Hong Kong for the sake of simplicity), despite some apparent Portuguese influence, such as *ananshu* 阿囝薯 (rice, from Portuguese *arroz*) and *baosha* 煲沙 (scholarship, from Portuguese *bolsa*). This multi-regional linguistic situation obviously increased means of entry for possible loanwords but with an increased possibility of duplicated loanwords too. Mutiple renderings of the same source word or term caused inconvenience. With increased cross-Strait exchanges and readjusted post-Cold War international relations since China's reform and opening-up in the 1980s, linguistic contact and inflow of loanwords have also become increasingly diversified. The situation where different renderings of the same source word or term (hence possible confusion), however, has not drastically changed, except for a handful of loanwords shared across the four regions, such as bashi 巴士, yapishi 雅皮士, kala OK 卡拉OK, and MTV. The following are some loanwords with different Chinese renderings across the mainland, Hong Kong (Macao included), and Taiwan. The source words are from English unless otherwise indicated.

Word of origin	Mainland	Hong Kong and Macao	Taiwan
ammonia	an 氨, amoniya 阿摩尼亚	yamoniya 亚摩尼亚	amoniya 阿摩尼亚
massage	anmo 按摩	anmo 按摩	anmo 按摩, mashaji 马杀鸡
show	biaoyan 表演, yanchu 演出	sao 骚, biaoyan 表演	xiu 秀, biaoyan 表演
size	chicun 尺寸, chima 尺码	shaishi 晒士	chima 尺码
jumbo	daxing feiji 大型飞机	zhenbaoji 珍宝机	zhenbaoji 珍宝机, daxing keji 大型客机
disco	disike 迪斯科	dishigao 的士高	disike 狄斯可/迪斯可
boycott	dizhi 抵制	beige 杯葛	beige 杯葛, dizhi 抵制

(*Continued*)

Word of origin	Mainland	Hong Kong and Macao	Taiwan
motor	diandongji 电动机, mada 马达	moda 摩打	mada 马达
golf	gaoerfu qiu 高尔夫球	geerfu qiu 哥尔夫球	gaoerfu qiu 高尔夫球
blog	boke 博客	boke 博客, buluoge 部落格	buluoge 部落格
hacker	heike 黑客	heike 黑客, haike 骇客	haike 骇客
jam	guojiang 果酱	guozhan 果占	guojiang 果酱
film	jiaojuan 胶卷	feilin 菲林	dipian 底片
card	kapian 卡片	ka 咭	kapian 卡片
carnival	(daxing gongkai) lianhuan huodong (大型公开) 联欢活动	jianianhuahui 嘉年华会	(daxing gongkai) lianyihui (大型公开)联谊会
captain	lingban 领班	kip⁵tən³⁵	lingban 领班
cheese	nailao 奶酪	zhishi 芝士	qisi 起司, rulao 乳酪
milkshake	naixi 奶稀, bingdannai 冰蛋奶	naixi 奶昔	naixi 奶昔, naixue 奶雪
cream	naiyou 奶油	jilian 忌廉	naiyou 奶油
deuce	pingju 平局	tieu⁵⁵si²¹	pingshou 平手
apple pie	pingguo tianbing 苹果甜饼	pingguopi 苹果批	pingguopai 苹果派
store	riza shipingdian 日杂食品店	shiduo 士多	zahuo shangdian 杂货商店
saxophone	sakesiguan 萨克斯管	seshifeng 色士风	sakesifeng 萨克斯风
sandwich	sangmingzhi 三明治	sangwenzhi 三文治	sangmingzhi 三明治
sauna	sangna(yu) 桑那(浴)	sangna(yu) 桑拿(浴)	sanwennuan 三温暖
sofa	shafa 沙发	shuhua 梳化	shafa 沙发
sashimi	shengyupian 生鱼片	yusheng 鱼生, cishen 刺身, sasimi	saximi 撒西米, shaximi 沙西米
stamp	youpiao 邮票	shidan 士担, youpiao 邮票	youpiao 票
Vatican	Fandigang 梵蒂冈	Fandigang 梵蒂冈	Fandigang 梵谛冈
Costa Rica	Gesidalijia 哥斯达黎加	Gesidanijia 哥斯达尼加	Gesidalijia 哥斯大黎加
Liberia	Libiliya 利比里亚	Libiliya 利比里亚	Laibiruiya 赖比瑞亚
Mozambique	Mosanbeigei 莫三鼻给, Mosangbike 莫桑比克	Mosanbiji 莫三鼻及	Mosanbike 莫三比克
Saudia Arabia	Shate Alabo 沙特阿拉伯	Shate Alabo 沙特阿拉伯	Shawudi Alabo 沙乌地阿拉伯
Sydney	Xini 悉尼	Xueli 雪梨	Xueli 雪梨
Singapore	Xinjiapo 新加坡	Xinjiapo 星嘉坡/新加坡	Xinjiapo 新嘉坡
Italy	Yidali 意大利	Yidali 意大利	Yidali 义大利
Chad	Zhade 乍得	Zhade 乍得	Zhade 查得
Disneyland	Disini leyuan 迪斯尼乐园	Disini leyuan 迪斯尼乐园	Disinai leyuan 狄斯奈乐园

Word of origin	Mainland	Hong Kong and Macao	Taiwan
Benz	Benchi 奔驰	Pingzhi 平治	Binshi 宾士, Pengchi 朋驰
Bush	Bushi 布什	Sushu 布殊	Suxi 布希
Reagan	Ligen 里根	Liegen 列根	Leigen 雷根
Nixon	Nikesong 尼克松	Nikexun 尼克逊	Nikesen 尼克森
Thatcher	Saqie'er (furen) 撒切尔(夫人)	Daizhuo'er (furen) 戴卓尔(夫人)	Chaiqi'er (furen) 柴契尔(夫人)
Stalin or Сталин (Russian)	Sidalin 斯大林	Shitailin 史太林	Shidalin 史达林

As can be seen from the above, some borrowed words were introduced in a different written rendering for each of the three regions, while for others, only one region is different from the other two. Some were in the same written form across the four regions prior to the 1950s but later turned different because of the political changes. Well aware that this deplorable linguistic situation will hinder mutual understanding or national reunification, many people have called for lexical unification of the Chinese language as soon as possible. While the four regions may have noticed such a need, it won't be realized overnight because it requires a concerted and sustained effort to strengthen inter-regional exchanges before the time is ripe.

2.6.4 Loanwords from non-Han ethnic groups in China

Each of the 55 non-Han ethnic groups in China had long been in close contact with their local Han Chinese, learning from each other's languages and thus assimilating some of their respective lexicons. But this did not affect the language system nationwide. Since the 1950s, however, non-Han ethnic cultures and loanwords which come from them have come to the national linguistic landscape as a result of national policies aimed at enhancing the status of ethnic groups, increased cultural exchanges between the Han and other ethnic groups, and dissemination by mass media. Since there has already been some discussion in this book of Chinese loanwords of Mongol and Manchu origin, the following section will offer a very brief survey of the loanwords from a few other ethnic groups.

2.6.4.1 Loanwords of Tibetan origin

Cultural exchanges started as early as the Tang dynasty, as with *fulu* 拂庐, one of the earliest loanwords, borrowed from the Tibetan *sbra*, meaning "yurt for upper Tibetans," and terms regarding Tibetan Buddhism and old institutional names. But the majority of the borrowing occurred after the 1950s. The following are some of those loanwords.

Manba 曼巴 or *menba* 门巴: doctor, from the Tibetan $mẽ^{55}pa^{54}$

Reba 热巴: Tibetan folk variety show or such performer, from $re^{11}pa^{54}$

Pulu 氆氇: a handmade woolen fabric that can be used to make clothes and bedspreads, from $pu^{55} ruʔ^{52}$

Kadian 卡垫: a Tibetan rectangular woolen rug, from $kʰa^{55} tẽ^{55}$

Zanba 糌粑: tsamba or tsampa, a roasted and ground meal from barley as the chief cereal food in Tibet, from $tsam^{55}pa^{54}$

Ke 克: a Tibetan unit of measurement for cultivated land (approximately 667 square meters), from $kʰẽ^{55}$

Qiema 切玛: a decorated container of Tibetan barley, mung beans, goat's head, etc. to express the wish for good luck or celebration of good harvests, from $tɕʰə^{55}ma^{55}$

Hada 哈达: kha-btag, a white ceremonial silk scarf used by Tibetans (as well as Inner Mongolians who believe in Tibetan Buddhism) as homage to deities, gift, greeting, etc., mostly in white but also in red, yellow, blue, or green, from $kʰa^{55} taʔ^{52}$

Zhaxidele 扎喜德勒: greetings indicating good luck, from $tsre^{55}ɕiʔ^{52}te^{11} ləʔ^{52}$

Guoxie 果谐, *guozhuo* 果卓, *guozhuang(wu)* 锅庄(舞): a Tibetan group folk round dance, from *skor gzhas* or *skor bro*

Genka 根卡: a three-stringed Tibetan musical instrument like *erhu*二胡 (a bowed, two-stringed Chinese vertical fiddle), from $ken^1 tɕʰa^{55}$

Bixiu 碧秀: a Tibetan whistling arrow game, from $mpi^{11} ɕu^{55}$

Linka 林卡: public garden, from $liŋ^{55}ka^{54}$

Gesanghua 格桑花: galsang flower, a most respected flower in Tibet, symbolizing happiness, from $ke^{55}sã^{52} nme^{11}tɔʔ^{52}$

Wanguojie 旺果节/望果节: a festival to pray for a bumper harvest, from $õ^{11} ko^{55}$

Lama 喇嘛: lama, from $la^{55}ma^{54}$

*Gexi*格西: a high degree for monastics in Tibetan Buddhism, with the highest one called *larangba gexi* 拉让巴格西 (from $la^{55}raŋ^{52}pa$), from $ke^{11}ɕiʔ^{52}$

Mani 吗呢/嘛尼/嘛呢: the second and third of the six-syllabled mantra in Tibetan Buddhism, seen as a condensed form of all the Buddhist teachings, from $ma^{11}ni^{54}$

Manidun 嘛尼堆: mani stones, stone plates, rocks, and/or pebbles, carved or inscribed with the six-syllabled mantra, from $ma^{11}ni^{54} do^{11} poŋ^{55}$

*Tangka*唐卡, *tangga* 唐嘎: thang-ka, tanka, Tibetan religious painting or drawing on woven material, usually five- to six-stories tall, annually rolled up for disciples to pay homage to, from $tʰã^{55}ka^{54}$

Gasha 噶厦: local Tibetan government prior to 1959, from $ka^{55} ɕaʔ^{52}$

Galun 噶伦: the four highest officials, only below the regent in the *gasha*, from $ka^{55}lø^{55}$

Kanbu 堪布: senior lama, who presides over the lamasery or commandments, or is a senior government servant, from $kʰẽ^{55}po^{54}$

Daiben 代本: a military officer commanding 500 men, from $ta^{11} põ^{55}$

Langsheng 朗生: home slave for a lord, from $nã^{11} sẽ^{55}$

2.6.4.2 Loanwords from the ethnic groups in Xinjiang

As China's northwesternmost province, Xinjiang is home to a number of non-Han ethnic groups, such as the Uighur, Kazakh, Kirgiz, Uzbek, and Tartar, who mostly follow Islam after converting from Zoroastrianism, Manichaeanism, and Buddhism. The Han Chinese have been in cultural and linguistic contact with those ethnic peoples in Xinjiang since the Han dynasty (206 BC). When exiled to Xinjiang, Lin Zexu, a Chinese scholar and official during the Qing dynasty, famous for his efforts to stop opium from being smuggled into China prior to the First Opium War of 1839–1842, wrote his 24-poem collection *Huijiang Zhuzhici* 回疆竹枝词, in which there was a lot of borrowing from Uighur words. In describing the celebrations at the Eid al-Fitr (Arabic for "Festival of Breaking Fast"), an Islamic canonical festival marking the end of Ramadan, one of them wrote to the effect that, during Ramadan, people cannot eat until they see the stars in the sky, they read the Quran every day, when the hook-shaped new moon appears the Eid al-Fitr gets started, and with the end of fasting tens of thousands are celebrating (*bazhai xudai jianxing can, jingjuan tongfan pulugan; xinyue rugou cai ruze, aiyidi hui wanren huan* 把斋须待见星餐, 经卷同翻普鲁干; 新月如钩才入则, 爱伊谛会万人欢). Here, *pulugan* 普鲁干 comes from the Uighur mistransliteration of the Arabic *quran* (Uighur *koran*); *ruze* 入则 from the Uighur *Rozi*, meaning "Eid al-Fitr"; and *aiyidi* 爱伊谛 from the Uighur q^hejt, meaning "end of fasting." Further investigations are needed before those Chinese transcriptions of Uighur words can all be called Chinese loanwords. They are more properly considered temporary and unstable phonetic transcriptions in Chinese, and that explains the appearance of such a bizarre phonemic loan of *pulugan*.

Fast forward to modern times. More loanwords from those ethnic groups settle more permanently in the modern Chinese lexicon. The following are some from Uighur:

Huda 胡大: Allah, the Supreme Being among Muslims, from the Uigur Xuda, from the Kazakh Qudaj, from the Persian k^huda
Namazi 乃玛孜: namaz, the ritual prayers prescribed by Islam to be observed five times a day, from the Uighur namaz, from the Persian *namaz*
Rouzijie 肉孜节: Eid al-Fitr, end of Ramadan, from the Uighur Rozi $q^həyt$, with Rozi from the Persian *Roza* meaning "fasting"
Kuerbangjie 库尔邦节, *guerbangjie* 古尔邦节: Corban or Korban, one major Islamic festival for sacrificial offerings, from the Uighur Qurban q^hejt, from the Arabic *id al-Qurban*
Yakexi 牙克西: very good, from *jaxʃi*
Roubayi 柔巴依: an ancient Uighur four-sentence poem, from *rubay*, from Persian
Kantuman 坎土镘: a kind of flat hoe, from *ketmen*

Kan'erjing 坎儿井: an underground irrigation system using thawed water from mountain snow, from *kariz*

Qiapan 袷袢: a collarless long robe worn by Uygur and Tajik men, from *ʧʰapan*

Nang 馕, *kaonang* 烤馕: naan, nan, a round flat leavened bread in Xinjiang made of white flour and baked in a clay oven (tandoor), from *nan*

Bazha 巴扎: bazzar, from Uighur *bazar*, from the Persian *bazar*

Maixirefu 买西热甫: Uighur family gala, from mesrep, from the Arabic *meʃrep*

Dawazi 达瓦孜: high-altitude rope walking, from *dawaz*

Rewafu 热瓦甫: Uighur plucked musical instrument with five or seven metal strings, from *rawap*, from *rabab*

Dutaer 独它尔/都塔尔: Uighur plucked musical instrument, thin and long with two strings, from the Uighur *dutar*, from Persian

Tanboer 弹拨尔, *tanbuer* 弹布尔: Uighur plucked musical instrument, similar to dutaer but with two strings, from the Uighur *tʰembur*, from Arabic

Dafu(gu) 达甫(鼓): hand drum, from dap, from the Persian *tabirah*

There are also some loanwords from ethnic groups other than the Uighur in Xinjiang, such as:

Nawu rouzijie 拿吾肉孜节, *nuonuzijie* 诺鲁孜节: a major Kazakh festival in December on the Islamic calendar, from the Kazakh *naw(ə)rəz*

Dongbula 冬不拉/东不拉: a Kazakh plucked musical instrument with two strings made from the intestine of a sheep, from the Kazakh *dombra*

Kebusi 柯布斯: a Kazakh stringed musical instrument with three strings, from the Kazakh *qobəz*

Aken 阿肯: a Kazakh title for a folk poet or singer, from the Kazakh *aqən*

Kumuzi(qin) 库木孜(琴): a Kirgiz three-stringed musical instrument, from the Kirgiz *qhomuz*, from Arabic. Kumuzi, *konghou* 箜篌, *huobusi* 火不思 (from the Turkic *qobuz* or *qupuz*) both played by the ancient Han Chinese, and similar musical instruments in the Middle East, may all have been originated from Arab countries.

Naren 纳仁: a kind of Kirgiz noodles with minced meat, from the Kirgiz *naren* or the Kazakh *narən*

Qiekeman 切克满: Kirgiz textile fabric woven from camel hair, from the Kirgiz *ʧʰekmen*

Dongbu 东布: a Uzbek plucked musical instrument, from the Uzbek *tumbur*

Xiegenai 斜格乃: a Uzbek triangle-shaped musical instrument, from the Uzbek *ʃaqne*

Kesaile 克赛勒: a Tartar thick drink made from wild grape, potato and sugar, from the Tartar *kʰesel*

2.6.4.3 Loanwords from the ethnic groups in Inner Mongolia and Northeastern China

Northeastern China and Inner Mongolia are home to the Mongol, Manchu, Korean, Daur, Orunchun, and Ewenki peoples, from which the Chinese language has borrowed some words. As has been discussed, Chinese already had plenty of loanwords from the Mongol and Manchu peoples prior to 1840, though, in modern times, the Manchu language has fallen into disuse, while Mongolian has still been in active use, with new loanwords coming into Chinese lexicon. Probably because of the unexpected Korean War, Korean culture and some of their words received more attention, with some entering the Chinese vocabulary.

Loanwords from Mongolian. Some loanwords had been borrowed earlier but were in active or prominent use in this period, such as

Sumu 苏木: a Mongolian administrative division previously equivalent to prefecture, not similar to township, from the Mongolian *sumu*, meaning "arrow"
Aobao 敖包: heaps of stones used by Mongolians and Tibetans as markings for roads or boundaries, from the Mongolian *obuga*
Haote 浩特: city or village, from the Mongolian *xota*
Kalun 卡伦: a military outpost at the border, from the Mongolian karon
Wulan muqi 乌兰牧骑: the troupe that travels on horseback for cultural performance in Inner Mongolia, established after the founding of the People's Republic in 1949, from the Mongolian *ulaan mocir*, meaning "red sprouts"
Andai 安代: a Mongolian group folk dance, from the Mongolian *andi*
Dairilicha 代日丽查: a kind of Mongolian standup comedy, from the Mongolian *kairalcaa*
Haolaibao 好来宝: a Mongolian folk standup comedy routine accompanied by a four-stringed *sihu* 四胡, two-stringed *erhu* 二胡, and the *matouqin* 马头琴 (literally "horsehead fiddle"), from the Mongolian *xolboga*
Nadamu 那达慕: nadaam, a Mongolian traditional sporting game combining sports, entertainment, and market fair, from the Mongolian *nagadum*
Taozi 桃子: lace or pattern at the edge of the robe worn by Mongolian women, from the Mongolian *togosu*

Loanwords from Korean:

Gudaling 鼓打铃: a Korean folk art form with the performer singing while beating the long drum attached to his/her body, from the Korean p^huk $t^ha\ riəŋk$
Pansuoli 判索里: a Korean folk art form with the performer singing accompanied with drum beating, from the Korean $p^han\ so\ ri$

Caitan 才谈: a Korean folk art form similar to two-person standup comedy, from the Korean *tse tam*
Sanlaoren 三老人: a caitan-based Korean standup comedy started in the late 1940s with three performers acting as different elderly people, from the Korean *samro'in*
Jiayeqin 伽倻琴: a broad, zither-like, plucked Korean musical instrument, from the Korean *ka ja kum*
Dongmu 冬木: comrade, widely used during the Korean War in the 1950's, from the Korean *toŋ mu*

Loanwords from other ethnic groups:

Kaotao 靠套: small knife, from the Ewenki k^hot^ho
Anda 安达: friend or businessperson, from Mongolian, from the Ewenki *anda(k)*
Wulileng 乌力楞: clan commune, tribe, from Ewenki or the Orunchun *urirən*
Xianrenzhu 仙人柱: a conical tent made from 32 wooden poles for one family to reside in or, by extension, a household composed of a couple and their children, from the Orunchun *ʃienrəntʃu*
Wuli'an 乌力安: a wooden horn-shaped whistle, about 1 meter long, making the sound of a male deer by inhalation, from the Orunchun *ulian*
Mukulian 木库连: a Daur plucked harmonica made from iron wire and steel reed, played by blowing while plucking the reed, from the Daur *mukulien*
Beikuo 贝阔: short for *boyikao polie* 波依靠颇列, a kind of hockey, from the Daur *boikoo pooliee*

2.6.4.4 Loanwords from ethnic languages in southern China

In terms of number, South China has the most non-Han ethnic groups, making up more than half of its population. Close interactions between the Han and these non-Han groups throughout history have produced not only some substrate words from those ethnicities but also quite a few *bone fide* loanwords, such as

Cha'erwa 察尔瓦: a cloak made from coarse wool felt, from the Yi language $va^{21}la^{33}$. Cha'erwa might have gone through phonetic inversion.
Bimo 毕摩: a male witch, from the Yi language $pi^{33}mo^{34}$
Atu ajia 阿土阿加, abbreviated as *ajia* 阿加: a married slave in old times, from the Yi language $ŋgatɕ^hu^{33}ŋga^{21}tɕe^{33}$
Gaxigaluo 呷西呷洛, abbreviated as *gaxi* 呷西: a lower-grade slave, from the Yi language $ka^{33}ɕi^{33}ka^{23}lo^{55}$
Dongba 东巴: a sorcerer in the traditional Dongba religion (a form of shamanism influenced by Tibetan Buddhism), from the Naxi language $to^{33}mba^{21}$

Arenren 阿仁仁: a kind of singing and dance at funerals among the Naxi people, from the Naxi language $uə^{33}ze^{21}ze^{21}$

Siweiwei 四喂喂: verse sung at weddings or funerals, from the Naxi language $sı^{55}uə^{55}uə^{55}$

Bawu 巴乌: a single-reed, flute-shaped wind instrument by the Hani people made from bamboo or plastics with a very thick sound, from the Hani language $ba^{55}u^{55}$

Youfang 游方: a kind of match-making event among the Miao people where the interested youth sing songs to each other to express mutual affection, from the Miao language $ze^{55}faŋ^{55}$, from Chinese

Malang 马郎: same as *youfang* 游方, from the Miao language $moŋ^{33}ła^{13}$

Tingcha 亭茶: same as *chating* 茶亭, literally a pavilion for tea but usually referring to a place where romantic youth gather and sing together, from the Zhuang language *dingzcaz*

Lebao 勒保: an appreciative title for a young man, from the Zhuang language lwg-*mbauq*

Bu 布: the number (of people), from the Zhuang language *boux*

Zanha 赞哈: folk singer among the Dai ethnic group, from the Dai language $tsaŋ^{33}xəp^5$

Tongpa 统帕: a square cross-body tasseled cloth bag favored by the ethnic minorities in Yunnan Province, China, from the Dai language $t^hoŋ^{35}pa^{55}$

Bai 摆: a Buddhist gathering among the Dai people, similar to temple fair, from the Dai language pai^{55}. Attending such an event is called *ganbai* 赶摆.

Meng 勐: place, originally used as administrative division, now only used in some place names, from the Dai language $məŋ^{51}$

Duoye 多耶: an art form among the Dong people characterized by song and dance in festivities, with multiple combinations in singing style, from the Dong language $to^{23}ye^{342}$

Galao 嘎老: a form of folk song among the Dai people, from the Dai language $qa^{55}lau^{11}$. Also known as gama 嘎玛, from $qa^{55}mak^{23}$.

Duanjie 端节: a traditional festival among the Shui people from the end of August into early October according to the Chinese lunar calendar, from the Shui language ton^{33}, from the Chinese *duanwu* 端午. Celebrating *duanjie* is called *jieduan* 借端, from the Shui language $tsie^{11}ton^{33}$

Da'ge 打歌: a kind of singing and dancing while tapping among the Bai people, from the Bai language $ta^{51}gau^{11}$

Lerong 勒绒: a reedless bamboo-made blowing instrument among the Jingpo people, with the main pipe and the pipe for expiration, 80–143 cm long, with five holes, one at the front and the others at the back, producing a soft bright sound of a broad range, from the Jingpo language $la^{55}zuŋ^{51}$

Bisun 毕笋: a kind of reedless blowing instrument among the Jingpo people, from the Jingpo language $pyi^{33}sun^{55}$

Mangluo 铓锣: a kind of convex gong, from the Jingpo language $pau^{31}moŋ^{33}$

Munao(wu) 目脑(舞): a massive song and dance among the Jingpo people with about 100 participants, from the Jingpo language ma^3nau^{31}

86 *A historical overview of Chinese loanwords*

Piqie 毕切: also known as *dongba*, a kind of reedless blowing instrument among the Jingpo people, from the Zaiwa *pyi^{33}k^{h}ye^{33}*

Zengjiang 增疆: a 1.66 meter-long drum among the Jingpo people, from the Zaiwa *tsiŋ^{51}kiaŋ^{51}*

Longdongge 龙洞戈: funeral dancing among the Jingpo people, from the Zaiwa *ʐum^{21}toŋ^{21}ko^{55}*

Suo 索: a folk tune among the Bulang people, from the Bulang language *so^{55}*

2.6.5 More borrowed loanwords in the late 20th century

Over the past decades, especially since China's reform and opening-up in 1978, there have been fundamental changes in Chinese social and political life. Its ties with the Western world have changed as well. Since the return of Hong Kong and Macao to China and the resumption of postal, transportation, and trade links across the Taiwan Strait, the lexical communication among the four regions has been gathering momentum. Along with the rapid advances in technology and industries worldwide come tremendous changes in people's ways of life, which naturally brings in wave upon wave of new words and expressions. This, in turn, leads to either active or passive lexical creation on the part of the Chinese language. The majority of this creation is semantic borrowing of foreign concepts or ideas, followed by phonemic loaning. There is also a remarkable increase in direct borrowing of abbreviations from the source language. Since the early 1980s, China's mainland, for example, has seen an uninterrupted flow of loanwords from a rich variety of sources, such as Hong Kong, Taiwan, Europe, America, and the greater Chinese community in southeast Asia. In addition to graphic loanwords from Japanese, many of those loanwords are assimilated through translation in China's mainland, especially the phonemic loans. All this indicates the country's urgent need for lexical borrowing of new ideas, concepts, and terminology from the outside in order to catch up and to grow. The following are some of the loanwords in the contemporary Chinese lexicon, placed into five different categories.

1. New technical and cultural loanwords:

    Kelong 克隆: from the English *clone*

    Paidian 派典: from the English *paradigm*

    Mai'se 脉塞, also written as *maishe* 迈射 or *weishe* 微射 in Taiwan, from the English acronym *maser*, short for "microwave amplification by the stimulated emission of radiation"

    Shengna 声呐/声纳: from the English *sonar*

    E'erninuo 厄尔尼诺, *ai'erninuo (xianxiang)* 艾尔尼诺(现象): from the Spanish *El Nino*

    Kanameisu 卡那霉素: a broad-spectrum antibiotic against intestinal infection, from the Latin *kanamycin*

A historical overview of Chinese loanwords 87

Xianfengmeisu 先锋霉素: also called *cephalosporin*, similar to penicillin in function, used particularly for urinary infection, from the Latin *cephalothin*

Lifuping 利福平: an antibiotic used chiefly to treat tuberculosis, from the Latin/English *Rifampin*

Baineiting 白内停: a kind of medicine to treat cataracts, from the Latin/English *Bernetin*

Limianning 利眠宁: trademark for chlordiazepoxide, a tranquillizer for better sleep, from the Latin *Librium*

Sumieshading 速灭杀丁: a broad-spectrum pesticide with low toxicity and high efficacy, from the English *Sumicidin*

Aizibing 艾滋病/爱滋病: from *AIDS*, acronym for "acquired immune deficiency syndrome"

Tuofu 托福: from *TOEFL*, short for "Test of English as a Foreign Language"

GRE: abbreviation for *Graduate Record Examination*

OA: abbreviation for *office automation*

CT: abbreviation for *computerized tomography*, a medical examination in which an image of the inside of someone's body is produced on a computer using X-rays.

IT: abbreviation for *information technology*

2 New loanwords for everyday life:

Bijini 比基尼: from *bikini*

Tixu T恤: from *T-shirt*

Mini- 迷你-: borrowed from Hong Kong first, from the English *mini-* as a prefix, such as *miniqun* 迷你裙 (miniskirt), *minijiuba* 迷你酒吧 (-mini-bar), and *minibashi* 迷你巴士 (mini-bus)

Xiangbo 香波: borrowed from Hong Kong or Taiwan first, from the English *shampoo*

Mosi 摩丝: borrowed from Hong Kong or Taiwan first, from the English *mousse*, a foamy preparation used in styling hair

Lisi 丽丝: a hair conditioner to make hair glossy, from the English *Liese*, a brand name by Japanese cosmetics company Kao

Hanbaobao 汉堡包: from *hamburger*

Bisabing 比萨饼, *pichabing* 皮查饼: from *pizza*

Zha 扎: a certain amount of beer, usually a large glass or a large jar, also used as a modifier, from *jar* or *draft*

Dishi 的士: borrowed from Hong Kong first, from *taxi*

3 New loanwords for entertainment and sport:

Disike(wu) 迪斯科(舞): from *disco*. *Dishigao* 的士高 in Hong Kong and *disike* 狄斯可 in Taiwan.

Hulaquanwu 呼拉圈舞: from *hula hoop* or *hula-hula*

Piliwu 霹雳舞: from *break dance*

Jialisuo 嘉力索: from *calypso*, a kind of Latin American (Trinidadian and Tobagonian) folk music

Xiha 嘻哈, xibeng 嬉蹦: from *hip hop*

Kala OK 卡拉 OK: borrowed from Taiwan first, from Japanese *karaoke* (*kara* for "empty" or "without," *oke* for "orchestra")

KTV: from KTV, or *karaoke TV*

MTV: from MTV, or *music TV*

CD: from CD, or *compact disc*

MP3: from MP3, a compressed digital file type, also a pocket device for playing such MP3 files

Lalisai 拉力赛: a race for cars, motorcycles, etc. over public roads, from *rally*

Kabadi 卡巴迪: a South Asian sport on a round sand court in which a player from one team tries to capture a player from the other team and must hold their breath while running, from English *kabaddi*

Shansexing 煽色腥: from *sensationalism*

New loanwords for organizations or their members:

Oupeike 欧佩克: from *OPEC*, Organization of Petroleum Exporting Countries

Youlika 尤里卡: from Greek *Eureka*, abbreviation for European Research Coordination Agency

APEC: from *APEC*, Asia Pacific Economic Cooperation

ECFA: from *ECFA*, Economic Cooperation Framework Agreement between China's mainland and Taiwan

Pitoushi 披头士: from *the Beatles*, a popular British rock-'n'-roll music group or its members

Yapishi 雅皮士: from *yuppies*

Xipishi 嬉皮士: from *hippies*

Dingke fufu 丁克夫妇, *dingkeshi* 顶客士: from *dink(s)* or double income no kids (a couple with two incomes and no children)

Pangke 旁客/庞克: from *punk* or urban unemployed youth who wear aggressively unconventional and often bizarre or shocking clothing, hairstyles, makeup, etc., and the defiance of social norms of behavior

4   New graphic loans from Japanese:

Budao 步道: pedestrian, from the Japanese *hodo*

Eping 恶评: bad review, from *akuhyo*

Niyin 拟音: imitated sound of the surroundings in stage play, film, or TV, from *gion*

Yangtai 样态: the way something is at work or what appears externally as opposed to the thing in itself, from the Japanese *yotai*

Anlesi 安乐死: euthanasia, from the Japanese *anrakshi*

Yuanzhu jiaoji 援助交际: *yuanjiao* 援交 for short, from the Japanese *enjo-kosai* えんじょこうさい or *enko*, a type of sexual transaction in which older men give money and/or luxury gifts to attractive young women for sexual favors

Among the Chinese graphic loanwords from Japanese are some return loans, which were originally borrowed from Chinese but with a new meaning imposed and returned to the modern Chinese lexicon near the end of the 20th century, such as:

Renqi 人气: popularity, from Japanese *ninki*, which originally meant "human life energy or human smell" as opposed to *guiqi* 鬼气, the life energy or smell of a ghost
Daren 达人: expert, from Japanese *tatsujin*, which originally meant "open-minded person"

It is generally agreed that there have been more than 400 new graphic loanwords from Japanese in the Chinese lexicon since China's reform and opening-up in 1978, and the number keeps going up, while most of the graphic loans from Japanese from the 1950s to 1978 indirectly entered the mainland via Hong Kong or Macao. Today, with thousands of Chinese mainlanders going to study in Japan every year and many Chinese who are good at Japanese, cultural and linguistic interchange between the two countries is increasing on an unprecedented scale. Borrowing from Japanese has become more convenient and direct than ever before. Given the increasing substitution of *gairaigo*, or words that are phonologically translated via katakana, for Chinese words/characters or kanji in the Japanese language, the Chinese language will borrow directly from Western languages for new ideas rather than indirectly from Japanese as it used to.

2.7 Contemporary Chinese loanwords (1978–2018)

2.7.1 Introduction

The 40-year period from 1978 to 2018 is when lexical borrowing can be best observed at close range. As the prelude to the upcoming wave of lexical borrowing, the first 20 years after China's reform and opening-up in 1978 only saw a tentative trial and resumption (more on this in Section 2.6.5 of this chapter); the full-scale wave for loanwords did not start in earnest until the late 20th and early 21st century.

In its first two decades, China's reform and opening-up went through a difficult period of hesitation, controversy, and baby steps before it charted a determined course after the second epoch-making inspection tour of South China by the late leader Deng Xiaoping in 1992. In the same year, it became easier for ordinary Chinese people to apply for passports and go abroad. In the 1980s, computers and PCs were a rarity, seen only in a few government or research institutions. Microsoft entered China in 1992, and PCs began to enter Chinese households in the mid-1990s. China's domestic internet started in 1984 but was not connected to the global Internet until April 20, 1994. Chinese Internet giants Sina, an Internet media company, and Baidu, a search engine, came into being in 1998 and 2000, respectively.

The latter 20 years in this period, up to 2018, saw the increased expansion, deepening, and maturity of China's reform and opening-up, bringing about profound changes to Chinese society. With China's accession to the World Trade Organization in 2001, huge numbers of Chinese people went to study, work, or travel abroad, though many returned upon completion of their academic studies. China increasingly engaged with the world, which was undergoing rapid technological, economic, political, and military transformation. As a result, new products, new technologies, and new ideas rapidly entered China. Significant improvement in cross-Strait relations led to a sustained linguistic interchange between the mainland and Taiwan. The communities and channels involved in Chinese lexical borrowing were drastically different from what had been before. The confluence of the institutional reform; the political, economic, and cultural opening-up to the world; and the technological and economic integration with the world all contributed to a tidal wave of foreign products and ideas to China. This constituted the social and political basis for a massive entry of loanwords.

Thanks to the policy of reform and opening-up, more Chinese people brought back new objects, new concepts, and new vocabulary from abroad. With the advancement of education, foreign languages and pinyin became known to more and more young people, so imported loanwords were brought in not solely by the elite few but by the general public in various fields. Borrowing of foreign words was not exclusive to foreign language or translation professionals but open to all people, even teenagers. This change constituted a new demographic basis for the entry of loanwords into Chinese.

With the rapid changes in the global political, economic, military, and cultural configuration, and the ever-evolving technological advances, China and the rest of the world were entering a rapidly changing era of information technology. This constant emergence of new things constituted a new referential basis for new loanwords.

The turn of the new century marked the beginning of a rapid expansion in China of new technologies and tools, such as personal computers, the Internet, video games, animation, and new media. Available to more and more young people in the 21st century, those new technologies, tools, and media became the new channels by which loanwords could enter China, thus constituting a new instrumental basis for lexical borrowing.

There are two obvious characteristics among the incoming loanwords during this period. One is broad distribution, and the other is quick appearance and disappearance, both occurring at a rate faster than ever before. This is closely related to contemporary communication tools, rapid replacement of new things, and economic globalization. Three typological features are worthy of attention here. The first is the comprehensive entry of loanwords from English into science, technology, politics, economy, military, and literature. The second is the massive entry of lexical borrowing from

Japanese into animation, entertainment, and special service industries. The third is the conspicuous popularity of alphabetic letter words.

2.7.2 *Phonemic loanwords*

Phonemic loans during this period are broad in scope and large in number, reflecting improved living standards across the board so that people begin to enjoy broader horizons and more variety in leisure pursuits. Most of these phonemic loanwords come from English, making it the primary source language for Chinese loanwords and indirectly suggesting its predominant position in the world. Two more aspects are also worthy of attention here. First, corresponding Chinese phonemic loanwords immediately come into being as soon as new things or concepts occur in a foreign source culture. The time delay for loanword assimilation, very obvious in the early years, is now almost negligible. Second, as a result of its opening-up, some things or concepts which have long been in existence abroad are now being introduced and borrowed into China, filling the knowledge gap at last. Both aspects prove an open and constructive ecology of Chinese society today. The following are some of the phonemic loanwords used in different fields.

A **Phonemic loanwords in technological and military fields**:

Caimang 彩芒: a television set or computer monitor, from the English *monitor*

Wubantu 乌班图: a Linux open-source operating system which runs from the desktop, from the English *Ubuntu*, pronounced /ùbúntú/, from the Zulu and Xhola languages, meaning "humanity to others" with a connotation of "I am what I am because of who we all are" and "allegiance"

Guge 谷歌: American-based search engine, the Chinese version first officially used in 2006, from the English *Google*

Tuite 推特: American-based social networking site founded in 2006, from the English *Twitter*

Biying 必应: search engine launched by Microsoft in 2009, from the English *Bing*

Anzhuo (*xitong*) 安卓 (系统): Linux open-source mobile operating system, from the English *Android* (Operating System)

Pika 皮卡: a light truck which has an open body with low sides used for carrying goods and tailboard, mounted usually on a passenger car chassis, from the English *pickup* (truck)

Fulexi 富勒烯: the third crystalline form of carbon after diamond and graphite, with properties of good conductivity and tension, from the English *fullerene*, from *buckminsterfullerene*, named after the American designer and architect Richard Buckminster Fuller

Mokuai 模块: the modified version, usually used in computer or video games, from the English *MOD*, from *modification*

Kelongka 克隆卡: cloned computer disk or banking card, from the English *clone card*

Apaqi 阿帕奇: a Boeing twin-turboshaft attack helicopter or a free and open-source cross-platform web server, from the English *Apache*

Sade 萨德: an American anti-ballistic missile defense system designed to shoot down short-, medium-, and intermediate-range ballistic missiles in their terminal phase, from the English acronym *THAAD*, from Terminal High Altitude Area Defense, originally Theatre High Altitude Area Defense

B **Phonemic loans in educational and medical fields**:

Muke 慕课: A massive open online course aimed at unlimited participation and open access via the web, from the English acronym *MOOC*, from *massive open online course*

Mimu 弥母 or *moyin* 模因: a hypothetical cultural element that is passed on by imitation, from the English *meme*, from the Greek *mememe*: "something imitated"

Aipu (kaoshi) 爱普(考试): an AP Examinations course managed by Educational Testing Service (ETS) designed for non-native speakers to prepare for studying in an English-speaking university, from the English acronym *APIEL*, from *AP International English Language* or *Advanced Placement International English Language*

Lehuo 乐活 or *Lehasi* 乐哈斯: a lifestyle that pursues healthy, organic, self-sufficient, self-renewing, and earth-preserving goods and services, from the English acronym *Lohas* (first officially used in 1998), from *Lifestyle of Health and Sustainability*

Huoerte 霍尔特: a type of portable device for cardiac monitoring, from the English *Holter*, a Holter monitor, a Holter ECG (electrocardiogram), named after its inventor, Dr. Norman J. Holter

Teluokai 特罗凯: a targeted medication for the treatment of cancer, also known as erlotinib, from the English *Tarceva*

Jiaoshameisu 交沙霉素: a macrolide antibiotic, similar to Erythromycin, against a wide spectrum of pathogens, from the English *Josamycin*

Amoxilin 阿莫西林: a penicillin-type antibiotic used to treat a number of bacterial infections, from the English *Amoxicillin*

Aositawei 奥司他韦: a commonly used drug for the treatment of influenza, most effective against avian influenza, swine influenza, and type A H1N1 virus, from the English *Osteltamivir*

Dafei 达菲: brand name, the same thing as Osteltamivir, from the English *Tamiflu*

Fenbide 芬必得: Ibuprofen, an analgesic, antipyretic, anti-inflammatory, non-steroidal sustained-release drug, from the English *Fenbid*, from Ibuprofen Sustained Release Capsules, from Spansule Capsulae Ibuprofeni

Bixin 比辛: a naturally occurring lantibiotic (an antibacterial peptide) discovered by Americans in 2015, from the English *Bisin*

Lukasu 露卡素: a revolutionary concept of diet therapy with low carbon, low sugar, high nutrition, anti-glycation, anti-oxidation, and organic raw food, from the English *low carbs* or low carbohydrate

Nuolisu 诺丽素 or nuolijiaosu 诺丽酵素: an enzyme produced by the noni fruit after purification and fermentation, from the English *noni*, a fruit-bearing tree in the coffee family found from Southeastern Asia to Australia

Sailuoning 赛洛宁: an early enzyme as one of the basic elements that regenerate and restore the cells or alkaloid necessary for normal biochemical reactions synthesized in the human body, from the English *Xeronine*

Haifudao 海扶刀: a non-invasive therapy that uses focused ultrasound waves for cancer treatment, from English acronym *HIFU*, high intensity focused ultrasound

Shashi 沙士: Severe Acute Respiratory Syndrome, from *SARS*

Nuoru bingdu 诺如病毒: a virus that can cause nonbacterial acute gastroenteritis, from the English *Norovirus*

Ereying 二恶英 or 二噁英 or Daiaoxin 戴奥辛: a carcinogenic and teratogenic chlorinated triaromatic toxic substance, from the English *dioxin*

Shawu 沙雾: a drug using methamphetamine as raw material, from the Filipino *shabu*

C **Phonemic loanwords in financial, trade, and textile fields**:

Liuyisi guaidian 刘易斯拐点: a point at which a country would move from a vast supply of low-cost workers to a labor shortage economy, from *Lewis turning point*, named after British economist W. Arthur Lewis

Buerxian zhibiao 布尔线指标: a technical analysis tool developed by John Bollinger for stock price trends, from the English *Bollinger Bands*

Bitebi 比特币: a cryptocurrency that can be sent from user to user on the peer-to-peer network, from the English *bitcoin* (bit + coin)

Tewolun 特沃纶: a para aramid fiber, similar to Kevlar, with ultra-high molecular weight developed in Japan, from the Japanese-made English *Twaron*

Beitelun 贝特纶: a multi-purpose, high-performance synthetic polymer elastic short fiber, from the English *Bettera*

Weiketelun 维克特纶: a high-performance, high-strength, multifilament fiber composed of liquid crystal polymer (co-polyarylate), from the English *Vectran*

Ouke 欧刻: a new smart heating fiber, from the English *OK*

Modaier 莫代尔: a cellulose regenerated wood pulp fiber with high wet modulus viscose fiber, from the English *Modal*

Tiansi 天丝: a pure natural regenerated fiber of silk nature, from the English *tencel*

Amani 阿玛尼: an Italian luxury fashion brand founded by Giorgio Armani for clothing and shoes, from the Italian *Armani*

D **Phonemic loanwords in sports, leisure, and entertainment**:

Debi 德比 or debizhan 德比战: the game between the two most important teams (mainly football) within the same region, from the English *derby*

Wuwuzula 呜呜祖拉: a long, plastic horn that makes a loud, monotone sound, typically blown by South African fans at soccer matches, from English, from the Zulu *vuvuzela*: "making vuvu-like noise"

Bulazuka 布拉祖卡: the official match ball of the 2014 FIFA World Cup, held in Brazil between June 12 and July 13, from the Portuguese *Brazuca* ("our fellow" or slang for "Brazilian")

Shebin 舍宾: an all-around sport that pursues bodily beauty and flexible form, from the English *shaping*

Wukelili 乌克丽丽: a small four-stringed guitar of Hawaiian origin, from the Hawaiian *ukulele* (*uku* gift or award, *lele* coming; or "jumping flea")

Buji 布吉: a dance music or art originating in the black American community in the 1960s, from the English *boogie*, meaning "swinging the body"

Labuladuo(quan) 拉布拉多(犬): a breed of dog originating in Newfoundland and used in hunting to retrieve felled game or as a guide for a blind person; from *Labrador dog* or *Labrador retriever*

Hashiqi(quan) 哈士奇(犬): a powerful dog used in the Arctic for pulling sledges, from the English *husky* or *Siberian husky*

Taidiquan 泰迪犬: a small curly poodle, from the English *Teddy dog*

Kejiquan 柯基犬: a small, short-legged hound or guard dog, from the English *Welsh corgi*

E **Phonemic loanwords in food**:

Miqilin 米其林: an authoritative institution which provides ratings for the catering industry, from the French *Michelin*

Xingbake 星巴克: American company that is the largest coffeehouse chain in the world, from *Starbucks*

Nuoli(guo) 诺丽(果): a nutritious potato-shaped fruit from Morinda Citrifolia from the English *Noni*

Xiaweiyiguo 夏威夷果: a round, beige to light brown, hard-shelled nut cultivated extensively in Hawaii, from *Hawaii nut*, also known as macadamia nut or Queensland nut

Gala (*pingguo*) 嘎拉(苹果) or *jinaguo* 姬娜果: an American apple cultivar with a mild and sweet flavor, from the English *Gala apple*

Xinqishi(*cheng*) 新奇士(橙): a red-flavored orange or navel orange in the United States, first borrowed from Hong Kong, from the English *Sunkist orange*

Baixiangguo 百香果: an egg-shaped purple or yellow fruit from the perennial vine plant Passiflora, from the English *passion fruit*

Bigenguo 碧根果: the nut of the American hickory tree, from the English *pecan*, from *paccan*, from the American Indian Algonquian dialect: *pakan* or *pukan* meaning "crack nuts"

Bulun 布仑: American plum, from *plum* or *black plum*

Maka 玛咖: the root of an edible herbaceous biennial plant of the family Cruciferae, from the English/Spanish *maca*, an Incan Peruvian dialect for "mother"

Makalong 马卡龙: a colorful French almond pastry with sandwich filling, from the English macaroon, from the French *macaron*

Babaluowa 芭芭罗瓦: a French dessert similar to pudding and mousse, from the French *bavarois*

Bulangni (*dangao*) 布朗尼 (蛋糕): an thick, black, American chocolate cake, from the English *brownie* or *chocolate brownie*

Napolun(*dangao*) 拿破仑(蛋糕): a French-style cream crisp cheesecake, from *Napoleon*, mispronunciation of Naples

Tilamisu 里拉米苏: an Italian layered cake with coffee and wine flavor, from the English *tiramisu*, from the Italian *Tiramisù*: "take me away" or "remember me"

Magelite 玛格丽特: a cake with egg yolk and butter, from the English *Margaret*

Bafei 芭菲: an ice cream jelly filled with chocolate and fruit served in a tall glass, from the French *parfait*: "perfect"

Madaicha 马黛茶: leaves of an evergreen shrub native to South America used as one of the three main beverages (the others being coffee and tea), from the Spanish *maté* or *yerba maté*

Alabika(*dou*) 阿拉比卡(豆): small oval coffee beans, with good aroma and sour taste, which are one of the two major varieties in the world, from the English *Arabica*

Maqiduo (*kafei*) 玛奇朵 (咖啡): a strong black Italian coffee with a dash of frothy steamed milk, from the English *macchiato*, from the Italian *macchiato*: "stained or marked (coffee)"

Kelibing 可丽饼: a small thin French pancake, from the English *crepe*, from the French *crêpe*

Sikangbing 司康饼: a small British cake made from flour and fat, usually eaten with butter, from the English *scone*

Boliduo(*juanbing*) 波丽多(卷饼): a Mexican dish made with a flat thin bread folded around meat or beans with cheese, from the Spanish *burrito*

Pita(bing) 皮塔(饼): a pocket-shaped wheat flour pancake in the Middle East, from the Greek *pita*, from the Hebrew *pat*: "bread"

Dongyingong 冬荫功: a Thai sweet and sour soup made with prawns, from the English *tom yum goong*, from the Thai *tom yum* or *tom yam*: "cooked in sweet and sour + *goong* "prawn"

Tatajiang 塔塔酱: a sauce made of mayonnaise dressing with chopped pickles, olives, capers, and parsley, from the English *tartar sauce*

Saersa(jiang) 萨尔萨(酱): a spicy sauce of tomatoes, onions, and hot peppers, from the English *salsa (sauce)*

Mianbaokang 面包糠: tiny pieces of dry bread used in cooking, from the English *breadcrumb*

Kule 酷乐: a cold drink of mixed white wine and juice, from the English *cooler*

Tequila(jiu) 特奎拉(酒): a strong alcoholic drink made in Mexico, from American Spanish, after *Tequila*, a town in west-central Mexico

Asibatian 阿斯巴甜: an artificial non-saccharide sweetener, formally methyl ester of the aspartic acid/phenylalanine dipeptide, 150 to 200 times sweeter than sucrose, from the English *Aspartame*

Ansaimi 安赛蜜: acesulfame potassium or dioxoxazone potassium, the most stable sweetener (200 times sweeter than sucrose), from the English *acesulfame-K* or *acesulfame potassium*

Xuekebei 雪克杯: a container in which drinks are mixed by shaking or stirring, from the English *shaker*

F **Phonemic loanwords for a specific group of people or special gear**:

Feite(zu) 飞特(族): member of a group who chooses to work part-time or hold down odd jobs, even while full-time employment is available, so as to enjoy more flexibility and freedom, from the English *freeter*, probably from the English *free* and the German *arbeiter* "laborer"

Bobozu 波波族: member of a social class of well-to-do professionals who adopt bohemian values and lead bourgeois lives, from *bobo*, from *bourgeois* and *Bohemian*

Nitezu 尼特族: member of a social class of people who don't go to school, work, study, or do anything else, from *neet*, acronym of "Not in Education, Employment or Training"

Mensao 闷骚: a romantic person who is calm and deep in appearance but full of thought or insight, borrowed from Hong Kong, from the English *man show*

Luolita 洛丽塔: a beautiful, open, and seductive adolescent girl who already has secondary sexual characteristics, from English *Lolita*

Lianjini 脸基尼: a mask designed for swimmers and beachgoers which covers the head and reveals only the eyes, nose, and mouth, invented by a Chinese person from Qingdao, from the English *facekini* (face + bikini)

Halunku 哈伦裤: loosely fitted women's trousers that are gathered at the ankle, from the English *harem pants*

Bomiqun 波米裙: a colorful bohemian-style skirt, from bohemian skirt

Buka 布卡: a loose enveloping garment, usually with veiled eyeholes, that is worn in public by Muslim women, from the English *burka*, from the Hindi *burqa*, from the Arabic *burqu*

Nikabu 尼卡布: a veil covering the face below the eyes, worn by Muslim women, from the English *niqab*, from the Arabic *niqāb*

Bubuzhuang 布布装: a long flowing garment worn by men and women in parts of Africa, such as Mali and Senegal, from the English *bou-bou*

Shatushi (*pijian*) 沙图什(披肩): a shawl made of high-quality wool from the neck hair of the Himalayan chiru, an endangered Tibetan antelope, from *shahtoosh*, from the Persian *šāh* king + Panjabi *tūś*, Kashmiri *tośa* fine shawl-stuff

Bobotou 波波头: a very short to shoulder-length haircut on a woman or child that hangs evenly all round, from *bob*, *bob haircut*, or *Sassoon bob*, named after British hairstylist Vidal Sassoon

G **Phonemic loanwords in daily life**:

Hai 嗨: a friendly informal greeting used to attract attention, used by contemporary young people, from the English *hi*

Hai 嗨: sing, shout, suck, or eat excitedly; extremely excited, from the English *high*

Ye 耶: an exclamation to express agreement, surprise, or cheers, from the English *yeah*

Tieshi 贴士: a small but useful piece of practical advice, from the English *tip(s)*

Shai 晒: to show your life, experience, and mood online to share with others, from the English *share*

Kou 蔻: beautiful, petite, cute, avant-garde or fashionable, from the English *cute*

H **Homophonic transliteration as quasi-affix**:

Apart from its phonetic proximity with the source word, homophonic transliteration, or phonetic-cum-semantic loaning, sometimes makes its transliterated word, so semantically close to the source word as well as if the transliteration functions as a ready-made autochthonous Chinese morpheme. Once it is following a fixed pattern, this morpheme may become a special quasi-affix which semantically deviates from the original character. This type of quasi-affix makes the resultant phonemic loanword appear closer to the autochthonous Chinese lexicon and easier for users to accept. One example is -*ke* 客.

Boke 博客: blog (the earliest form of citizen media) or blogger, first created in 1997 and first introduced to the Chinese mainland in 2000, from the English *blog*, from *weblog* and *blogger*

Boke 播客: a person who is fond of downloading online programs and listens to them wherever possible, from the English *podcaster*

Baike 摆客: someone who regularly rides a bicycle for work or daily life, first used in Taiwan, from the English *biker*

Baike 拜客: a member of a group of people who prefer to live in the past, from the English *backer*

Jike 极客: a knowledgeable and obsessive person enthusiastic about computer or social life, from the English *geek*

Pake 趴客: a person who engages in the activity of planking or lying facedown with their arms by their sides in a rigid, "plank-like" pose and getting a friend to photograph them, usually with the intention of posting the resulting snapshot on social media sites, from the English *planker*

Saike 赛客: personal blog on science, from *sciblog* or *sciblogger* (science + blog)

Weike 维客: a Wikipedia follower, from *wikier*

Weike 威客: a web-based system whereby users can exchange and purchase services and information, and share knowledge and experience in order to save time and money, from *witkey*

Another similar quasi-affix is -*kong* 控 from Chinese lexical borrowing from Japanese -*kon* (-*con*) or "complex" in the sense of "preoccupation with a subject or situation." Deriving from such loanwords from Japanese as *luolikong* 萝莉控 (Japanese *rori-kon* or *lolicon*: sexual attachment to a young, generally prepubescent, girl), *zhengtaikong* 正太控 (Japanese *shota-kon*: a sexual complex where an adult is attracted to a young boy), and *yujiekong* 御姐控 (Japanese *onee-con*, elder sister complex: sexual attachment to an elder mature girl or lady), Chinese -*kong* is used to create its own neologisms, such as *dashukong* 大叔控 (a girl's sexual attachment to an elder man), *weibokong* 微博控 (excessive attention to reading or writing *Weibo* or Chinese micro-blogs), *duanfakong* 短发控 (excessive attraction to having a short hairstyle or sexual attachment to anybody with a short hairstyle), and *yanjingkong* 眼镜控 (excessive attraction to the collection of glasses or sexual attachment to anybody who wears glasses).

2.7.3 Loanwords of Japanese origin

Since Japanese switched to katakana transliteration of Western terms, it is no longer a bridge for Chinese assimilation of Western technological vocabulary. The words borrowed from Japanese during this period (1978–2018) are still largely made up of kanji or Japan-made Chinese characters, with a considerably shifted focus. Most of the borrowed words relate to what is distinctively Japanese, such as anime, services, food, and fruit. Other borrowed words are those in the Western languages which Japan had translated into Chinese characters earlier but that did not enter China until the turn of the new century, after having first been in popular use in Taiwan or

A historical overview of Chinese loanwords 99

Hong Kong for some years. Entering the 21st century, however, the mainland quickly changed to direct assimilation of words from Japan. Most of these loanwords were originally represented in kanji.

Loanwords of Japanese origin are predominantly read according to the on-yomi pronunciation scheme, namely, Japan-made kanji composed of Chinese morphemes (*wasei kango*), which can be divided into the following semantic categories.

A **Loanwords related to business or food**:

Liangfan 量贩: sell in a large amount with a small profit, from *ryōhan*
Peisong 配送: delivery, from *haisō*
Kanban 看板: billboard, first borrowed in Taiwan, from the Japanese *kanban*
Jingsuan 精算: accurate calculation, first *jingsuanshi* 精算师or actuary, then *jingsuan*, from *seisan*
Zhinajin 滞纳金: punitive payment as a result of arrears, from *tainōkin*
Rongjilu 容积率: the measurement of a building's floor area in relation to the size of the lot/parcel that the building is located on, or floor area ratio, from *yōsekiritsu*
Hanfangyao 汉方药: traditional Chinese medication, first borrowed in Taiwan, from the Japanese *kanpō-yaku*
Nadou 纳豆: a traditional sticky Japanese food made from fermented soybeans, from *nattō*
Qiancai 前菜: a small amount of food that is served before the main course of a meal, from *zensai*
Biandang 便当: a single-portion take-out or home-packed meal, from *bentō*
Wanglin pingguo 王林苹果: a Japanese cultivated apple with yellow-green skin and sweet and sour flavor, from *ōrin ringo*

B **Loanwords related to leisure and entertainment**:

Huiben 绘本: picture-book, from *ehon*
Shudu 数独: sudoku, a number game in which a number between 1 and 9 is filled in each small box of a 9x9 square, from *sūdoku*
Toushou 投手: pitcher, the player in baseball or softball games who delivers the ball to the batter, from *tōshu*
Wansheng 完胜: total victory, from *kanshō*
Erciyuan 二次元: a purely ideal virtual fictional world used in anime, reflecting an unrealistic worldview, from *nijigen*
Danmu 弹幕: comments appearing on the screen at the same time as the film and television video is shown, from *danmaku*
Shijuexi 视觉系: a movement among Japanese musicians characterized by the use of varying levels of makeup, elaborate hair styles, and flamboyant costumes, from *shikaku-kei* or *visual kei*
Shengyou 声优: a voice actor, especially for anime, from *seiyū*

C **Loanwords to describe a particular kind of persons**:

Shunu 熟女: a type of mature Japanese woman between 30 and 50 years old who is considered attractive, from *jukujo*

Funu 腐女: a female fan of manga and novels that feature romantic relationships between men or, by extension, any lady who has some peculiar hobbies, from *fujoshi*

Dushe 毒舌: a person who is particularly bitter and harsh in speaking, from *dokuzetsu*

D **Loanwords related to some buzzwords**:

Zhengzhi xianjin 政治献金: donation to a political party in exchange for a guarantee of your own interests, from *seiji kenkin*

Minsu 民宿: a family-run, guesthouse-style lodging in the owner's home, from *minshuku*

Shaozihua 少子化: decline in birth rate, from *shōshika*

Guolaosi 过劳死: karoshi, sudden death from physical or mental overwork, from *karōshi*

Hunhuo 婚活: marriage hunting, searching for a potential partner with the purpose of marriage, from *konkatsu*

Xiaoquexing 小确幸: little but certain happiness, from *shōkakkō*

Zhai 宅: a young person who is obsessed with computers or particular aspects of popular culture to the detriment of their social skills, from *otaku* (*taku* "home")

Aside from those predominantly Japanese kanji on on-yomi reading, other loanwords of Japanese origin are words on kun-yomi reading or a combination of on-yomi and kun-yomi.

Here are some loanwords on kun-yomi reading composed of autochthonous Japanese morphemes:

Fuhei 腹黑: an evil-hearted person, from *haraguro*

Yujie 御姐: a type of young women aged 20 to 36 who are mature in appearance and mind, calm and strong in personality, intellectually self-confident, elegant, considerate, and charming, from *onē* or *onee* 御姉: elder sister

Ganwunu 干物女: a young woman who is as boring and uninteresting as dried food, from *himono-onna*

Suren 素人: amateur, layman, from *shirōto*

Shouda 手打: handmade, from *teuchi*

Meng 萌: (a girl) cute and appealing, from *moe*

Here are some loanwords on a combination reading of on-yomi and kun-yomi:

Chunsheng 纯生: genuine draft beer, from *junnama*

Huizhuan shousi 回转寿司: fast-food sushi which are served on plates that sit on a rotating conveyor belt which runs through the restaurant by every table and counter seat, from *kaiten sushi* or *kaiten zushi*

Fengshuili 丰水梨: Japanese cultivated pear with light reddish brown skin, from *Hōsui nashi*

Baomai 爆买: an explosive tourist shopping spree, created in 2014–15 when tourists from China began their intensive bulk buying in Japan, from *bakugai*

Zhichang 职场: office or workplace and its general environment for career development, from *shokuba*

Bishaji 必杀技: a finishing move or coup de grâce, often in contexts such as pro wrestling or video games, from *hissatsu waza*

The following are some of the loanwords on a combination reading of kun-yomi and on-yomi:

Yuzhaizu 御宅族: a type of people who shut themselves in at home without social or professional pursuit, from *otaku*

Yingwuzhe 影武者: a shadow warrior or a person who manipulates behind the scenes, from *kagemusha*

Beichangtan 备长炭: hard charcoal, charcoal made from black oak and green wood, from *binchyōzumi* or *binchyōtan*

Finally, there are also a very small number of loanwords from Japanese which were originally written in Japanese kana or a combination of kana and Chinese characters, such as *wudong(mian)* 乌冬(面) (Japanese *udon*, thick Japanese noodles made with wheat flour served in soup or broth, probably from the Chinese *huntun* 馄饨 or "dumpling") and *yujiekong* 御姐控 (Japanese *onee-con*, elder sister complex).

2.7.4 Alphabetic letter words (zimuci in Chinese)

As a type of "quasi-loanwords" in the Chinese, borrowed alphabetic letter words continue to pour in in the 21st century, with the appearance of new words almost on a daily basis, covering various fields. Mostly abbreviations of terms marked by complicated concepts and extreme technicality, they would require a long string of characters, ranging from seven to more than a dozen, were they represented in Chinese. Their short and distinct written form explains why they immediately capture the imagination of the technological and cultural sector as well as that of the younger generation. Without presenting the source words in full, these abbreviation-type letter words have greatly distanced themselves from the source words, making them more accessible and thus acceptable to those users who are not well trained in foreign languages. The apparent lack of transparency (i.e. no semantic indication from the lettered form) becomes an advantage in the sense that users, especially those without much training in foreign languages, simply take these lettered words as they are without having to think about how they relate to their foreign source words, thus greatly reducing any possible resistance toward their entry into the Chinese lexicon. There are now hundreds of such alphabetic letter words,[4] with various degrees of assimilation into Chinese, and their impact certainly deserves our attention. The following are some examples, used in various fields.

A **Borrowed letter words in science and technology:**

APP: application store, from APP Store
iPad: a tablet computer developed by Apple
OLED: organic light-emitting diode
LCD: liquid crystal display
MP4: a multi-functional player integrating audio, video, picture browsing, e-book, and radio, from English MPEG-4, an audio and video compression standard introduced in 1998
ETC: a wireless system to automatically collect the usage fee or toll charged to vehicles using toll roads, from the English *Electronic Toll Collection*
VR: virtual reality
PM2.5: atmospheric particulate matter (PM) that is less than 2.5 μm in diameter, from *particulate matter*
PPT: PowerPoint or slides
PS or P: photo adjustment software, from Photoshop
BRT: bus rapid transit
TMT: technology, media, and telecom as an industry grouping that includes the majority of companies focused on new technologies, from *Technology Media Telecom*
Wi-Fi or WiFi: a wireless networking technology that provides users with wireless high-speed Internet and network connections, from *wireless fidelity*
LiFi: a wireless optical networking technology that uses light for data transmission, from *light fidelity*
Loft: a 30 to 50 square-meter small apartment or a flexible, open and stylish multifunctional space that can be used for business or residence.

B **Borrowed letter words in education and health:**

MFA: Master of Fine Arts
IBO: a non-profit foundation for multinational education system, serving international schools and providing high-level pre-university programs, from *International Baccalaureate Organization* (IBO), now International Baccalaureate (IB), founded in 1968
SCI: Science Citation Index, originally produced by the US Institute for Scientific Information (ISI)
SARS: severe acute respiratory syndrome, a form of atypical pneumonia which broke out in 2002 in China

A historical overview of Chinese loanwords 103

Q re Q热: a natural systemic infectious disease, from Q fever or query fever

SPA: a place with therapeutic services, such as massage, sauna, bath, and manicure, probably from Solus Por Aqua or Solubrious Par Aqua

X dao X刀: a device that cuts by means of X-ray, from X-ray

Gama dao 伽马刀 or γ dao γ刀: stereotactic gamma-ray radiosurgery or gamma knife, from gamma knife

C **Borrowed letter words in political or economic fields**:

RCEP: a proposed free trade agreement in the Indo-Pacific region between 16 Asia-Pacific countries—the 10 members of ASEAN, plus China, Japan, South Korea, Australia, New Zealand, and India, from Regional Comprehensive Economic Partnership

NGO: nongovernmental organization

FTA: Free Trade Agreement

ISIS: the terrorist organization "Islamic State," established in 2014, from "*Islamic State in Iraq and Syria*" or "Islamic State in Iraq and al-Sham"

HR: human resources

PPP: a cooperative arrangement between the government and business, from *Public-Private Partnership*

CBD: central business district

Logo: a small design or symbol that is the official sign of a company or organization, from *logo*, *logotype*

FDI: foreign direct investment

ICO: the cryptocurrency (blockchain) industry's equivalent to an Initial Public Offering (IPO), from *Initial Coin Offering*

Polo shan Polo 衫: knitted tennis shirt, from *Polo shirt*

O2O: online-to-offline business model

SDR: an international type of monetary reserve currency created by the International Monetary Fund (IMF), from *special drawing rights*

M2: a calculation of the money supply that includes all elements of cash and checking deposits (M1) as well as savings deposits, money market securities, mutual funds, and other time deposits, from *money*

K xian K 线: a type of price chart used in technical analysis that displays the high, low, open, and closing prices of security for a specific period, from *candlestick*

POS(ji) POS(机): point of sale (terminal)

K: one thousand, from *kilo*

D **Borrowed letter words in sport and entertainment**:

U20: football game for players under the age of 20, from *Under-20*

VAR: a match official in association football who reviews decisions made by the head referee, from *video assistant referee*

PU paodao PU 跑道: running track paved with Polyurethane, from *PU* or *Polyurethane*

KO: in fighting or boxing, a blow that makes an opponent fall to the ground and be unable to get up so that he or she loses the fight, from *knockout*

LOL: a multiplayer online battle arena video game, from *League of Legends*

Da call 打 call: a form of interaction at the concert where the audience cheer and wave glow sticks to the rhythm of the music, from *da* (semantic marker "act") + *call* (pronounced /kāo/ in Chinese) from the Japanese *kōru*, phonemic loan from the English *call*

Cosplay: performance art or party of dressing up as a character from a work of fiction, such as anime and manga, from the Japanese *kosupure* for cosplay, from costume + play

C wei C位: the position for the strongest player in a game performance or competition, from *C* for center

ACG: a collection or culture of anime, comic and games, from *anime, comic and games*

K ge K歌: go to the karaoke, from *karakoke*

E **Borrowed letter words as popular buzzwords**:

V or *da V* 大 V: very important person, from *VIP*

Boss: from English *boss*

Hold: control, grasp, pronounced /hōu/, from the English *hold*

Out: out of fashion, outdated, disqualified, from the English *out*

NG: poorly done, worthless, defective, from *no good*

N or *N duo* N多: numerous to the nth degree or by extension to a great degree, from *N* as a mathematical symbol, indicating an indefinitely large number

PK: Player killing or knocking out opponents in competition, from *player killing* in games

btw: (netspeak) by the way

B4: (netspeak) before

f2f: (netspeak) face-to-face

Notes

1 For their corresponding Babylonian terms, please refer to *Yiwenhua de shizhe: wailaici* 异文化的使者——外来词 (*Messenger for foreign cultures: loanwords*. Shi, Youwei. 1991) and *Wailaici: yiwenhua de shizhe* 外来词——异文化的使者 (*Loanwords: messenger for foreign cultures.* Shi, Youwei. 2004).

2 This section, 2.5.3.1 and 2.5.3.2, specifically, is mainly based on the research by Federico Masini (1993) and Shen Guowei (1994/1995/2011).

3 This is confirmed by the statistics in *Language and Philology* (1923) by Roland G. Kent on 20,000 English words and *Understanding English* (1958) by Paul Roberts on 140,000 English words, as summarized below:

English words and their sources:

Source	20,000 by Roland Kent	140,000 by Paul Roberts
Autochthonous English words	19%	14%
Latin origin	15%	36%
French origin	36%	21%
Greek origin	13%	4.5%
Nordic origin	7% (Dutch and German included)	2%
Italian or Spanish origin	1%	3%
Others	9%	19.5%

For statistics on the origin of the English lexicon from a 1,000,000-word sample, please refer to the research by Gu Jiazu 顾嘉祖 (1990).

4 There are 239 acronyms or words beginning with Greek or Latin letters listed at the end of the *Xiandai hanyu cidian* 现代汉语词典 (The Contemporary Chinese Dictionary. 6th edition, 2012) and more than 2,000 words beginning with Latin letters in the *Xinhua wailaici cidian* 新华外来词词典 (Xinhua dictionary of Chinese loanwords. 2019) in which at least 400–500 are borrowed ones, excluding those Chinese self-made letter words and those yet to become the established "quasi-loanwords".

3 The characteristics and functions of Chinese loanwords

3.1 Multiple characteristics of the loanword

3.1.1 Three semiotic identities

As part of the lexicon of a particular language, the loanword is necessarily a semiotic representation of that language. It is also one of the vehicles of cultural transmission, so it is undoubtedly a semiotic representation of culture. At the same time, the loanword is a participant in social activities in the sense that it reflects social changes, ethnic exchanges, and the social stratification of people who use it. So, like it or not, the loanword is also symbolic of a society. In short, the loanword assumes three semiotic identities: linguistic, cultural, and social, all of which we can observe and study for the purpose of understanding it. In fact, it is not just the loanword but any semiotic representation of a language that must have these multiple identities or attributes. The only problem in that regard is that, for a long time, we have been paying attention only to the loanword's linguistic attribute, so much so that we are unable to have a systematic observation and understanding of the other two identities. Of course, there is nothing wrong with giving considerable attention to the linguistic aspect because it constitutes the loanword's distinguishing feature as compared with other symbols. But our understanding of the loanword cannot be complete or holistic unless its linguistic, cultural, and social attributes are all taken together for observation.

Additionally, the loanword is made by and used for human beings, who are, by definition, creatures with a mind and soul. So, its linguistic, cultural, and social aspects may also be tinged with some psychological implications that call for additional attention. In terms of its written form in particular, the loanword may trigger some opaque and convoluted psychological reactions due to its compositional heterogeneity, which is in conflict with the homogeneity of the native language in general, something worthy of further attention.

Take *bingqilin* 冰淇淋, a Chinese loanword from the English "ice cream," for example. In terms of language form, this is a combination of both indigenous Chinese morphemes and elements from a foreign language through phonetic transliteration, the latter of which have already been naturalized in pronunciation. So, in that sense, the Chinese and the foreign are integrated into one. The word's components, *bing* and *qilin*, are semantically integrated because we are unable to clearly explain what Chinese *qilin* is, and *bing*, here, is not real ice at all. An even further examination would reveal that this cold sweet food may probably have originated from China: *uta* in Manchu is a prototype of ice cream, and a still earlier version appeared in China's Ming dynasty. Westerners in China at the time took it home and refashioned it to suit the tastes and style of the West. This is such interesting and living proof of cultural exchange. As ice cream dominates the dessert and soft drink market today, it also reminds us of its social implications. As a symbol of contemporary society, it may represent "being modern or contemporary" and the infiltration of Western into Eastern culture.

It is true that *bingqilin* may not trigger any special psychological reaction, but *Kekou kele* 可口可乐, a Chinese loanword from the English Coca-Cola, is different. This is a product from a very specific manufacturer of a specific country and a symbol that has evolved from a specific trademark. So, oftentimes, it represents an invasion of trade and culture from that specific country into another and triggers various psychological reactions. As for the Chinese word itself, some love it, some hate it, others are jealous, and still others hold it in contempt. Whatever the reaction, *Kekou kele* is the very epitome of American culture and a representative symbol of contemporary society.

There is also no ignoring the fact that similar loanwords, like *kala OK* 卡拉 OK and *DNA*, present some extremely heterogeneous forms, thus provoking an antipathetic or inexplicably mixed reaction from the Chinese. The opposition to or controversy over the 239 entries which begin with Western letters in the 6th edition of China's most widely used *Xiandai hanyu cidian* (The Contemporary Chinese Dictionary), published in 2012, is a clear manifestation of that.

3.1.2 *The linguistic and cultural characteristics*

In a broad sense, language contact between national, racial, or ethnic communities is contact between different cultures, which will, over time, bring about cultural integration. Cultural integration is embodied not only in physical artifacts but also in institutions and the depth of consciousness. The loanword is still another field in which cultural integration is manifested. Language exists both outside and inside a culture. So, broadly speaking, it is a kind of culture in itself or might be called "linguistic culture." What is more, it is an extremely important type of culture, a "meta-culture,"[1] so to speak, which can interpret and condition other aspects of culture within a certain scope and to a certain degree. Seen from this perspective, the loanword is no doubt a kind of representation of this linguistic culture. With its linguistic attribute being identified as such, we can discover and appreciate more of the special nature of the loanword. This product of direct and indirect contact between national, racial, or ethnic communities will, as a matter of course, integrate different languages and cultures, thus possessing a dual linguistic and cultural identity.

3.2 Linguistic and cultural integration as reflected in the loanword

The loanword necessarily results from the integration of at least two languages and cultures, and this integration is reflected in two aspects: the semantic and grammatical content on the one hand and the phonetic, compositional, and written forms on the other hand.

3.2.1 Integration in terms of the content

3.2.1.1 Integration in semantic content

As far as the content is concerned, what most loanwords have introduced are undoubtedly loaned concepts, but many of those loaned concepts which have taken root in the recipient language usually turn out to deviate from the original ones. In their interactions and exchanges, nations or inter-ethnic communities are bound to encounter many distinct things, including natural objects, man-made artifacts, institutions, and behaviors. Whether natural or artificial, they are all arbitrarily perceived by human beings as long as they are signified with a language and given a specific word; therefore, there will already be some human subjectivity in their cognition. Things in the natural world are thus endowed with humanistic attributes. Mandarin ducks, for example, once known by the Han Chinese, take on connotations beyond their apparent natural properties, such as beauty, love, and loyalty. In their natural state, mandarin ducks cannot be said to be loyal to each other, but Han Chinese people still prefer to view them as a symbol of love and fidelity. Given this consideration, naming and assignment of meaning are in fact some kind of contrivance by mankind, a human effort in its adaptation to and modification of Mother Nature. So, the meaning and form which are associated with naming will possess cultural attributes to varying degrees. In terms of semantic content, there are three basic scenarios for the Chinese loanword.

1. Chinese did not have a word with the same meaning as the loanword until the lexical borrowing. Having been in use for many years, some loanwords essentially keep their meaning(s) unchanged. What these words signify are mostly concrete names and/or descriptions of things, and, on occasion, some few abstract nouns. The following are a few examples.

Putao 葡萄 (borrowed from *badaga* in Dayuan 大宛, the language in ancient Central Asia, meaning "grape"). It was introduced to China more than

2,000 years ago from Central Asia. It has been so called and used in such semantic reference ever since.

Niepan 涅槃 (from the Sanskrit *nirvana* or the Pali *nibbana*). With its entry into the Chinese language, along with the introduction of Buddhism before 1900, the loanword has kept its original meaning, "the final beatitude in Buddhism that transcends suffering, life, and death through the extinction of desire and individual consciousness" or "the passing away of Buddha," unchanged, despite the multiple changes in its phonemic shape.

Luoji 逻辑 (from the English *logic*). Since its entry in the early 20th century, this has consistently meant the laws governing one's way of thinking and a science that deals with the subject.

When they are entering into the Chinese language, the meanings of some of the loanwords in this category are partially chosen before they become a full member of the Chinese lexicon, and, therefore, they are not entirely equivalent in meaning to their foreign source words. The following are two examples.

Shalong 沙龙 (from the French *salon*). Besides referring to a regular gathering of people of social or intellectual distinction, at which they talk about art or politics, the French source word also means a sitting room, a reception party, and an exhibition of works of art. When the French word was introduced to Chinese, *shalong* not only adopted this first meaning but also removed its original restriction to upper society. The other meanings of the French source word, along with their accompanying connotations of upper society, have all been absent in *shalong*.

Beige 杯葛 (from the English *boycott*). The English source word can either mean refusing to buy goods as a punishment (or protest) or withdrawing from commercial or social relations for the same reason. *Beige*, the monosemous Chinese phonemic loan from boycott, however, only adopts this first meaning.

2. Building upon the original meaning of the borrowed word, the Chinese loanword then evolved some new meaning. These words are in their totality no longer the same in meaning as the borrowed words (further details in Section 4.1.1 in Chapter 4). The following are a few examples.

Pusa 菩萨 (from the Sanskrit *bodhisattva*). In Buddhism, bodhisattva refers to the title given to Sakyamuni before he reached nirvana. In the Chinese school of Buddhism, *pusa* also refers to a person who preaches Buddhist teachings to promote universal salvation. When the term was introduced to China, the general public used it to respectfully refer to those decorous and compassionate-looking people. In *Xiyouji* 西游记 (*Journey to the West*), the foremost Chinese comic novel in the 16th century, monks and nuns also used *pusa* as a reverential title for alms givers and disciples. In short, the laity now broadens the meaning of *pusa* to being "greatly merciful and compassionate."

Zhan 站 (from the Mongolian *jam*). This originally referred to a courier station where a horse-riding courier took a break or changed horses. Since its introduction into Chinese in the Ming dynasty, it gradually transformed itself into the station as we understand today. It also refers to those grass-roots bodies, such as health and epidemic prevention station, weather station, publicity station, and broadcasting station.

Ximingnaer 习明纳尔 (from the Russian семинар, meaning "seminar"). The Chinese loanword adopted the partial meaning of classroom discussion at the time of its borrowing. It should have been a mistranslation because it deviated from the meaning of its Russian source word, which, in fact, not only refers to a method of teaching but also means a teaching unit that is equivalent to a class. Incidentally, it is perhaps because of its insufficient borrowing that this Chinese loanword did not go very far before it was replaced by *yantaoban* 研讨班 and *taolunban* 讨论班.

Qudi 取缔 (from the Japanese *torishimaru*). The Japanese source word means "supervise" or "manage," but the Chinese loanword changed it to mean "cancel". Japanese has both the verb "*torishimaru*" and the noun "*torishimari*," but the Chinese loanword only took the verb for use.

3. The loanword has the same lexical meaning as the existing indigenous or self-originated Chinese words. Loanwords of this kind do not bring about new concepts; instead, they bring a synonym, in a borrowed form, into the existing Chinese lexicon. There are not many of this kind, and they do not play a major role among Chinese loanwords.

Haluo 哈罗 (from the English *hello*). As an exclamation or greeting, it does not itself constitute a concept, and it is exactly the same as the Chinese indigenous greeting *wei* 喂.

Baibai 拜拜 (from the English *bye-bye*). It means the same thing as Chinese autochthonous *zaijian* 再见 and does not bring in anything conceptually new.

Bo 波 (from the English *ball*). The loanword *bo* simply means the Chinese indigenous word *qiu* 球, which was written in ancient China as 毬, the same as *ju* 鞠. *Qiu* had already come into being in China between 420 and 589 AD. This borrowed *bo*, which was first used in the Cantonese dialect and then extended to modern standard Chinese, does not add anything new at all in terms of lexical content.

3.2.1.2 Grammatical integration

To be naturalized into the Chinese lexicon, foreign loanwords must necessarily be influenced by Chinese lexical usage, subject themselves to Chinese grammar, and accommodate Chinese users. These processes are reflected in the restrictions on choice of parts of speech, the determination of different functions of the words of similar parts of speech, and the functional changes in word formation. The following are a few examples to illustrate this integration.

Xian 仙 (from the English *cent*). This is used in Hong Kong and Macao as fractional currency. Chinese people used to borrow "cents," the plural of its English source word, as *xianshi* 仙士, but *xianshi* was used in some dialects as *tongyuan* 铜元 (bronze coin). So, *xian* is used in Hong Kong and Macao for both the singular and the plural.

Youmo 幽默 (from the English *humor*). The source word under the Chinese borrowing is a noun, but its Chinese loanword *youmo*, except for its rare use as a noun (e.g. *you youmo* 有幽默 meaning "has a sense of humor" and *yizhong youmo* 一种幽默 "a kind of humor"), mainly functions as an adjective and can also be used as a split verb. For instance, *tai youmo le* 太幽默了 "too humorous," *youmo jile* 幽默极了 "extremely humorous," *youbu youmo* 幽不幽默 "humorous or not," and *youle ta yimo* 幽了他一默 "bantered him."

Baibai 拜拜 (from the English *bye-bye*). The source word is an exclamation, and its loanword is also used as such when being introduced into Chinese. But it can also be used as a verb, such as *baibai le* 拜拜了 "said bye-bye" and *genta baibai le* 跟他拜拜了 "part company with him." In addition, there is a unique use of the word in the local Beijing vernacular as *baibai le nin na!* 拜拜了您哪! either as a polite way of saying, "goodbye" or as a jocular way of saying, "I won't come here again."

3.2.2 *Integration in terms of form*

The word "form" in this section mainly refers to phonetic and compositional form, though some forms of writing will also be touched upon. Though the phonemic loanword is phonetically influenced by the borrowed source word and a certain phoneme or phonemic combination from the source word may be assimilated into Chinese, the loanword as a whole must always be subjected to the Chinese phonetic system, thus making it more or less different from its source word. Chinese phonology will, to varying degrees, modify these "foreign guests," making them naturalized. This kind of modification mainly happens phonetically and structurally; it may also include changes to the written form.

3.2.2.1 *Phonetic adjustment for the phonetically borrowed part*

This adjustment only affects the pronunciation of the phonetically borrowed part, either by tweaking the sound, adding or deleting the syllable, or phonetic shortening. The following are a few examples to illustrate how the adjustment is carried out.

Laise or *laize* 莱塞/莱泽 (now replaced by semantic loan *jiguang* 激光, both from the English *laser*). The two-character Chinese loanword phonetically imitates the two-syllable source word by using Chinese compound vowel /ai/ for English diphthong /ei/ and voiceless consonant /s/ or voiced /z/ for English /z/. Its more recent and popular variant *leishe* 雷射/镭射, introduced from Hong Kong and Macao, is an adjustment combining near homophony and *huiyi* 会意 (ideogrammic compound, one of the six types of Chinese character formation)—a combination of elements thought to be logically associated: the first characters are near homophones of the first syllable of the English word, while the second combines the sound and meaning by using a Chinese retroflex consonant /sh/.

Saiyinsi 赛因斯 (phonemic loan from the English *science*). This was the complete form of the more popularly known *sai xiansheng* 赛先生 (Mr. Sai, taking its first syllable from *saiyinsi*) in the May Fourth Movement, and it has now been replaced by *kexue* 科学, the semantic loan from *science*. The English source word has two syllables, while its Chinese phonemic loan *saiyinsi* has three. This expedient method is a reluctant means to the end of adapting foreign sounds to Chinese phonological form as there is no phonetic form of "front compound vowel + nasal sound" in Chinese, nor does it have an affricate consonant without any vowel at the end.

Si 锶 (a soft silver-white metal, from the New Latin *strontium*). If this two-syllable source word were transliterated sound by sound, its Chinese loanword would have had to use five characters, as in *sitelongtianmu* 思特隆田姆. Obviously, the now one-syllable Chinese word is adopted instead to suit the Chinese language characterized by monosyllabic morphemes and, with the monosyllabic *si*, to make it better able to form new words through combination.

Jialan 伽蓝 (temple or monastery, from the Sanskrit *samgharama*). The original transliteration *sengjialanmo* 僧伽蓝摩 has already made some phonetic changes, as compared with the source word. As a typical language dominated by one-syllable morphemes, Chinese, classical Chinese in particular, is not accustomed to four-syllable words. So, the transliteration has undergone further adaptation during its usage and finally been phonetically shortened to *jialan*.

3.2.2.2 Structural adaptation

Changes to lexical structure usually happen not in isolation but in combination with phonetic changes. The most common loanword is the completely phonetically translated one whose structural components (morphemes) form an integrated whole; they cannot be further atomized or differentiated in terms of grammatical unit but can only be seen as one morpheme. For example, *panchaxila* 潘查希拉 (meaning "Five Principles" of the Indonesian state philosophy, from the Sanskrit *pañca*, meaning "five," and *sīla*, meaning "principles") is a four-syllable word and cannot be further parsed into two or more meaningful or associated components. Even phonetic shortening of the initial form of *channa* 禅那 (a Buddhist method of self-cultivation through sitting in meditation, from the Sanskrit *dhyana*) and *mitu* 米突 (meter, from the French *mètre*) to present-day *chan* 禅 and *mi* 米, respectively, still does not change the nature of such pure phonemic loaning. In other borrowed words in Chinese, however, structural adjustment is carried out. There are three types of structural adjustment: partial semantic loaning, partial or complete homophonic transliteration, and addition of semantic marker.

1. Partial semantic loaning. This means that the rest of the loanword will go through phonetic loaning. The following are a few examples.

Bingqilin 冰淇淋 (from the English *ice cream*). As has been discussed, the first character *bing* results from semantic loaning, while the other two, *qilin*, choose to apply phonetic loaning by using words that are related to water (both *qi* and *lin* contain the radical 氵, meaning "water") in order to bring about the intended association.

Motuoche 摩托车 (from the English *motorcycle*). As has been discussed, the first two characters are obviously phonetic loaning, while the third and last characters are somewhat semantic loaning. *Che*, meaning "vehicle," as used in *zixing che* 自行车 (bicycle) and *sanlun che* 三轮车 (tricycle), is a hypernym to classify various road vehicles with wheels, as is the custom in the Chinese language.

X guang X光 (from the English *X-ray*). The first part, X, is both phonetic and graphic loaning. Its variant by means of part-phonetic and part-semantic loaning is *aikesiguang* 爱克斯光.

2. Partial or complete homophonic transliteration. Homophonic transliteration or translation through homophonic proximity with some semantic cues is the same thing as phonetic and semantic loaning combined. Homophonic proximity, *xieyin* 谐音 in Chinese, usually refers to words with identical or near homophony. It is used here to refer to translating the sounds of a foreign word with Chinese characters which are identical (or nearly identical) in pronunciation to the source word and which retain their lexical meanings—otherwise, it would merely be phonetic loaning. Strictly speaking, though, this still belongs to phonetic loaning, not semantic loaning in the real sense of the word, because it takes Chinese morphemes on the basis of homophonic proximity to the source word in order to create certain semantic ties with the source word. While some of these attempted ties are very close and direct, almost as in semantic loaning, most of the ties are indirect and semantically leaning. Others are rather far-fetched or said just for fun. Still others are just partial homophonic transliteration. Therefore, these words may also be regarded as Chinese neologisms which are both based upon and inspired by the phonetic form of the source words. The following are a few examples in order of homophonic proximity (also Section 4.1.2.1 in Chapter 4).

Shimintu 士敏土 (from the English *cement*). This is modern Chinese writer Lu Xun's trans-creation for *cement*, in which the last character, *tu*, is a case of homophonic transliteration with some semantic cues as it is both phonetically similar to the last sound, /t/, and semantically means "clay." A more popular alternative in Lu Xun's time was *shuimenting* 水门汀, in which the first character *shui* is homophonic transliteration with some semantic cues (phonetically close to the sound of the first syllable of the source word and literally meaning "water"), while the third *ting* is related to the meaning of the source word with its left-side component, which suggests water.

Mangguo 芒果/杧果 (from the Malay *manga*). This goes one step further (and is better) than the above *shimintu* in terms of word creation by combining 芒 *mang* or 杧 *mang*, a fairly good choice, to help people associate it with plants and 果 *guo* (meaning "fruit"), making the combination almost like an indigenous Chinese word.

Heike/haike 黑客/骇客 (from the English *hacker*). This goes even further (and is even better) than *mangguo* by using two common Chinese morphemes (*hei* and *ke*), the combination of which dovetails so nicely with the Chinese way of word formation that it is virtually identical to an indigenous Chinese or self-originated word.

Luoji 逻辑 (from the English *logic*). The homophonic transliteration with semantic cues is more covertly implied here. The first character, *luo* 逻, means inspecting, indicating acting according to a defined route, while the second, *ji* 辑, means editing, also implying acting in a certain order. The two words combined are therefore implicitly associated with "laws governing the way of thinking," to which its English source word "logic" basically refers. This covertly implied association in meaning is a corollary of the practice of homophonic transliteration with semantic cues. Similar words, namely, words created by means of covert homophonic transliteration, include *anqier* 安琪儿 (-from English *angel*).

Wayehu 瓦夜壶 (from the English *wife*). This farcical homophonic transliteration of "wife" to *wayehu*, literally meaning "chamber pot at night," would no doubt invite vociferous protests from wives. Similar cases include *mashaji* 马杀鸡 (literally "horse killing chicken," used in Hong Kong, Macao, and Taiwan) for English *massage*. It is surprising that customers in Hong Kong or Taiwan do not seem to feel intimidated about the word "kill."

3. Addition of semantic marker. Most semantic markers belong to what is called a "category marker," located at the end of the word. Some few belong to what is called a "modifier marker," located at the beginning of the word. Still others are "affix markers," located either at the beginning or the end (for more on this, please refer to Section 4.1.2.1.D in Chapter 4). The following are some examples.

Shading yu 沙丁鱼 (from the English *sardine*). One can only determine what kind of thing *shading yu* is through the character *yu* (meaning "fish"); in other words, one would not be able to make any sense of *shading* without *yu* as its category marker. In contrast, words like *baita you* 白塔油 (from the English *butter*), *balei wu* 芭蕾舞 (from the French *ballet*), *xiangbin jiu* 香槟酒 (from the French *champagne*), *tanke che* 坦克车 (from the English *tank*), and *gaoerfu qiu* 高尔夫球 (from the English *golf*) are usually used with the omission of their last component characters (*you*, *wu*, *jiu*, *che*, and *qiu*, meaning "oil," "dance," "wine," "vehicle," and "ball," respectively) as category markers. It is fair to say that, with their meaning perfectly intact, this omission of category markers is a regular pattern in the evolution of such loanwords.

"*Muhou*" 沐猴 (from the Tibeto-Burman language *m(j)uk* and the Burmese *mjok*). Many people take the first component character of the word too literally, wrongly assuming that *mu* 沐, which means "wash one's hair," is used here to suggest that the monkey loves wiping its face in a manner very similar to a lady washing her hair. As a matter of fact, *mu* here is a mere phonemic rendering of the source word to refer to a kind of monkey or ape. Therefore, *hou* (monkey) is added as a category marker to avoid any further misunderstanding.

Baolingqiu 保龄球 (from the English *bowling*). Probably because Chinese people had grown mature in lexical borrowing, a second phonemic version, with the same pronunciation, of the English word—保令球, with only the second component character different from 保龄球—quickly became obsolete after the borrowing of the word "bowling" into the Chinese language. One apparent reason for this is that the first two component characters (保龄) of the preferred version not only indicate the pronunciation (i.e. phonetic loaning) but also suggest some favorable implications, while the last character, *qiu* ("ball"), indicates what category of thing it belongs to.

Xianpalazi 线帕拉子 (meaning "cotton thread blanket without velvet," from the Uighur *palaz*). Lexically speaking, the word *xian* 线 (thread) is redundant because *palaz* is, by definition, made of cotton thread, but it is a necessary "modifier marker" from a cognitive point of view.

Ashe 阿蛇 or *a sir* 阿 sir (used in Hong Kong to address a policeperson, from the English *sir*). The component character *a* 阿 is typically used in the Chinese language as a prefix before a name.

A more recent one is *hazu* 哈租 (from the English *hire*). The first character, *ha* 哈, is a homophonic transliteration, but it does not carry over the meaning of "hire"—it usually means "apple-polish" or "admire." Only the second character means "hire." The two characters combined constitute a "V + O" phrasal structure, vividly suggesting the mentality of those people, though it is hard to classify such lexical borrowing as a particular type of loanword.

3.2.2.3 Graphic remolding for semantic association

This means choosing or remolding the Chinese characters used in phonetic transliteration in order to make the component radicals of the characters lexically associated, in a way, with the source word. Though not yet impacting morphemic atomization, this unique linguistic integration in Chinese provides some lexical association or ties and points to a potential direction for the further evolution of this kind of loanword. Once the loanword is smoothly abbreviated to a single character, it may become a character of *xingsheng* 形声 (phono-semantic compound), a type of character that combines a semantic element (i.e. a radical) with a phonetic element intended to remind the reader of the word's pronunciation. That means that a lot more words can be created out of this *xingsheng* character. The following are a few examples.

- *Ningmeng* 柠檬 (from the English *lemon*). Once transliterated as *limeng* 黎濛 but later replaced by the current *ningmeng*, which is better able to suggest a plant, with its invented characters featuring the left-side character component *mu* 木 (meaning "wood"). Then its first component character, ning, becomes something of a morpheme used in such new compound nouns as *qingning* 青柠 (lime), *ningguo* 柠果 (lemon fruit), *ningxiang* 柠香 (lemon-like flavor), *ninghongcha* 柠红茶 (black tea with lemon), and *mangningcha* 芒柠茶 (lemon mango tea).
- *Luotuo* 骆驼 (from the Hun or Xiongnu word *dada*, meaning "camel"). Entering into the Central Plain, the cradle of ancient Chinese civilization, more than 2,000 years ago, the loanword once took the form of *tuota* 橐它, but soon, a *xingsheng* character was invented for the desert animal—*tuo* 驼—so the word was replaced by *tuotuo* 駝驼 before it was transformed into *luotuo* 骆驼 due to an erroneous change of sound. The invention of *tuo* 驼 enables the Chinese language to shorten the two-character *luotuo* 骆驼 into one-character *tuo* 驼 and, with that, to create a host of new related words, such as *tuobei* 驼背 (hunchback), *tuoyuan* 驼员 (camel man), *tuofeng* 驼峰 (hump), *tuoling* 驼铃 (camel bell), *tuomao* 驼毛 (camel hair), *tuorong* 驼绒 (camel's down), and *tuolu* 驼鹿 (moose).
- *Shizi* 狮子 (from the East Iranian word *se* or *si*). The loanword was initially written as *shizi* 师子 when introduced from Central Asia and later graphically remolded for semantic association by adding a radical 犭 as animal indicator to the left side of the character *shi* 师, turning the word into the current form 狮子, which, in turn, makes it possible to use *shi* 狮 in isolation. *Shi* has since become a very active one-syllable morpheme in creating new words, such as *shiwu* 狮舞 (lion dance), *shihou* 狮吼 (roaring of or like a lion), *shizi'e* 狮子鹅 (lion-like goose), *shishi* 石狮 (stone lion), and *wushi* 舞狮 (have a lion dance).
- *Bingqilin/bingjiling* 冰淇淋/冰激凌 (from the English *ice cream*). The last two characters in both variants act, as it were, in concert without previous arrangement through their use of the left-side component radical of 氵,

indicating "water," in order to stay consistent with the first component character, *bing*, in type and to maintain a phonetic formation similar to the source word.

Since Chinese is a language largely based upon mono-syllable morphemes, these newly abbreviated morphemes naturally become the best choice for the invention of new words. This will, in turn, exert an influence on the written form of loanwords. The fact that the Chinese phonemic loanword *putao* 葡萄 ("grape") has gone through many graphic modifications in history, such as 蒲陶, 蒲桃, 蒲萄, and 葡陶 (all with the same pronunciation as the currently used 葡萄), makes clear the significance of such a graphic written form to the national psyche and lexical formation. But once reaching the above-mentioned stage of homophonic transliteration that borders on semantic loaning, the loanword becomes stable, thus facilitating the graphic finalization of the lexicon.

3.3 Cultural conflicts reflected in the loanword

Since loanwords embody the integration of different cultures, those diverse cultures, while they are carried along through loanwords, will also naturally bring in various reactions on the part of loanword users. Some of the reactions are harmonious, meaning that users are happy to embrace them, while others are not so, meaning that they resist or reject them to varying degrees, which would either help force further adjustments to be made to the loanword or have it disappear from the scene. There are two possible reasons that help explain the inharmonious reactions. One is that conflicts in social, political, ideological, and cultural traditions may have been shifted onto the loanword; the other is that one's native linguistic and cultural elements are inadequately or incorrectly represented in the loanword.

Cultural conflict itself is a natural response in the process of cultural integration, another form of representation of the integration process. As a kind of conflict between two different cultures which are defined in a broader sense, cultural conflict reflected in the loanword can be observed in two areas: one between words and the other between words and non-lexical aspects. These conflicts will lead to the selection, elimination, or modifications of the loanword in question, the purpose of which is to maintain a stable yet tense equilibrium between the two cultures, linguistic cultures included.

3.3.1 *Conflicts between words*

3.3.1.1 *Conflicts between loanwords and non-loanwords*

Laise 莱塞 vs. *jiguang* 激光 vs. *leishe* 雷射/镭射. Initially phonetically transliterated from the English *laser* (light amplification by stimulated emission of radiation), *laise* was perceived as too technical to be understood and used by ordinary people, thus prompting the birth of *jiguang* (literally "stimulated light"), a form of semantic loaning. Easier to understand from its graphic representation, *jiguang* very quickly became popular. Words and expressions used in Hong Kong and Macao following China's reform and opening-up in 1978 have flowed into the mainland. Among them was *leishe*, a commercial-sounding homophonic transliteration from *laser*. With its peculiar lexical combination (雷射 "thunder + emission" and 镭射 "radium + emission"), *leishe* attracted many users. However, *jiguang* did not phase out as a result; instead, both hold their respective areas for use: *jiguang* basically keeps its original "sphere of influence," while *leishe* is limited to some commercial context (e.g. when laser video or CD is commercially available) and related premises in Hong Kong and Macao.

Mitu/mida 米突/密达 vs. *gongchi* 公尺 vs. *mi* 米. *Gongchi* and *mitu* (or *mida*) almost simultaneously became the earliest translations of the French word "mètre," though 米突 and 米 were probably initially borrowed in the Cantonese dialect of Chinese. Despite both having two syllables, they have had different destinies. Characterized by its frequency in use and considerable stability, a system of weights and measures is an important part of a nation's culture and customs. In the eyes of the general public, the best choice of a name for a new unit of measurement would be the one which is able to be associated with the traditional system. So, with some conflict and practice, the public finally chose *gongchi* 公尺 because *chi* 尺 is such a familiar and traditional unit to the Chinese people. Meanwhile, thanks to its monosyllabic advantage, *mi*, the shortened form of *mitu*, won the day in the scientific community and was thus adopted to replace *mitu*. Since China's reform and opening-up in 1978, internationalizing and standardizing terminology for the measurement system was gathering momentum so as to promote cross-national exchange. Against this background, the national government promulgated—in the form of a decree—a unified system of measurement units. Since then, the status of *mi* has continued to shoot up, while the use of *gongchi* has dwindled, and its frequency in use consequently keeps going down.

Weitaming 维他命 vs. *weishengsu* 维生素. While the former is a homophonic transliteration of the English "vitamin," and the latter is a semantic loaning, the latter is obviously influenced by the former and came into being after being made more scientific. They now hold their respective "spheres of influence": the mainland stipulates using *weishengsu*, while Taiwan and Hong Kong keep the original transliteration of *weitaming*. But with the reform and opening-up on the mainland, *weitaming* is quietly returning to the mainland in some commercial circles.

DNA vs. *tuoyanghetanghesuan* 脱氧核糖核酸. As a typical alphabetic graphic loan, DNA does not mean much to most people, but it is broadly received by the general public due to its brevity and simplicity. As a semantic loan from its source word DNA, *tuoyanghetanghesuan* accurately captures the meaning but is obviously too long to remember. So, the latter is only used occasionally within the scientific community as a technical term. There are many similar pairs of loanword versions, such as UFO vs. *bumingfeixingwu* 不明飞行物 and GPS vs. *quanqiudingweixitong* 全球定位系统, where the original acronyms are preferred over their semantically rendered long versions.

3.3.1.2 Conflict between loanwords of different types

Making a choice between different types of loanwords also reflects various considerations associated with the means by which the loanword is formed. Some are affected by academic considerations, while others are affected by political ones. The following are a few examples.

Gelangma 葛郎玛 vs. *wenfa* 文法 vs. *yufa* 语法. *Gelangma* made its debut in 1898 in *Mashi Wentong* 马氏文通 (*Ma's Grammar Guide to Literary Chinese*), the first grammar book of the Chinese language, which was a semantic loan from the Greek word "γραμματική" (*grammatikḗ* or *grammaticae* in Latin). But almost at the same time and in the same breath, Ma's book borrowed *wenfa* 文法 from Japanese *bunpo* 文法, which, in turn, was borrowed from Old Chinese. Since this loanword from Japanese was originally from China,[2] and it would be easier for something new to be introduced by some familiar old means—such as *wenfa*—so that it would be understood and accepted, *wenfa* then replaced *gelangma*. In 1913, the Chinese language borrowed the term *yufa* 语法 from the Japanese *goho* 語法, which, in turn, was borrowed from Old Chinese. So, *wenfa* and *yufa* coexisted at the time, while people made their own choice on which one to use. In the tug of war between the two in the 1950s, *yufa* finally won. This represents another kind of lexical conflict and its resolution.

Puluolietaliya 普罗列塔利亚 vs. *puluo (dazhong/jieji)* 普罗(大众/阶级) vs. *wuchan jieji* 无产阶级. The English or French word "proletariat" used to be phonetically translated in full into Chinese, but the result—*puluolietaliya*—is such a long, multi-syllable word that it is unacceptable to the general public. In terms of phonological rhythm, two-syllable words are generally preferred in the Chinese language, so it was soon replaced by *puluo, puluo dazhong*, and *puluo jieji*. Over time, however, they were replaced by yet another loanword, "*wuchan jieji*," which, this time, was graphically borrowed from the Japanese *musankaikyuu* 無産階級 (obviously, a semantic loan literally meaning "property-less class") and sounds much more Chinese than the previous phonemically rendered versions.

Aizibing 爱滋病 vs. *aizibing* 艾滋病. Soon after the syndrome was discovered, the term AIDS was borrowed into the Chinese-speaking community, with a variety of translated versions, including "*aisibing*" 爱死病 (literally "deadly love disease") and "*aizhibing*" 爱之病 ("disease of love"), on top of the two above. China adopted 爱滋病 (literally "love-caused disease") at the beginning, but later, after considering the possible negative implications that "love-caused" might inspire, its Ministry of Public Health required the change to the currently used 艾滋病 as the proper Chinese equivalent to AIDS.

Airen 爱人 is another interesting case to study here. Though used on both sides of the Taiwan Strait, it doesn't mean the same thing (or person rather) on the Chinese mainland and in Taiwan: spouse for the mainland and lover/paramour for Taiwan. Both meanings were probably borrowed from the Japanese word *aijin*, which, in turn, was directly borrowed from the Old Chinese 爱人. The source word *aijin* indeed has two meanings in Japanese: a person who one loves and a lover. The Chinese language used to borrow the former only, and the meaning of spouse was developed from parts of the mainland before the 1950s, later becoming popular across the mainland. The meaning of lover, as used in Taiwan and some overseas Chinese communities, comes directly from Japanese. Quite a few people on the mainland today are against the use of *airen* simply because it is prone to misunderstanding due to the alternative meaning of lover/paramour in Taiwan. There doesn't seem to be any easy solution to this conflict for now or in the immediate future. So, we just wait and let actual use by the public run its course.

3.3.2 Conflicts between lexical and non-lexical aspects

This conflict is in fact closely related to the background against which the loanword is used and the content it suggests. In most cases, other conflicts between two nations happen first and then are reflected in the languages concerned, such as the refusal to use some loanword which contains the perceived undesirable connotations of the other culture, leading to its disappearance from the scene or making it a thing of the past forever. Such a scenario does not happen very much and mainly concerns the words which are related to the historical invasions and humiliations which China once suffered. The following are a couple of examples.

Zhongguo 中国 vs. *Zhina* 支那. Originally, *Zhina* was a phonemic loanword from the Sanskrit *Cina* (meaning "China") in the Buddhist scriptures. It had no offensive implication; in fact, it was a complimentary term. Over the 100 years following the late Qing dynasty, the ever-declining China suffered invasion after invasion by the rising militarist Japan, culminating in China's crushing defeat in the Sino-Japanese War of 1894–1895. As a result, the *Zhina* (*Shina* in Japanese pronunciation) that was frequently used in the Japanese became entirely associated with a weak nation and its defeated military. Added also to its connotation were contempt and insult. All these factors helped transform *Zhina* 支那 from an appreciatory to a neutral and then finally to a derogatory term in Japan, so all patriotic Chinese people refused to use *Zhina* 支那. What is more, Chinese students in Japan at the time publicly protested against the use of the term by the Japanese right. For instance, Yu Dafu 郁达夫 (Yu Ta-fu, 1896–1945), an influential Chinese writer in the 1920s, wrote in his *Chenlun* 沉沦 (*Sinking*, 1921): "All Japanese call us Chinese '*Zhina ren*' 支那人 (*Zhina* people). In Japan that term sounds even more offensive than the Chinese swear word '*jianzei*' 贱贼 (meaning 'despicable wretch')." For this reason, *Zhina*, the term that the Chinese people phonetically translated themselves to refer to their country, exited the linguistic stage, except for its occasional appearance in such indirect references as *Yindu Zhina* 印度支那 (Indo-China).

Zhumu langma feng 珠穆朗玛峰 vs. *aifo lesi feng* 埃佛勒斯峰. *Zhumu langma feng* 珠穆朗玛峰 or Mount Qomolangma (Chomolungma) is a holy mountain to Tibetan Chinese people, so, a very long time ago, they named it $dzjo^{13}\ mo^{13}\ lang^{55}\ ma^{55}$ in Tibetan, meaning "Goddess Mother of the World." In contrast, *aifo lesi feng* 埃佛勒斯峰 (from the English "Mount Everest") is the name forced upon the mountain during British rule in India, after George Everest (1790–1866), Surveyor General of India from 1830 to 1843, who was believed to "discover" this peak. This English naming and its phonemic loan undoubtedly reflect jealousy, expansionist intention, and insult. No doubt the Chinese people would not accept or tolerate it.

Aside from the above, it is more often the case that a loanword becomes disused for some social reason but later gradually comes back again. This can be illustrated by a historical episode that occurred during the Qing dynasty. After the defeat of the Sino-Japanese War in 1895, Zhang Zhidong 张之洞 (Chang Chih-tung, 1837–1909), a late Qing scholar-official and reformer, was dedicated to establishing a new school system, asking his aide, surnamed Lu, to draft an outline. When he saw the word *jiankang* 健康 (meaning "health") in the prepared outline, Zhang immediately flew into a rage, warning in writing that "*jiankang* is a noun [*mingci* 名词 in Chinese] from Japan; using it feels extremely detestable" before throwing it back to Lu. Lu, who happened to be knowledgeable about Western learning and Japan, was quick to spot something in Zhang's writing to his advantage. So, he replied back, "*Mingci* itself is also a noun from Japan; using it feels particularly detestable." The Chinese word *mingci* 名词 that both used is a graphic loan from the Japanese *meishi* 名詞, meaning "noun." This episode reflects the prevalence of Chinese lexical borrowing from the Japanese lexicon at the time as well as the post-war hatred which the Chinese government felt toward Japan, though this sentiment was shifted onto Chinese loanwords from Japan.

Similar things also happened to other sectors of society at the time. For instance, in his book *Mangrenxiama zhi xin mingci* 盲人瞎马之新名词 (*New nouns: blind men riding blind horses*), first published in 1915 in Tokyo and expanded in 1931, Japan-educated Peng Wenzu 彭文祖 poured ridicule and sarcasm on Japanese words that first entered China. He enumerated 65 such words—though some of them are actually indigenous Chinese words—as morphologically ungrounded, compared them to the proverbial "blind men riding blind horses," and proposed that some of them be modified or replaced.

Among the 65 words are *qudi* 取缔, *quxiao* 取消, *shouxu* 手续, *yindu* 引渡, *daxiao* 打消, *mudi* 目的, *changhe* 场合, *daijia* 代价, *yaosu* 要素, *faren* 法人, *wenping* 文凭, *jingji* 经济, *yinyang* 引扬, *zhifu* 支拂, *xiangchang* 相场, *qieshou* 切手, *shouxing* 手形, *quli* 取立, *rangdu* 让渡, *chaiya* 差押, and *disanzhe* 第三者. In addition, Peng suggested that, among these graphic loanwords from Japanese, *changhe* 场合 be changed to *shi* 时, *shi* 事, or *chu* 处 depending on the context; *daxiao* 打消 to *feizhi* 废止 among others; *mudi* 目的 to *zhuyan* 主眼 among others; *qudi* 取缔 to *jinzhi* 禁止 or *guanshu* 管束 among others; *quxiao* 取消 to *quxiao* 去销; *shouxu* 手续 to *cixu* 次序 or *chengxu* 程序; and *yindu* 引渡 to *jiaofu* 交付 or *jiaochu* 交出.

Of course, the fact of the matter is that many of these words—over 20, at least—are still alive and kicking in the Chinese language because they refer to concepts which are indispensable in modern life. Even those who lambasted them and proposed changes could not avoid using quite a few graphic loanwords from Japanese due to the need for some concepts. The following words, for instance, are still in use:

> *cailiao* 材料, *chengren* 承认, *cunzai* 存在, *dingyi* 定义, *fouren* 否认, *ganshi* 干事, *geren* 个人, *huanjue* 幻觉, *jiguan* 机关, *jinianwu* 纪念物, *jin'e* 金额, *meiguan* 美观, *minfa* 民法, *quedian* 缺点, *renge* 人格, *renquan xuanyan* 人权宣言, *renzhi* 认知, *shehui* 社会, *shiji* 世纪, *shiwusuo* 事务所, *guanshui* 关税, *tiaojian* 条件, *xitong* 系统, *xianfa* 宪法, *xinli* 心理, *yijue* 议决, *zhaiquan* 债权, *zhuyi* 主义, and *zizhi tuanti* 自治团体.
>
> (Shen 1994)

What Peng and Zhang did both reflect a complicated or ambivalent state of mind in China's intellectual and political circles at the time after its humiliating defeat in the Sino-Japanese War. On the one hand, they hoped to import a new lexicon, new knowledge, new technology, and new weaponry in order to renovate and strengthen their country. On the other hand, they shifted their hatred toward enemy Japan onto loanwords from Japanese. This also gives a glimpse of the divergence of opinion among Chinese intellectuals at the time. Alongside those enthusiastic advocates for borrowing those Japanese-made Chinese words, there were quite a great number of people who, for a long period of time, took a critical, resistant, and even sarcastic attitude towards lexical borrowing from Japanese or denied the significance in number or proportion of those loanwords in the Chinese lexicon. This provides a good footnote to and explanation for the cultural conflict encountered by loanwords.

Another kind of conflict between lexical and non-lexical aspects is caused by linguistic narrow-mindedness or misunderstanding and cultural differences.

For instance, one particular form of address went viral on some university campuses in Shanghai in the late 20th century. It was –sang 桑, borrowed from the Japanese さん (-san), which is used after the name of a person (either male or female) in Japan to express a certain measure of respect. In fact, the two-character word xiansheng 先生 (meaning "mister" or "sir") is often phonetically condensed into the pronunciation of sang 桑 in the Shanghai dialect, which is very similar to that of -sheng –生, a reverential suffix attached to a person's name in ancient China. So, that popular mode of address on campus already had some linguistic foundations in Shanghai; incidentally, some research suggests that the Japanese -san was actually borrowed from the Old Chinese sheng 生.

Since there is no appropriate Chinese translation of the Japanese form of address, it was rendered into lao- 老- ("senior") or xiao- 小- ("junior"), depending on the age of the addressee, which is of course very inconvenient and improper. There do exist a lot of forms of address in Chinese, but what the language lacks is one that is universally applicable, regardless of age or gender. So, what the college students introduced, namely, the use of –sang to address people, was actually convenient and presumably above reproach. However, it still received criticism from the public, who called it a form of "pidgin" (that is, impure language) and demanded that it be stopped. The fact that these narrow-minded remarks were even published in local newspapers reflects the considerable forces behind such a conservative linguistic mentality. There is no knowing whether this resistance had anything to do with the previous wars which happened between the two countries.

Here is another case related to the conflict between lexical and non-lexical aspects. In 1996, a Japanese eyewear manufacturer opened up a store selling its Nojiri eyeglasses in Shanghai but soon received criticism from the public, complaining that the Chinese equivalent to its trademark Nojiri (野尻 in Chinese characters), which literally means yepigu 野屁股 (or "wild buttocks" in English), is indecent, and therefore, it should be outlawed. It soon caused quite a stir, unnerving foreign enterprises and very likely affecting foreign investment in China. The truth is that, as a Japanese surname, Nojiri means "the end of an open field," and there is nothing unwholesome, as it was alleged. It is common for many places in Japan to use kao 尻 and wei 尾 (also meaning "end") in their names, and some Japanese people take place names that contain these characters as their personal names. Kao 尻, used in this way, is also found in ancient China, such as in the verse "Kunlun xuanpu, qikao anzai?" 昆仑悬圃，其尻安在？ (Oh, the sky-high peak of Mount Kunlun, where is its base?)" in Chuci 楚辞·天问 (Songs of the Chu), a compendium of ancient Chinese poetic songs from the southern state of Chu 楚国 during the Zhou dynasty 周朝 (1046–256 BC). Today, phrases like jietou xiangwei 街头巷尾 and jietou xiangtun 街头巷臀, both literally meaning "from the beginning to the end of the streets and lanes" or "everywhere in the town," are still in use. Since such avoidable lexical conflicts are in fact caused by misunderstanding and ignorance, it is necessary to learn to treat things coming from the outside, including loanwords, in a more discreet manner so as to avoid unnecessary conflict.

3.4 The linguistic and cultural dual nature of the loanword

3.4.1 Introduction

Chinese loanwords necessarily presuppose the coexistence of autochthonous language and culture represented by Han Chinese characters on the one hand and non-indigenous languages and cultures by non-Han ethnic or Western words on the other hand, making it possible to examine them from both of the angles of Chinese and non-Chinese or foreign languages. Such coexistence or integration naturally leads to the dual nature of loanwords. Without this knowledge, it would be impossible for non-Chinese speakers to understand some apparently bizarre modifications made to Chinese loanwords. In *Chaguan* 茶馆 (*Teahouse*, 1957) by Chinese contemporary playwright Lao She (1899–1966), for example, the loanword *tuolasi* 托拉斯 (from the English *trust*, meaning "a large company that has monopolistic control of a market") was phonemically parsed into three separate actions undertaken: *tuo* 拖, or towed away; *la* 拉, or pulled up; and *si* 撕, or torn apart. This amusing effect is achieved by parsing or rendering the loanword as if it were an indigenous Chinese word composed of detachable characters. A good understanding of such parsing leads people back to the actual meaning of the loanword *trust*, which necessarily reflects foreign concepts or culture. The sarcastic remark of "whoever it is, Tietuo or Nibatuo" by former Chinese Communist party leader Mao Zedong 毛泽东 (Mao Tse-tung, 1893–1976) is another example of the Chinese language perspective toward the loanword. Tito (1892–1980), the former Yugoslav leader, is transliterated in mainland China as *Tietuo* 铁托, literally meaning "iron buttressed"; hence the jocular nonce word of *nibatuo* 泥巴托, literally "mud buttressed." By the same token, a good understanding of the comparison of Tito to the buttress mud necessarily leads readers back to what kind of person Tito was perceived to be by the speaker in context.

On a more serious note, if the insecticide *dipterex* were merely phonemically rendered as *diputelaikesi* 狄普特莱克斯 rather than both semantically and phonemically crafted as *dibaichong* 敌百虫 (literally "killing 100 pests") in current use, or if the German *Gestapo* were merely transliterated as *gaisitabo* 盖斯塔波 rather than both semantically and phonemically engineered as *gaishitaibao* 盖世太保, it would not be hard to imagine that few people could easily remember these two loanwords. Since each component character has a meaning relevant to the borrowed source word, it is much easier to understand the overall meaning of the newly invented word than it would be with a mere transliteration. The first component character, *di*, in *dibaichong* means "fight"; the second, *bai*, means "one hundred," and *chong* means "insect." The first two, *gaishi*, in *gaishitaibao* mean "unparalleled," while the last two, *taibao*, mean "an imperial official or a brigand." So this combination of phonetic approximation with semantic cues represents the dual linguistic and cultural nature of loanwords. Unlike pure semantic loaning, lexical loaning through phonetic approximation with semantic cues might considerably deviate from the original meaning of the source word but make it more accessible to the average Chinese person. The process and end product of this phonetic approximation with semantic cues represent a commingling of the borrowing and borrowed cultures.

3.4.2 *Tentative quantification of the linguistic and cultural dual nature*

The idea of quantifying the linguistic and cultural dual nature of loanwords is to numerically indicate the extent to which a certain loanword is influenced both by the language and the culture of the source word, and by the recipient language and culture, respectively, so as to have a new understanding of what constitutes a loanword or the criteria for being a loanword. We arbitrarily assign the highest impact of either the source or the recipient language/culture to a value of 10 and the lowest to 0, and posit that each loanword has five component factors, each with a highest assigned value in parenthesis: semantics (2), phonetics (5), morphemics (1), word form (1), and character form (1).

Take *bingqilin* 冰淇淋 (ice cream), which was discussed at the beginning of this book. First, let us assess the impact of the source language/culture on the word. Since the meaning (semantics) of this loanword is completely borrowed, its semantics is therefore assigned the value of 1. Since half of the word is phonetically borrowed from the source word (i.e. *qilin* from cream), its phonetics is assigned 2. Morphemically borrowed from ice and cream, it is assigned 1. The value in word form is assigned 0.5 because *bingqilin* is half (*bing*) from the source language and half (*qilin*) from the recipient, but the value in character form is assigned 0 since all the characters (*bing*, *qi*, and *ling*) are purely Chinese rather than from the recipient language. Now let us assess the impact of the recipient language/culture on *bingqilin*. Since it contains the autochthonous Chinese one-character word *bing* for ice, its semantic value is assigned 0.5. Since it is pronounced entirely the Chinese way, the phonetic value is assigned 5. Similar to the impact of the source, the morphemic value is 0.5. The value in word form is also 0.5, while the value in character form is 1.

To visually clarify such an impact in numerical terms, here, we have created a table of different types of Chinese loanwords and the impacts of both source and recipient cultures in terms of the above-mentioned five aspects.

126 *Characteristics of Chinese loanwords*

Type	Loanword	Impact culture	Semantics	Phonetics	Morphemics	Word form	Character form	Overall impact score
Semantic loan	Moshui 墨水 (English ink)	Source culture	2	0	0	0	0	2
		Recipient culture	1	5	1	0.5	1	8.5
Return graphic loan from Japanese	Geming 革命 (Japanese kakumei)	Source culture	2	0	0	1	0	3
		Recipient culture	1	5	1	1	1	9
Loan translation	Zuqiu 足球 (English football)	Source culture	2	0	1	0	0	3
		Recipient culture	1	5	1	0.5	1	8.5
Japan-made Chinese character + semantic marker	Xueyu 鳕鱼 (Japanese tara)	Source culture	2	0	0.5	0.5	0.5	3.5
		Recipient culture	1.5	5	1	0.5	0.5	8.5
On-yomi Sino-Japanese word	Jiji 积极 (Japanese sekkioku)	Source culture	2	0.3	0.5	1	0	3.8
		Recipient culture	1	5	1	0.5	1	8.5
Kun-yomi Sino-Japanese word	Shouxu 手续 (Japanese tetsuzuki)	Source culture	2	0	1	1	0	4
		Recipient culture	0.5	5	0.3	0	1	6.8
Phonetic semantic approximation + semantic loan	Nihongdeng 霓虹灯 (English neon light)	Source culture	2	2	0.5	0.5	0	5
		Recipient culture	0.7	5	1	0.5	1	8.2
Phonetic + semantic loan	Motuoche 摩托车 (English motorcycle)	Source culture	2	2.3	0.5	0.5	0	5.3
		Recipient culture	0.5	5	1	0.5	1	8

Type	Example	Culture						Total
Phonetic loan + semantic marker	*Kache* 卡车 (English *car*)	Source culture	2	2.3	0.5	0.5	0	5.3
		Recipient culture	0.5	5	0.5	0.5	1	7.5
Graphic loan + semantic marker	*A sir* 阿 sir (English *sir*)	Source culture	1.5	2.5	0.5	0.5	0.5	5.5
		Recipient culture	1	4.8	1	0.5	0.5	7.8
Graphic + semantic loan	*TDK Bei* TDK 杯 (*TDK Cup*)	Source culture	2	2.5	0.5	0.5	0.5	6.5
		Recipient culture	0.5	4.7	0.5	0.5	0.5	6.7
Semantic loan from Japanese	*Xian* 腺 (Japanese *sen*)	Source culture	2	2	1	1	1	7
		Recipient culture	0.5	5	1	0	0.5	7
Phonemic loan from Japanese	*Wasi* 瓦斯 (Japanese *gasu*)	Source culture	2	3.5	1	1	0	7.5
		Recipient culture	0	5	0	0	1	6
Phonetic semantic approximation	*Didiiti* 滴滴涕 (*DDT*)	Source culture	2	4	1	1	0	8
		Recipient culture	0.2	5	0.5	0	1	6.7
Humorous phonemic loan	*Wayehu* 瓦夜壶 (*wife*)	Source culture	2	4	1	1	0	8
		Recipient culture	0	5	1	0.5	1	7.5
Partial phonetic semantic approximation	*Aolun* 奥伦 (*orlon*)	Source culture	2	4.3	1	1	0	8.3
		Recipient culture	0.5	5	0.5	0.2	1	7.2
Phonemic loan	*Yakexi* 雅克西 (Uighur *yahxi*)	Source culture	2	4.5	1	1	0	8.5
		Recipient culture	2	5	0	0	1	8
Blend phonemic loan	*Kala OK* 卡拉 OK (Japanese *kalaok*)	Source culture	2	4.5	1	1	0.5	9
		Recipient culture	0	5	0	0.5	0.5	5.5
Graphic + phonemic loan	*T xu* T 恤 (*T-shirt*)	Source culture	2	4.5	1	1	0.5	9
		Recipient culture	0	4.5	0	0.5	0.5	5
Alphabetic graphic loan	*DNA*	Source culture	2	4.7	1	1	1	9.7
		Recipient culture	0	4	0	0	0	4

Among those types, the return graphic loan from Japanese refers to a word that already existed in ancient Chinese texts but had now been borrowed by the Japanese to translate Western words as a semantic loan. The on-yomi Sino-Japanese word refers to a Japan-made Chinese word that is read according to the pronunciation of the kanji characters in the originating Chinese dialect at the time the word was introduced into Japanese. The kun-yomi Sino-Japanese word refers to a Japan-made Chinese word that is read with the Japanese pronunciation system called kun-yomi.

Though it may not encompass all possible types (for further details, please refer to Section 4.1.2 in Chapter 4), all major types of loanwords can be found in the above table. Arbitrary as the assigned values obviously are, they may well be able to provide a general picture of the impact of the source versus recipient culture/language on the loanword in question. It can be seen that the first five types, such as semantic loan, return graphic loan from Japanese, loan-translation (calque), and on-yomi Sino-Japanese word, all have a low value (less than 4) in terms of the overall score of the impact of the source culture on the loanword. It is exactly those five whose identity as loanword is most controversial. From the type of phonetic/semantic approximation + semantic loan onward, none of the overall scores of the impact of the source culture on the loanword is less than five; those loanwords, including hybrid words, semantic loan from Japanese, and phonemic loan from Japanese, are least controversial.

It can also be seen from the table that the more linguistic influence of the source culture/language a loanword falls under means the less influence of the recipient culture/language it comes under, and vice versa.

A considerable number of scholars would not regard alphabetic graphic loans, the last type in the table, as *bona fide* loanwords. Some pronounce these words the way they are said in their native language, while others say them the Chinese way. Whether those letter-composed quasi-loanwords are or become *bona fide* depends on the grammatical naturalization, cognitive acceptance, duration, size, and frequency of their actual use.

Still some other potential loanwords, which are not listed in the table, are those Chinese inventions which apparently imitate or sound like Western words, such as phonetic/semantic imitations (e.g. *meijiajing* 美加净, with its own invented English *Maxam*, a Chinese brand of toothpaste), phonetic imitations (e.g. *bosideng* 波司登, a Chinese wool sweater, which sounds like the Chinese word for Boston 波斯顿), partial borrowing (e.g. *angongzuo* 安宫唑, with its invented English word *panazol*, and *qiangdisong* 强的松, with its invented English word *paednisone*), and phonetic derivatives (e.g. *hongke* 红客 and its invented English word *honker*, arbitrarily derived from *heike* 黑客 "hacker"; and words formed by blending the elements of several phonemic loanwords, such as *diba* 迪吧 from *disike* 迪斯科 "disco" + *ba* 吧 "bar").

3.5 Functions of the loanword

The loanword exists to be used; only through actual use can its value and *raison d'être* be justified. Loanwords generally serve three primary functions (linguistic, cultural, and social) and one secondary function (psychological).

3.5.1 Linguistic function

The most prominent and important function of the loanword is the linguistic function because it compensates for some inadequacies in the lexicon of the recipient Chinese language and promotes its tendency of compound word formation, poly-syllabication, and lexical enrichment. As a heterogeneous strain in the Chinese lexicon, the phonemic loanword, for example, strengthens the power of its word formation by providing new and broader approaches. Four aspects of the linguistic function of the loanword deserve our attention here.

Promotion of affixation-type of word formation. Loan-translations and some phonemic loans, particularly graphic loans from Japanese, have introduced, through Chinese morphemes, a great number of derivatives in the Western languages. In the process, many of the affixes—suffixes and prefixes included—of those derivatives have been permanently matched in meaning with certain Chinese characters, bringing in a corresponding number of new Chinese affixes (or quasi-affixes) which are more practically meaningful than those existing Chinese suffixes, such as *–zi* 子, *-er* 儿, and *-tou* 头. The acceptance of those newly introduced affixes, in turn, also means new methods of word formation to the Chinese language. Those like *–xing* 性, *-de* 的, *-lun* 论, *-quan* 权, *-jie* 界, *-jia* 家, *-shuo* 说, *-zhi* 制, *-xin* 心, *-shui* 税, *-shang* 上, *-yuan* 员, *-fa* 法, *-dian* 点, *-li* 力, *-pin* 品, *-zhang* 长, and *-xue* 学, borrowed from Japanese, are more or less like affixes, easily generating numerous words, such as *duoyang-xing* 多样性 (diversity), *xiandai-hua* 现代化 (modernization), *fuwu-yuan* 服务员 (waiter), *meishu-jia* 美术家 (fine artist), *gongyi-shi* 工艺师 (craftsman), *cuichan-su* 催产素 (oxytocin), *lixiang-zhuyi* 理想主义 (idealism), *ya-redai* 亚热带 (sub-tropical), *zhun-junshibudui* 准军事部队 (para-military), *ban-fengjian* 半封建 (semi-feudalism), and *mini-dianshiji* 迷你电视剧 (mini-series). Each being of Chinese morpheme, they have different meanings and serve different functions here. This great number of newly evolved affixes exerts a far-reaching influence on the Chinese language, particularly its lexical power. As a result, an ever-increasing number of readily formed new expressions or terms continues to enter the contemporary Chinese lexicon, such as *beida-ren* 北大人 (current member or alumni of Peking University, from *beida* PKU + suffix *ren* person); *duomian-shou* 多面手 (all-rounder, from *duomian* many sides + suffix *shou* or hand); *gaige-pai* 改革派 (reformists, from *gaige* reform + suffix *pai*: a school of people sharing the same ideals); *dian-ba* 电霸 (power grid bully, from *dian* electricity + *ba* bully); *dushu-re* 读书热 (popular craze for reading, from *dushu* reading + *re* or craze); *xiao-xing* 笑星 (joking star, from *xiao* laugh + *xing* star); *zu-tan* 足坛 (football community, from *zu* foot + *tan* circle); *junyong-pin* 军用品 (military supplies, from *junyong* military use + *pin* articles); *fa-mang* 法盲 (law ignorant person, from *fa* law + *mang* blind); *huihe-dian* 汇合点 (converging point, from *huihe* converge + *dian* point); *zhufan-nan* 住房难 (housing issue, from *zhufang* housing + *nan* difficulty); *chihe-feng* 吃喝风 (wining and dining spree at public expense, from *chihe* eating and drinking and *feng* craze); *chao-nengli* 超能力 (extraordinary power, from prefix *chao* super + *nengli* capacity); *hou-xiandai* 后现代 (post-modern, from prefix *hou* post- + *xiandai* modern); *ci-changyong* 次常用 (second most common, from *ci* sub + *changyong* commonly used); *fan-zhizi* 反质子 (antiproton, from *fan* against + *zhizi* proton); *gao-xiaofei* 高消费 (high level of consumption, from *gao* high + *xiaofei* consumption); *wei-dianzi* 微电子 (micro-electronics, from *wei* micro- + *dianzi* electronics); and *fan-taipingyang* 泛太平洋 (Pan Pacific, from *fan* pan- + *taipingyang* Pacific). Words of this kind are obviously inspired, either directly or indirectly, from calques and other forms of borrowed words.

Birth of discrete word formation. Generally speaking, the compound word is semantically and structurally cohesive or confluent in that a totality of meaning for the word is the semantic aggregation of its component characters, words, or morphemes. This is the cohesive type of word formation. In contrast, discrete word formation means that there is no connection in meaning between or among the component Chinese characters of the word. This semantic discreteness is a generally followed principle in choosing component Chinese characters for a pure phonemic loanword in order to ensure that each component character be used solely for its phonetic approximation to, rather than semantic association with, the corresponding part of the source word. In other words, characters in most phonemic loans are expected to be purposefully discrete, stand-alone components, so it is impossible to arrive at a reasonable totality of meaning by aggregating the literal meaning of the component characters. In Chinese autochthonous words and semantic loanwords, however, all component characters (morphemes) are expected to relate to each other so that their related semantic aggregates constitute a totality of meaning for the word in question. In other words, characters in each of those words are generally semantically similar (at least on the surface) and therefore are not semantically and structurally discrete but confluent (or cohesive) in nature.

Examples of such discrete phonemic loans are *kaqu* 卡曲 (from car coat), *kaisimi* 开司米 (cashmere or cassimere), *bolangning* 勃朗宁ʻ (Browning automatic pistol), and *pushier* 蒲式耳 (bushel). Some others also contain elements of semantic approximation with semantic cues, such as *baobo* 胞波 (close relative, from Burmese *pau^{955}p^{h}o^{33}*), *kudieda* 苦迭打 (*coup d'état*, the component characters *ku*, "bitter," and *da*, "strike," both semantically related to the violent taking of the government), and *Koudan* 蔻丹 (nail polish from Cutex, the component character *dan* meaning "red"). Though some phonemic loans are of fully semantic approximation, their component characters do not simply add up to a cohesive whole, such as *Dititi* 滴滴涕 (from DDT, a chemical used to kill insects that also harm crops), *Xuebi* 雪碧 (Sprite, a brand of carbonated drink), and *Futumei* 富图美 (Fotomatic, a brand of photoflash).

Influenced by this discrete element in semantic loaning, some Chinese neologisms also start to take on this discrete form, especially for names of a product or firm, such as *Jiebili* 洁碧丽, a cosmetic brand, and *Yumeijing* 郁美净, a brand of detergent. Some brands are counterintuitively given an existing Western word before being matched with a Chinese term through something of transliteration, as with *Bolong* 伯龙 (a cosmetic brand for men, from the English *baron*) and *Aoqi* 奥琪 (a cosmetic brand, from *orchid*). Others may have taken both Western phonetics and Chinese naming culture into account, such as *Kangfushou* 康福寿 (a Chinese tonic, with is self-made English-like version *Konfuso*) and Lekoufu 乐口福 (a malted milk product, with its self-made English-like version *Locavo*). Still others seem to use a term transliterated from a foreign one, such as *Bosideng* 波司登, a major Chinese brand of down jackets, with its own proprietary English brand, BOSIDENG, which sounds very much like Boston, an American city of knowledge. Those invented words are, strictly speaking, not *bona fide* loanwords but "imitation loanwords" at best.

Consolidation of the status of the words in or containing alphabetic form. Inspired by the appearance of alphabetic graphic loans, Chinese people start to invent words or terms for themselves in a similar manner. Here are some examples:

San S yanjiuhui 三S研究会 (The Three-S Society, where S's refer to Edgar Snow, Anna Louise Strong, and Agnes Smedley, three American sympathizers of the Chinese communists during the Chinese Civil War in the 1930s and 1940s)

Guowei VC 果味VC and *VC Qishui* VC汽水, two Chinese drinks containing vitamin C

BB ji BB机, beeper, from its name in Taiwan, BB-call, named after the sound it makes

A gu A股 (shares for domestic purchase), *B gu* B股 (shares for overseas individual purchase), *H gu* Hu股 (shares listed in Hong Kong)

TCL (a Chinese electronics company, self-made abbreviation for *The Creative Life*)

HSK (Chinese abbreviation for *Hanyu Shuiping Kaoshi*, Test of Chinese as a Foreign Language)

GB (Chinese abbreviation for *Guojia Biaozhun*, national standard, used for identifying coded characters set by China)

Increased probability of new phonemes or phonemic combinations entering the Chinese lexicon. The use of phonemic loans, especially the direct use of alphabetic graphic loans, brings in some new phonemic components to a varying degree of steady use acceptable to certain communities of people, making it possible to transcend the relatively closed Chinese phonetic system, as has been seen in the letters V, C, B, H, S, G, and L, which have already gone beyond the Chinese phonetic pinyin system.

3.5.2 Cultural, social, and psychological functions of the loanword

3.5.2.1 Cultural function

As a messenger of other cultures, loanwords can bring not only exotic diversity to the Chinese language community but also modern arts and science. A certain loanword may be able to offer a new perspective or even open up a new world. Though a bit exaggerated, the size of loanwords in a language may be considered one of the criteria by which the cultural development and social openness of that language community are measured. The inflow of other cultures is realized through the introduction of their things or ideas, which, in turn, is made possible by means of semantic borrowing as well as phonemic borrowing, which spreads relatively fast. In practice, however, a considerable number of those foreign things or ideas are very difficult to semantically translate within the existing system of autochthonous Chinese morphemes, and this is all the more true for an accurate and concise version. So, each major wave of non-Han or foreign culture inflow in Chinese history is, without exception, accompanied by the appearance of a large number of phonemic loans. The introduction of Buddhism into China, for example, simultaneously brought in many phonemic loans on Buddhism. Seven hundred and ninety-four entries of phonemic loans of Sanskrit origin are listed in the *Hanyu wailaici cidian* 汉语外来词词典 (Liu et al. 1984); this number is 2,602 if the 1,808 entries of their variants are counted. The second major wave of foreign culture inflow, which happened from the modern period up to the 1940s, saw the introduction of Western science and culture. Along with this wave of cultural inflow were 2,030 loanwords of English origin, or 5,430 if the 3,400 entries of their variants are counted, according to the *Hanyu wailaici cidian*. Considering loanwords of Russian, French, and German origin combined, there are 2,630, or 6,260 when the 3,630 variants are counted. On the whole, it is safe to say that there are far more than 3,000 Chinese loanwords of Western origin. In the *Xinhua wailaici cidian* 新华外来词词典 (Xinhua dictionary of Chinese loanwords, Shi 2019), for example, there are more than 6,600 Chinese loanwords of English origin and over 3,000 of Japanese origin. It would not be hard to imagine how profoundly the two waves and the attendant linguistic borrowing influenced the Chinese language, and, as far as the number of borrowed words is concerned, the second wave was much more influential than the first. Through the phonetic forms of those loanwords, we may also gain insights into the geographic information and trajectory of cultural exchange at the time.

3.5.2.2 Social function

As a special part of the lexicon and semiotic representation of a society, loanwords may demonstrate different features at different social sectors in terms of their acceptance and actual use. Therefore, they may reveal the social identity and status of the people involved in a certain society. Just as ancient Chinese people had no idea what *chuzuche* 出租车 (taxi), *qiaokeli* 巧克力 (chocolate), or *motuoche* 摩托车 (motorcycle) was, people today probably have no idea what *bazheluo* 跋折罗 (Sanskrit *vajra*, the scepter of the god of thunder and lightning, with which he slays the enemies of Buddhism), *sanmiao sanputi* 三藐三菩提 (Sanskrit *samyak-sambodhi*, complete enlightenment in Buddhism), or *sumuzhe* 苏幕遮 (Old Persian, a particular rhyme scheme and tonal pattern in Chinese poetry popular in the Tang and Song dynasties) is either.

By the same token, some loanwords are region-specific: Shanghainese say *sidike* 司的克 (walking stick from the English *stick*), Beijingers say *laolao* 佬佬 (nonsense, from the Manchu *longlongseme*), Northeasterners say *maitai* 埋汰 for dirty, Cantonese say *bo* 波 for ball, Taiwanese say *haike* 骇客 for hacker, and Hong Kongers say *a sir* 阿 sir to address a policeperson. When one is in these places, little knowledge of community-specific loanwords could easily get one into trouble. Which or what loanword is uttered may also readily reveal which geographic or linguistic region the speaker is probably from. For instance, a person most probably hails from Hong Kong or Taiwan who is used to *Leigen* 雷根 instead of *Ligen* 里根 for "Ronald Reagan," *Gannaidie* 甘乃迪 instead of *Kennidi* 肯尼迪 for "John F. Kennedy," *Hangshiji* 杭士基 instead of *Qiaomusiji* 乔姆斯基 for "Noam Chomsky," *Niuxilan* 纽西兰 instead of *Xinxilan* 新西兰 for "New Zealand," *leishe* 雷射 instead of *jiguang* 激光 for "laser," *tuokouxiu* 脱口秀 instead of *dankou xiangsheng* 单口相声 for "stand-up comedy," and *tonghe* 统合 instead of *zhenghe* 整合 for "integration."

As far as frequency in use is concerned, loanwords may also suggest different social sectors of a community. *Kala OK* (karaoke), *Maidanglao* 麦当劳 (McDonald's,) and *KTV* are faddish symbols for contemporary teens. *Haluo* (hello), *OK*, and *Misi* (Miss) are used by those who intend to declare that they are not rustic but very urbane and modern. Those who say *dige* 的哥 (taxi driver), *xiaomi* 小蜜 (mistress), *paomi* 泡蜜 (pick up hot chicks), and *bengdi* 蹦迪 (go to the disco) are most probably young people who value unprincipled friendship and seize the pleasures of the moment without concern for the future. Scientists, however, might look down upon those words but mention *kelong* 克隆 (clone), *kasite* 喀斯特 (karst), UFO, or DNA. Every now and then, words like CEO, offer, and HR flow from the lips of those urban professionals. So, it is all too obvious to see the social function of loanwords at work.

3.5.2.3 Psychological function

As the phonemic loan generally follows the principle of discreteness to ensure that its component Chinese characters are not semantically cohesive or aggregate, it is barely possible to ascertain what the word actually means by deciphering the component characters and thus securing an intended stylistic aura or a sense of mystery. This distinctive psychological effect translates into a feeling of extraordinariness or other-ness. When describing a plant popularly known as the devil's trumpet, for example, a Chinese essay writes, "No, do not forget that it has got a beautiful name—*yangjinhua* 洋金花 and a noble name as well—*mantuoluo* 曼陀罗!"[3] While *yangjinhua* is clearly confluent in terms of word formation, with each of its component characters semantically associated with the other (*yang*, "exotic" or "elegantly foreign"; *jin*, "golden"; and *hua*, "flower"), *mantuoluo*, apparently phonemically borrowed from the English *metel*, is obviously discreet in that its semantically unassociated component characters signify nothing semantic but a feel of being foreign, mysterious, or romantic.

In a similar vein, the rationale behind the choice of exotic names over domestic-sounding ones for some brands or products does nothing but make them appear high-sounding, mysterious, and exquisite so as to grab public attention for marketing purposes. The preference of *Aoqi* 奥琪 (Chinese phonetic approximation of "orchid") over *Lanhua* 兰花 (Chinese word for "orchid") for the cosmetic brand is an obvious example. Yet it should be clear that, with the ever-increasing frequency in the use of phonemic loans, this exotic feeling, however high-sounding, will diminish to nothing over time. Inner quality and inherent merit count in the long run.

Notes

1 As the earliest and most essential form of human cultures, 'meta-culture' here refers to a kind of culture which may, to a certain extent, control and explain other cultures. This author believes that at least the concept of human body and gender, the concept of nature versus human beings, music, and languages are somewhat qualified candidates as elements of meta-culture.
2 The word *wenfa* 文法 can be found in Old Chinese, as in "weiren lian, jinyu wenfa" ("为人廉，谨于文法") from *Shiji* 史记·李将军列传 (Shiji: Biography of General Li), an early history of China written in about 85 BC by Sima Qian (145–87 BC). There, *wenfa* meant "laws and regulations." It was not until the Yuan dynasty that *wenfa* obtained the meaning of "the art and craft of writing." Its current usage, meaning grammar, is borrowed from Japanese. The word *yufa* 语法 can also be found in Old Chinese as in "yufa, liangren jiaohu nai decheng xiang" ("语法，两人交互乃得称'相'") from the annotation by Confucian scholar Kong Yingda 孔颖达 (574—648) on *Zuozhuan* (Tso-chuan) 左传, Tso-chuan, an ancient commentary on the *Chunqiu* 春秋 ("Spring and Autumn Annals", covering the period 722–479 BC) and the first sustained narrative work in Chinese literature. Here, *yufa* means "unity and coherence in writing." The word *yufa* also appeared in the *Da zhidu lun* 大智度论 (Great Treatise on the

Perfection of Wisdom, Chinese translation of the Buddhist scripture *Mahāprajñāpāramitāśāstra* in Sanskrit) in 405 AD by Buddhist scholar Kumarajiva (343–413 AD): "tianzhu yufa: zhong zi hehe chengyu, zhongyu hehe chengju. Ru pu wei yizi, ti wei yizi, shi er bu hehe ze wuyu; ruo hehe mingwei puti, qinyan wushang zhihui." ("天竺语法:众字和合成语,众语和合成句。如菩为一字,提为一字,是二不和合则无语,若和合名为菩提,秦言无上智慧". *Da zhidu lun.* Volume 44). Here, *yufa* refers to the rule governing how syllables make a word and how words make a sentence. The above two usages are close to the modern meaning of the word but still does not touch upon the structural rule.

3 See Wang Zifu 王梓夫. "Yangjinhua" 洋金花. *People's Daily* (Overseas Edition) 人民日报. October 14, 1996. Page 7.

4 Classification of Chinese loanwords

4.1 Determining factors and formal types

4.1.1 Determining factors for the loanword

To determine whether a particular word or a particular type of words is a loanword can be very tricky because there is no simple straightforward or absolute rule to go by; instead, there are a combination of various and occasionally arbitrary or fuzzy factors to consider. Specifically, they include character type, semantic variation, phonetic affiliation, grammatical domestication, cognitive acceptance, and user diffusion, which can roughly be simplified as four major factors in loanword determination or identification—way of borrowing, usage and its frequency, user community, and semantics—which, in turn, help classify loanwords into different types. These factors roughly correspond to the three primary functions which have been discussed in Chapter 3: way of borrowing, usage, and frequency mainly relate to the linguistic function, the community factor mainly relates to the social, and the semantic factor mainly relates to the linguistic/cultural function. In other words, loanword classification based on the four major factors naturally involves discussion of its functions. Hopefully, this integrated investigation will provide a new perspective on the old issue of what exactly makes a loanword.

4.1.2 Formal types

Ideally, the phonemic and graphemic components of a word should correspond to each other, but in reality, there may always exist some discrepancy between the two aspects in a given language as long as it has its orthography and a relatively long history. This discrepancy is far more pronounced in Chinese because it is essentially an ideographic language. In addition to the phonetic and lexical components shared by all languages, therefore, the graphemic shape is uniquely important to Chinese, distinguishing itself from all Western or Romance languages. Considering the phonetic, graphemic, and lexical/semantic aspects, there are four formal types of Chinese

Classification of Chinese loanwords 137

loanwords. The following is an extended discussion which may somewhat overlap with some sections in the previous chapter (Sections 3.2.2 and 3.4 in Chapter 3).

4.1.2.1 Phonemic loaning

The phonemic loan involves both phonetic and lexical borrowing, and happens orally first before it is transcribed in a written form, which is generally presented in Chinese characters but is occasionally mixed with Roman letters or even fully in the original letters, though they are all pronounced or read in the Chinese way, whatever the specific graphic form. Since the pronunciation of a specific loanword is influenced by both the time and place of its initial appearance, a comparison with the sound of its source word may provide us with a temporal and spatial trajectory as regards its history of borrowing. Phonemic loans can be divided into the following types.

1   *Pure phonemic loaning.* Some words in this category have already been mentioned in this book, such as *kehan* 可汗 (supreme ruler, from the Turkic *qaghan*), *biqiu* 比丘 (a fully ordained male monastic in Buddhism, from the Sanskrit *Bhiksu*), *dishi* 的士 (Cantonese borrowing, from *taxi*), *pasi* 派司 (Shanghainese borrowing, from *pass*), *kaqiusha* 喀秋莎 (Northern Chinese borrowing, from the Russian *КАТЮША*), and *Kala OK* 卡拉 OK (Taiwanese borrowing, from the Japanese *karaoke*).
2   *Homophonic transliteration.* Homophonic transliteration, or translation through homophonic proximity (wording with identical or near homophony) with semantic cues, is essentially phonemic and semantic loaning combined. It chooses some Chinese characters which are phonetically close to and semantically related with the source word. The literal meaning of this type of loanword, however, may be considerably different from that of the source word. Loanwords of homophonic transliteration can be further divided into two kinds: those of the more commonly seen phonetic-cum-semantic approximation and what might be called humorous phonemic loans (for further details, please refer to Section 3.2.2.2 in Chapter 3). Here are some additional examples.

    Wutuobang 乌托邦 (from *Utopia*). This is generally considered one of the best examples in part-phonemic and part-semantic loaning: *wu* 乌 in Early Middle Chinese did mean "not" or "without," which corresponds to Greek *ou* or "not" in Utopia. However, few average Chinese today know that meaning ("not") of the character *wu*.

    Yecha 夜叉: a human-eating demon in Buddhism, homophonically transliterated from the Sanskrit *yaksa*. *Ye* 夜 or "night" implies the time when the demon is active, while *cha* 叉 or "fork" suggests its viciousness in attacking humans. Taken together, this fragmented

and limited literal meaning of *yecha* is considerably removed from the original meaning of *yaksa*.

Buxin 补心: a removable metal lining for a round hole, from the English *bushing*. It is unclear how this humorous phonemic loan, literally meaning "patch heart," has anything to do with a removable metal lining, apart from its homophonic proximity to the source word.

Jiantouman 尖头鳗 (literally "sharp-ended eel"): a humorous phonemic loanword from *gentleman*. Another such utterly facetious loanword of phonetic-cum-semantic approximation is *heiqibandeng* 黑漆板凳 (literally "pitch-dark bench") from *husband*.

Some humorous phonemic loanwords, such as *shafa* 沙发 (from the English "so fast"), exclusively used in the Chinese cyberspace, and *fensi* 粉丝 (from the English "fans," meaning "admirers"), broadly used in the art and entertainment circle, are slightly different; they are simply some already existing Chinese words which happen to be approximately homophonic with the new source words (*shafa* with "so fast" and *fensi* with "fans"). As a result, the Chinese word arbitrarily takes on a new meaning which corresponds to that of the source word and takes advantage of its usual collocations in expanded usage (e.g. *zuo shafa* 坐沙发, literally "sitting in a sofa," can now refer to a situation in which someone is the first to publish his or her post in an online message board). *Shafa* (a loanword itself from English *sofa*) originally referred to a piece of furniture, and *fensi* originally meant vermicelli made from the starch of sweet potato, beans, etc.

Some other phonemic loans also contain some elements of semantic approximation, such as *bao* 胞, meaning "of the same parents or nation" in *baobo* 胞波 (close relative, from the Burmese $pau^{955}p^{h}o^{33}$); *lun* 纶, meaning "synthetic fibre" in *nilun* 尼伦 (same as *nilong* 尼龙, from *nylon*); and *fu* 氟, meaning "fluorine" in *tefulong* 特氟隆 (from *Teflon*).

Still some few come from acronyms, such as *wanweiwang* 万维网 (from *WWW*, World Wide Web), in which only the initial consonants of the source word are approximated phonetically, making them more like semantic loans.

It must be pointed out that there are drawbacks to homophonic transliteration. Its semantic cue is often obscure or vaguely related, such as in *youmo* 幽默 (both *you* 幽 and *mo* 默 here mean "quiet") and *luoji* 逻辑 (*luo* 逻 means "patrol," and *ji* 辑 means "collect"). Efforts in semantic approximation may also result in inaccurate phonetic approximation, such as *piliwu* 霹雳舞 (from *break dance*) and *paidian* 派典 (from *paradigm*), where many phonemes in the source word are lost in the process, or *anchuantong* 安喘通 (medicine to treat cough, asthma, and bronchitis, from *Asmeton*), which simply distorts the sound of the source word.

3   *Phonemic loaning with graphic adaptation.* This is to indicate the semantic category with which the new loanword is to be associated. With a

long history in practice (such as *putao* 葡萄 and *luotuo* 骆驼 and *boli* 玻璃 in ancient China), this kind of phonemic loaning typical of the ideographic language usually resorts to inventing new characters by adding certain graphic radicals to existing characters. Here are some examples which first occurred in modern China before 1949:

Binglang 槟榔: a digestive and worming tropical Asian palm called areca or its betel nut, phonemically loaned first in the Chinese Fujian dialect from the Malay *pinang*. Originally written as *binlang* 宾朗, it was then combined with the radical *mu* 木 or "tree-type plant" to the left side of each character of the word, giving it its current graphemic shape: 槟榔.

Leiding 镭锭 or *lei* 镭: the radioactive chemical element of atomic number 88 (symbol: Ra), phonemically loaned from *radium*, initially written with the radical *jin* 钅 ("metal") imposed on both component characters of *lei* 镭 and *ding* 锭 to indicate that this chemical element is a metal. *Leiding* was later shortened to *lei*, the first character.

An 氨: a gas with a strong bad smell (chemical formula NH_3), from *ammonia*. Initially rendered *amoniya* 阿摩尼亚 or *anmoniya* 安摩尼亚, it was later abbreviated into an invented semantic-phonetic compound character by combining the radical *qi* 气 and the phonetically indicating character *an* 安. Chemicals related to ammonia are rendered in a similar manner in Chinese, such as *an* 胺 (with the radical *yue* 月 here suggesting organic matter) for *amine*, an organic compound derived from ammonia via replacement of one or more hydrogen atoms by organic radicals (RNH_2) and *an* 铵 (with the graphical radical *jin* 金 suggesting its relation to metal) for ammonium, a positively charged radical.

4   *Phonemic loaning added with a semantic marker.* The semantic marker or indicator mostly uses an autochthonous Chinese character with a clear indication of semantic categorization and occupies the critical end position modified by the component character(s) before it, which can be called post-modifier semantic marker. Some few semantic markers are at the front position, serving as a pre-modifier semantic marker. Still a handful of others function as an affix (prefix or suffix), which can be called an affix-type semantic marker. The marker may sometimes be omitted or simply phased out for loanwords whose phonemically loaned part is polysyllabic but not for monosyllabic ones. Here are some examples.

In *kapian* 卡片 (from card) and *kache* 卡车 (from car), semantic markers *pian* 片 (meaning "piece") and *che* 车 ("vehicle") for *kapian* and *kache*, respectively, are commonly used words for taxonomic purposes themselves.

Jiaomutang 胶姆糖: chewing gum, from the English *gum* + semantic marker *tang* 糖 ("sugar") and *jiao* 胶 ("sticky substance") as near semantic rendering of *gum*.

Bailandi(jiu) 白兰地(酒): from brandy + an optional semantic marker *jiu* 酒 "alcoholic drink." Similar loanwords include *balei* 芭蕾 (or *baleiwu* 芭蕾舞) from *ballet*, *basong* 巴松 (or *basongguan* 巴松管) from *bassoon*, and *fuge* 赋格 (or *fugequ* 赋格曲) from *fugue*. In other words, all the above semantic markers can be omitted without changing the meaning.

Jiuba 酒吧: from *bar* with what may be called a semantic pre-marker *jiu* 酒 to suggest a place where alcoholic drinks are served.

Danta 蛋挞: an open pastry containing egg, from *tart*. First borrowed by people in Hong Kong, the word also contains a semantic pre-marker *dan* 蛋, meaning "egg."

Ashe 阿蛇: sir, used in Hong Kong to refer to cops, phonetically translated from *sir* with a semantic pre-marker *a*阿.

Yanggangzi 洋杠子: vulgarized Chinese in Xinjiang meaning "elder sister-in-law," from the Uighur *yaenggae* plus a common suffix *zi* 子 or "person."

Besides all the above noun-type loanwords, semantic markers may also appear in the few verb-type ones, in which the markers serve as something of a grammatical object or supplement to the verb. Examples include *dangji* 宕机/当机 "(of a computer) not working," with *dang* phonetically rendered from the English adjective source word *down* and *ji* or "machine" added as object- or supplement-like semantic marker (supplement-type marker for short), and *pache* 泊车, with *pa* phonetically rendered from the English verb *park* and *che* or "vehicle" added as supplement-type marker. *Shuqiu* 述球 "shoot (baskets)," used in the Teochew dialect in Malaysia, is phonemically borrowed from the English verb *shoot* or noun *shot*, with a supplement-type marker *qiu* ("ball"). While *xiu* 秀 and *xiao* 逍—both also phonemically loaned from the same English source word in Beijing and Shanghainese dialects, respectively—can both be used monosyllabically without the potential marker of either *qiu* (ball) or *lan* (basket) at the end, *shuqiu* cannot go without its end marker *qiu*.

4.1.2.2 Phonemic and graphemic loaning

Phonemic and graphemic loaning is the most thorough form of lexical borrowing. As part of this, alphabetic graphic loaning (*zimuci*) is the most heterogeneous and is considerably constrained at present because of the Chinese linguistic features and user cognitive schema. So, it is not supposed to be large in number but may have great potential for growth which adapts to the Chinese language as exchange with the rest of the world and foreign language education continue to advance. There are three main types under phonemic/graphemic loaning.[1]

1   *Alphabetic graphic loans*, such as OK, DNA, DVD, WTO, and BBC.
2   *Phonemic loans from Chinese words of Japanese origin.* Unlike the direct borrowing of Western alphabetic letters above, some Chinese loanwords are from phonemic loans in Japan, which use Chinese words, not autochthonous Japanese words, though they may not be pronounced exactly the same due to the different pronunciation systems in Chinese and Japanese, respectively. In contrast to Chinese loanwords of Western origin, however, these phonemic loans and their Japanese source words share considerable phonetic similarity and linguistic lineage so they can at least be considered of quasi-phonemic/graphemic type. Examples include *wasi* 瓦斯 (from Japanese *gasu* 瓦斯, which is phonemically loaned from *gas*), *huliela* 虎列拉/虎列剌[2] (from the Japanese *korera* 虎列剌, which is phonemically loaned from the Dutch *cholera*), *julebu* 俱乐部 (from the Japanese *kurabu* 俱樂部, which is phonetically approximated from *club*).
3   *Semantic loans from Japanese-coined Chinese characters.* The Japanese self-made Chinese characters in this kind of loanword are either those which combine a semantic element added with a phonetic element intended to remind the reader of the pronunciation of the character (the method being called *xingsheng* 形声 or phono-semantic compound) or those which are formed by a combination of elements thought to be logically associated (the method being called *huiyi* 会意 or ideogrammic compound) plus *xingsheng*. But their phonemic borrowing is at times obvious too because the pronunciation of these self-made characters must depend on that of the source word. *Xian* 腺, for example, directly borrowed from the Japanese 腺, pronounced *sen*, a word invented by Japanese as a semantic loan from English *gland*, an organ in the body which secretes particular chemical substances. *Cuizang* 膵脏, an obsolete word for the currently used *yi* 胰 (meaning "pancreas"), is also directly borrowed from the Japanese 膵臟, pronounced *suizo*, which is the Japanese semantic loan from English *pancreas*.

4.1.2.3 Hybrid loaning

Hybrid loaning or phonetic-cum-semantic loaning is also known as half-phonemic, half-semantic loaning, such as *daolinzhi* 道林纸 (a kind of high-quality offset printing paper made from wood, from *Dowling paper*, with *daolin* phonemically translated from *Dowling* and *zhi* semantically translated from *paper*), *nihongdeng* 霓虹灯 (from *neon light*, with *nihong* phonetically approximated from *neon* and *deng* semantically rendered from *light*), and *xinxilan* 新西兰 (from *New Zealand*, with *xin* semantically rendered from *New* and *xilan* phonetically approximated from *Zealand*).

4.1.2.4 Graphic loaning

Graphic loaning refers to the borrowing of graphic shape in Chinese characters, while its pronunciation is carried out in the Chinese way, which can

142 *Classification of Chinese loanwords*

be very different from that in the source language. Most graphic loaning comes from the Japanese language, with some few coming from other countries where Chinese characters are part of the writing system. It can be divided into the following two types.

1   *Graphic loaning with no phonetic association with the source word.* This mainly refers to those Japan-made Chinese words that are read with the Japanese pronunciation (kun-yomi) or other graphic symbols whose pronunciation has nothing in common with that of the Chinese equivalents, such as

> *Shouxi* 手续: administrative procedure in getting something done and the approved documentation thereof, from the Japanese 手続, pronounced *tetsuzuki*
> Qudi 取缔: outlaw, from the Japanese 取り締まる, pronounced *torishimaru*, which originally meant "supervise" or "manage"
> 卍: a non-textual symbol borrowed from India the (Sanskrit *swastika*). It originated in the Middle East or West Asia in the form of an equal-armed cross with each arm continued at a right angle, all in the same rotary direction, used in clockwise or anticlockwise form, symbolizing virility, reproduction, origin, and aegis. When entering South Asia, it was adopted by Buddhism as a symbol of the sun, fire, holiness, and good luck. It entered imperial China's Tang dynasty in 693 AD when Wu Zetian 武则天 (624–705), the imperial concubine turned empress, authorized the symbol as a Chinese character, meaning "the aggregate of auspice and virtue," and ordered it to be used anticlockwise and pronounced the same as *wan* 万.

2   *Graphic loaning of the same graphemic and phonetic origin with the source word.* This graphic loaning refers to those mainly Japan-made Chinese words that are read according to the pronunciation of the Chinese characters in the originating Chinese dialect at the time the word was introduced into Japanese, called on-yomi. Examples include:

> *Xiangdui* 相对: from the Japanese 相対 *sotai*, which is directly borrowed from ancient Chinese by Japanese as a semantic loanword for English *relativity*
> *Malingshu* 马铃薯: from the Japanese *baleishio*
> *Yanwen* 谚文: the current alphabetic writing in the Korean language, from the Korean *o:nmun*
> *Zinan* 字喃: Chinese characters previously used in the Vietnamese language, from the Vietnamese *chu'nôm*

Among the above phonemic, phonemic-graphemic, phonetic-semantic, and graphic types of loaning, the first is the most representative in the strict sense of loanword. Alphabetic graphic loanwords of the second type can easily be pronounced in their original rather than in the Chinese way, so they are in a kind of swing state. The third type is a hybrid, a kind of loan blend. The first subtype under graphic loaning should be considered loanwords proper as their semantic and graphic components are both borrowed, while the second subtype may be taken as quasi-loanwords or loanwords in a broad sense.

4.1.3 Self-made words from foreign linguistic elements

Like Japanese-coined Chinese characters/words, there also exist in Japan a lot of Japanese-coined English words called *wasei eigo* 和製英語. They follow the typical English phonetic and graphic formation but are generally used by and for the Japanese. English as they look, they are neither authentic English nor authentic Japanese and are not recognized in the English-speaking world unless they have been assimilated into it. Examples include *mook* (Japanese bend of *magazine* and *book*), *pasokon* (*personal computer*), and *pachinko* (a Japanese pinball-like gambling machine). As has been discussed, there are also a great number of Japanese self-made Chinese words, such as *guoli* 国立 (pronounced *kokuritsu*), *baifenlu* 百分率 (pronounced *hyakubunritsu*), *anlesi* 安楽死 (pronounced *anraku shi*), and *baojian* 保健 (pronounced *hoken*). Unless they have been assimilated into, and regularly used by, Chinese, like the above, they are considered not proper Chinese words but Japanese-coined Chinese words called *wasei kango* 和製漢語.

The same is true with Chinese-coined English words such as *motuoka* 摩托卡 (a Shanghainese blend of motor and car), *dika* 涤卡 (dacron + khaki), *lekoufu* 乐口福 (Lacavo), and *Fushikang* 富士康 (Foxconn, a Taiwan-based IT contract manufacturing company). Unlike the rich variety of Japanese self-made English words, Chinese ones are not large in number and are different in their types of composition.

This linguistic phenomenon raises interesting theoretical questions: is the extent to which one language assimilates elements of a foreign language correlated with the intrinsic characteristics of the receptive language? How differently do receptive languages assimilate foreign linguistic elements? How does the extent of assimilation also relate to the depth of language contact and the capacity to assimilate on the part of receptive languages? Lying in a linguistic limbo, this might be a field yet to be fully explored for students of linguistics in general and those of loanwords in particular.

4.2 Functional types

4.2.1 Four types of application in the loanword

A typical loanword is one frequently used over a long period of time on a given occasion in the recipient language; its usage must be extremely natural and cannot, in the extreme case, even be substituted with other words. It has already taken root in the Chinese language system, becoming part of the

Chinese lexicon. These words, such as *shafa* 沙发 and *bingqilin* 冰淇淋, can be taken as archetypal loanwords against which to measure how typical a loanword is. On the other hand, the functional type of loanwords can be discussed in terms of application and frequency in use. The type of application is determined by its purposes and, in turn, often determines its frequency in use. Those archetypes are reflected in both the type of application and frequency in use. There are four types of application in loanwords.

4.2.1.1 Use-oriented application

This application type is used to introduce foreign words into one's own community for use since there is an obvious lack, in one's native language, of the notion or pragmatic overtone which is conveyed by such a foreign word. Therefore, frequent use or priority in use is expected of such words. Examples include *shizi* 狮子 (lion, from the old East Iranian *se* or *si*), which did not exist in Asia; *lama* 喇嘛 (lama, from the Tibetan *lama*), whose Tibetan Buddhism is drastically different from Han Buddhism; *caokulun* 草库伦 (enclosed pastureland unique in Inner Mongolia, from the Mongolian *obson xuree*); *jiaokeshu* 教科书 (textbook, from the Japanese *kyokasho*), which is a modern systemically compiled book for the study of a particular subject drastically different from the Chinese classics used in ancient China's kindergarten- or primary school-like education, such as the *Sanzijing* 三字经 (Trimetric Classic), *Baijiaxing* 百家姓 (Hundred Family Surnames), *Qianziwen* 千字文 (Thousand Character Classic), and *Sishu wujing* 四书五经 (Four Books and Five Classics); *UFO* or *youfu* 幽浮 (from UFO, *unidentified flying object*); and *baibai* 拜拜 (bye-bye), which exudes an exotic flavor and is used as frequently as, if not more than, the autochthonous word *zaijian* 再见.

Like most loanwords, the above six are borrowed in the fullest sense of the source words. For some, however, their lexical extension may have gone through some adaptation, usually getting narrower. When the word *xiezhen* 写真, originally a true-to-life portrait in Old Chinese, was adopted in premodern times by Japanese as a graphic loan pronounced *shashin*, its meaning was changed to "photo-taking," "photo," or "photography." When it flew back to modern Chinese, a good part of the Japanese *xiezhen* introduced to Hong Kong and Taiwan at the time was erotic or pornographic, so the word has since taken on a narrow meaning of sexually explicit photos or photography. *A she* 阿蛇 or *a sir* 阿 sir, a Cantonese word used in Hong Kong, is from the generic *sir*, used specifically to refer to cop. *Hafu* 哈夫, a Shanghainese loanword from *half*, is used as its verb *halve* only. *Sa'ei* 撒诶, another Shanghainese loanword from English *side* is used specifically when a ball is hit out of bounds.

Since they selectively take some attribute(s) from their source words, a handful of Chinese loanwords are figurative in usage. *Denglupu* 邓禄普, for instance, a Shanghainese loanword from *Dunlop*, the English tire-manufacturing company and its products, takes the attributes of thick rubber surface and durability to specifically describe those people who are shameless. *Asan* 阿三, another Shanghainese loanword from *sir* (probably also borrowed from the Hong Kong Cantonese *a sir* 阿蛇), was used to refer pejoratively to Indian police (*hongtou asan* 红头阿三, literally "red-head" *asan*) serving the British concession in Shanghai in the early 20th century and later to refer to monkeys. Originating from the Gandhari or Prakrit *bosa*, which was from the Sanskrit *Bodhisattva* "enlightenment," *pusa* 菩萨 originally referred to the title given to Sakyamuni before he reached nirvana or a person who preaches Buddhist teachings to promote universal salvation in the Chinese school of Buddhism, but later, it also referred to a greatly merciful and compassionate person.

These figurative-type loanwords are used more frequently in local dialects, where there are not as many constraints as in the formal written form. Both figurative and adaptation features, however, can sometimes be seen on the same loanword. This dynamic variation as a result of lexical comparisons between the source word and the loanword will stand in marked contrast to the semantic and lexical discussions over the loanword alone later in this chapter. Considering the current related research, we believe that this dynamic contrastive analysis deserves much more academic attention.

4.2.1.2 *Information-oriented application*

This application type is intended not to borrow those foreign words but, through those words, to provide some related social or cultural background against the source language. Compared with archetypal loanwords, they are merely formal ones, not reaching the status of fully fledged ones yet. Those words necessarily reflect elements of other cultures which may differ from, and therefore complement or enrich, those of one's own. They may even be adopted for daily use and, over time, assimilated into one's own language system. For instance, in its overview of Central and Western Asia (what was then called "the Western Regions") in the *Wei Shu* 魏书 (Book of Wei), a Chinese classic describing the history of the Northern Wei and Eastern Wei from 386 to 550 AD, there is the following passage about Persia:

> People here call the king *yizan* 医囋 [Phonemic loan from the Old Persian *Ixsed*], imperial concubine *fangbulu* 防步率 [Old Persian *banbusn*], king's children *shaye* 杀野 [Old Persian *satrya*]. Important imperial leaders include *mohutan* 摸胡坛 [Old Persian *magudan*] in charge of domestic civil and criminal justice, *nihuhan* 泥忽汗 [Old Persian *nexurghan*] in charge of national treasury and imprisonment, *dibei* 地卑 [Persian *dipibara*] in charge of archives and miscellaneous affairs. Lesser officials include *eluohedi* 遏罗诃地 [Persian *argabides*] in charge of the king's private affairs and *xuebobo* 薛波勃 [Persian *sipahbad*] in charge of military forces.

Had they wished to borrow those terms, no such disrespectful words as *sha* 杀 ("kill") or *bei* 卑 ("lowly") would have been used in introducing those senior titles for government officials.

Take a more recent example. In the Qing dynasty, many of the scholars and government officials who had been to Japan on missions or tours published informative books on the country they had visited when they returned. The *Ce'ao zazhi* (My miscellaneous studies on Japan, 1889) by Ye Qingyi, for example, was not intended to introduce Japanese words for their use in China but to tell his fellow Chinese about Japan and Japanese culture. Here is a short passage:

> *Xiaozi* 硝子 refers to glass so the Japanese have what they call *xiaozi zhizaohuishe* 硝子制造会社, which means glass factory. I do not know why, but *zuoguan* 左官 here refers to bricklayer. *Xueyin* 雪隐 means lavatory. *Babaiwen* 八百问 or *babaiwu* 八百屋 (やおや) refers to greengrocer. *Babai* or 'eight hundred' is used to indicate that there is a rich variety of vegetables, gourds, melons, and other fruits, as many as eight hundred! *Yudeyong* 御徳用 is an alternative name for candle by Japanese.

None of the Japanese words listed above entered into the Chinese lexicon; they were introduced merely for informative purposes. In fact, the word *xiaozi* had its first attestation in China's Ming dynasty, referring to "artificial crystal," which was then borrowed by Japanese to refer to glass. Having received sustained introduction or promotion later on, some Japanese words provided in Ye's book, however, have morphed from information-oriented into use-oriented application and thus become a regular part of Chinese vocabulary, such as *roushu* 柔术 (Japanese *jujutsu* 柔術), *shangye* 商业 (Japanese *shogyo* 商業), *gongzhai* 公债 (Japanese *kosai* 公債), and *xiashuidao* 下水道 (Japanese *gesuido* 下水道).

Here is a contemporary example—a short passage from the overseas Chinese edition of *Renmin Ribao* 人民日报 (*People's Daily*) about Tibetan people:

> Tibetan people call themselves *Boba* 博巴 because, according to historical records, they slowly evolved from one sub-branch called *Boqiang* 发羌 [in ancient Chinese *fa* 发 was pronounced as *bo* 博] out of *Xiqiang* 西羌 ethnic group during the Western and Eastern Han dynasties [206 BC–280 AD].

Here, *boba* (from the Tibetan $p^ho?^{13}pa^{54}$ or poe^{q31}) is informative in function. As both *Tubo* 吐蕃 and *Zangzu* 藏族 have been in the Chinese language for a long time, referring to the Tibetan ethnic group, so *Boba* is now used in Chinese for information purposes only, unlike the direct adoption of the names of *Menba* 门巴 (from $m\tilde{o}^{13}pa^{55}$ or $m\tilde{o}^{35}pa^{53}$) and *Luoba* 珞巴 (from Tibetan *łopa*), minor ethnic groups living in Tibet, according to the observance principle that name-giving should be based on the originating person (or place). This does not rule out, however, the possibility that *Boba* might move up from the information-oriented to the use-oriented type of loanword under certain circumstances.

4.2.1.3 Source-providing application

Neither for practical use nor for explanatory purposes, this application type is intended to provide the source word for the foreign thing or concept under discussion. This source-providing, one-time note of formal etymology is not expected to be in actual use in the Chinese language, so it cannot be considered *bona fide* loanwords, nor even *pro forma* ones; instead, it makes something of pseudo-loanwords, though a few words of this type might over time elevate themselves into information-oriented or even use-oriented application. Here is how *Minglitan* 名理探 (*A study of logic*), which was translated from Latin by Francois Furtado and Li Zhizao 李之藻 in the early 17th century, introduced Western terminology:

> In the West, a subject of study which loves to explore wisdom and learning is called *feilusuofeiya* 斐录琐费亚 [Phonemic rendering from the Latin *philosophia*], which actually means a collection of all kinds of studies that try to understand how things work…There are three aspects concerning language. The first is *tanyi* 谈艺, called *elemadijia* 额勒玛第加 [from *grammatical*] in the West; the second is *wenyi* 文艺, called *ledulijia* 勒读里加 [from *rhetorica*]; the third is *bianyi* 辩艺, called *luorijia* 络日加 [from *logica*]. In the West, *shi* 史 ["history"] is called *yisiduoliya* 伊斯多利亚 [from *historia*] and *shi* 诗 ["poetry"] is called *bo'edijia* 博厄第加 [from *poetica*].

It should be noted that translation at the time was not rendered strictly according to the original but was combined with relevant explanations to facilitate readers, such as the wording "In the West…is called," which did not exist in the original Latin text of *Categories* by Aristotle but was added by the translators as the source of the already semantically rendered translation. Indeed, *feilusuofeiya* and the like, i.e., the above words of source-providing application, have not been in actual use in the Chinese language. In hindsight, such awkward phonetic representation may be the lesser evil, so to speak, because at the time (400 years ago, from the time at this writing), Western languages were so very alien and unknown to the Chinese readers, and there was no official and effective phonetic representation in practice. Today, handy phonetic systems like the Romanized *pinyin* or the source words in their original spelling (or graphemic shape) would obviously replace *feilusuofeiya* and the like. Even with that, words of source-providing application are, in essence, still foreign words, not really part of the Chinese lexicon *per se*, as is the case of the word "internet," following

148 *Classification of Chinese loanwords*

its Chinese equivalent *hulianwang* 互联网 in brackets. In this case, of course, it is easier for the Chinese representations in characters (e.g. *hulianwang*) to become *bona fide* loanwords or be mistaken as such at least.

4.2.1.4 Inquiry-oriented application

This application type is used to study or probe into the etymology, meaning, first attestation, etc. with regard to the word in question. Since this application is, in nature, more like linguistic or humanities research, how the word is actually used in real life or its frequency in usage is beyond its concern. Nor can inquiry-oriented application indicate the proximity of the word to the so-called archetypal loanwords as the previous three application types can.

A very common form of inquiry-oriented application is that which is used for academic purposes. Take the term *taohuashi* 桃花石, for example. Throughout Chinese historical literature and records to date, it appeared only twice in actual use. In *Changchun zhenren xiyouji* 长春真人西游记 (*The Journey to the west by Qiu Chuji*) by Li Zhichang 李志常, documenting the journey in Xiyu, the Western Regions to then China, by Li's Taoist mentor Qiu Chuji 丘处机 (1148–1227) at the imperial request of Genghis Khan, it wrote (in English translation), "(The Alima aboriginals) also saw the Chinese water-drawing utensils and said happily: 'Everything made by *Taohuashi* is smart.' *Taohuashi* means Chinese Han people." The word *taohuashi* probably originated from the Turkic *Tabgac* in the Tang dynasty or the Uighur *Tapkac* in the Yuan. Merely for information purposes, the term has never been used by Chinese people to address themselves. But since the publication of *Changchun zhenren xiyouji*, there have been at least 100 academic monographs or papers probing into its corresponding original form in the source word and the semantic evolution of *taohuashi*. However, they are all inquiry-oriented in nature, and it is dubbed not an actual loanword due to its information function.

Another form of inquiry-oriented application is for political purposes. For example, for a long time in history, the Japanese government took an attitude of evasion and denial toward its acts of aggression against Asian countries. Their further lack of sincere apology and repentance has to this day been reflected in claiming their aggressions as *shinshutsu* or *jinchu* 進出 in kanji, meaning "advance into," "break into," or "squeeze in." This has evoked strong condemnations from the Chinese government and people. As a result, this Japanese term *jinchu* has been quoted hundreds of times in Chinese writing. Certainly not accidental, its high-frequency appearance is not intended for actual use in the Chinese language but for laying bare the rightist views in Japan and exposing the Japanese government's ulterior motives.

It is worth pointing out that the differentiation between the first three application types (use orientation, information orientation, and source provision) is not fixed but dynamic; occasionally, they might each, in an incremental manner rather than all of a sudden, morph into other application types.

4.2.2 Frequency types of the loanword

There are roughly four frequency-in-usage types in loanwords: most frequent, frequent, less frequent, not frequent, and rare. It goes without saying that frequency in usage is very volatile; a certain loanword which is occasionally used at the moment may well turn out to be frequent in its use after some period of time or might have been very popular in ancient times. However, it may still reveal the dynamic nature of loanwords in a particular society—which words are dead, obsolete, or transient and which are alive and kicking—as long as sufficiently large chunks of relevant data are available, and their analyses are feasible. In today's information technology (IT) era, when large-scale electronic resources, including databases and corpuses, are available, and cloud computing is being used at an accelerating rate, research into loanword frequency holds alluring prospects for further development.

4.3 Social stratifications

4.3.1 Introduction

The social stratification of a loanword refers to a community which speaks a specific language and borrows and routinely uses the word in that language. For a specific small community, any borrowed word can no doubt become a loanword to a varying degree of proximity to the archetypal one. However, if the whole nation is taken into account, things become more complicated as the community varies in size. In terms of the scope of loanword use, there are generally at least three tiers of language community when we talk about the Chinese language: global community, primary community, and secondary community; in terms of the connections among different communities, there can be central and regional communities; and, in terms of the relations—both subjective feelings and objective manifestations—between the language users in question and the local residents, there can be naturalized and un-naturalized communities.

4.3.2 Global language community

This encompasses all members across the world who use Chinese as their native language. In pre-modern times, the Chinese-speaking community was basically limited to present-day China. Chinese immigrants overseas, self-initiated or involuntary, such as those in Southeast Asia and the US, were insignificant in size. So, the loanwords which were prevalent in the

Chinese-speaking community were practically legacy ones, i.e., those historically accumulated loanwords, such as *putao* 葡萄, *luotuo* 骆驼, *muxu* 苜蓿, *shizi* 狮子, *fo* 佛, *pusa* 菩萨, *luohan* 罗汉, *liuli* 琉璃, and *boli* 玻璃. Since modern times, however, more and more Chinese have emigrated or began living abroad, meaning that the Chinese-speaking community now spans the whole world. This community is characterized by a huge user population and broad yet more or less concentrated areas which are variously inter-connected. Within such a community, whose boundaries are relatively vague, despite its clearly defined core, the popularity of a certain loanword will necessarily depend on a host of factors, not least linguistic, political, economic, ethnic, and cultural considerations. But, given the worldwide prevalence of the English language as a successful precedent, it is reasonable to expect the same from the Chinese language as long as it has standardized its usage and globalized its dissemination. Modern loanwords like *youmo* 幽默 ("humor"), *fanshilin* 凡士林 ("Vaseline"), *sangba(wu)* 桑巴(舞) ("samba"), *anqier* 安琪儿 ("angel"), *faxisi* 法西斯 ("fascism"), *leida* 雷达 ("radar"), *shouxu* 手续 ("procedure"), *wuzhi* 物质 ("material"), *mudi* 目的 ("purpose"), *tanpan* 谈判 ("negotiation"), and *geming* 革命 ("revolution") have all gained currency in the global Chinese language community.

4.3.3 Primary community

A primary community refers to one which people inhabit with a long history and which they view as their ancestral homeland. The greater Chinese community across the Taiwan Strait constitutes the primary Chinese language community, which forms the bulk of the global community. A primary community is usually one for naturalized residents and can be further divided into central and regional sub-communities.

4.3.3.1 Central community

As an administrative and linguistic concept, a central community is one in which a standard language is used as the primary language of communication. Based on a specific area or region, a central community may to some extent transcend the strictly geographic boundaries and may under certain circumstances even become what might be called the language administration center. In the case of Chinese, it is a community where its members view Beijing as the center of residence and *Putonghua* 普通话 (literally "common language," also known as Mandarin or Modern Standard Chinese) based on the Beijing dialect as the primary language of communication. This central community is shaped and strengthened as a result of the increasing uniformity in the primary community and the consolidation of the centralized governance. Historically, China witnessed a succession of powerful central governments which basically viewed the heartland of the nation, or *Zhongyuan* (the Central Plains), as the center; hence, the central community which has gradually used the Northern Chinese dialect as the standard literary and official form of Chinese. This central community obviously has had its ups and downs, going through various adaptations and relocations, due to dynastic changes and the capacity of dynastic governance across the country. Loanwords which are actively used in the central community are mostly adopted across the global language community; they not only come from the community itself but are constantly coming from regional communities as well. Loanwords which are borrowed at the central community level and universally adopted across the global community include, among others, *youmo* 幽默, *luoji* 逻辑, *jihe* 几何, *modeng* 摩登, *mote'er* 模特儿, *anqier* 安琪儿, *shalong* 沙龙, *langman* 浪漫, *kekou kele* 可口可乐, *mian'ertong* 眠而通 (from *Miltown*, the proprietary name for a mild tranquilizer called meprobamate), *kelikong* 克里空, *wutuobang* 乌托邦, *julebu* 俱乐部, *shehui* 社会, *shouxu* 手续, *huashengdun* 华盛顿, *qiujier* 丘吉尔, and *yingjili* 英吉利. Loanwords which are borrowed at the central community level but whose use extends only to the primary community include, among others, *baobo* 胞波, *Panchaxila* 潘查希拉 (Five Principles, the Indonesian state philosophy, formulated by the Indonesian nationalist leader Sukarno, from *Pancasila*), *bulaji* 布拉吉, *aizibing* 艾滋病, *pangke* 旁客, *kennidi* 肯尼迪, *ligen* 里根, and *xinxilan* 新西兰.

Many of the loanwords used in the primary community are either absent in other Chinese-speaking communities, such as *Panchaxila*, *ximingna'er*, *bulaji*, and *baobo*, or represented in a slightly different phonemic or graphemic form, such as *aizibing* 艾滋病, *bangke* 傍客/*pengke* 朋客, *gannaidi* 甘乃迪, *liegen* 列根, and *niuxilan* 纽西兰, which correspond to the last five words in the previous paragraph. Common loanwords like *shafa*, *qiaokeli*, *mitu* 米突 (from *meter*, replaced by *mi* 米 now), *pijiu*, and *baituoyou* 白脱油 (from *butter*) were first borrowed by people in the greater Shanghai area; *kuaiba* 快巴 (from *fiber*), *bashi*, *dishi*, and *T xu* T恤 were first borrowed in the Cantonese-speaking area based in Hong Kong and Guangzhou; and *Kala OK*, *KTV*, and *MTV* were first borrowed in Taiwan, then Hong Kong.

4.3.3.2 Regional communities

Regional communities are variously located sub-communities surrounding the central community, such as those regions in which various Chinese dialects are spoken by the majority Han people and the regions where Chinese-speaking Muslims (the Hui people) concentrate—excluding those Hui people who migrated to Russia from Gansu and Shaanxi in the late 19th century as they later formed a distinct ethnic group called *Tungani* (or *Donggan* 东干族 in Chinese), and their language has obviously creolized. The Chinese-speaking community has long since expanded to Taiwan, making it another regional community.

Though influenced by the central community, a regional community usually enjoys a certain measure of autonomy by giving more weight to its own considerations in tackling language issues and therefore bears the cultural hallmark of that particular dialect. In fact, a regional community itself may also have central and peripheral parts, such as the provincial capital Guangzhou vis-à-vis the rest of Guangdong province. The characteristic marginality of the regional community is an important source of variation and creation. So, the more distinctively regional or local the community is, the more creative its loanwords are in terms of assimilation and type, making it a significant contributor to the rich variety of the loanwords in the central community. The pre-1950s Shanghai and the post-1950s Hong Kong are prime examples in this regard. Here are some representative regional communities (Taiwan and Hong Kong will be discussed separately in Section 4.3.4 of this chapter).

1 **Shanghai Wu dialect community.** Encompassing a variety of Chinese dialects, the Wu language 吴语 is a major cluster of Chinese dialects spoken in East China's Yangtze River Delta (i.e. Shanghai, Jiangsu, and Zhejiang province) by more than 8% of the national population. Centered in cosmopolitan Shanghai, with its highest level of education in foreign languages and its most extensive ties with the rest of the world, this Wu-speaking region has culturally been well ahead of other regions in China since the 1920s. Traditionally a magnet for aspiring people from the neighboring Jiangsu and Zhejiang provinces, Shanghai has also been a center for the inflow of loanwords. Before the founding of the People's Republic in 1949, there were a number of foreign concessions in the city, so English was widely used, bringing in a multitude of Chinese loanwords of English origin to various sectors of society. Many of them have been adopted in the primary community already while a considerable number of others are still used in the Shanghai dialect in various fields, such as sports. Though they usually appear in a spoken rather than a written form, here are some such localized phonemic loanwords presented in tentative phonetic and graphic forms for the sake of simplicity: $la\textipa{P}^5fi^1li^2$ 辣斐理 (from *referee*), $go^2\textipa{*}^{12}$ 搞尔 (goal or goalkeeper, from *goal*), sa^1he^2 撒诶 (ball being hit out of bounds, from *side*), $\textipa{G}io^1$ 肖(shoot a basket, from *shoot*), $\textipa{\ae}ian^2bo^2$ 强搏 (steal the ball, from *jump ball*), p^ha^1 派 or 帕 *(pass the ball, from pass)*, and $do^2ba\textipa{P}^5\textipa{*}^{10}$ 道勃尔 *(double hit in a volleyball, from double).*

Here is a short description from a mainstream newspaper in the 1940s about the popularity of loanwords in Shanghai at that time:

> When the foreign walking stick was first introduced to Shanghai, one buzz phrase among the local residents there was '*Keluoke* on your eyes, *jialike* in your mouth, *sidike* in your hand.' Armed with these three *ke*'s, a man would look every bit like a foreign gentleman and felt free to strut up and down like a peacock.

In this description, three items which were fashionable at the time are mentioned. *Keluoke* 克罗克 was the phonemic loanword from *Crookes*, a brand of glasses designed to diminish the transmission of ultraviolet rays; *jialike* 茄力克 was the phonemic loanword from *Garrick*, a top-brand cigarette at the time; and *sidike* 司的克 was the phonemic loanword from *stick* or walking stick. Obviously, the three *ke*'s mentioned in the passage refer to the above faddish items.

2 **Guangzhou Cantonese dialect community.** As one of China's earliest treaty ports and having thus experienced the First Opium War (1839–1842), Guangzhou, formerly known as Canton in the West, is contiguous to Hong Kong, and English has long been a major language for international communication there. It is no wonder that the city, or in fact this Guangzhou-based Cantonese dialect community (apart from Hong Kong), has seen a lot of borrowing from English. Due to the distinctive features of the Cantonese dialect, the use of many of the loanwords in this regional community and their written forms have largely been limited to the community itself. Here are some such Cantonese-sounding phonemic loanwords, followed by the Modern Standard Chinese equivalents and their source words:

Shuhua 梳化: shafa 沙发, from *sofa*
Huachen 花臣: liuxing shiyang 流行式样, from *fashion*
Kelijia/tilijia 克力架/体力架: binggan 饼干, from *cracker*
Zhuguli 朱古力: qiaokeli 巧克力, from *chocolate*
Quqi(bing)/quqishi 曲奇饼/曲奇士: naiyou tiansubing 奶油甜酥饼, from *cookie*
Mai/me 唛/嚜: paizi 牌子, from *mark*
Leng 冷: maoxian 毛线, from the French *laine*, meaning "woollen yarn"
Bo 波: qiu 球, from *ball*
(Che)tai 车呔: chetai 车胎, from *tire*
(Ling)tai 领呔: lingdai 领带, from *tie*
Mai 迈/咪: yingli 英里, from *mile* (mai 迈 in this meaning has been assimilated into Chinese)
Mai 咪: kuoyinqi 扩音器, from *microphone*
Shidan 士担: youpiao 邮票, from *stamp*
Cheka 车卡: huoche chexiang 火车车厢, from *car*
Bandai 扮带: diaodai 吊带, from *band*
Baiwulong 摆乌龙: nongcuo 弄错, from *wrong*
Mixian 咪仙: lianmeisu 链霉素, from *streptomycin*

3 **Southern Fujian language community.** The southern part of China's eastern province Fujian, the *Minnan* 闽南, as it is abbreviated in Chinese, is centered on the Xiamen-Zhangzhou-Quanzhou triangle and has had active ties with the rest of the world since ancient times. Once the largest sea port in southern China, Quanzhou had sea-faring links with south and southeast Asia, and later Xiamen (also known as Amoy) caught up. Since modern times, the southern Fujian dialect or Minnan dialect

154 *Classification of Chinese loanwords*

闽南语 (known as Hokkien in Singapore and Malaysia) has assimilated a number of spoken words from Southeastern Asian languages, particularly from Malay, including Indonesian (the latter being based on the former). Here are some examples:

Lanfu 滥斧: Western-style lamp, from the Malay *lampu* from the English *lamp*
Dongge 洞葛: walking stick, from the Malay *tongkat*
Tsim¹: kiss, from the Malay *chium*
Wujiaoji 五脚忌: *qilou* or *tong lau*, an arcade running alongside the road for pedestrian use, from the Malay *gokhaki*
Basha 巴刹: market, from the Malay *pasar* from the Persian *bāzār*
Laojun 老君: doctor, from the Malay *dukun*
Daolang 道朗: assistance, from the Malay *tolong*
Xuewen 雪文: soap, from the Malay *sabon*

4 **Northeast China language community.** Though the closest to the Beijing dialect, the Northeast China language community is the ancestral homeland of the Manchu people, and a considerable number of Russians once emigrated to the area close to the border. Many of its loanwords therefore come from Manchu, and some come from Russian. Various other ethnic groups in Northeast China, such as the ethnic Korean group in the border prefecture of Yanbian 延边, have also made contributions. Some of the loanwords in this community are still in use, while others have been replaced with other expressions. Here are some examples:

Luosuo 洛索: indecisive, not neat, from unknown Manchu
Maitai 埋汰: dirty, from unknown Manchu
Moxing 嫫性: ugly and large, from unknown Manchu
Tele 特勒: slovenly, from unknown Manchu
Lieba 裂粑/黑列巴: bread, from the Russian хлеба
Biliqi 壁里砌/壁里气: Russian fireplace, from the Russian печь
Mashen 马神: machine, farming machine, from the Russian машина
Jimiqi 积米琪: kimchi, Korean spicy pickled cabbage, from the Korean *kimtsʰi*
Meiyuntang 梅云汤: spicy soup made with little fish and vegetables, from the Korean *mai'unthang*
Daolaji 道拉吉: Chinese bellflower, from the Korean *toratsi*

5 **Beijing Manchu community.** Manchu people have long since lived in Beijing and taken it as their primary place of residence, thus bringing in a good number of loanwords of Manchu origin to the Beijing dialect, while ethnic Manchu have also retained some of their own words. However important, the Beijing dialect is just one of many Chinese dialects, serving and therefore having to adapt to its regional Han community. Here are some of the words generally limited to the community of Chinese-speaking Manchu people in Beijing:

Ama 阿玛: father, from the Manchu *ame*
Eniang 额娘: mother, father's concubine, from the Manchu *eniye*
A'ge 阿个/阿哥: young son of a rich or noble family, from the Manchu *a'ge*
Gege 格格: young daughter of a rich or noble family, from the Manchu *gege*
Dalami 达拉密: boss, person in charge, from the Manchu *dalambi*
Tata'erda 塌塌儿搭: a local bully, from the Manchu *tatan i da*, "local chief"
Keshi 克什: sacrificial food shared among people after service, from the Manchu *kesi* "sacrificial offerings"
Naiwuta 奶乌他: milk cake, from the Manchu *uta*
Wadan 挖单: double-layered clothes wrapper or cloth cover for jugglers, from the Manchu *wadan*
Duomohu 哆嗼壶: an inter-layered pot to warm liquor, from the Manchu *dolmombi*, "add more liquor"
Duoluo 哆罗: a Mandarin jacket, from the Manchu *delehe*
Halaba 哈拉巴: shoulder blade or the flesh around it, from the Manchu *halba*
Dede 得得: shiver, from the Manchu *ededei* "tremble"
Motuozi 磨驼子: dilly-dally or such a person, from the Manchu *modo*, "tardy"
Wusu 恶愫: disgust or irritated, from the Manchu *usun*
Se 嗖: a shout asking the camel to lie down, from the Manchu *sohu*, "sit"

A few other words of Manchu origin are not only used in Beijing but broadly accepted in larger communities, such as *kandahan* 堪达罕 or *handahan* 犴达罕 (moose, from the Manchu *kandahan*), *bashi* 把式 (a skillful master good at martial arts, from the Manchu *baksi*; already discussed in Section 1.1.2 in Chapter 1), and *saqima* 萨其马 (candied fritter, from *sacima*; already discussed in Section 2.4.2.4 in Chapter 2).

6 **Ethnic Hui community**. Most Hui people are concentrated in a few particular regions, but many scatter across the country. Except in Tibet, ethnic Islamic Hui people usually speak Mandarin Chinese and are characterized by both their regional distinction, common among other Chinese-speaking communities, and their own ethnicity. There is a strong sense of cohesion among the Hui people in Beijing, for instance, so they have retained much of their distinct ethnicity, which is reflected in their use of some specific loanwords amongst themselves, largely from Turkish, in addition to the common lexicon used in Beijing. Here are some such loanwords from the Hui people in Beijing:

Baba 爸爸: paternal grandparent, from the Turkish *baba* "elders"
-Ba(er)- 爸(儿): elder uncle, used after the name, from the Turkish *baba*
-Baer -巴儿: sir, used after the name, from the Turkish *baba*
Daba 大爸/大把: elder uncle, from the Turkish *baba*

156 *Classification of Chinese loanwords*

Nietie 乜贴: charity, from the Turkish *niyet*

Samosa 撒摩萨: a triangular fried pastry with mutton fillings, from the Turkish *samsa*, "sweet pastry"

There are also many religious loanwords among the ethnic Hui people across the country, including, for example, Linxia Prefecture in Gansu Province and Xunhua in Qinghai Province, such as

Zhuma 主麻: Jumu'ah, Friday Prayer, Congregational Prayer that Muslims hold every Friday, from the Arabic *jum'ah*

Yimani/yiman 伊玛尼/伊曼: God's blessing, belief in Allah, from the Arabic *iman*

Hadi 哈的 or *kadi* 卡迪: religious judge in Islam who presides over a wedding or mourning ceremony, from the Arabic *khadi*

Nikahan 尼卡罕: union, Islamic wedding ceremony, from the Arabic *nikah*

Zhenaze 者那则: Islamic funeral ritual, from the Arabic *janazah*

4.3.4 Secondary community

A secondary language community is transplanted outside of the primary community and enjoys great linguistic autonomy as the primary community exerts far less influence upon it. A typical example is the Chinese-speaking communities among overseas Chinese. The differentiation between the primary community and the secondary community, however, is not absolute as the latter may rise to the former's status under certain circumstances. The English-speaking community in early America, for instance, used to be secondary to the primary community in Britain, viewing British English as authentic. The end of World War II, however, saw the rapid rise of the US in international standing and the corresponding rise of American English as equally important to British English, making US and the UK both primary English-speaking communities. Indeed, American English seems to be in an increasingly advantageous position as it exerts more influence than British English.

Though, like a primary community, a secondary community may also have its central and regional sub-communities, they all still belong to their primary community as a dialectal region. Therefore, unless the secondary community has grown to a considerable degree, there is not much point in discussing its central or regional divisions. Instead, what is outstanding in the secondary community is the differentiation between naturalization and non-naturalization (while primary communities are, needless to say, all naturalized ones by definition).

4.3.4.1 Naturalized sub-community

Members in a naturalized sub-community view the place where they live as their homeland and themselves as permanent local residents rather than temporary visitors. Practically all Chinese communities in Southeast Asia, most typically, Singapore and Malaysia, belong to this category. Their Chinese lexicon reflects many of their marginal features. In Singapore, for example, local Chinese have already adopted many of the Chinese language norms prescribed in mainland Chinese, but their loanwords are still considerably peculiar, such as

Baxian 巴仙: percent, from the English *percent*
Basha 巴刹: food market, from the Malay pasa,r from the Persian *bāzār*
Balengdao 巴冷刀: a kind of long sword, knife for cutting wood, from the Malay *parang*
Baba 峇峇: a Chinese male born in Singapore, Malaysia, or Indonesia and strongly influenced by the local culture, from the Malay *baba*; such a Chinese female is called *nianre* 娘惹 from the Malay *nyonya*
Badi 峇迪: a fabric with patterns printed by using removable wax on the parts that will not be dyed, from the Malay *batek* (same as *batik* in Indonesian, also referring to Indonesia traditional clothing)
Manbowu 曼波舞: a lively dance originating from Cuban black people, with syncopated music in 4/4 time, from *mambo*
Yaxi'an 亚细安: the Association of Southeast Asian Nations, from its acronym *ASEAN*

Though some communities have already transformed themselves from temporary residents to permanent naturalized ones, some sectors of the host country may still view them as an outsider group, evoking in these groups' members a sense of alienation, however fleeting. One obvious example is the Chinese-speaking community in Indonesia. Naturalized as they have been, they suffer from nativist harassment and estrangement from time to time. Only in a country like Singapore, where the Chinese-speaking community has categorically been recognized as an inalienable and major part of the nation, enjoying equality in all rights and obligations with other members of the society, can its naturalized host status be fully attained and maintained.

4.3.4.2 *Un-naturalized sub-community*

An un-naturalized sub-community refers to a community either living outside of the primary community or in a non-native region where its members experience noticeable isolation from the local society; feel psychologically alien; and, to some extent, are treated as such. Such a sub-community will not usually maintain such a transitional status for long unless it is treated by the host society explicitly as an outsider—exceptions do exist where alienation lingers among the third or even later generations of a community. For instance, some Chinese-speaking communities in Southeast Asian countries are evolving, or have already evolved, into naturalized host status as Chinese speakers, while others are being integrated, or have already been integrated, into local language communities.

As marginal groups, un-naturalized Chinese-speaking sub-communities may demonstrate more linguistic variations. When building up their loanword lexicon, they are physically in a foreign country and surrounded by the omnipresent and powerful linguistic/cultural "otherness." So, besides being strongly localized, their loanwords tend to be more informal, involuntary, temporary, or even perfunctory. Representative of this category are new Chinese immigrant communities since the 1950s, such as Mandarin-speaking communities in the US and Japan.

There are, in fact, two types of Chinese community in Japan: one composed of the second- or third-generation settlers and the other composed of new immigrants. The first generation of the former may still have a habit of using Chinese within the family or with relatives, but the language they use is punctuated with Japanese words. What is more, from the second generation on, most of them start to wean themselves off Chinese. Owing to the Japanese policy, these people still have a strong sense of living as an alien guest in a foreign host country. The latter new immigrant community is either from the Chinese mainland or from Taiwan. To better secure a job, many immigrants from Taiwan become naturalized Japanese citizens. Since the 1970s, however, most immigrants from the mainland have come to Japan for study or work on a temporary basis, so they have a much more palpable sense of being a visitor. This community is broadly dispersed, with a few clusters across Japan. They communicate in Chinese and have several Chinese language newspapers in which to express their views and follow what is going on in the community. Their Chinese, however, often borrows words of Japanese origin in various forms (mostly in speaking but sometimes also in formal writing): Sinicized pronunciation of Japan-made Chinese words, phonetic approximation of Japanese words usually according to Japanese pronunciation, and abbreviations in Latin letters. Quite diverse in scope, these Japanese words are rather casually used and thus basically in an off-and-on state of borrowing.

1. Sinicized pronunciation of Japan-made Chinese words: *liushou dianhua* 留守电话 (answering machine); *xiedai dianhua* 携带电话, popularly known in mainland China as *dageda* 大哥大 (first-generation heavy and large cellular phone); *huishe* 会社 (company); *mianjie* 面接 (interview); *xiushi* 修士 (master's degree holder); *yuansheng* 院生 (graduate student); *daxueyuan* 大学院 (graduate school); *fuzhi* 福祉 (welfare); *feichangqin jiaoshi* 非常勤教师 (temporary teacher); *liaoli* 料理 (cuisine); *geyin* 割引 (discount); and *buyongpin* 不用品 (unwanted articles)
2. Phonetic approximation of Japanese words according to Japanese pronunciation: *saximi* (from Japanese *sashimi*), *wapulo* (word processor, from *wapuro*), *lusibang* (answering machine, from *rusuban* 留守番), *pasokong* (personal computer, from *pasokon*), *tagoyaki* (a ball-shaped Japanese snack or appetizer made of a wheat flour-based batter and cooked in a special molded pan, from *tagoyaki*), *sixi* (sushi), *xiokelimu*

(a cream-filled dessert, from *shokurimu*), *alubayido* (part-time job, from *arupaito*), *mangxiong* (mansion, high-end apartment, from *manshon*), *apado* (apartment, from *apato*), *bonsai* (bonus pay, from *bonasu*), *hotelu* (hotel, from *hoteru*), and *paqinko* (a Japanese pinball-like gambling machine, from *pachinko*)

3   Abbreviations in Latin letters: *CD, DVD, FAX, PHS* (Personal Handyphone System, a lightweight portable wireless telephone that functions as a cordless phone in the home and as a mobile phone elsewhere, called *xiaolingtong* 小灵通 in China), *NHK*, and *LED*

As can be seen from the above, these borrowed Japanese words are not typical loanwords as their original shape remains largely intact, more like distorted versions of the Japanese originals. This linguistic situation may apply to many other un-naturalized sub-communities.

4.3.5 Special regional language communities

Some special cases may occur under certain social, political, historical, or other circumstances in which one ordinary regional language community becomes physically isolated and partially linguistically deviates from its primary community. This physical isolation and linguistic deviation has been in place for a considerably long period of time, making it a special regional community which enjoys greater linguistic autonomy than other regional ones. Such special communities include Hong Kong, Macao, and Taiwan, each with its own distinctive features. From a historical point of view, however, this linguistic specificity is not static and may change accordingly as the relevant political and economic conditions evolve. Though this special community can be subsumed under the primary one for discussion, a separate inquiry may be of more value due to its distinctive nature. The following is a brief look at the Taiwan and Hong Kong language communities, respectively.

4.3.5.1 Taiwan linguistic community

Ceded to Japan in the late 19th century and reclaimed in the 1940s, Taiwan was soon in a state of standoff and isolation with its mainland as a result of the civil war between the communists and the nationalists, with the latter being driven to the island. Faced with this political reality, the two sides across the Taiwan Strait went their separate ways in their interactions with the rest of the world. The mainland secured close ties with the former Soviet Union, while Taiwan continued its history of close ties with Japan and at the same time strengthened its special relationship with the US. Away from the otherwise unified language communication and distanced from the traditional central language community, the Taiwan linguistic sub-community continued the standard *Guoyu* 国语 (literally "national language"), which had been authorized in the mainland by taking it as the "official" language in its educational system and daily life across the island. As a result, loanwords in this unique community are characteristically at once both marginal and somewhat central. Specifically, the loanwords during the first 50 in its past over 100 years in Taiwan were predominantly of Japanese origin, indicating Japan's powerful colonial imprint; the loanwords in the next 70 years were predominantly of English origin, while many of those existing loanwords from Japanese remained in use (mostly by the old generation and indigenous peoples), with a continued inflow of new ones from Japanese. Here are four different types at a glance.

1   **Loanwords of Japanese origin** (more in Section 2.7.2 in Chapter 2):

   Duijue 对决: duel, confrontation, from *taiketsu*
   Chuzhang 出张: business trip, from *shutchyo*
   Tuiyuan 退院: hospital discharge, from *tai-in*
   Kanhufu 看护妇: nurse, from *kangofu*
   Liaoli 料理: cuisine, from *ryori*, from Early Chinese
   Shoudang 手当: subsidy, from *te-ate*
   Mamasheng 妈妈生: female boss of a hotel or eatery, from *mamasan*
   Xianu 下女: female servant, from *gejo*
   Mashaji 马杀鸡: massage, from *massaji*, from the English *massage*, from French
   Yinghua 映画: film, from *eiga*
   Qihua 企画: planning, from *kikaku*
   Zhenghe 整合: integrate, from *seiko*
   -Ting -町: neighborhood, township, from *-machi*/*-cho* (such as *Ximenting* 西门町 in Taipei)
   -Zu -族: a group of people sharing the same feature, from *-zoku* (such as *hongchunzu* 红唇族 or people who love to chew betel nuts; *tianjizu* 田鸡族 or people who habitually wear glasses; *qingchunzu* 青春族 or fashionable youth; *bailingzu* 白领族 or white-collar professionals; *kaichezu* 开车族 or people who drive a car to and for work; *kuzu* 酷族 or people who stay cool; and *luoyongzu* 裸泳族 or nude swimmers)

   Some others stay in local dialects in a more or less localized form such as those in Taiwanese Minnan dialect:
   $Lai^{53}ta^{21}$: cigarette lighter, from the Japanese *raita*, from the English *lighter*
   $La^{22}dzi^{55}o^{11}$: radio, from the Japanese *raji-o*, from the English *radio*
   $O^{44}to^{55}bai^{53}$: auto-bicycle, from the Japanese *otobai*, from the English *autobicycle*
   $T^{h}o^{22}la^{55}ku^{21}$: truck, from the Japanese *torakku*, from the English *truck*
   $P^{h}aŋ^{53}$: bread, from the Japanese *pan*, from the Portuguese *pao* or the Spanish *pan*
   $Se^{33}bi^{55}lo^{53}$: Western-style business dress, from the Japanese *sebirofuku*
   $Hu^{55}lo^{53}$: bathtub, from the Japanese *furo*

Classification of Chinese loanwords 161

The above loanwords are still used in speaking among the older generations, including indigenous peoples, while younger people seldom know or use them as they are mostly exposed to Guoyu (standard Chinese) and American English.

2 **Loanwords of English origin.** Taiwan inherited many loanwords of Western origin from people who moved to Taiwan from the mainland in and around 1949, many of which were first created in Shanghai. Isolated from the mainland and encouraged by political considerations, Taiwan had borrowed more loanwords from English since the 1950s. Phonetic and semantic approximation is very popular among phonemic loans, especially for commodity and brand names. Here are some examples:

Dakelong 达克龙 or *dakelun* 达可纶: from *Dacron*
Pangke 庞克/*pangkezu* 庞克族: from *punk*
Ku 酷: fashionably attractive or impressive, from *cool*
Peiji 培基: Basic, a computer programming language, from *Basic*
Miniqun 迷你裙: from *miniskirt*
Tuokouxiu 脱口秀: from *talk show*
-*Xiu*, in the last word above (same as -*sao* -骚 in Hong Kong), functions as a highly active suffix which keeps creating new compound words that are popular across the island, such as *zhengzhixiu* 政治秀, *mingrenxiu* 名人秀, *toumingxiu* 透明秀, *niurouchangxiu* 牛肉场秀 *gongdixiu* 工地秀, and *cantingxiu* 餐厅秀

3 **Loanwords of proper names.** As on the mainland, phonetic and semantic approximation is preferred (even more so in Taiwan) for proper names, such as:

Piaoya 飘雅: a shampoo brand, from *Pure*
Gaolujie 高露洁: a toothpaste brand, from *Colgate*
Jiaosheng 娇生: a brand of baby oil, from *Johnson & Johnson*
Lishi 丽仕 (known as *Lish* 力士 on the mainland, which is suggestive of masculinity, while the Taiwanese one is completely feminine): a soap brand, from *Lux*
Pailide 拍立得: a small camera that can take, develop, and print a photograph in a few seconds, from *Polaroid*
Lipawen 利怕蚊: a brand of mosquito repellent, from *Repellun*
Bianda 必安达 (*baoma* 宝马 in Hong Kong): a car brand, from *BMW*
Fuhao 富豪: a car brand, from *Volvo*

Taiwan also prefers Sinicizing loanwords of foreign personal names by choosing a typical Chinese family name for the first character and making the full name syllabically shorter so as to make them both phonetically and semantically a typical full Chinese name, such as:
Aisenhao 艾森豪: American President *Eisenhower*
Kelindun 柯林顿: American President *Clinton*

162 *Classification of Chinese loanwords*

Kasichu 卡斯楚: Cuban President *Castro*
Oubama 欧巴马: American President *Obama*

4 **Abbreviations in Lain letters**. The Taiwan language community has consistently been open, and seems to be more courageous than the mainland, in assimilating abbreviations in Latin letters. Invented in Taiwan, the peculiar yet unique blend of *Kala OK* 卡拉OK is a good example. Most such words are direct borrowings of the written forms of the English originals, such as *NG jingtou* NG镜头 (wrong or bad camera shot), *VS* (versus), *LD* (laser disc), *MTV* (music TV), and *DIY* (do-it-yourself)—as in *DIY jiaju* DIY 家具 (DIY furniture).

After the 1970s, when the two sides across the Strait resumed contact, there was a very sharp increase in bilateral communication over a very short period of time. With that came a two-way flow of various words and expressions. Taiwanese loanwords such as *Kala OK*, *KTV*, *leishe* 雷射, *mini-* 迷你-, *Tuofu* 托福 (TOEFL), and *biaozhi* 标致 (Peugeot) were instantly accepted and used on the mainland. Some words and expressions from the mainland were also adopted in Taiwan. Considering the current people-to-people interactions in terms of language use, the linguistic differences between the two sides will reduce to a manageable state, and the discrepancy is expected to narrow as well. With continued improvement in cross-strait relations and expanding ties, Taiwan's linguistic community might be expected to gradually return to a more common regional one.

4.3.5.2 *Hong Kong linguistic community*

Under British rule for over 100 years, Hong Kong had been comprehensively influenced by the English language in all sectors of society besides its language. As a result, the Cantonese dialect in Hong Kong became somewhat different from the original Cantonese in Guangzhou. One outstanding difference is loanwords and mixture with English on the part of the former. This is why some argue that the Chinese language used in Hong Kong, that is, the Hong Kong-style Cantonese dialect, is the most Westernized version of Chinese. After its return to China in 1997, the special intermediary status of the Hong Kong linguistic community is expected to gradually return to its regular regional status, yet the "high degree of autonomy" it has since enjoyed would mean that, for a long time to come, its great linguistic autonomy and strong intermediary nature will stay unchanged. All this can be reflected in its loanwords, as shown below.

1 *Loanwords with a fixed written form*. Some loanwords in Hong Kong have conventionally accepted written forms, and some even use invented dialectal characters solely to serve this purpose. Here are some examples (more in Section 3.3.2 in Chapter 3): *zheli* 遮喱/啫喱 (jelly), *gat¹* 咭 (card), *shidi* 士的

(walking stick, from *stick*), *zak*[1] 仄 (a printed form used to make payments from your bank account, from *check*), *wenna* 温拿 (winner), *pache* 泊车 (park a car, from *park*), *boshi* 波士 (boss), *shiduopili* 士多啤梨 (strawberry), *fei* 飞 (the money a passenger on public transport has to pay, from *fare*), *feilao* 肥佬 (not pass the test, from *fail*), *li* 軨 (elevator, from *lift*), *bo* 波 (ball, also female breast, from *ball*), *shalu* 沙律 (salad), *sheguo/diliguo/dilisheguo* 蛇果/地厘果/地厘蛇果 (an American red apple called Red Delicious, from *Delicious*), and *xiezhen* 写真 (pornographic photo, from Japanese *shyashin* from Early Chinese *xiezhen* "true-to-life portrait")

2   *Loanwords without a written form.* In Hong Kong, there are a lot of loanwords which do not have a specific or fixed written representation in Chinese characters—except their English source words—but only exist in its spoken communication, such as *feiʃi* (as in losing "face," from *face*), *fit* (as in keeping "fit," from *fit*), *fækʃi* (fax), *sen* (send), *fænʃi* (groupies, from *fans*), and *fulen/fæn* (friend/fan). Others simply take the foreign source word as (part of) its form, such as the previously mentioned *a sir* 阿 sir (male cop or teacher, sometimes facetiously written as *ashe* 阿蛇, though both the component "sir" and "she" here are pronounced /sœ/) and *call ji* call 机 (pager, "call" pronounced /kʰo/).

Considering British colonial rule, with its robust efforts to promote the use of English and a lack of official norms in Chinese usage in Hong Kong, loanword marginality in Hong Kong is far greater than in Taiwan. With increasing ties and interactions between Hong Kong and the mainland since its return in 1997, that marginality has been decreasing, and Hong Kong is bound to become linguistically closer to the mainland.

4.4 Semantic types

It is common practice to analyze a potential loanword from the perspective of its forms before we determine or identify whether it is a *bona fide* loanword. Actually, it can be analyzed and identified from the semantic angle by observing its possible conversions in semantics. Loanwords can be semantically divided into generic and proper-name types. Most of the former are conceptual in meaning and highly significant in terms of cognition and abstraction, while the latter do not have conceptual meanings and instead only have referential significance. That is why the latter are typically not included in the discussion of loanwords. The types may change from one to the other, usually from proper names to generic ones. For instance, the loanword *oumu* 欧姆 (*ohm*), the SI unit of electrical resistance, is named after German physicist Georg Simon Ohm, so, while Ohm is a proper name, ohm has been converted to a generic conceptual loanword. Since different makes of aircraft manufacturer *boying* 波音 (Boeing) are usually named in the pattern of the company's name followed by numbers and/or letters, Boeing changes from a proper name to a generic word for any airplane made by

Boeing. Conversely, once used in Media Center (*Meidiya* 梅地亚 in Chinese) as the name of a company and its office tower, the generic noun "media" becomes a proper noun. When the loanword *daban* 达坂 (mountain pass, from the Urdu *daban*) has been repeatedly used in referring to a certain mountain pass, it may gradually turn into a proper name, as in a well-known Chinese folk song titled "The Girl from Daban Cheng" (Daban Cheng meaning "the City of Daban"). So, this dichotomy between semantically generic and proper-name loanwords is anything but static.

4.4.1 Generic-word type

4.4.1.1 Three types of generic-word loans

Unlike proper nouns, the generic word refers to a whole class of things or concepts sharing the same characteristics rather than to one specific instance alone. Its semantic universality and abstraction determines that what is signified are many rather than one. Generally recognized loanwords are of a generic-word type, which can be divided into three kinds: conceptual, exclamatory, and onomatopoeic loanwords, though an undisputed one in the latter category is yet to be found. Theoretically speaking, there could also be function loanwords, which only perform some grammatical functions without any real semantic meanings, but with grammatical meanings instead, similar in function to Chinese particles, such as *de*的 or *le*了. To date, the Chinese language has not borrowed any such function words from others. This might prove that there are self-contained linguistic mechanisms and functions inherent in Chinese, as is the case with other major mature languages. Nevertheless, there are cases in which the Chinese language learns from other languages in terms of enhancing or expanding its linguistic functions, such as the borrowed new usage of *de* 的 in "noun + *de* + verb," like "zhebenshu *de* chuban" 这本书的出版 (literally "this book *de* publish," meaning "publication of this book") and "haizi *de* chusheng" 孩子的出生 (literally "child *de* born," meaning "the birth of the child"). However, this is beyond the scope of this book.

1. *Conceptual loanwords.* Conceptual loanwords are those which semantically describe the nature or essential attributes of the signified, such as boli 玻璃 (glass, from the Sanskrit *sphatika*), bocai 菠菜 (spinach, from the Nepalese *palinga*), puke 扑克 (poker), mengtaiqi 蒙太奇 (montage), liuming 流明 (a unit for measuring the rate of flow of light, from *lumen*), and saizuo 噻唑 (thiazole). Most of the Chinese loanwords borrowed now belong to this category.
2. *Exclamatory loanwords.* Very few in number, exclamatory or interjectory loanwords are those which are spoken to express an emotion or response without any conceptual meaning, such as haluo 哈罗 (hello), hayi 哈伊 (hello, from the Japanese *hai*), yaxia(xun) 亚夏(逊) (hurrah, from the Uighur *yasya* or *yasisun*), and wula 乌拉 (hurrah, from the Russian *ypa*).

4.4.1.2 Statistics about generic loanwords

1 *Parts of speech*. Loans of generic-word type are relatively stable, and conceptual loanwords can be nouns, verbs, adjectives, or adverbs. Here are the statistics on the number of loanwords included in the *Hanyu wailaici cidian* (Liu et al. 1984) according to their particular part of speech:

Word class	Number of occurrence	Example words
Noun	7,344	kexue 科学, guti 固体, anbu 安瓿 (ampule), puke 扑克 (poker)
Verb	122	quxiao 取消, qudi 取缔, paiqian 派遣, paoguang 抛光 (polishing)
Verb/noun	123	panjue 判决, piping 批评, xiangxiang 想象, niepan 涅槃
Adjective	89	zhudong 主动, sili 私立, neizai 内在, saiyin 塞音 (good, from Mongolian *sain*)
Adjective/noun	6	xiangdui 相对, ouran 偶然, modeng 摩登
Adjective/verb	1	mingque 明确
Adverb	7	nengdong 能动, qiangzhi 强制, wulun 勿伦 (not yet, from Malay *belum*)
Interjection	12	zha 喳 (yes or ok, from Manchu *ja*), wei 维 (yes or ok, from French *oui*)

The classification above, however, is broad and relative. There are several reasons for this. First, without sufficient textual and historical context of the word in question, it can only be an educated guess at best on the word class according to its semantic meaning. Second, in the Chinese language system, the usage of some loanwords is gradually developed only after their borrowing, not at the time at which they are borrowed. Third, some word classes cover so large a scope. Chinese nouns, for example, include those concerning the amount or number of a material or immaterial thing and those concerning location or position; Chinese adjectives also include attributive words (apart from predictive ones) and such lexical units, such as "subject + adjective," like *qisai* 其赛, which is borrowed from the Mongolian *ci sain* (literally "you good") but is lexicalized after its entry into Chinese). For all those complexities, we may still draw some general conclusions. Chinese loanwords predominantly borrow concepts of things. Adverb- and interjection-type loanwords are generally information-oriented rather than use-oriented. Those loanwords, which can each function, depending on the context, in the capacity of different word classes (e.g. verb and noun or adjective and verb), are mostly borrowed from Japanese. This is, for one thing, closely related to the fact that, in some cases in the Japanese language system, the same kanji has both noun and verb functions or uses (some nouns become a verb once added with する "suru").

166 Classification of Chinese loanwords

	English	Russian	French	Latin	Sanskrit	Arabic	Persian	Khitan	Mongolian	Tibetan	Manchu	Uighur	Malay	Japanese	Others	Total
Politics	225	35	21	18	7	7	15	47	105	99	49	17	2	142	171	960
Military	77	11	2	3	0	5	0	10	18	8	7	0	0	39	22	202
Economy	214	10	13	2	2	3	1	0	3	6	0	1	6	63	17	341
Industry	486	41	8	1	1	0	3	0	5	1	0	0	2	43	8	599
Science	645	9	7	7	3	0	0	0	1	0	0	0	0	93	2	767
Education	122	9	2	26	20	3	0	0	4	1	0	0	0	124	10	321
Health	370	24	6	1	18	4	4	2	3	2	4	0	0	58	9	505
Sport	337	139	23	2	10	1	3	0	17	24	2	18	0	60	114	750
Religion	112	6	2	7	408	63	9	1	65	43	2	12	0	9	43	782
Daily life	374	65	18	2	61	15	16	10	74	48	22	24	24	63	161	977
Agriculture	14	5	0	0	1	0	0	0	15	3	0	3	0	6	14	61
Measurement	59	13	39	4	6	1	0	0	0	1	19	1	1	13	11	149
Nature	344	29	11	4	160	19	33	8	53	10	19	3	25	25	101	844
Others	47	5	10	11	77	2	0	6	37	10	23	6	16	144	52	442
Total	3426	401	162	88	780	117	84	84	400	256	128	85	76	882	734	7704

Note: Here is a brief description of the 14 subject areas under which each loanword is listed in the table.

2   *Semantic statistics.* We take the loanwords included in the *Hanyu wailaici cidian* as the source data for our observation. Each loanword is categorized into 1 of the 14 topical areas (see the note below for a brief description). While those foreign languages from which at least 70 loanword entries in total are borrowed will be separately identified, those from which less than 70 are borrowed will simply be subsumed under "others" as their source language. Since data collection and word class categorization are all manually conducted, occasional deviations may be inevitable, and classification such as this is no doubt relative and arbitrary as some words simply defy easy grouping. These imperfections notwithstanding, the big picture is still clear, as shown in the above tabulation of the number of loanwords from a specific foreign source language in 1 of the 14 subject areas.

1 **Politics**: hierarchical ranks, titles, etc. in politics, law, society, or among individual persons
2 **Military**: military forces, war, casualties, etc.
3 **Economy**: economic terms, currencies, etc.
4 **Industry**: industry, industrial products, technologies, etc.
5 **Science**: natural sciences, psychology, etc.
6 **Education**: social sciences, humanities, archeology, philosophy, logic, education, publishing, etc.
7 **Health**: medical science, health, medical treatment, medicine, etc.
8 **Sport**: culture, literature, art, sports, entertainment, etc.
9 **Religion**: religion, religious titles, religious holidays, etc.
10 **Daily life**: daily life, general public holidays, general forms of address, etc.
11 **Agriculture**: forestry, fishery, husbandry, hunting, etc.
12 **Measurement**: general weights and measurements
13 **Nature**: animals, plants, minerals, precious metals and stones, natural landscape, celestial bodies, days, etc.
14 **Others**: all other subject areas which cannot be included in the above 13 categories

As can be seen from the above data, what the Chinese language community cares about or needs the most, as far as lexical borrowing is concerned, are terms related to the fields of politics, economics (including industry), natural sciences (including medicine and health), daily life, and the natural world.

4.4.2 Proper name-type loanwords

A proper name is a symbol or word that designates a unique individual, place, event, brand, institution, etc. Some institutional names are composed of a combination of both proper and common nouns, such as "Harvard

University." What will be discussed in this section is the proper name in a narrower sense (e.g. "Harvard") rather than in a broad sense (e.g. "Harvard University"). This kind of proper name is generally not conceptual in reference or associated with the essential attributes of the signified but instead is a mere marker. Theoretically speaking, all foreign proper names can become loanwords of one's own nation, and those loanwords are mostly phonemic ones, though such borrowing *en masse* would certainly not be as meaningful, in practice, as with those of a non-proper name type. Considering this, it is quite understandable that loanwords in the narrower sense of the term are often limited to those of a generic type, i.e., of non-proper name type. Still, what is referred to in quite a few proper name-type loanwords may contain strong cultural overtones, so those proper names themselves are subsequently tinged with similar connotations or even extended figurative implications, so much so that they are not merely bland proper names but ones given some special significance, such as *Yesu* 耶稣 (Jesus), *Shijiamouni* 释迦牟尼 (Shakyamuni, the founder of Buddhism), *Aiyinsitan* 爱因斯坦 (Einstein), *Haolaiwu* 好莱坞 (Hollywood), and *Kekou kele* 可口可乐 (Coca Cola). Proper name-type loanwords can generally be divided into marker-only proper names and associative ones.

4.4.2.1 Marker-only proper names

These loanwords are mere markers or indicators of a unique individual, place, event, brand, or institution without any conceptual connotation. They can be further divided into the following three kinds:

1 Phonemic loans in Chinese characters. These are the most common and most widely used words, such as *Engesi* 恩格斯 (Engels), *Kennidi* 肯尼迪 (Kennedy), *Liening* 列宁 (Lenin), *Lundun* 伦敦 (London), *Niuyue* 纽约 (New York), and *Bali* 巴黎 (Paris).
2 Graphemic loans in the original Latin letters. Graphemic loanwords in the original Latin letters are usually read according to the pronunciation of the component source letters. These loans are mostly corporate or brand names in abbreviated forms. Their somewhat indicative functions are limited to phonetic or graphemic aspects rather than the essential attributes of the signified, so they remain under the category of marker-only proper names. Examples include USA, IBM, AT&T, SONY, NHK, and BBC.
3 Graphemic loans in Chinese characters. These are all borrowed from Japanese as some proper names in Japan, mainly those of places, are written in Chinese characters which do not mean anything except for the proper name, such as *Naba* 那霸 (place name, from the Japanese *Naha*), *Fushi* 富士 (place and personal name, from *Fuji*), and *Jiuliumi* 久留米 (place and personal name, from *Kurume*).

4.4.2.2 Associative place names

These loanwords are such that their graphemic forms can partially suggest the attributes of the signified. They can be further divided into the following two kinds:

1. Semantic Sinicization. Words of this kind are phonemic loans but semantically Sinicized through the use of some highly associative Chinese characters. Typical Chinese family names, for example, are chosen to phonetically approximate the sound of the first syllable of the foreign name. This is very popular practice in Hong Kong and Taiwan, such as in *Daizhuoer/Chaiqier/Sheqier Furen* 戴卓尔/柴契尔/佘契尔 夫人 ("Madame Thatcher," known as "Saqieer Furen" 撒切尔夫人 in mainland China, from *Thatcher*), *Hangsiji* 杭斯基 (linguist Noam Chomsky, known as "Qiaomusiji" 乔姆斯基 in mainland China, from *Chomsky*), *Haidi* 海地 (Haiti), *Fandigang* 梵蒂冈 (Vatican), and *Luoshanji* 洛杉矶 (Los Angeles).
2. Graphemic loans in the original Chinese characters. Historically, names were written all in Chinese characters in North and South Korea, Vietnam, and Japan. Though Chinese characters are not used in Vietnam any longer, its personal and place names still match their corresponding Chinese characters. Loanwords of this kind are most often borrowed from Japanese, followed by Korean. Characters in many of those proper names do contain some meaning, but the meaning is irrelevant to the essential attribute of the signified, such as in *Dajiangjiansanlang* 大江健三郎 (Japanese writer, from the Japanese *Oe Kenzaburo*), *Jinli* 金笠 (Korean satirical poet, from the Korean *Rip Kim*), *Liuchonglu* 刘重庐 (Vietnamese writer, from the Vietnamese *Lưu Trọng Lư*), *Dongjing* 东京 (from the Japanese *Tokyo*), *Daban* 大阪 (from the Japanese *Osaka*), *Hancheng* 汉城 (now *Shouer* 首尔, from *Seoul*), and *Xinyizhou* 新义州 (a border city in North Korea, from the Korean *Sinŭiju*).
3. Phonemic semantic loans, such as *Xin Yinggelan* 新英格兰 (New England), *Xindeli* 新德里 (New Delhi), *Dazhongma* 大仲马 (Alexandre Dumas, père), and *Xiaozhongma* 小仲马 (Alexandre Dumas, fils).

4.4.3 Terminology-type loanwords

When the scope of use or application is added into the current semantic classification of loanwords, those of generic-word type can be further divided into terminology and daily-life (non-terminology) subtypes. Terminology, needless to say, refers to the special terms used in a special subject, such as *jiyin* 基因 (gene), *leida* 雷达 (radar), *aizibing* 艾滋病 (AIDS), *kelong* 克隆 (clone), *kexue* 科学 (science, from the Japanese *kagaku*), *zhengfa* 蒸发 (evaporate, from Japanese *johatsu*), *DNA*, and *GPS*. In contrast, non-terminology or daily-life loanwords include words such as *baibai* 拜拜, *T xu* T恤, *xiangbo* 香波, *bulaji* 布拉吉, *weizhisu* 味之素 (a Japanese food and biotechnology corporation well-known for its original MSG product, from the Japanese *ajinomoto*), *kanban* 看板 (a scheduling system for lean manufacturing and just-in-time manufacturing, from the Japanese *kanban*), *e'niang* 额娘, *anda* 安达, *reba* 热巴, *zhe* 嚡, and *OK*. These two subtypes do not always have a fixed line of demarcation but may overlap or change from one to the other. The daily-life loanword *zhan* 站 (meaning "stop" or "post," from the Mongolian *jam*), for example, can become a technical term in communication or transport science. The originally technical term *weitamin* 维他命 (vitamin) has also become part of the everyday lexicon through frequent use.

Beyond the above examples, terminology-type loanwords may, in a broader sense, encompass the technical or special terms or expressions used in a business, industry, art, science, religion, or special subject, such as *fanshilin* 凡士林 (vaseline), *biji* 哔叽 (beige), *pusa* 菩萨, *jialan* 珈蓝, *niepan* 涅槃, and *ahong* 阿訇 (a Persian title for an Islamic cleric, from the Persian *akhund*). Seen from this broad perspective, it seems that a majority of loanwords of the generic-word type are associated in one or another way with terminology; those of Sanskrit origin are predominantly Buddhist terms.

Serving the most meaningful and valuable part of the lexicon in facilitating socio-cultural development, terminology, especially in the narrow sense of the word, is something of a node, marked by its unambiguous referential meaning in the conceptual network of a particular subject, cause, or industry and a section in the epistemological deductive system from which to infer more new concepts or nodes so as to push back the cognitive boundaries of cultural and social understanding.

Well aware of the significance of terminology to science and society in this regard, Chinese scholars have for quite a long time been dedicated to studying loanwords from the angle of terminology, such as in their research on terms in chemistry, including chemical elements. It is therefore hoped that research taking this approach will enjoy greater and more enduring growth.

4.5 Loanwords of Japanese origin

4.5.1 Etymological disputes in the Sino-Japanese lexical exchanges[3]

Japan-made Chinese words which are read according to the pronunciation of the kanji characters in the originating Chinese dialect at the time during which the word was introduced into Japanese (on-yomi) are not treated as Japanese *gairaigo* (loanwords). Japanese was originally a blend of the aboriginal language and an Altaic language from the northwest. Since their coming to Japan in the 1st century, a considerable number of Han Chinese people have entered the Japanese ruling hierarchy, making the Han Chinese language the only official written language in Japan. Through integration over a long period of time between Han Chinese and local Japanese people, Chinese was also integrated as part of the Japanese language by means of lexical form and word formation. Since Chinese was a participant in the later stages of linguistic blend, Japan never considers the Chinese used in the Japanese language *gairaigo*. By the same token, those borrowed words which originated in Japan and formed according to the Japanese means of character combination had long been denied the status of loanwords, until the 1950s, when such statuses started to be recognized but were still differentiated from other loanwords. Indeed, except for a few, it is impossible to distinguish Japan-made on-yomi words from autochthonous Chinese words. For lack of a better word, many of those pairs are temporarily termed "words of the same graphic form" because they are so inextricably intertwined that it is often the case that those which have previously been confirmed by many scholars as autochthonous Chinese (or Japan-made Chinese) now reexamined with newly discovered evidence ,and it is discovered that the opposite is true.

The relevant research so far indicates that Sino-Japanese lexical exchanges in modern times were a two-way process rather than moving just from Japan to China. For example, recent research shows that the word *qianbi* 铅笔 (pencil), which used to be considered a loanword from Japanese, turns out that it was first used or invented in the Chinese language as a semantic loan from English. In both the original *Huaying tongyu* 華英通語 (*Chinese and English Phrase Book*), compiled by Chinese scholar Ziqing 子卿 in 1855, and the later version, expanded with phonetic transcriptions and Japanese interpretation in kana (a Japanese syllabic writing, as distinguished from Japanese written in kanji or Chinese characters) in 1860 in Japan by Japanese educator Fukuzawa Yukichi, the Chinese loanword *qianbi* was included under its original English meaning, "lead pencil." Indeed, *qianbi* had already appeared in various writings in China in the 1860–1870s. For example, the *Ziyu huijie* 字语汇解 (*An Anglo-Chinese Vocabulary of the Ningpo Dialect*), published in 1876 by William T. Morrison, an American Presbyterian missionary based in eastern China's treaty port of Ningbo (Ningpo), and the *Yinghua zidian* 英华字典 in 1882 both rendered the entry word "pencil" or "lead pencil" as *qianbi*. In Japan, by contrast, it was in 1873 that *qianbi* appeared in a German-Japanese dictionary; it also appeared in an English-Japanese dictionary in 1885.

Take *Tianzhu* 天主 (Lord of Heaven or God) as a second example. Many scholars think this is borrowed from Japanese, but it had already been used as early as 1584 in the *Tianzhu shengjiao shilu* 天主圣教实录 (*True Meaning of the Lord of Heaven*), published in Guangzhou by Italian Jesuit priest Michele Ruggieri. In 1704, both *tianzhu* and *tianzhujiao* 天主教 were used in imperial China's translation of a papal interdict in which it was stated that "the two-character word *tianzhu*" had been "in use for a long time" (*yijing rijiu*) in China. All these historical facts refute the argument that it was originated from Japanese.

Jidu 基督 (Christ) is another case in point. It has long been held that this word originated from the Japanese translation *Jilisidu* 基利斯督, later abbreviated in the current form, and was then introduced to China. The fact is that Westerners came to China before they came to Japan. Italian Jesuit priest Matteo Ricci (1552–1610), popularly known as Li Madou 利玛窦 in China, lived in imperial China's Ming dynasty in the late 16th century. The dissemination of Western religions in East Asia also started in China before it expanded to Japan and the rest of the region. It is simply impossible that the translation and authorization of such major proper names in religions had not already been done until after they entered Japan. Phonetically speaking, "Christ" in Japanese is actually *Kirisuto*, while *Jilisidu*, according to the Japanese pronunciation system, would be Ki-ri-shi-toku, which is generally believed to be from the Portuguese Cristo/Christo. Compared with *Kirisuto* and Ki-ri-shi-toku, Jilisidu in the Cantonese pronunciation /gei¹lei⁶si¹duk¹/ is clearly more in line with the sound of the original Western word. In *Xinyizhaoshu* 新遗诏书, Robert Morrison's Chinese version of the New Testament, "Christ" was already translated as *Jilishidu* 基利士督, and in 1837, the word *jidu* also appeared in the December issue of the *Dongxiyangkao meiyue tongjizhuan* 东西洋考每月统记传 (*Eastern Western Monthly Magazine*), the first modern Chinese-language magazine founded by the Prussian Protestant missionary Karl Gützlaff. Therefore, it is most probable that "Christ" was first translated into Chinese before being introduced to Japan via missionaries.

Take *huaxue* 化学 (chemistry) as one last example. In Japan, the Chinese word first appeared in the 1860s in the early Meiji era, whereas it had already been used in 1856 in the *Gewu tanyuan* 格物探原 (*In search of the Roots of Science*) by Alexander Williamson, a British missionary in China. Again, it is very probable that the Chinese word of *huaxue* for the term "chemistry" was first used in China.

It should be admitted that Western missionaries have made great contributions to both the cultural exchanges between China and the rest of the world, and the introduction of modern science to China. One of the best known was Matteo Ricci, who came to China in 1582, wrote books in Chinese, including *Wanguo tushuo* 万国图说 and *Qiankun tiyi* 乾坤体义, and co-translated *Euclid's Elements* with Xu Guangqi 徐光启, all of which disseminated, among other things, Western knowledge of the world geography, astronomy, and geometry across China. In terms of lexicographical contribution and translation of terms, Western missionaries, along with their Chinese assistants, carried out impressive and practical research in the early 19th century into the Chinese language by compiling books and dictionaries. These Chinese-English dictionaries include *Huaying zidian* 华英字典 (*A Dictionary of Chinese Language*, 1815–1823) and *Guangdongsheng tuhua zihui* 广东省土话字汇 (*Vocabulary of the Canton Dialect*, 1828), both by Robert Morrison; *Hanying yunfu* 汉英韵府 (*A Syllabic Dictionary of the Chinese Language*, 1874) by Samuel Wells Williams; *Hanying xiuzhen zidian* 汉英袖

珍字典 (*A Chinese and English Pocket Dictionary*, 1874) by George C. Stent; *Guangzhou fangyan hanying cidian* 广州方言汉英辞典 (*A Chinese Dictionary in the Cantonese Dialect*, 1877) by Ernest John Eitel; and *Huaying zidian* 华英字典 (*A Chinese-English Dictionary*, 1892) by Herbert Giles. Their English-Chinese dictionaries include *Yinghan zidian* 英汉字典 (*English and Chinese Dictionary*, 1847–1848) by Walter Henry Medhurst, *Yinghua zidian* 英华字典 (*English–Chinese Dictionary*, 1866–1869) by Wilhelm Lobscheid, and *Ziyu huijie* 字语汇解 (1876). Most of these dictionaries were compiled for Cantonese speakers, except for the last one, which was prepared exclusively for speakers of the Ningbo sub-dialect, part of the Wu dialect in East China.

Research into these dictionaries (and other historical resources) also reveals that many of what have hitherto been regarded as loanwords of Japanese origin were actually invented by Chinese people or the missionaries stationed in China, and later introduced into Japan and accepted in its dictionaries for widespread use. Below is a very brief comparison based on four dictionaries (two from each country) which were all published in the 19th century. The two dictionaries in China are *Yinghan zidian* by W. H. Medhurst and *Yinghua zidian* by W. Lobscheid. The two dictionaries in Japan are 英和対訳袖珍辞書 or えいわたいやくしゅうちんじしょ (*A Pocket Dictionary of the English and Japanese Language*) by Hori Tatsunosuke (PD for short), the very first English-Japanese dictionary in Japan, and 附音挿図英和字彙 (*An English and Japanese Dictionary, Explanatory, Pronouncing, and Etymological, Containing All English Words in Present Use, with an Appendix*) by Masayoshi Shibata and Takashi Koyasu (EJD for short).

Borrowed source word	Yinghan zidian 1847–1848	Yinghua zidian 1866	PD 1862	EJD 1873
Adjudge	shenpan 审判	shenpan 审判	罪ヲ言ヒ付ル, panduan 判断	裁判スル
Apostle	shitu 使徒	shitu 使徒	zongtu 宗徒, shitu 使徒	耶苏ノ徒弟
Lord	Tianzhu 天主	Tianzhu 天主	N/A	N/A
Christ	Jidu 基督	Jidu 基督	Xijiao 西教	Jidu 基督
Passion	nu 怒, xingqing 性情	shounan 受难	教祖ノ受タル难	耶苏ノ苦难
Catholicism	N/A	Tianzhujiao 天主教	罗马宗旨ノ人	罗马教
Propagate	chuanjiao 传教	xuanchuan 宣传	弘メル	弘ル, 博ル
Meditation	canchan 参禅	moxiang 默想	思ヒ计ル	moxiang 默想
Truth	zhenli 真理	zhenli 真理	xinyi 信义, xinshi 信实	xinshi 信实, xinyi 信义

Again, it can be seen from the above table of comparison that, in the early stage, many of the borrowed words were actually first invented in the dictionaries published in China whose translated language was Chinese or by scholars or officials in China. Obviously heavily influenced by this, Japan then could possibly have started to use those words. Thanks to their necessary advice and aid in the compilation of the dictionaries by the missionaries, those Chinese assistants played an indispensable role in the actual wording of a particular translated term. So, it is reasonable to argue that many of the borrowed words in Japan at the time were not only from Chinese but also half-directly and half-indirectly influenced by it.

However, since those missionary-compiled dictionaries were largely used within the church or its related activities in South China at the time, they were not widely disseminated and therefore did not really take root on Chinese linguistic soil. Once introduced to Japan, however, they were quickly absorbed into the Japanese language in renovating some of the Japanese borrowed words. The works aimed to introduce Japanese culture by those Chinese officials and scholars who had been to Japan received a similar reader response. It was at the turn of the last century that those words had a return flow and gradually took root in China.

The humiliating Chinese defeat in the First Sino-Japanese War (1894–1895) triggered a reform movement that attempted to renovate the government, which, in turn, started to send funded students to study in Japan and the US. From 1903 to 1904 alone, many books were translated by those students overseas. Publication of these translated works in the Chinese homeland drastically changed the vernacular lexicon of the urban public, especially in such coastal cities as Shanghai, where new terms in law and social sciences filled the press clamoring for modern civilization. The extent of their impact on China at the time can be gleaned from the many borrowed words which were either of Japanese origin or return loans from Japan (more on this in Section 2.5.3 in Chapter 2).

This impact can be seen from a brief illustration of three English-Chinese dictionaries in China in the early 20th century. The *Yinghua dacidian* 英华大辞典 (*English-Chinese Standard Dictionary*, The Commercial Press, 1908) by US-educated Chinese scholar Yan Huiqing (Weiching Williams Yen) 颜惠庆, clearly acknowledged that it had drawn on the wisdom of Japan's English-Japanese dictionaries. The *English-Chinese Dictionary of the Standard Chinese Spoken Language and Handbook for Translators, including Scientific, Technical, Modern, and Documentary Terms* (Statistical Department of the Inspectorate General of Customs, 1916), by German Karl Ernst Georg Hemeling at the invitation of Yan Fu 严复, stated in its Preface that the modern terms were built on its assimilation from ancient Chinese and Japanese. The *Zonghe yinghan dacidian* 综合英汉大辞典 (*A Comprehensive English-Chinese Dictionary*, The Commercial Press, 1928) by Huang Shifu 黄士复 and Jiang Tie 江铁 obviously copied a lot of nouns and loanwords from Japanese dictionaries. Used in the titles of two of the above three dictionaries, the word *cidian* 辞典 (dictionary) itself was also an obvious borrowing from Japanese *jiten* 辞典 as *zidian* 字典 had been the conventional word for "dictionary" in China. For easier illustration, nine English words are selected; the *Yinghua zidian* (1866) is also included here for comparison.

Source word	Yinghua zidian 1866	Yinghua dacidian 1908	ECD 1916	Zonghe yinghan dacidian 1928
Science	xue 学	xue 学, zhi 智, zhuanmenxue 专门学, kexue 科学	kexue 科学[n]	kexue 科学
Revolution	bian 变, luan 乱, panni 叛逆	biange 变革, geming 革命, neibian 内变	geming 革命, biange 变革[a]	geming 革命
Cadre	N/A	liandui zhi bianzhi 连队之编制	ganbu 干部[n]	(army) liandui zhi ganbu 连队之干部
Philosophy	lixue 理学	aizhi 爱智, zhexue 哲学	zhexue 哲学	zhexue 哲学
Space	difang 地方, jian 间	kongjian 空间, kongchu 空处	kongjian 空间	kongjian 空间
Abstract	chan 禅, xuexin 虚心	lilunde 理论的, chouxiangde 抽象的	xuanxiang 悬想[a]	chouxiang 抽象
Century	yibainian 一百年	yibainian 一百年	yibainian 一百年, shiji 世纪	shiji 世纪
Procedure	fa 法	fa 法, zhixu 秩序, cidi 次第	shouxu 手续[n]	shouxu 手续
Formalities	lifa 礼法	chengfa 成法, changli 常例	shouxu 手续	shouxu 手续

Note: In the ECD (*English-Chinese Dictionary of the Standard Chinese Spoken Language and Handbook for Translators*), any word with a superscript "n" means that the ECD marked it as a new term, while any word with a superscript "a" means that the ECD marked it as one authorized by the then Ministry of Education.

The above comparison roughly echoes the general view that the *Yinghua zidian* was independently compiled, while the other three were variously influenced by Japan. The more recent the dictionary was, the more influence it accepted from Japan. Specifically, both the *Yinghua dacidian* and the *ECD* still did part of their independent work in translating new terms, apart from drawing on the wisdom of Japanese dictionaries, but the *Zonghe yinghan dacidian* was so slack that almost all of its contents were directly copied from Japanese dictionaries. It is little wonder that it is criticized for "plagiarizing Japanese and the annotations being interspersed with many confounding Japanese words."[4] It is no wonder either that Wang Li 王力 (1900–1986), the founder of modern Chinese linguistics, pointed out that "itching for

176 *Classification of Chinese loanwords*

convenience, those Chinese compilers of dictionaries of Western languages (especially English) simply copied the translated wording from Western language dictionaries compiled by Japanese" (1958:528). Wang's remark suggests that it is not only the compilers of the *Zonghe yinghan dacidian* who did this; in fact, it became common practice. To be fair, that dictionary, or its likes, did so not on the spur of the moment but as an attempt to follow both the tradition and the trend at that time. That somewhat explains why many of the terms adopted in that dictionary are still in use today, almost 100 years later. It also proves the view that the faster the borrowing and the more the borrowed words, the quicker the development of the borrowing nation. In that sense, dictionaries of this category still deserve due credit for their contribution to the establishment and dissemination of properly translated terms and the development of the modern Chinese lexicon.

4.5.2 Classification of the loanwords originated from Japanese

It must be admitted that, whether they are original loans (autochthonous Japanese words) or return loans (terms that already existed in earlier Chinese texts and still have the same meaning but, through their use in Japanese, later came back into use in Chinese), loans of Japanese origin are one form of cultural exchange between the two countries and therefore should receive serious academic attention. So far, there have already been different classifications of Chinese loans from Japanese.[5] A proper approach to such a classification should consider the way in which Chinese as the borrowing language corresponds to Japanese as the borrowed language. What is critical here is the means of borrowing in not only phonemic but also graphic and semantic aspects. When all three aspects are taken into account, such loanwords, with their distinctive features, can adequately be differentiated from those of non-Japanese origin while still remaining under the same broader category as the latter. Considering the above three aspects, loanwords of Japanese origin can be divided into the following three categories, each of which is further divided.

4.5.2.1 Graphic loans in which the meaning of the kanji used is applied

This category holds the largest number and constitutes the core of the loanwords of Japanese origin. Seen from the Japanese origin, these words can be pure semantic loans of Western words, phonemic semantic loans, or graphic loans of Chinese words upon which new meanings are imposed.

Semantic loans of Western words. There are five kinds of such loanwords.

1. Loanwords which already existed in Early Chinese but were borrowed into Japanese as semantic loans of Western words. These words can be perceived to have their original meanings extended or transformed;

hence, a kind of "quasi-loanwords" or "quasi-autochthonous Chinese words," depending upon which language direction they are perceived in. There are quite of few words of this type.

Jingji 经济: used in Japan as a semantic loan of the English "economy," later with an extended meaning of "economical." As the abbreviation of the phrase *jingshi jimin* 经世济民 in Early Chinese, *jingji* was used to administer the society and help the populace. The term was used in the biography of Wang Anshi 王安石 (1021–1086), a Chinese prose writer and governmental reformer best known for his advocacy for "New Policies" (1069–76), contained in the *Songshi* 宋史, the official dynastic history of the Song dynasty (960–1279), in which there was an impressive evaluation of him by Zhu Xi 朱熹 (1130–1200), a great Confucian scholar: "On Anshi, Zhu Xi once remarked that he was renowned for his excellent writing and character but, on top of that, he felt duty-bound to be moral, to *administer the society, and to help the populace* (朱熹尝论安石，以文章节行高一世，而尤以道德经济为己任)." *Jingji* is also extended to mean "economics."

Geming 革命: used in Japan as a semantic loan of the English "revolution." The word originally appeared in the *Yijing* 易经 (or *I-Ching*, meaning "*Classic of Changes*"), an ancient classic on divination and fortune-telling, especially esteemed by the Confucians: "With the change on heaven and earth came the smooth running of the four seasons. The first kings of the Shang and Zhou dynasties both *launched a revolution* because it followed both the mandate of heaven and the will of people (天地革而四时成。汤武革命，顺乎天而应乎人)." Later on, *geming* was also used as a verb and an adjective.

Jiaotong 交通: used in Japan as a semantic loan of the English "traffic." In Early Chinese, the word originally meant "communicate" or "make friends" as it appeared in the *Shiji* 史记 ("Historical Records"), early history of China, written in about 85BC by Sima Qian: "All the acquaintances he made were either of outstanding talent or very treacherous (诸所与交通，无非豪桀大猾)."

Jiaoshou 教授: used in Japan as a semantic loan of the English "professor." In Early Chinese, it originally meant "teach and impart learning," as it appeared again in the *Shiji* on one of the prominent disciples of Confucius: "Zixia went to live in Xihe, engaging in teaching and became private teacher of the founding king of the Wei (子夏居西河教授，为魏文侯师)."

2 Japanese loanwords in which Chinese morphemes (i.e. kanji characters) are innovatively combined to form individual words by the Japanese language as semantic loans of Western terms. Though also considered "quasi-loanwords," they are closer to the archetypal or *bona fide* loanword. Words of this type have the largest number, such as *ganbu* 干部

(from the Japanese *kanbu*) for the French *cadre*, *paiqiu* 排球 (Japanese *haikyu*) as semantic loan of volleyball (but now an equivalent phonemic loan is used in Japan instead), and *meishu* 美术 (Japanese *bijutsu*) for art.

3 Loanwords formed by Japan-made kanji. Not many in number, words of this type are created either by adding an already existing semantic element (called "radical") to an already existing phonetic or semantic element. Since both the sound and the meaning of the newly formed word either correspond to or are associated with those of their respective original kanji, they are also put under this general category,[6] such as *xian* 腺, *nian* 鯰 (from the Japanese *nen* or *namazu*, semantic marker *yu* 鱼 or "fish" + phonetic element *nian* 念, replaced by *nianyu* 鲇鱼 now), and *zhi* 膣 (vagina, from *chitsu*).

4 Loanwords formed with Japanese morphemes but written in kanji (i.e. taking a *kun-yomi* reading) as semantic loans of Western terms. These words are not many, such as *zuhe* 组合 (association or union, from the Japanese *kumiai*; mathematical combination, from the Japanese *kumiawase*), *jiefang* 借方 (debit, from the Japanese *karikata*), and *yindu* 引渡 (extradition, from *hikiwatashi*).

5 Loanwords formed with Chinese characters on a half-*kun-yomi* and half-*on-yomi* reading. Words of this type are extremely few, such as *shengfushou* 胜负手 (win-or-lose move, from the Japanese *shobu-te*) and *shouzukoubing* 手足口病 (hand, foot, and mouth disease, from the Japanese *teashikuchi-byo*).

Phonemic semantic loanwords. Extremely few, these words mainly borrow phonemically but also use kanji for semantic purposes. They are divided into the following three kinds:

6 *Kun-yomi*-type phonemic loans in which Early Chinese words are used, such as *maijiu* 麦酒 (Japanese *biru*) as a kun-yomi phonemic loan of the Dutch *bier* ("beer" in English). *Maijiu* was not the same thing as beer today but was instead wine made from barley as it was used in the *Houhanshu* 后汉书 (*Book of the Later Han*, covering the history of the Han dynasty from 6 to 189AD): "When Wang Huan was promoted to the governor of Hanyang and about to leave for Hanyang, Fan Ran then along with his younger brother Fan Xie carried *maijiu* on foot and waited for Wang on the road (奂迁汉阳太守，将行，冉乃与弟协步赍麦酒，于道侧设坛以待之)."

7 *On-yomi*-type phonemic semantic loans, such as *julebu* 俱乐部 (club) and *huliela* 虎列辣 or 虎列剌 (cholera).

8 Loanwords formed by Japan-invented kanji by adding a semantic element as the radical to another semantic element with an extended meaning and phonetically treated as phonemic loans or according to *kun-yomi*. Words of this type are very few, such as *li* 粴 (Japanese *senchimetoru*, as a phonemic loan of *centimetre*) and *xue* 鳕 (cod, from Japanese kun-yomi *tara*, a combination of *yu* 鱼, "fish," + *xue* 雪, "snow," suggesting the cold region where cod lives).

Graphic loans of Chinese words upon which new meanings are imposed. Words of this category are not translated from Western languages but are mainly representative of things very distinctive in Japanese society. They are not many but can be divided into two classes.

9 Japan-made Chinese words formed with *on-yomi* kanji, such as *huadao* 花道 (*kado*, the Japanese art of flower arrangement), *paiju* 俳句 (*haiku*, a type of short Japanese poem with three lines, consisting of five, seven, and five syllables), *renliche* 人力车 (*jinrikisha*, rickshaw, a light, two-wheeled hooded vehicle drawn by one person), *jizhong* 集中 (concentrate or focus, from the Japanese *shuchu*), renxuan 人选 (candidate, from the Japanese *jinsen*), and *richeng* 日程 (agenda or schedule, from the Japanese *nittei*)

10 Words borrowed from Early Chinese to express Japanese things, such as *roudao* 柔道 (judo), which, in Early Chinese, originally meant "soft or gentle way or means," as said by Emperor Guangwu 光武帝 (5 BC–57 AD) of the Han dynasty in the *Houhanshu*: "I would also act in a gentle soft way to govern the country (吾理天下, 亦欲以柔道行之)," and *langren* 浪人 (tramp, from Japanese *ro-nin*), which, in Early Chinese, meant "a person without a settled home or regular work who wanders from place to place," as in the *Lichi zhuan* 李赤传 (Biography of Li Chi) by Liu Zongyuan 柳宗元 (773–819), Chinese poet and prose writer: "Li Chi is a *langren* (李赤, 江湖浪人也)."

11 Words from kanji on a kun-yomi reading. Words of this type are not many, such as *changhe* 场合 (occasion, from the Japanese *ba-ai*), *shouxu* 手续 (procedure, from the Japanese *te-tsuzuki*), and *daxiao* 打消 (cast aside, abandon an idea, from the Japanese *uchikeshi*, originally meaning "cancel some motion or proposal through a certain procedure").

4.5.2.2 Graphic loans in which the meaning of the kanji used is not applied

12 Words which are autochthonous Japanese or as phonemic loans of Western terms and are written in kanji on an on-yomi reading. Since none of the kanji keeps its meaning, there is an element of phonemic borrowing when it is loaned from Japanese to Chinese, somewhat similar to the phonetic adjustment within different dialects. Chinese pronunciation of these words is considerably different from that of their Japanese source words. Quite a few in number, words of this kind also differ from other Chinese phonemic loanwords from Western languages. Examples include *shousi* 寿司 (sushi), *wasi* 瓦斯 (from the Japanese *gasu* as a phonemic loan of the Dutch *gas*), *jiadaer* 加答儿 (now *kata* 卡他 in contemporary Chinese, from the Japanese *kataru* as a phonemic loan of the Dutch *catarrh*), and *caoda* 曹达 (*suda* 苏打 in contemporary Chinese, from the Japanese *sōda* as a phonemic loan of the Dutch *soda*).

4.5.2.3 Chinese phonemic loans of Japanese origin

13 Chinese phonemic loanwords from Japanese. Extremely few in number, these words are those which are phonemic loans (all or partially in Chinese characters) of Japanese terms, which are usually written in kana or in the combination of kana and kanji, such as *kala OK* 卡拉OK (karaoke, from Japanese *kara-oke*, *kara* meaning "empty, without" and *oke* meaning "orchestra"), *sinaku* 斯纳库 (a small, slightly porn-style hotel provided with simple meals and girls accompanying alcoholic drinking, from the Japanese *sunakku*, borrowed from the English *snack* bar), *duosang* 多桑 (father, used in Taiwan, from the Japanese *tosan*), and *oubasang* 欧巴桑 (old lady, used in Taiwan, from the Japanese *obasan*).

14 Some few phonemic loanwords with semantic approximation, such as the previously discussed pajinku/pajingong/bajinku 扒金库/扒金宫/拔金库 (Japanese *pachinko*).

15 Some Japanese homemade Romanized acronyms, such as NHK (Nippon Hoso Kyokai 日本放送協会, Japan Broadcasting Corporation).

4.6 Pidgin English (*Yangjingbang*) and linguistic mixture

4.6.1 Yangjingbang

Yangjingbang 洋泾浜 (also *Yangkingpang* or *Yang King Pang*) used to be a natural stream of water in Shanghai, which became its southern border canal during the British concession in 1845 and later separated the French from the British and American concessions. To local Shanghainese or perhaps even all Chinese, this long culverted canal on which Avenue Edward VII (now Yan'an Dong Lu 延安东路) was built in the 1910s has taken on a new meaning, apparently not related to the name of a river any more but a makeshift mixed spoken language formed with foreign words arranged in Chinese syntax and sometimes even combined with some Chinese words. This kind of language is called "*Yangjingbang* speech" 洋泾浜话 or "pidgin" in English, and is used mostly for speaking rather than in formal writing. Actually, Chinese pidgin originated in Macao and Guangzhou (formerly known as Canton) in the early 18th century and later developed in Shanghai in the mid-19th century.

The naming of this kind of pidgin is, of course, related to the location of the creek. Flanked by two concessions at the time, Yangjingbang and its surrounding area were quickly influenced by the Western business environment and became one of the busiest districts, teeming with tea houses, stores, theatres, and brothels, attracting people of all kinds. In his published diary, Wang Tao 王韬 (1828–1897), one of the pioneers of China's modern journalism, also described the bustling and flourishing scenes in 1858. Yangjingbang was almost synonymous with the concessions since it often appeared in the regulatory agreements signed between the local government and the concessions. When interacting with the foreigners in the concessions, some less-educated local Chinese people had to speak broken English with Chinese grammar and a strong Chinese dialect, sometimes even jumbled with Chinese words. The locals called this Pidgin English. Apart from those Chinese, ordinary locals there also occasionally flirted with such Pidgin English or Chinese utterances peppered with some English words. Without a prescribed set of rules, this Pidgin speaking convention was very idiosyncratic and remained at a spoken level until, later on, some tentative efforts were made to standardize and develop it into a written form, with the publication of some crash course books on it. A book titled *Yangjingbang yingyu riyong shouce* 洋泾浜英语日用手册 (*An Everyday handbook of Yangjingbang English*), for example, was published in the late 19th century. Because such books were compiled mostly by Ningbo natives, the provided Chinese pronunciation was strongly affected by their Ningpo dialect, as reflected in the following mnemonic lines popular at the time (English translation in this book, with the original omitted)[7]:

Lai 来 is called *kemu* 克姆 (come), *qu* 去 is called *gou* 狗 (go)
Yiyuan 一元 is called *wendela* 温得拉 (one dollar)
Ershisi 二十四元 is called *tundifu* 吞的福 (24)
Shi 是 is *yesi* 也司 (yes), *wu* 勿 is *na* 拿 (no)
Ruciruci 如此如此 is *shaxianyusha* 沙咸鱼沙 (so and so)
Qiaoti 翘 (choose) 梯 (tea) is have a tea
Xuetang xuetang 雪堂雪堂 is please sit down
Hongtou asan 红头阿三 kaipodu 开泼度 (keep door)
Zijia xiongdi 自家兄弟 is called *bolacha* 勃拉茶 (brother)
Ye 爷 is *facha* 发茶 (father), *niang* 娘 is *maicha* 卖茶 (mother)
Zhangren abo 丈人阿伯 is *fachalao* 发茶佬 (father-in-law)

As can be seen from these examples, the syntax, if it is worthy of the term, of *Yangjingbang* English is jumbled and very unstable. In an English local travel guide book published in 1912 in Shanghai, Yanngjingbang English was ridiculed as *gezi yingyu* 鸽子英语 ("pigeon English" or "English spoken by pigeons") as the word pidgin is homophonous with pigeon. The following brief comparison with Standard English was provided for illustration in the booklet:

Standard English	Pidgin English
Do you understand?	Savvy?
Can you tell me what this is?	What thing this b'long?
Can you do this for me?	Can do?

Some Pidgin or *Yangjingbang* English expressions even flow back as Standard English for informal use, such as "Long time no see," which is presumably based upon the Chinese expression "*haojiu bujian*" 好久不见. Influenced by the Chinese language, *Yangjingbang* English adopted some peculiar

182 *Classification of Chinese loanwords*

quasi-suffixes, such as -*pisi* or -*piecee* (for "piece," similar to a Chinese partitive after numbers), -*said* (for "side" or prepositional function after locational nouns or pronouns related to location), and -*taim* (for "time" after nouns related to time). What is more, the grammatical number and case in nouns are absent in Chinese Pidgin English. Here are some examples.

> tupisi man: two men
> forpisi tebal: four tables
> hi hous said: He is at home. (hi = he, hous = house)
> doksaid: at the dock
> maisaid: my side
> distaim: this time

In addition, the syntactic order is very close to that of Chinese, such as in "Ning-Po mo far" (mo = more) for *Ningbo yiyuan* 宁波以远 (beyond Ningbo). Some early Chinese immigrants in the US also spoke Pidgin English of similar syntactic order, such as in "No tickee, no washee" (No wash without ticket) among early Chinese laundrymen.

Similar to its grammar, the Pidgin lexicon is extremely primitive, rough, and volatile. Just as it comes into being under certain social circumstances, so it evaporates into thin air when those circumstances are no longer present. On the positive side, however, pidgin not only serves as a makeshift vehicle of communication between the two sides but may also bring some loanwords to the local language. Speaking pidgin on a regular basis definitely has an influence on the mother tongue of the very interlocutors, and other people around, making some frequently used words more and more popular before even becoming part of the standard Chinese lexicon, as seen in early Cantonese pidgin English, such as *sanwenzhi* 三文治 (sandwich), *zhishi* 芝士 (cheese), *shidan* 士担 (stamp), and *mai* 麦 (trade mark), and words in early Shanghainese dialect, such as $ba^2 ɦe^2$ (bye-bye), $sən^1 k^h əʔ^4 jə^2$ (thank you), $ge^2 vu^2 mi^2$ (give me), $wən^2 dəʔ^5 foʔ^4$ (wonderful), $ve^2 le^2 gu^2 dəʔ^5$ (very good), $laʔ^5 fi^1 li^2$ (referee), $dʑiaŋ^2 bo^2$ (jump ball), $ɕio^1$ (shoot, shoot the basketball), $sa^1 ɦe^2$ (side, ball going outside), and $gɔ^2 ə^{12}$ (goalkeeper).

All of the above words originally came from pidgin but later on became popular among ordinary people. Though not often seen in writing, they were *bona fide* loanwords in real life. Most of them disappeared as a result of the political upheavals and language standardization movement since the founding of the People's Republic in 1949, and it was not until 1978 when the country started its reform and opening-up that such loanwords as *baibai* 拜拜 came back to life, spoken again by everyone ever since.[8]

4.6.2 Linguistic mixture

In essence, pidgin is a strong and distorted form of linguistic mixture (or language mixing) in which a foreign language dominates. Linguistic mixture is, to a lesser degree, a common phenomenon among foreign language learners who have attained a certain level of proficiency in a particular environment.

It is not uncommon at all for presentations or discussions at an academic conference to be punctuated with foreign technical terms (mostly English); utterances by local Hong Kong or Taiwan residents are often interspersed with English words, and some Japanese words are habitually used in the everyday interactions among Chinese students in Japan. Linguistic mixture is common in second-language teaching too, such as English mixed with Chinese among Chinese teachers of English for Chinese students and Chinese mixed with some foreign language among Chinese teachers of Chinese for speakers of other languages.

It is a viable language tactic to use commonly agreed-upon terms in a foreign language, such as English, in an academic environment because this serves to facilitate discussion by avoiding misunderstanding caused by different renderings for the same technical terms. What we hear from people in Hong Kong and Taiwan, as has just been described, reflects either a fairly good command of a foreign language among local residents or a linguistic fashion among them, formed under foreign influence. What Chinese students in Japan have experienced is the natural result of what might be called language osmosis under the powerful foreign language environment. The final situation among foreign language teachers also reflects a language tactic by which the linguistic mixture is intentionally presented to make it easier for students to understand another language or to help enhance their listening and familiarity with the language in question. Linguistic mixture of all these normally occurs in speaking rather than in formal writing or written communication. So, no fixed usage is formed as it varies from person to person and situation to situation. In fact, this phenomenon is common throughout history. A colloquial-style Chinese mixed with Mongolian, for example, became popular in China's Yuan dynasty in the 13th and 14th centuries, so much so that it was even seen on the steles, with inscriptions written in a mixture of Chinese and Mongolian, and in the popular literary genre of music drama called *yuanqu* 元曲. Later, in the Qing dynasty (1644–1912), many Manchu words could be found in the *zidishu* 子弟书 (literally "bannermen tales"), a popular storytelling genre created by the Manchus in early 18th-century Beijing. More examples can be found in modern and contemporary times, such as one comic verse in the Shanghai dialect mixed with English, which the author of this book learned in childhood: "Father mather *jingbingzhe* 敬禀者: I *lela* 勒拉 school, *bieyang* 别样 *gongkelze*[2]/ 功课侪 good, *zhiyou* 只有 English *wujige* 勿及格 (To my respected father and mother: I am at school. Other courses are all good. Only English I do not pass)."

As a linguistic fad or game, this did not contribute to any loanword *per se* because the pronunciation of the English words used in the above maintains their essential phonetic attributes, despite the influence of the Shanghai accent, and this did not happen in a normal communicative context.

184 *Classification of Chinese loanwords*

However provisional and unstable, linguistic mixture may help create a favorable condition for the possible entry of loanwords. Indeed, a considerable number of foreign words, in the process of such linguistic mixture as Yangjingbang English and other forms of pidgin, are gradually borrowed for routine use and lexically Sinicized, and finally become part of the regular Chinese lexicon.

4.6.3 *The so called Xieheyu* 協和語 *(Kyowa-go)*

For a time, on a considerable scale, though not in polite company, some Chinese people used to imitate some of the expressions which had been used in the Japanese army in China during the War (1937–1945), such as *mixi mixi* 米西米西 (have meal, from the Japanese *meshi* "meal") and *bageyalu* 拔格亚路 (you stupid bastard, from the Japanese *baka yaru* "stupid jerk"), which are, of course, special loanwords used under special circumstances. Apart from that, during the period of the War of Resistance against the Japanese Aggression, there existed another form of pidgin. In the 1930s and 1940s, in the occupied northeastern part of China, called Manchuguo by the Japanese at the time, the *Xiehehui* 協和會 (Concordia Association or Concordia Society) appeared at various levels across the region to show allegiance to the Japanese. Members of the *Xiehehui* developed a pidgin-like spoken language called *Xieheyu* (or *Kyowa-go* in Japanese, literally "Concordia language" or "Commonwealth language") to accommodate pidgin Chinese spoken by the Japanese stationed there. Later, any similar Chinese expression mixed with some Japanese in China's northeast was also generally called *Xieheyu*. Based on Chinese, with various distortions, such *Xieheyu* was not only interspersed with Japanese lexical elements, such as *ding* 町 ("town" or "district") and *fandi* 番地 ("house number" or "address") but also mingled with some specious Japanese syntax. Reflecting unmitigated colonial rule and self-puppetization, this strange pidgin only had limited use among certain social classes, and no fixed form or norm was developed.

Without popular support, *Xieheyu* couldn't make itself a true language. Indeed, with the disappearance of the conditions for its birth—the surrender and defeat of the Japanese in the war—*Xieheyu* or *Kyowa-go* met the end of its short life cycle. Even this weird form of pidgin still left a few loanwords in the Chinese language. For example, since the railway system in the so-called Manchukuo and the puppet army there were both controlled by the Japanese, the word *manin* 満員 (at full strength, full capacity), frequently used in both systems at the time, was later assimilated into Chinese (*manyuan* 满员) and extended to other military and railway systems during that period and even after the Japanese surrender, making it synonymous with the autochthonous Chinese *keman* 客满 (full house, full capacity), though it was still used in a different context.

Notes

1 Broadly speaking, phonemic/graphemic loaning might also include that, with a semantic marker such as *a sir* 阿 sir, which is used by Hongkongers for "cop," and *PC ji* PC 机. Some people even put the previously mentioned *BP ji* BP 机 in this category, but this is actually a fake loanword. While there are indeed radio pagers or paging receivers in the West, also popularly known as pager or pocket pagers in the US, none of these terms is shortened as beeper or bell pager, as some Chinese claim. BP ji is actually erroneously borrowed from BB ji BB 机, which is from the term BB-call (also known as *Call ji* Call 机 or *kaoji* 拷机), which was created in Taiwan, imitating the sound that the radio pager makes. When entering the Chinese mainland via Hong Kong, it was initially called *BB ji* BB 机 or *bibiji* 哔哔机, soon erroneously regarded as a graphic loanword, seducing people into seeking its supposed source word, and somehow erroneously transformed into *BP ji* at the same time.

2 It is inappropriate that the *Hanyu wailaici cidian* 汉语外来词词典 complied by Liu et al. lists *huliela* 虎列剌 as etymologically originated from Japanese and *huliela* 虎列拉 from English. The first syllable /kɔ/ in English cholera may never be pronounced remotely like the Chinese sound /hu/. This originally Japanese loanword (written in kanji) graphically evolved from *geliela* 格列剌, *kuliela* 酷烈剌, *gelieya* 革列亚, and *huliela* 虎烈剌 before finally settling as *huliela* 虎列剌 in Japan. Since the character 剌 is deceptively similar to another kanji *ci* 刺, 虎列剌 is invariably changed to homonphonic 虎列拉 in modern Chinese to avoid confusion in both writing and pronunciation (as in the case of *alabo* 阿拉伯, which has replaced its homophonic predecessor 阿剌伯). Therefore, micro-changed by Chinese based on the Japanese 虎列剌, 虎列拉 should be considered of Japanese origin, not English.

3 This section draws a lot of insights from *Jindai zhongri cihui jiaoliu yanjiu* 近代中日词汇交流研究 [*A study of modern lexical communications between China and Japan*] (Shen 2010).

4 See Dong Qiusi 董秋斯. 1956. *Fanyi gongzuo zhong de hanyu guifanhua wenti* 翻译工作中的汉语规范化问题 (*Issues on the standardization of Chinese in translation*).

5 In his paper *Xiandai hanyu zhong cong riyu jielai de cihui* 现代汉语中从日语借来的词汇 (1958a), Wang Lida divided loanwords of Japanese origin into nine classes: (1) words which in Japanese were phonemic loans but written with Chinese characters (kanji), such as wasi 瓦斯 and jiada'er 加答儿; (2) autochthonous Japanese words written with kanji but read with Japanese pronunciation (kun-yomi), such as shouxu 手续, danshu 但书, and rukou 入口; (3) words attested in earlier Chinese texts but used for the first time by the Japanese to express a new modern meaning, such as jingji 经济 and geming 革命; (4) Chinese words newly invented by Japan in modern times, such as juedui 绝对, zhipei 支配, zhexue 哲学, and yiyuanhua 一元化; (5) Japanese words which had acquired a new meaning in Chinese, such as laodongzhe 劳动者 and bianhushi 辩护士; (6) function words which correspond to their equivalents in hiragana, such as duiyu 对于 and jiyu 基于; (7) Kanji invented by Japanese, such as xian 腺, zhi 膣, chi 呎, and cun 吋; (8) now obsolete Chinese words, such as laodong zuhe 劳动组合 and laonong zhengfu 劳农政府; and (9) pidgin-like Chinese words (xieheyu 协和语), such as ting 町, fandi 番地, and manyuan 满员. This kind of classification is obviously inappropriate because different rather than uniform criteria have been applied to different classes.

6 In the paper *Xiandai hanyu zhong congriyu jielai de cihui* 现代汉语中从日语借来的词汇 (1958a), Wang Lida listed *ai* 癌 under the category of Chinese loanwords of kanji invented by Japanese, but actually, the word was created in China as early

as the Ming dynasty. For more details, please refer to *Ai yi*癌疑, in *Ciku jianshe tongxun* (Shi 1998).

7 There was an alternative version of these mnemonic lines, as recorded by Qian Nairong 钱乃荣 (1989). Here it is (provided with possible English original words except for those already mentioned in the first version): lai is kangmu 康姆, qu is gu 谷, ershisi is tundifu, shi is yesi, wu is na, ruciruci is shaxianyusha, zhenzhan shizhi 真崭实质 is foligu 佛立谷 (very good), xue 靴 is putuo 蒲脱 (boot), xie 鞋 is xue 靴 (shoe), yanghangmaiban 洋行买办 is jiangbaidu 江摆渡 (comprador), xiaohuolun 小火轮 is sidingba 司汀巴 (steamboat), qiaotiqiaoti is have a tea, xuetang xuetang is please sit down, hongshanyu 烘山芋 is putietu 朴铁秃 (potatao), dongyang chezi 东洋车子 is likexue 力克靴 (rickshaw), dapigu 打屁股 is banpuqu 班蒲曲 (bamboo chop), hunzhang wangba 混账王八 is danfenglu 蛋风炉 (damn fool), namowen 那摩温 (number one) is ada 阿大, paojie xiansheng 跑街先生 is shalaofu 杀老夫 (shroff), maike maike 麦克麦克 (mark) has lots of money, bideshengsi 毕的生司 (pihtihsansy or empty cents) has lots of pawn tickets, hongtou asan 开泼度 (keep door), zijia xiongdi is bolacha, ye is facha niang is maicha, and zhangren abo is fayinluo 发音落 (father-in-law).

8 In China's northwest region of Xinjiang where most Uighur people live, there also exists something of *Yangjingbang* Chinese or pidgin Chinese, which is locally called *Tuhanyu* 土汉语 (roughly "provincial Mandarin"). Many in this *Tuhanyu* are formed by the combination of Uighur words with a Chinese suffix *zi* 子 or other modifying components. Some of them flow back to standard Chinese as loanwords used by local Han Chinese people there, such as *xianpalazi* 线帕拉子 ("cotton thread blanket without velvet," from the Uighur *palaz*; *xian* or "cotton thread" as modifying marker and *zi* as suffix), balangzi 巴郎子 ("kid," from the Uighur *bala* or *balang*; *zi* as suffix), *yanggangzi* 洋缸子 or 洋岗子 ("young married lady," from the Uighur *yênggê*; *zi* as suffix), and *dadangzi* 大当子 ("father," from the Uighur *dada* or *dadang*; *zi* as suffix).

5 Trends in and standardization of Chinese loanwords

5.1 Trends in Chinese loanwords

5.1.1 Historical trends

From its earliest recorded appearance, the loanword in the Chinese language has a history of at least 2,000 years, with two long-running major waves and two brief minor ones. The first major wave lasted from the Eastern Han to the Tang dynasty, while the second lasted from the late Qing dynasty to modern China. As regards the two minor ones, the first happened in the Yuan dynasty, with a massive borrowing of Mongolian words, followed by their fleeting evanescence, while the second, less massive than the first, occurred during the Qing dynasty, ruled by the non-Han Manchus, when words from Manchu were borrowed mostly in China's northeast and the northern region surrounding the capital of Beijing. Thanks to the Manchu enthusiasm for Han Chinese culture, a better part of those Manchu words, under residual substrate influence, have remained with the Chinese-speaking Manchu community as substrate loanwords. Despite—or rather thanks to—the vicissitudes of the rise, decline, and longevity among those loanwords over the last two millennia, we may be able to observe some general historical trends in terms of lexical stability and shifts in forms of borrowing.

5.1.1.1 Trends seen from lexical stability

Loanwords in the *Hanyu wailaici cidian* (1984), the most comprehensive collection to date, can be roughly divided into phonemic borrowing, which includes phonetic approximation and phonemic semantic loaning, and graphic borrowing, which is semantic loaning in essence and mainly refers to kanji of Japanese origin. While the latter is obvious, the former predominantly comes from Western languages, mostly English, followed by Sanskrit, Mongolian, and Russian as well as a small amount from foreign ethnic languages in ancient times and modern ethnic minority languages in China. There are 6,822 phonemic loanwords (excluding those from Japanese, which will be discussed separately below) and 4,817 graphic variants of the above words,

188 *Standardization of Chinese loanwords*

making up a total of 11,639 dictionary entries. Here are some simple calculations. The ratio of phonemic loanwords to total entries is 6,822:11,639 = 1:1.7. The rate of average use per dictionary entry can be defined as the number of words divided by the number of entries, which is 6,822/11,639 ≈ 59%, while the rate of average repetition per entry is defined as the number of variants divided by the number of entries, which is 4,817/11,639 ≈ 41%.

Bear this in mind, and look at the general situation of the Chinese phonemic loanwords of 15 major foreign (or non-Han Chinese) language sources of origin (with at least 50 loanwords per language), as shown in the table below.[1]

Source language	Number of phonemic loanwords	Total dictionary entries	Ratio of phonemic loanwords to total entries	Use rate	Repetition rate
Sanskrit	780	2,589 (1,809+780)	1:3.31	30%	70%
Persian	84	167 (83+84)	1:1.98	50%	50%
Turkic	52	98 (46+52)	1:1.88	53%	47%
Arabic	117	209 (92+117)	1:1.78	56%	44%
Khitan	84	122 (38+84)	1:1.45	68%	32%
English	3,426	5,456 (2,030+3,426)	1:1.59	62%	38%
Russian	401	482 (81+401)	1:1.20	83%	17%
French	162	286 (124+162)	1:1.76	56%	44%
Latin	88	98 (10+88)	1:1.11	89%	11%
Malay (Indonesian excluded)	74	108 (34+74)	1:1.45	68%	32%
Mongolian	400	525 (125+400)	1:1.31	76%	24%
Tibetan	256	336 (80+256)	1:1.31	76%	24%
Manchu	128	175 (47+128)	1:1.40	73%	27%
Uighur	85	123 (38+85)	1:1.44	69%	31%
Ewenki	54	59 (5+54)	1:1.09	91%	9%

It can be seen from the above that the smaller the ratio of the total number of phonemic loanwords to total entries, the lower the lexical stability becomes. Conversely, the higher the rate of use, the higher the lexical stability; and the higher the rate of repetition, the lower the lexical stability.

It must be admitted that, as with any analysis, the above statistics and observations are subject to data availability and accuracy. For example, contrary to what is indicated above, Chinese loanwords of Ewenki origin should in fact be fewer than those of Chinese ethnic Tai origin (49:54) or German origin (30:55).

The above statistics on phonemic loanwords can be compared with those on graphic loans of Japanese origin. But before that, some clarifications are needed. It is generally agreed that there exists in the dictionary of the *Hanyu wailaici cidian* a considerable amount of inappropriate inclusion concerning loanwords of Japanese origin. Zhu (1993) divides the loanwords of Japanese origin included in that dictionary into nine categories and points out that four out of the nine should not be considered of Japanese origin. By Zhu's account, there are 188 such cases in that dictionary, such as *qianbi* 铅笔, *tianzhu* 天主, *jidu* 基督, and *jidujiao* 基督教, which, according to him, have inappropriately been included in the dictionary as loanwords of Japanese origin. But, considering the fact that even more loanwords from Japanese should have been included in that dictionary, we take its data as is. Along those lines, there are 882 graphic loans of Japanese origin and another 7 graphic variants (not including words from the Ezo (Emishi), a Japanese tribal group in the northern districts of Honshu), as compared with 887 by Zhu's account. Among them, 21 plus 1 variant may be considered indirect phonemic loans because they are from Japanese phonemic loans of Western origin, such as huliela, julebu, wasi, linba, jiadaer, baisidu 百斯笃 (pest), zhifusi 窒扶斯 (from German "Typhus" or "typhoid" in English), guininie 规尼涅 (from Dutch "kinine" or "quinine" in English), wa 瓦 (from French "gramme"), guke 古柯 (coca), caoda, tatami (a traditional Japanese floor covering made from dried rushes), and wodu 沃度 (from German "Jod" or "iodine" in English); 2 are direct phonemic loans: namely, aobasang 奥巴桑 (Japanese *oba-san*, old aunt or lady) and jidi 吉地 (Japanese *geta*, wooden clogs for outdoor wear by Japanese people); and 8 are invented characters as phonemic loans of Western units of measurement which include 3 quasi-phonemic loans of zhe 粍 (millimeter, pronounced *mirimeetoru* in Japanese), li 糎 (centimeter, pronounced *senchimeetoru* in Japanese), and qianwa 瓩 (kilogram, pronounced *kiro-guramu* in Japanese).

Here is the comparison of graphic loans (from Japanese) with phonemic ones:

Loanword type	Number of phonemic loanwords	Total dictionary entries	Ratio of phonemic loanwords to total entries	Use rate	Repetition rate
Graphic loans from Japanese	882	889 (7+882)	1:1.007	99.3%	0.7%
Phonemic loans	6,822	11,639 (4,817+6,822)	1:1.7	58%	42%

This comparison indicates that there are hardly any repetitions (in the form of variants) among Chinese graphic loanwords of Japanese origin, with one dictionary entry matching exactly one loanword. This means that this graphic loaning maintains extremely high lexical stability, which stands in sharp contrast to phonemic loaning: the use rate among graphic loans

190 *Standardization of Chinese loanwords*

is 70% higher than that among phonemic loans, and the repetition rate is 97% lower. In short, lexical stability proves that semantic loaning—as those graphic loanwords from Japanese are essentially their semantic loans of Western terms—is more adaptable to Chinese than phonemic loaning.[2]

5.1.1.2 Trends seen from shifts in the forms of borrowing

1   *Shift from phonemic to semantic loaning.* Among a total of 794 phonemic loanwords of Sanskrit origin listed in the *Hanyu wailaici cidian* (1984), only a little over 50 are still in use today, taking up 1/16 of the total.[3] Other loanwords of Sanskrit origin have shifted to various forms of semantic loaning or can only be found in Buddhist scriptures and Buddhist communities, and thus have a minimal impact on language or society as a whole.

Apart from Sanskrit, the shift from phonemic to semantic loaning happens quite often among words from other languages too, such as *maikefeng* 麦克风→*kuoyinqi* 扩音器/*huatong* 话筒 (microphone), *buerqiaoya* 布尔乔亚→*zichanjieji* 资产阶级 (bourgeois), *puluolietalieya* 普罗列塔列亚→*wuchan jieji* 无产阶级/*laodong renmin* 劳动人民 (proletariat), *peinixilin* 配尼西林→*qingmeisu* 青霉素 (penicillin), *pasi* 派司→*yuepiao* 月票/*tongxingzheng* 通行证/*zhizhao* 执照 (pass), *laise* 莱塞→*jiguang* 激光 (laser), *mada* 马达→*fadongji* 发动机/*diandongji* 电动机 (motor), *danbagu* 淡巴菰→*yancao* 烟草 (tobacco), *baituoyou* 白脱油→*huangyou* 黄油/*naiyou* 奶油/*niuyou* 牛油 (butter), *kangbaiyin* 康拜因→*lianheshougeji* 联合收割机 (combine harvester), *ximingnaer* 习明纳尔→*ketangtaolun* 课堂讨论/*yantaoban* 研讨班 (from the Russian семинар, meaning "seminar").

One interesting scenario is that some existing semantic loaning first shifts to (or is added in coexistence with) phonemic loaning and later shifts back to its original semantic loaning. This happened around the May Fourth Movement in the early 20th century when the so-called "Mr. De" (democracy) and "Mr. Sai" (science) were considered, among other things, critical to the intellectual revolution and sociopolitical reform movement. Thus, the semantically rendered *minzhu* 民主 (democracy) coexisted with the phonetically rendered *demokelaxi* 德莫克拉西 but has since reverted to the semantic *minzhu*. *Kexue* 科学 (science) coexisted with *saiyinsi* 赛因斯 before returning to *kexue*, as it is used today. *Sidike* 司的克 (phonemic loanword from "stick") coexisted with the semantic *shouzhang* 手杖, but only the latter is in use today. And *misituo* 密斯脱 (phonemic loan from "mister") coexisted with *xiansheng* 先生, but only the latter is still in use.

The above statistics and observations tell us that, though it may not replace phonemic loaning completely, semantic loaning should remain a predominant form of lexical borrowing for the foreseeable future.

There are at least two underlying reasons for the predominance of Chinese semantic loaning over phonemic loaning. First, homogeneous with other Chinese conventional words or expressions, semantic loanwords are more accessible and receptive. Second, semantic loaning enjoys greater semantic transparency, the degree to which the meaning of a word can be correctly inferred from its component characters. Despite the possibility of erroneous interpretation based on the seemingly transparent surface structure, high transparency can still more easily lead the average language user to the threshold of a correct semantic understanding. With almost no semantic transparency, however, phonemic loaning does not provide such facility but has to be learned as an apparently unintelligible whole because it simply defies meaningful morphemic analysis. After all, Chinese is an analytical language which is characteristically composed of monosyllabic morphemes, and its words are so structured that they go hand in glove with its monosyllabicity. Over a long period of time, the dual linguistic nature has gradually helped to shape the analytical nature in the Chinese cognitive schema as a whole. Incidentally, this also marks one of the unique features (or perhaps advantages) of the Chinese language over its Western counterparts.

2 *Evolution from pure phonemic borrowing to semantically more intelligible phonetic approximation with semantic cues.* With up to 40 in total, these are rare in number and negligible in linguistic significance. Examples include the shift of *gaisitabo* 盖斯塔波 to *gaishitaibao* 盖世太保 (Gestapo), from kaobuling 考不令 to kaobeilun 靠背轮 (coupling), and from *youmo* 酉酞 to *youmo* 幽默 (humor).

3 *Evolution from semantic to phonetic loaning and/or phonetic approximation with semantic cues.* This is even rarer and can be divided into three different situations. First, phonemic loaning later replaces semantic loaning due to the latter's failure to accurately express meaning, such as the substitution of *mingxue* 名学/*lunlixue* 论理学 with luoji 逻辑 (logic), *zonghui* 总会 with *julebu* 俱乐部 (club), *huizhang* 徽章 with *tuteng* 图腾 (totem), *anleyi* 安乐椅 with *shafa* 沙发 (sofa), and *Huijiaotu* 回教徒 with *Musilin* 穆斯林 (Muslim). Second, considering various factors (e.g. length), phonemic loaning is ultimately chosen over the otherwise coexisting semantic loaning, such as in *aizibing* 艾滋病 over *houtian huodexing mianyili quefa zonghezheng* 后天获得性免疫力缺乏综合征. Third, both phonemic and semantic versions exist but are used on different occasions. For example, both being borrowed from "fair play," *fei'epolai* 费厄泼赖, the phonemic loaning, is reserved for literary use, while *gongping jingsai* 公平竞赛/*gongping duidai* 公平对待, the semantic one, is used more generally. Both being borrowed from *Kurban* or *Eid al-Adha* (Arabic for "Festival of Sacrifice"), *Gu'erbangjie* 古尔邦节 is used as the official term for this major Muslim festival, while *Zaishengjie* 宰牲节 is used in an explanatory context. Both from the Mongolian *gudum* or "alley," the phonemic *hutong* 胡同 is typically used in the northern parts of China, while the autochthonous Chinese synonyms *xiaoxiang* 小巷 and *lilong* 里弄 are used in the south. While *jiantouman* 尖头鳗 is

occasionally used on jocular occasions as a humorous phonemic loanword of "gentleman," *shenshi* 绅士 is used on all other formal occasions. Overall, however, such coexistence is infrequent, with one fairly recent exception: in the last two decades of the 20th century, phonemic loanwords, mostly pre-existing, also came back into use, along with their dominant semantic equivalents, such as phonemic *misi* 密斯, with semantic *xiaojie* 小姐, for Miss, and *leishe* 雷射, with *jiguang* 激光, for laser. Obviously, this phenomenon seems to go hand in hand with the opening-up of Chinese society.

As may be seen from above, the shift from semantic to phonemic loaning is not very common, but the latter is on a gradual increase. In fact, with increased opening-up and foreign language education, it will be no surprise to see more and more phonemic loaning, including phonetic approximation with some semantic cues, such as more recent loanwords of *boke* 博客 from *blog* and *heike* 黑客/*haike* 骇客 from *hacker*.

5.1.2 Contemporary trends

5.1.2.1 Actual proportion of phonemic to semantic loaning

Difficult as it is to calculate the actual proportion, Chinese loanwords from English and Japanese, which both started to come into Chinese after 1840, can serve as sample data in order to get a general idea. While there are 3,426 loanwords from English and only 882 (allowing for possible deviation due to manual calculation) from Japanese in the *Hanyu wailaici cidian* (1984), the actual number of loanwords from the latter is five to six times as large, indicating its conservative approach to the inclusion of the latter. There are more than 3,000 entries for words of Japanese origin and over 6,600 for words of English origin in the recently published *Xinhua wailaici cidian* 新华外来词词典 (*Xinhua dictionary of Chinese loanwords*. Shi 2019). In the dictionary *Xin Erya* 新尔雅 (Wang and Ye 1903), there are 2,728 newly introduced semantic loanwords from Japanese (excluding 21 phonemic or "quasi-phonemic" ones), approximately half of which are direct borrowings of Japanese kanji words; the other nearly half were Chinese semantic loans, with some negligibly few autochthonous Chinese words, such as *wugong* 蜈蚣 (centipede). So, considering the ongoing direct borrowing of Japanese kanji words and other semantic loaning, the total number of Chinese semantic loans far exceeds that of phonemic loans from English.

5.1.2.2 Active use for the contemporary period

The *Hanyu wailaici cidian* is not an appropriate choice for the observation of the active use of loanwords for the contemporary period because it is a collection of Chinese loanwords both in ancient, modern times and today, some still in active use, while others are long obsolete. In other words, the dictionary notes which loanwords have existed but does not provide any clue as to which have survived or which were in active use during a specific period in history, given the fleeting evanescence of many of the loanwords included. With that in mind, we put that dictionary aside and use the following three contemporary Chinese dictionaries for analysis.

1. Xiandai hanyu cidian 现代汉语词典 (The Contemporary Chinese Dictionary, 1978). As a medium-sized dictionary of standard modern Chinese, this does not impose any different or extra restrictions on the inclusion of loanwords. Thus, it can more or less fairly reflect the state of their active use for the period covered by the dictionary, though the number of the loanwords in active use exceeds that included there. Below is a brief data analysis of Japanese loanwords borrowed into Chinese, based on this dictionary.

Types of loaning	General purpose words	Single character technical terms	Multiple character technical terms	Proper names	Total
Phonemic loaning (subtotal)	476+23	121+4	17+0	77+9	691+36 =727
(1) Pure phonemic loaning	238+19	119+4	17+0	25+6	
Japanese kanji	3+0	1+0	–	1+0	
Subtotal	241+19	120+4	17+0	26+6	404+29 =433
(2) Phonetic approximation	30+1	–	–	–	
Japanese kanji	1+0	–	–	–	
Subtotal	31+1	–	–	–	31/1 = 32
(3) Quasi-phonemic loaning	138+2	–	–	3+0	
Japanese kanji	–	1+0	–	–	
Subtotal	138+2	1+0	–	–	142+2=144
(4) Phonemic loaning + semantic marker	65+1	–	–	47+3	
Japanese kanji	1+0	–	–	1+0	
Subtotal	66+1	–	–	48+3	114+4=118
Graphic loaning (subtotal)	761+0	4+0	–	3+0	768+0=768
Latin letters	–	–	–	–	
Japanese kanji	761+0	4+0	–	3+0	

Note: The figure before the plus sign "+" is the number of loanwords, and the figure after it indicates the number of variants.

Overall, there are 691 phonemic loanwords and 768 graphic (mostly semantic) loanwords. Given that those semantic loanwords borrowed from Japanese are not included in the dictionary, taken together, there may be at least twice as many as phonemic loanwords from Japan. Among the phonemic loanwords, 58% are pure phonemic loaning, which proves their mainstream status, while phonetic approximation makes up 4%, suggesting minimal use. In between are half-phonemic, half-semantic loaning (21%) and phonemic loaning + semantic marker (17%), which, taken together, account for a little over one-third, indicating their relative linguistic vitality.

2   *Xiandai hanyu xinci xinyu cidian* 现代汉语新词新语词典 (*A dictionary of new Chinese words and expressions.* Yu 1994). There are 7,655 total entries, among which only 65 are, to the best of our judgement, phonemic loanwords, taking up 0.84% of the total.
3   *Dangdai xin shuyu* 当代新术语 (*New contemporary technical terms.* Jin, Yongkang, and Xiejun 1988). There are 2,197 entries of new terms, among which 134 are loanwords in a very broad sense (5 phonemic loans, 98 quasi-phonemic, 27 composed or partially composed of Latin letters, 4 numeric or alphanumeric ones), making up 6.1% of the total.

In sum, contemporary Chinese still adopts semantic loaning as the major means of lexical borrowing from the outside, and the use of phonemic loaning is greatly limited. This will be very instructive in designing a language standardization scheme.

5.1.3 Trends as seen from the Chinese language features and user cognitive schema

The examination of both historical and contemporary use of loanwords consistently and unambiguously demonstrates that semantic loaning takes a dominant position, while much of phonemic loaning will over time be replaced by semantic loaning, despite its initial boom. This certainly does not happen by accident; underlying it are some fundamental reasons, i.e. the unique characteristics of the recipient Chinese language in general and user cognitive schema.

5.1.3.1 The Chinese language and its ideographic written characters

1   *Language factors.* The lexical composition of the Chinese language is mainly determined by the distinctive characteristics of its length of linguistic units and its ideographic written characters. Unlike English, in which one morpheme is often expressed by two syllables, and two morphemes may be contained in one syllable, each Chinese morpheme is one syllable long, with a general correspondence between morpheme and syllable. For a clear semantic articulation within the length of just

one syllable, the enunciation must be properly elongated so that its consonant and vowel are given fullness. That is why, in general, the Chinese syllabic sound is relatively long, excepting some shorter ones in the northern Chinese dialects. This is the defining feature of the Chinese morpheme and syllable. What is more, many of the two-syllable words in modern Chinese are not exactly the same as the words in Western languages. When lent to Chinese, foreign loanwords normally translate to more than two syllables, which is obviously incongruous with the Chinese monosyllabic feature. This syllabic clash, however unobtrusive or slow-moving, usually tends to move in the conciliatory direction so that the loanword becomes more accessible to the average user and assimilable to the Chinese lexicon. These conciliatory efforts include phonetic approximation with some semantic cues, syllabic shortening and lexical Sinicization through semantically suggestive phonetic approximation, and the addition of semantic markers.

Perfect phonetic approximation with some semantic cues only occurs in few cases, if any. Partial approximation in varying degrees, however, is quite common with Chinese loanwords, such as *diedi* 爹地 (daddy), *mami* 妈咪 (mummy, mommy), *baobo* 胞波 (close relative, from the Burmese $pau^{955}p^ho^{33}$), *anbu* 安瓿 (ampule, ampoule), *shuiting* 水汀 (steam heating, from *steam*), and *xiuke* 休克 (shock).

In addition, Chinese loanwords are often made monosyllabic and therefore result in single morphemes as well, thus creating a favorable condition for lexical derivatives and reproductivity. Examples abound, such as *sengjia* 僧伽 being abbreviated to➔seng (male Buddhist), *biqiuni* 比丘尼➔ni (a fully ordained female monastic), *tapo* 塔婆➔ta (a Buddhist burial mound), *chaduoluo* 刹多罗➔cha (temple), *mitu* 米突/*mida* 密达➔*mi* 米 (meter), *wate* 瓦特➔wa (watt), *pingpoluo* 蘋婆罗➔*pingguo* 苹果 (apple), *bolengcai* 菠棱菜➔*bocai* 菠菜 (spinach), and *kaluli* 卡路里➔*ka* 卡/*daka* 大卡 (calorie). The new morpheme of *di* 的, derived from *dishi* 的士 (taxi), has been used to create new words, such as *dige* 的哥 "taxi-driver" and *dadi* 打的 "take a taxi." Similarly, *bo* 玻 has been used in inventing words like *boguan* 玻管 (glass tube) and *tuobohua* 脱玻化 (devitrify).

Finally, semantically suggestive phonetic approximation, semantic loaning, and addition of semantic markers can also make the loanword approximate to an autochthonous Chinese word in morphemic composition, hence leading to lexical Sinicization. Some loanwords form an indivisible cohesion as a result of full phonemic approximation, such as *weitaming* 维他命 (vitamin), *youfu* 幽浮 (UFO), and *diqueliang* 的确良 (Dacron). Other loanwords of fully phonemic approximation have not formed an indivisible whole, such as *diditi* 滴滴涕 (DDT), *luoji* 逻辑 (logic), and *liuming* 流明 (lumen). There are fully semantic words, like *heiban* 黑板 (blackboard), *lanqiu* 篮球 (basketball), and *tielu* 铁路 (railway); half-semantic, half-phonemic loans, like *bingqilin* 冰淇淋 (ice-cream), *denggere* 登革热 (dengue fever), and *anpeiji* 安培计 (ammeter);

and phonemic loaning combined with a semantic marker, like *chanhui* 忏悔 (Ksama), *kapian* 卡片 (card), and *jipuche* 吉普车 (jeep).

2   *Factors of Chinese ideographic written characters.* Dovetailing nicely with the quintessentially monosyllabic and mono-morphemic language (and, of course, an essential part of it too), Chinese written characters are strongly ideographic, so much so that this language tends to "semanticize" every component character in a word in at least three ways.

The first way is to reserve or create a character with the morphemic or lexical meaning uniquely befitting some borrowed word or take a semantically appropriate and phonetically similar but already existing word, such as *seng* 僧, *ta* 塔, *mo* 魔, *lao* 酪, and *fo* 佛 in Early Chinese, and *lei* 镭, *nai* 氖, *zong* 腙, and *ka* 胩 in modern Chinese. The second is to find semantically indicative words of phonetic approximation, including fully approximate ones, such as leida (radar), shengna (sonar), liuming (lumen), and wutuobang (utopia), and partially approximate ones, such as manguo (mango, *guo,* "fruit"), shalong (sarong, a garment traditionally worn in Southeast Asia, *sha,* "fabric"), and luohan (arhat, *han,* "man"). The third way is to affix a radical to the borrowed phoneme as a semantic marker. There are dual-character words such as *putao* 葡萄 (*ao* 艹, "grass"), *luotuo* 骆驼 (*ma* 马, "horse"), *ningmeng* 柠檬 (*mu* 木, "wood" or "plant"), *jiasha* 袈裟 (*yi* 衣, "garment"), *liuli* 琉璃 (*yu* 王, "precious stone"), *mengma* 猛犸 (*quan,* 犭 "dog" or "canine"), *pulu* 氆氇 (*mao,* "wool"), and *kafei* 咖啡 (*kou* 口, "mouth"). There are also single characters contained in words such as *shayu* 鲨鱼 (*sha* 鲨, composed of *sha* 沙 as phonemic borrowing from *shark* + *yu* 鱼, "fish"), *bocai* 菠菜 (*bo* 波, composed of *ao* 艹, "grass," and *bo* 波, as phonemic borrowing from *palinga* + *cai* 菜, "vegetable"), and *handahan* 犴达罕 (*han* 犴, composed of *quan* 犭, "dog" or "canine," + *gan* 干, as a phonemic component, from the Manchu *kandahan* "moose").

In sum, all those intrinsic linguistic features of the Chinese language are instrumental in reinforcing its tendency toward the prevalence of semantic loaning over phonemic loaning.

5.1.3.2 User cognitive schema for the Chinese language

It is generally agreed that the Chinese language community is more used to analytical cognition as opposed to synthetic cognition when it comes to words. This is the inevitable corollary of the absolute predominance of monosyllabic words in Early Chinese and traditional education on Chinese lexis, which has naturally influenced modern and contemporary Chinese, contributing to the great flexibility and advantage that the modern Chinese lexicon enjoys in forming both single morpheme words and compound words on different pragmatic occasions while at the same time making its linguistic cognition more accessible to analysis. Specifically, monosyllabic Chinese verbs, including formal ones, prevail in the dynamic colloquial environment, while disyllabic words prevail in the more static, written language environment.

This lexical composition and user cognitive schema is reflected in various aspects. Monosyllabic words remain the backbone of the modern Chinese lexicon. Four-character words and temporarily coined words are commonplace. Component morphemes in a word can often be substituted by another for the nonce (hence, nonce words). There are a very large number of *liheci* 离合词 or "separable verbs" in the Chinese language, which can be used as a single verb or can be separated and used as a verb + object phrase. Mutually reinforced by the monosyllabicity and ideography of Chinese characters, of course, this tendency also helps shape a linguistic cognitive schema on the part of the language user, which is commensurate with this quintessentially analytical language. This is one of the fundamental reasons behind the prevalence of semantic loans and Japanese kanji in the modern Chinese lexicon.

In sharp contrast, the English language community seems to be accustomed to more synthetic than analytical cognition when it comes to words. Clear proof of this is the overwhelming proportion of phonemic borrowing in the entire lexicon of the English language: more than 50% out of its vocabulary of one million words are phonemic, which mostly come from French and other Romance languages derived from Latin.[4]

Easier access to phonemic loaning does not necessarily suggest the superiority of English over Chinese; instead, it merely proves that each language may have a distinctive means of evolutionary development. As long as it can rapidly and effectively assimilate a complementary lexicon from other languages, it is a good language.

5.2 Standardization of Chinese loanwords

5.2.1 Flexible standardization

5.2.1.1 The flexibility principle

Both historical and current trends indicate that flexibility should be a general principle in standardizing Chinese loanwords. The flexibility principle means that while recognizing the uncertain nature in language standardization and multiple factors in affecting such an effort, we should put to work a model involving those factors by which to guide the standardization with different schemes for different cases. The viability of this principle can be seen from both theoretical consideration and historical practice.

From a linguistic point of view, the cultural duality of loanwords is even more pronounced and intense in the Chinese language system, and there could be all kinds of possible choices or conflicts between the two languages and/or cultures in the integration of one language into the other. Therefore, there is no one-size-fits-all yardstick out there. What is feasible is to stay maximally close to the borrowed language while accommodating the Chinese user environment.

Historical and current practice also disproves such a one-size-fits-all approach. Through active use, most viable loanwords have gone through initial tension between the two languages upon contact, followed by a period of natural selection and mutual accommodation, gradually culminating in some standardized form. It sometimes means that no intervention is required until some unmistakable trend or preference reveals itself. Then a prescriptive linguistic decision may be made for public guidance, as in the Chinese Ministry of Public Health (now National Health Commission)'s promulgation of the use of *aizibing* 艾滋病—as opposed to homophonic but misleading 爱滋病 (literally, "love-induced disease") for its inappropriate association with *ai* 爱, "love,"—as the standardized Chinese phonemic loanword of AIDS.

5.2.1.2 Five influencing factors

There are at least five influencing factors to consider in the construction of a model for formal selection and adjustment.

1. *Syllabic structure.* Sufficient consideration should be given to the full and clear articulation of the component sounds in this tonal language, and it is not advisable to invent some tone-less words or a lexical structure in a consonant cluster.
2. *Word length.* The optimal length of a Chinese word is between one and four syllables. Words with more syllables should be avoided.
3. *Choice of characters.* Sufficient consideration should be given to the ideographic feature of Chinese characters. In most cases, connotatively neutral or bland characters are preferred; avoid those component characters whose potential semantic association or interaction may cause misinterpretation of the compound word.
4. *User cognitive schema.* Sufficient attention should be given to the collective cognitive schema among native speakers of Chinese, which prefer, among other things, the *prima facie* credibility in lexical composition and the ideographic consideration in each component character. Adequate consideration should also be given to the younger generation, who is more exposed to the latest science and technology, and therefore potentially more receptive to foreign languages and cultures.
5. *Durability in active use.* As the ultimate determinant, durability in active use can best indicate how well the above four factors can go together in a given loanword.

5.2.1.3 Four aspects or rules for standardization

Considering the above five influencing factors and the criteria for phonemic loaning, we may go by the following four rules in loanword standardization. First, only durable, everyday use leads to public acceptance. Second, characters should be weighed and chosen with great discretion. Chosen characters should match the source word in tone, style, and connotation. Avoid rarely used characters or characters with too many component strokes and inventing new words unless absolutely necessary. Phonemic loans should choose characters which best fit the source word phonetically. Third, they should be short and easy to enunciate. The maximum syllabic length is usually four syllables. The component syllables should be in harmonious rather than cacophonic combination. Lastly, proper guidance is necessary. Phonemic loaning and loanword Romanization used to be the planned goal in China, but realistically, it takes much longer periods of time for such a goal to be attained or even conceived as a possibility. It certainly calls for familiarity of the general public with foreign languages and cultures, such as the enhanced feasibility and popular use of *hanyu pinyin* 汉语拼音, the official system adopted by the People's Republic of China in 1979 for transcribing the pronunciation of Standard Chinese using the Roman alphabet, and the public promotion of phonemic loaning. When appropriate, relevant national regulatory bodies may also publicize recommended versions of loanwords for the purpose of proper guidance, as in the previously discussed case of *aizibing*.

5.2.2 Standardization of loanword in practice

The above flexibility principle in standardization can be applied in practice to both the means of borrowing and the different types which loanwords signify.

5.2.2.1 Standardization with regard to the means of borrowing

1 *Phonemic versus semantic loaning.* While they each have their respective pros and cons, phonemic loaning facilitates synthetic interpretation, and semantic loaning is preferable for analytical understanding. Due to different language features and cognitive schemata, some language communities are accustomed to analytical ways of thinking, while others prefer synthetic ways. Though it is not impossible for human cognitive schema to change, it would normally take a long period of interaction for some fundamental change to happen. Foreign borrowing in the Japanese language has evolved from one dominated by semantic loaning in kanji for a long period to the present one, dominated by phonemic loaning in katakana. So, the extent of the maturity or openness of a language community cannot simply be determined by the number or prevalence of either phonemic or semantic borrowing. Indeed, as long as a language community can quickly borrow new ideas it needs for active use through various forms of lexical loaning, it should be considered a mature and open community.

   In case of multiple semantic and phonemic versions for the same source word, an appropriate semantic one, if any, is preferred; otherwise, a phonetic word is chosen according to the above-mentioned rules for standardization. If one of the versions has already enjoyed a considerable advantage over all others, it can be taken as the standard word, while others are kept aside so as to avoid chaos or endless debates. As long as it has been publicly accepted for consistent use, the loanword is considered stable and durable, however old or ill-translated it may be.

One focus of standardization is on new terms, in which phonemic loaning is preferred, while semantic loaning or, if applicable, Japanese kanji is not excluded from consideration. Phonemic loaning was initially used to serve practical purposes. Later, loanword users would have ample time to weigh its semantic alternative or consider whether the phonemic word should be replaced with the new semantic one. Whichever is used, the rules about the appropriate choice of characters and the ease of enunciation should always apply.

2 *Phonemic loaning or phonetic approximation with some semantic cues.* In case of multiple versions of phonemic loaning, the primary rule of standardization or choice remains public acceptance as a result of durable everyday use. If one particular version has already been broadly used, while others are in disuse, it naturally becomes the standard one. If several versions are all in active use, then the one which is used the most and tends to have an advantage over others becomes the principal candidate. If all these versions are still in their seemingly chaotic rivalry, a certain phonemic version may be chosen according to the rules on appropriate choice of characters and ease of enunciation. While phonetic approximation with semantic cues generally contributes to lexical stability, it may sometimes turn out inappropriate, though perhaps in a nuanced manner, as has been shown in the case of the two Chinese loanword versions for the English word *AIDS*.

3 Graphic transcription.

Graphic transcription of Chinese characters. Most of Japanese kanji can be directly transferred for use, but some measure of graphic transcription is still needed so that they adapt to the existing form of modern Chinese characters. Ever-increasing interconnectedness as a result of the Internet and social media popular among the younger generation in the 21st century can easily lead to hasty embracing of Japanese kanji without proper adaptation. Take *yujiekong* 御姐控 (from the Japanese *onee-con*, elder sister complex: sexual attachment to an elder mature girl or lady), for instance. The kanji character 御 (/o/ on the Japanese kun-yomi pronunciation scheme) is a noun-indicator prefix in Japanese, completely different from the usual literal meaning of "royal" in Chinese. Without proper adaptation to something of *dajiekong* 大姐控 or *ajiekong* 阿姐控, the verbatim borrowing of *yujiekong* from Japanese may be prone to easy misinterpretation and even throw the Chinese morphological structure into confusion.

Graphic transcription of loanwords composed of Roman or Latin letters. Many alphabetic languages take on unique spelling features and variant letters, so graphical transcription is needed for limited use within a certain scope on certain occasions. For now, such loanwords are mainly abbreviations, followed by personal or place and brand names. Given that many countries using alphabetic languages have their own transcription system based on Roman letters, there is also a need for China to gradually put in place a similar transcription system exclusively serving the Chinese language, in which the optimal length may be one to four syllables, seven at the maximum, and letter combinations which may sound awkward to Chinese people should be restricted or properly adjusted. Of course, such restrictions must be based on public surveys and experiments on user cognitive schema. Additionally, considering the initial public reception, it is better to have such graphic transcription followed by its Chinese equivalent when it first appears in a text.

Phonetic readjustment. When loaned to Chinese, both loanwords composed of Roman letters and those from Japanese kanji must be phonetically converted or readjusted to the pronunciation system of modern standard Chinese, without which such loanwords could not take root in the Chinese language. Many proponents of direct transcription for loanwords fail to take this necessary intermediary step of phonetic readjustment. Language regulatory bodies must also assume their due responsibility in this regard.

The discrepancy between transcription and phonetic readjustment, and therefore the necessity for the latter are seen in the following three examples. The Chinese loanword from the English word "pass" (meaning "a permit, ticket, or authorization to come and go at will") is 派司 in two-character graphic transcription. The first character, 派, used to be invariably pronounced /pai/ in pinyin, but this particular case is granted an exception, so 派 is tweaked in sound and pronounced /pa/ here to accommodate the pronunciation of the source word /pɑːs/. Similarly, as 快巴 was originally borrowed by Cantonese from the English "fiber," it is actually pronounced in Cantonese as /fɑibɑ/, which differs from its normal pronunciation, /kuaiba/, in modern standard Chinese. In the same vein, 沙士, as the loanword by Taiwanese from *sas*, the arbitrarily abbreviated form of sarsaparilla, a sweet drink, is pronounced not as /shashi/ as it should be but as /sazi/. The cause for this discrepancy between graphic transcription and phonetic readjustment is that such loanwords come into use first through speaking and therefore in phonetic forms, while graphic transcriptions come later as an inaccurate but tolerable written symbolic representations. So, it would be inappropriate to have all lexical borrowings invariably end in fixed written representation in Chinese characters; readjustment to the written representation, when necessary, would help facilitate their public use in daily speaking.

5.2.2.2 Standardization with regard to the different types which loanwords signify

1. *General conceptual terms* (including terminology in the broad sense, except strictly technical or scientific terms) *and words for everyday life*. These types of words are borrowed mainly through semantic loaning, supplemented by phonemic loaning. Under current conditions, phonemic loaning should be reserved for limited facilitation to avoid overuse.
2. *Scientific/technical terms* (terminology in the narrow sense). Phonemic loaning and semantic loaning are used in parallel, and generally, there is no need for the invention of new characters. These types of words constitute the focus or center of all standardization efforts. When necessary, administrative intervention is required. Proper guidance is also needed for tackling the considerable grey area between general conceptual terms and strictly technical terms.
3. *Personal and place names.* The universally acknowledged principle that name-giving should follow the will of the originating person or place (*mingcong zhuren* 名从主人 in Chinese) can be applied in a broad manner: namely, not only phonetically but also semantically and graphically. The myriad languages around the world are not represented in alphabetic phonetics only, let alone just the Latin alphabet. Even if only the phonetic part of the observance principle is followed, many practical issues would make this hard to implement. For one thing, the phonological system can vary drastically from language to language. Proper names, once borrowed, are intended for the recipients, the actual users. So, ease of use and accommodation to the phonological system and acceptability of the recipient language should be added as another principle in borrowing personal and place names. A more appropriate approach would be to duly respect the originating person or place, while sufficient consideration should also be given to the target users.

  Take Seoul as an illustration. Fully respecting South Korea's decision that the Chinese name for its capital Seoul be changed from *Hancheng* 汉城 to *Shouer* 首尔, China followed this change. The Chinese version of Obama is another case in point. The mainland Chinese loanword for former US President Obama is *Aobama* 奥巴马 (phonemic loaning of ao-ba-ma for O-ba-ma), while the US says that what phonetically corresponds to the "O" in Obama should be the Chinese character *ou* 欧, not *ao* 奥. To this, China responds that, since the general public is already accustomed to the current translation of "*Aobama*," and the original sound of "O" in Obama sits somewhere between *ao* and *ou*, the rendering of *ao* is not improper, so the existing use of *Aobama* is upheld.

  In short, what this observance principle means at the present stage is that for general readers, phonemic transliteration is the principal means and representation for the borrowing of foreign proper names and follows its very first appearance with the original word in parentheses.

For advanced (academic) readers, the borrowed original word can be directly used, with its Chinese characters in phonemic transliteration attached to it at its very first appearance. Again, whenever possible, semantic loaning is generally adopted for the borrowing of common names. Graphic loaning or matching Chinese morphemes with their corresponding component characters in the borrowed source word is generally adopted and maintained for Chinese lexical borrowing from Japanese, Korean, and Vietnamese.

4 *Other proper names.* Depending on the case, semantic, phonemic, or a combination of the two can be adopted for the borrowing of those proper names. In the case of countries, social organizations and other public or private institutions, the general approach is phonemic loaning for the proper-name part of the institutional name and semantic loaning for the common-name part, such as *Meilijian Hezhongguo* 美利坚合众国 (United States of America), *Ximenzi dianqi gongsi* 西门子电器公司 (Siemens Electric Company), and *Boyin feiji zhizao gongsi* 波音飞机制造公司 (Boeing Aircraft Manufacturing Company). Graphic transcription is generally adopted for Japanese institutional names, such as Riben waiwusheng 日本外务省 (Ministry of Foreign Affairs of Japan), Qingying yishu daxue 庆应义塾大学 (Keio University), and Songxia dianqi chanye zhushihuishe 松下电器产业株式会社 (Matsushita Electric Industrial Co., Ltd.). For those business institutions which take abbreviations as their corporate names, direct borrowing via phonemic and graphic loaning can be adopted for proprietary trademark or brand considerations, such as IBM, AT&T, and SONY. The same applies to other commercial or industrial institutions. No additional intervention is necessary in the process of direct lexical borrowing unless the original name contains publicly offensive, obscene, colonialist, chauvinistic, or other negative material.

Language being a system of great flexibility, we have to live with it in a flexible manner. What we should do is observe linguistic activities more and longer, rather than leaping to conclusions. No administrative intervention or linguistic guidance is warranted unless it is deemed necessary. It is sometimes the best policy to let the specific lexical borrowing, be it phonemic, semantic, or graphic loaning, run its course.

5.2.3 *The future of the loanword*

Since standardization plays the role of guidance and prediction, the discussion in this chapter so far states that loanwords are indispensable in the development and enhancement of a nation and its language. In fact, historical evidence shows that the size of loanwords in general, semantic loans in particular, and their frequency of use are directly proportional to the prosperity of a nation (and its language). Unless we hope to fall behind, it is essential that we take an active and balanced attitude toward the assimilation and use of foreign lexical heritage and, in particular, phonemic and semantic loaning.

When a nation gets into a regular habit of alphabetic reading, speaking, and writing, and, with sustained enhancement in foreign language education and international exchange, its people gradually become accustomed to the synthetic approach to lexical cognition, they will be in a better position to embrace phonemic loaning. Near the end of the 20th century, people expected that the next century would witness considerable growth in this form of Chinese lexical borrowing or, for that matter, even direct use of abbreviations in Latin letters, accompanied by a relative decrease in the proportion of semantic borrowing. Thanks to ideographic Chinese characters, however, semantic borrowing will still keep its comparative advantage in the long run. Now comes the end of the second decade of the 21st century, and the above predictions have proven true. What is more, with the massive inflow of loanwords come new linguistic and social issues. Lacking sufficient respect and love for their native language of Chinese, the younger generation seems to be uncritically attracted to exotic culture and to indiscriminately embrace foreign words. Particularly in the case of alphabetic-lettered loanwords, they simply take and use whatever comes to them without proper consideration of the context in which to use them, so much so that the general public feels overwhelmed. This may over time call for another round of linguistic guidance for standardization.

Notes

1 Due to the limited space of the Dictionary, *Hanyu wailaici cidian* (1984) deleted nearly 2,000 entries upon publication, mostly variants on main entries. Despite few misidentifications, if any, the manual calculation and data analysis of the Dictionary in this book will not affect the overall picture presented in the Dictionary about Chinese loanwords. Also, besides the 15 major language sources for Chinese loanwords listed on this page, there are another 69, as briefly listed below in descending order of the number of loanwords, with the total dictionary entries (number of loanwords plus their variants) in brackets: Jurchen 49 (64), Tai 49 (54), Xianbei 48 (55), Yi (Lolo) 38 (47), German 30 (55), Spanish 30 (38), Xiongnu 28 (58), Korean 23 (29), Kazakh 22(26), Indonesian 21 (29), Italian 18 (26), Wa (Kawa) 18 (18), Naxi (Nakhi) 17 (18), Zhuang 14 (15), Jingpo (Kachin) 14 (15), Elunchun (Orochon) 13 (13), Old Iranian 11 (19), Kyrgyz 10 (12), Thai 9 (14), Dong (Kam) 9 (10), Zaiwa (Tsaiwa, Atsi) 8 (9), Sogdian 8 (8), Kangju Sogdian 7 (14), Daur (Dawo'er) 7 (9), Burmese 7 (9), Portuguese 7 (8), Vietnamese 7 (8), Li (Hlai) 7 (7), Nepalese 6 (12), Lisu (Lisaw) 6 (7), Uzbek 6 (6), Kuchean (Tocharian B) 5 (21), Java 5 (7), Syrian 5 (6), Hani (Woni) 5 (5), Miao (Hmong) 5 (5), Greek 4 (4), Hindustani 4 (4), Bai (Bo) 3 (3), Tatar 3 (3), Swedish 3 (3), Pali 2 (3), Bengali 2 (3), Tajiki 2 (3), Baiyi 百夷语 2(2), Danish 2 (2), Shui (Sui) 2 (2), ancient Dayuan 大宛 1 (5), ancient Khotanese (Saka) 1 (3), Urdu 1 (2), Ainu 1 (1), Egyptian 1 (1), Babai 八百 1(1), Bantu 1 (1), Polish 1 (1), Bulang (Blang) 1 (1), Finnish 1 (1), Gaoshan (indigenous Taiwanese) 1 (1), Kyrgyz 1 (1), Czech 1 (1), Kucong (Lahlu) 1 (1), Tamil 1 (1), Turkish 1 (1), Tocharian (Tokharian) 1 (1), Tuyuhun (Azha) 吐谷浑 1 (1), Wuhuan 乌桓 1 (1), Xibo (Sibe) 1 (1), and Emishi (Ezo) 1 (1).

2 There are altogether over 13,300 loanwords and over 7,170 variants in the *Xinhua wailaici cidian* 新华外来词词典 or Xinhua dictionary of Chinese loanwords (Shi 2019). Compared with the *Xinhua* dictionary, we see a considerable increase in the number of loanwords from the major source languages: entries for those of English origin total 6,600, compared to 3,400 in the *Hanyu wailaici cidian* (Liu et al. 1984), and those of Japanese origin total 3,000 (excluding those very few variants), compared to 800 in the *Hanyu* dictionary. Even for the loanwords borrowed from the now dead language of Sansrikt, there are over 900 entries in the *Xinhua* dictinary, a slight increasee as compared with the 789 in the *Hanyu* dictionary.

3 Among those 50-strong loanwords are *fan* 梵, *fo(tuo)* 佛(陀), *pusa* 菩萨, *(a)luohan* (阿)罗汉, *namo* 南无, *emituofo* 阿弥陀佛, *mile* 弥勒, *lushenafo* 卢舍那佛, *weituo* 韦陀, *niepan* 涅槃, *puti* 菩提, *mantuluo* 曼荼罗, *heshang* 和尚, *seng* 僧, *toutuo* 头陀, *biqiu* 比丘, *biqiuni* 比丘尼, *shamen* 沙门, *shami* 沙弥, *yanluo* 阎罗, *mo* 魔, *yecha* 夜叉, *mantuoluo* 曼陀罗, *jialan* 珈蓝, *cha* 刹, *futu* 浮屠, *jie* 偈, *yujia* 瑜伽, *chan* 禅, *chan* 忏, *jie(bo)* 劫(波), *jiasha* 袈裟, *chana* 刹那, *tuoluoni* 陀罗尼, *yulanpen* 盂兰盆, and *zhina* 支那.

4 See Baugh, Albert G. 1957. *A History of the English Language*, p. 9. Also refer to Note 3 at the end of Chapter 2 of this book.

6 An overview of Chinese loanword studies

6.1 Areas of loanword studies

The linguistic, cultural, and social functions intrinsic to any lexicon mean that the loanword, as part and parcel of it, is the semiotic integration of language, culture, and society. From that, we can explore the following five areas, which each include further concentrations for loanword studies.

With loanword studies a part of language research, we may have an investigation of:

1 The etymology of the loanword to examine which language it comes from and the lexical and semantic origin of the word
2 Lexical identity, such as criteria to be used to determine the identity, qualifications, tier, and type of the loanword, and to prevent any false or pseudo-words from entering into the category or to remove such words which have already entered
3 Lexical composition to analyze the various representation forms and modes of composition so as to help determine the type and stratum of the loanword
4 Semantic evolution to ascertain the initial meaning of the word at the time of borrowing and how it has evolved into the present meaning
5 Written representation to analyze how the loanword is presented in writing and how it affects the borrowing language and its loanword assimilation in order to work out a viable scheme for written representation
6 Phonetic representation: how the loanword is actually pronounced in real life and how it phonetically varies between different geographic regions and demographic communities
7 Linguistic impact: how the loanword influences the borrowing language in terms of word formation, phonetics, syntax, pragmatics, and rhetoric, and how it affects the lexicon of the language as a whole

With loanword studies part of cultural studies, we may examine through loanwords:

An overview of Chinese loanword studies 207

8   Cultural exchange: the background of the cultural exchange behind the lexical borrowing, the trajectory of the borrowing, the cause and effect, the driving forces or the potential resistance, and its resolution in such exchanges
9   Cultural functions and implications of the loanword
10 Cultural integration which loanwords represent and potential cultural conflicts which they may bring

With loanword studies part of social studies, we may look into:

11 Different social strata of loanwords according to their social background and functions
12 Social purposes and the role the loanword plays as a social symbol
13 Interactive impact to observe the interactions between society and language

With loanword studies part of cross-disciplinary studies, we may also focus on:

14 Relevant statistics relating to the size and dynamic frequency of loanwords of various types and from various languages
15 Lexical collation and lexicography of various types and for different purposes based on solid etymological research
16 Loanword standardization to understand issues involving the actual use of the loanword and factors influencing its use so as to work out a viable standardization scheme and measures for its implementation
17 Process observation with regard to the initial borrowing, evolution, natural selection, decline, and disuse; the underlying causes or influencing factors; and relevant documentation.
18 Diachronic analysis of the loanword to prepare specific adjustment plans for its future development.
19 Contrastive investigation of the similarities and differences in terms of the above 18 aspects among loanwords from various source languages and from the same language in different historical periods so as to reach some general observations and offer possible advice for the development of those languages concerned

As efforts to develop loanword studies as an academic discipline, we can engage in:

20 Observing the spoken and written utterances in which loanwords appear and establishing various types of corpora to serve different purposes in further research
21 Terminology research. Though not strictly within its sphere *per se*, terminology is closely related to loanword studies and thus deserves

necessary attention. Just as Confucius stated more than 2,500 years ago in his *Analects* that "what is necessary is to rectify names" (*bi ye hu zhengming* 必也乎正名) and "if names be not correct, language is not in accordance with the truth of things" (*ming buzheng, yan bushun* 名不正,言不顺) (English translations by the 19th century Sinologist James Legge), so terminology today concerns the principle of naming or nomenclature and the bounds of the conceptual denotation and connotation, which closely relates to the loanword as it involves cross-lingual interactions in various terms.

22 Methodological and epistemological issues in loanword studies to build up theoretical underpinnings for loanword studies as an academic discipline

The above research concentrations are not mutually exclusive but strongly interconnected, so actual research activities will most probably turn out to be multi-threaded or cross-disciplinary in nature. What is more, as required by the development of any academic discipline, analytically rigorous and pertinent comment on the Chinese academic scene is found sadly wanting and will therefore be highly anticipated in the future.

6.2 Etymological research on the loanword

Etymology is an at once foundational and extremely challenging research upon which other relevant research is based. It is therefore very comprehensive work which requires cross-disciplinary awareness and capabilities such as expertise in foreign languages, natural and human history, geography, culture, folk customs, and archaeology.

Chinese loanword etymology did not start in earnest until the first half of the 20th century, when some predominantly Western scholars dedicated themselves to the textual archaeology of the Chinese borrowing of specific nomenclature, such as in the investigation of the Chinese borrowing of Central Asian plant and mineral names in *Sino-Iranica* by Berthold Laufer (1874–1934), American anthropologist and Sinologist, and separate research into the names of Central or Southeast Asia-originated physical things and places which appeared in classical Chinese texts by Sinologists Paul Pelliot (1878–1945), Sir Marc Aurel Stein (1862–1943), Henri Paul Gaston Maspero (1883–1945), Émmanuel-Édouard Chavannes (1865–1918), Sylvain Lévi (1863–1935), Léonard Eugène Aurousseau (1888–1929), and Gabriel Ferrand (1864–1935). Most of the latter research was published in France in *T'oung Pao*, the oldest international journal of Chinese studies; the *Journal Asiatique*; and the *Bulletin de l'École française d'Extrême-Orient*. Around the same time, some Japanese scholars also made contributions to Chinese lexical archaeology, including Shiratori Kurakichi (1865–1942), who studied, among many other areas of "Oriental history," the titles used among the Hun (Xiongnu) people in the 300s and 400s AD; Haneda Tōru (1882–1955), in his research on Turkic physical culture; and Tokuno Oda (1860–1911) and Shinko Mochizuki (1869–1948), in their exploration into and collation of the source words for Buddhist terms.

It should be admitted that Chinese indigenous scholarly efforts on loanword etymology were first inspired by these Western and Japanese counterparts and built on their achievements. Prior to 1949, when the People's Republic was founded, well-known Chinese scholars related to the field included Feng Chengjun 冯承钧 (1887–1946), Feng Jiasheng 冯家升 (1904–1970), Chen Yinque 陈寅恪 (1890–1969), Chen Yuan 陈垣 (1880–1971), Han Rulin 韩儒林 (1903–1983), Ji Xianlin 季羡林 (1911–2009), Xu Fu 徐复 (1912–2006), Cen Zhongmian 岑仲勉 (1886–1961), Xiang Da 向达 (1900–1966), and Guo Moruo 郭沫若 (1892–1978), who conducted admirably meticulous investigations into some Chinese loanwords in their study of Chinese history, such as the etymological efforts on Chinese loanwords of the Hun language in *Xiongnu minzu jiqi wenhua* 匈奴民族及其文化 (1937) by Feng Jiasheng; the pronunciation of the names of the Hun queens (in the sense of the official wife of the king) in *Yanshi yindu kao* 阏氏音读考 (1945) by Xu Fu; the names of Modu (c.234–c.174), the founder of the empire of the Xiongnu in ancient China's early Han dynasty, in *Modu zhi yuyuan jiqi yindu* 冒顿之语源及其音读 (1948) by Cen Zhongmian; the early Turkic official titles in *Tujue guanhao yanjiu* 突厥官号研究 (1940) by Han Rulin; and the Chinese names for Islam and its disciples in *Huihuijiao ru zhongguo shilue* 回回教入中国史略 (1940) by Chen Yuan. Perhaps the most outstanding work from this period is *Xiyu diming* 西域地名 (1955, first edition) by Feng Chengjun, later updated in 1980 by Lu Jungling 陆峻岭, a textual archaeology and compendium of the names of the places west of ancient China, generically called the Western Regions.

It must be pointed out that all these Chinese scholars were historians by training, and they happened to engage in textual archaeology (loanword etymology as its by-product, so to speak) only with the aim to better interpret history, their main field of study. Thus, there has been virtually no etymological study of loanwords solely from the linguistic perspective; in fact, it might be safe to say that, since its inception, Chinese loanword studies has been inextricably intertwined with culture, society, and many other fields of study.

The etymological study of Chinese loanwords of Japanese origin, unlike those of Western origin, is mainly involved in the determination of the true identity of the words in question. To date, the earliest work in this regard was *Xin mingci xunzuan* 新名词训纂 (*Collection of new words*) in 1913 by Zhou Qiyu 周起予, which did an admirable job of questioning and distinguishing 606 new Chinese terms, many presumably from Japanese, mostly from the angle of their origin in Early or Ancient Chinese.

After 1949, etymological research was conducted off and on, mostly still incidentally to research into other fields, such as natural and human history, geography, and ethnic studies, with little involvement from scholars in linguistics. Its achievements, therefore, were fragmented and did not make a marked impression or impact. Notwithstanding, some valuable contributions were still made during this period. The re-examination of the Mongol ceremonial *zhisun* robes 质孙服 in the Yuan dynasty by Ye Yiliang 叶奕良 (1936–2015) corrected the previously held view that the word *zhisun* originated from the Mongol *jasun*, "color," and pointed out that, instead, it came from the Early Persian word *jashn*, meaning "ritual," and, hence, the ceremonial robes granted by the emperor (see Ye's article in *Dongfang yanjiu lunwenji* 东方研究论文集. Beijing: Peking University Press. 1983). The etymological re-examination by Cai Meibiao 蔡美彪 (1928–) of the character 乣, which was used in the Khitan Liao, Jurchen Jin, and Mongol Yuan dynasties in ancient China, concluded that jiū, jiǔ, yòu, and yǒu (in Chinese phonetic *pinyin*) are all incorrect pronunciations of the word, which was originally a phonetic loan from an ancient Mongol word meaning "chicken," a variant of *jiu* 鸡, and the sub-standardized written form for both *jiu* 纠 and *zha* 札, and should therefore be pronounced *zhá* or *chá*, meaning "impure species or people." That is why, proves Cai, the term 乣民 at the time referred to people of the conquered ethnic groups, while 乣军 referred to an army made up of those people (see "乣yu 乣军zhi yanbian" 乣与乣军之演变 in *Yuanshi luncong* 元史论丛, Vol. 2. Beijing: Zhonghua Book Company. 1983). The research by Yang Zhijiu 杨志玖 on the Khitan word *tama* 挞马 (*tama*) and that by Jia Jingyan 贾敬颜 on the Mongol word *tanmachi* 探马赤 (*tamachi*) separately concluded that both originated from the Turkic *damozhi* 答摩支 (*tapmachi*), whose meaning evolved from "bodyguard for senior officials" to "vanguard cavalry or regional garrison soldiers," thus correcting the long-held misinterpretation by the *Yuanshi guoyujie* 元史国语解 in the late 18th century, the authorized history book of the Yuan dynasty.

The latter part of the 20th century started to see more Chinese scholars in linguistics joining the etymological efforts. These included, among others, the study of the etymological timeline for the three waterbirds *ya* 鸭, *ou* 鸥, and *wu* 鹜 by Wen You 闻宥 in 1980; the annotated revision of the *Datang xuyuji* 大唐西域记 (*Records of the Western Regions of the Great Tang Dynasty* by Xuanzang (Hsuan-tsang) 玄奘, Buddhist monk and Chinese pilgrim to India who translated the sacred scriptures of Buddhism from Sanskrit into Chinese) by Sanskrit scholar Ji Xianlin in 1990; the exhaustive etymological investigations in 1978 by philologist Zhang Qingchang 张清常 of *hutong* 胡同 and other Chinese loanwords of Mongol origin (one, for example, in which he discovered that the word *sai* in *sainiang* 赛娘, "beautiful girl," frequently used in variety plays popular in the Yuan dynasty, is abbreviated from the loanword *saiyin* 赛因 from the Mongolian *sain*, meaning "good"); and the etymological enquiry into many words, including *gesuer* 格素尔, by Liu Zhengtan 刘正埮 in 1984 in his co-compilation of the highly respected loanword dictionary *Hanyu wailaici cidian*, and the lexical examination of *feilian* 飞廉 (the Chinese god of wind) by Yuchi Zhiping 慰迟治平 in 1995. In his lexical examination of the adverb *bai* 白 as it was used in the mid-18th century classical novel *Hongloumeng* 红楼梦 and the 19th-century popular novel *Ernu yingxiong zhuan* 儿女英雄传, Hu Zengyi 胡增益 (1989, 1995) concluded that the adverb was loaned from the Manchu *bai/baibi*, which had, in turn, been borrowed from earlier Chinese. Lexicologist Zhang Yongyan 张永言 (1992b) proved through his research that the *mu* in *muhou* 沐猴 (macaque) was phonemically borrowed from the Tibetan *muk/mjuk* and that *huntuo* 浑脱 (a leather sack made from a whole stripped animal skin) was not a phonemic loanword.

The same period also saw similar efforts and achievements by international scholars. In his *The Golden Peaches of Samarkand: A Study of Tang Exotics* (1962), Sinologist Edward H. Schafer examined many words borrowed in the Tang dynasty. Sustained research led Japanese China expert Kiyohide Arakawa (1987, 1990, 1997) to conclude that the Chinese word *redai* 热带 ("the tropics") was created not in Japan but in China, while *huiguixian* 回归线 ("tropic") was indeed invented in Japan. The landmark monograph by Italian scholar Federico Masini (1993) made a massive investigation into the formation of the modern Chinese lexicon, especially its borrowing of loanwords. His work confirms the fact that Chinese first translated the new concepts or ideas implicit in the Western lexicon and, with his meticulous enquiry into the lexical exchange between Japan and China, also proves that many of the Chinese words previously considered pure graphic loans of Japanese origin were in fact those which Japan had borrowed from Chinese first.

Given the great complexity involved in lexical exchange between Japan and China, determining Chinese loanwords of Japanese origin is treacherously challenging and calls for far more effort than do those from Western languages. That is why we are so pleased to see the work undertaken by a number of Chinese scholars well versed in Japanese, Shen Guowei 沈国威 and Zhu Jingwei 朱京伟 chief among them. Through his rigorous re-examination, Shen (1994, 2010) proved Chinese provenance for a number of words previously considered of Japanese origin and confirmed some *bona fide* Chinese loanwords from Japanese. Almost every year since 1993, Zhu has published his etymological research on Chinese loanwords of Japanese origin. Peng Guanglu 彭广陆 also conducted a substantial case study of such words as *liaoli* 料理, *guolaosi* 过劳死, *xianjin* 献金, *zhengfa* 蒸发, *xiezhen* 写真, *wenti* 问题, and the suffixes -*zu* -族 and -*wu* -屋. As shining examples of scholarship, their academic rigor and research have made significant contributions to the maturity of loanword studies in China.

In addition, Lin Meicun 林梅村, a contemporary expert in Tocharian and the Western Regions in ancient China, published his brilliant etymological explorations of many Chinese words borrowed from the Western Regions, such as *jinglu* 径路, *wengzhong* 翁仲, and *qilin* 麒麟. His work demonstrates solitary and painstaking dedication that is extremely rare among his peers.

Again, we are particularly grateful to Professor Feng Chengjun 冯承钧 (1887–1946), who devoted practically his entire life to the translation of over 100 papers by Western scholars and the compilation of the voluminous *Xiyu nanhai shidi kaozheng yicong* 西域南海史地考证译丛 (*Collections of translated works for the study on historical geography of the Western Regions and the regions surrounding the South China Sea*). The first four volumes of his historic work were first published in 1934, and the remaining five were posthumously published in 1956–1958. Without Feng's admirable effort, it would be impossible for scholars of this field to be where they are today, academically speaking.

Founded in 1993 by the Chinese Language Society of Hong Kong, *Ciku jianshe tongxun* 词库建设通讯, a journal dedicated to loanword and related studies, has made impressive headway over the past four years (at the time of writing this book in 1997). Led by Yao Te Hwai 姚德怀, then head of the society, *Ciku* focuses its research on "conceptual loanwords," which include both general and semantic words, by constructing a data bank for Chinese conceptual loanwords as well as one for Cantonese used in Hong Kong and yet another for plant names, which also contain a considerable number of conceptual loanwords. Thanks to the journal, which attracts attention from interested scholars from home and abroad, hundreds of related words have been rigorously examined in terms of etymology and lexical/graphic formation, bringing in lively open discussions. Building on this momentum, Huang Heqing 黄河清 (1996) proposed the construction of a "lexical chronology" in order to make etymological enquiry systematic (for more details, please refer to Section 6.5 of this chapter). In short, it is fair to say that what *Ciku* has done is a major milestone in contemporary Chinese loanword studies.

In addition, by pure coincidence, He Huazhen 何华珍 (1998) and Shi Youwei 史有为 (1998) have simultaneously (but separately) conducted a careful, detailed examination on the origin of the word *ai* 癌 (with the earliest meaning of ulcer-like sore used in traditional Chinese medicine), concluding that the word was indeed made in China rather than Japan, and its later correspondence with cancer or malignant tumor was first made by Japanese scholars. Shi (2008, 2016b) also proves that the word *ma* 码 ("yard") is not from Japanese, as has been claimed by some, but an internal semantic loan from the Chinese Min or Cantonese dialect. The 21st century is seeing a new wave of etymological and other research into newly emerging loanwords, with many scholars resuming the work on neologisms which was halted during the Cultural Revolution. We would expect to see more of this down the road.

6.3 Cultural and social aspects of loanword studies

6.3.1 Cultural aspects of loanword studies

Loanwords have long been considered a means by which to probe into the cultures with which they are associated. This can be seen in many examples of scholarly research, such as the monumental *Sino-Iranica: Chinese contributions to the history of civilization in ancient Iran, with special reference to the history of cultivated plants and products* (1919) by American anthropologist Berthold Laufer, "Sur l'origine des Hiong-nou" [*On the origin of the Xiong-nu*] (*Journal Asiatique*, série 11:202/203.1923) by Japanese Sinologist Kurakichi Shiratori, and *Yuyan yu wenhua* 语言与文化 (1950) by prominent Chinese linguist Luo Changpei 罗常培 (1899–1958). As Luo points out in this ground-breaking work on Chinese cultural linguistics (1950:18), careful investigations into this mutual lexical borrowing throughout history may very well provide interesting explanations for the history of cultural evolution. The size and scope of the two-way lexical borrowing, for example, can offer a rough idea of China's cultural relations with other ethnic communities. By examining loanwords of general subjects, place names, and personal names in the book, Luo studied racial/ethnic origins, migrations, and religious beliefs as well as inter-racial or -ethnic cultural exchanges. The investigation of the loanword *shizi* 狮子/师子 ("lion"), for example, unveils its long historical route of entry into ancient China via Persia, the Yuezhi kingdom (ruling ancient Sogdiana and Bactria in what is now part of Afghanistan, Uzbekistan, and Tajikistan), and the Shule kingdom in what is now the city of Kashgar in China's southern Xinjiang province. Luo also traced its lexical formation back to Proto-Iranian. Citing research on place names by two other Chinese scholars, Luo pointed out that the characters *na* 那, *du* 都, *duo* 多, *gu* 古, *liu* 六, and *lu* 禄/陆 contained in place names across southern China's Guangdong and Guangxi provinces are all linguistic traces of Tai, the language spoken by the Zhuang people, the largest ethnic minority of South China. In fact, concluded Luo, the places whose names contained one of the above characters used to be where the Zhuang people had lived, which covered a larger area than where they currently live. In his book, Luo also encapsulated research by Xiang Da 向达 and Chen Yuan 陈垣 on the Sinification of personal names from the Western Regions and that of those Arab or ancient Uighur names by Ma Jian 马坚. Building on this, Luo offered a systemic and consistent interpretation of those phenomena from the angle of cultural interchange and reiterated his central argument that the Chinese nation originated in multi-tribal, multi-ethnic integration.

Another worth making note of is the monumental *Zhongxi jiaotong shiliao huibian* 中西交通史料汇编 (*Collated resources on historical communications between China and the rest of the world*) by Zhang Xinglang 张星烺. First published in 1930 and later expanded and collated by Zhu Jieqin 朱杰勤 in six volumes in 1977, the tome collects all the relevant research-worthy data available at the time, ranging from ancient classics to textual research from modern times. With the resources arranged along temporal and geographical lines in the volumes, loanwords were discussed mostly to sketch the cultural exchanges of ancient China with Europe, Africa, Arabia, Armenia, Central Asia, Persia, and India as well as with the Jewish people. Later research into this area all builds on this admirable work.

At the same time, other Chinese scholars were also trying to study such cultural exchanges from loanwords. As discussed in Sections 2.1.2 and 2.1.3 in Chapter 2 of this book, for example, Guo Moruo discovered the close etymological association of the ancient Chinese names for the 12 years and months with Babylonian. From his observation that *sheti(ge)* and *chanyan*, both names for different years, and *gu* and *tu*, both names for different months, probably originated from Babylonian, Guo inferred that there existed a certain relationship between Chinese culture in the Shang dynasty (1766–1122 BC) and Babylonian civilization. Having noticed that in Chinese Buddhist scriptures, *fo* 佛 appeared counter-intuitively in advance of *fotuo* 佛陀, both meaning "Buddha," and that the Chinese sound /l/ was used to correspond to Sanskrit apical consonants /t/ and /d/, Sanskrit scholar Ji Xianlin took the two as clues and discovered that Buddhist scriptures had been translated from Central Asian languages, such as Tocharian, until the Sui dynasty (581–618 AD), and only after the Sui were they gradually translated directly from Sanskrit.

Since 1949 there have not been many published monographs, or papers on historical cultural exchange from the loanword perspective. As a general enquiry, *Xiandai hanyu wailaici yanjiu* 现代汉语外来词研究 (1958) by Gao Mingkai 高名凯 and Liu Zhengtan 刘正埮 emphasized the great significance of loanwords in modern Chinese to international cultural exchange and illustrated the focus of what has been borrowed in the process through observing the semantically classified loanwords. As the first monograph on modern Chinese loanwords, this has made landmark contributions, but, considering its collected data and the emphasis on loanword standardization, their research is not an in-depth analysis on cultural exchange *per se*.

However, there is some more relevant and in-depth research in this regard. *Sichou zhilu yu xiyu wenhua* 丝绸之路与西域文化 (1981) by Chang Renxia 常任侠 (Ch'ang Jen-hsia) investigates historical contact between ancient China and the Central Asian "Western Regions" through its examination of the "seven modes and seven tones" which was generally attributed to Sujiva (Sujipo苏祇婆), a great player of the ancient *pipa*, or the pear-shaped lute, from the Kingdom of Kucha in the 6th century during the Northern Zhou dynasty and ancient Iranian dance music. The phonological tracing of the words *dao* 稻 and *he* 禾, "plant that produces rice" and "cereal plant," respectively, in *Fangyan yu zhongguo wenhua* 方言与中国文化 (1986) by Zhou Zhenhe 周振鹤 and You Ruchang 游汝昌, and in *Zhongguo wenhua yuyanxue yinlun* 中国文化语言学引论 (1993) by You Ruchang reveal the historical trajectory of those cereal plants and the cross-border cultural communications behind the plants. Quite a few scholars of language and culture have published research on the relations between loanwords and Sino-Japanese cultural exchange in modern times too, such as Wang Xiaoqiu 王晓秋 (*Jindai zhongri wenhua jiaoliu shi* 近代中日文化交流史, 2000), Zhu Jingwei (*Liang Qichao yu riyu jieci* 梁启超与日语借词, 2007), and Shen Guowei (*Jindai zhongri cihui jiaoliu yanjiu* 近代中日词汇交流研究, 2010). Backed by a multitude of facts, documentation, and lexical evidence, their enquiries have provided an impressive picture of inter-lingual, cross-national communications in modern history.

Cultural communication studies are also approached from the perspective of translation. In its chronicling of major translation activities, ranging from those on Buddhist scriptures in the Eastern Han dynasty (25–220 AD) all the way through to those on Western science, technology, and social sciences which happened between the late Ming (1368–1644) and the time prior to the May Fourth Movement around 1917, *Zhongguo fanyi jianshi* 中国翻译简史 (1984) by Ma Zuyi 马祖毅 has in effect shown how various forms of translation—phonemic loaning of foreign words included—historically helped the introduction of modern technologies and social sciences and the humanities to China. Combining chronological investigation and conceptual classification in his two books, Shi Youwei (1991, 2000) provides a comprehensive survey of historical cultural interchange in loanwords and an approach to examining cultural exchanges in terms of the impact of loanwords on Chinese lexical formation. Liang Xiaohong 梁晓虹 (1992, 1994) also traces the historical cultural activities between China and India through Buddhist terms and the influence of the lexicon on Chinese culture.

6.3.2 Social aspects of loanword studies

There has not been much research in this area. In his *Yuyan he ren* 语言和人 (1994), Chen Yuan 陈原 dedicates five sections (loanwords, language contact, linguist mosaic, terminology, and Chinese characters) to linguistic loaning and cultural exchange, which have also touched on some related social factors (Sections 5.1–5.3, 6.6, and 7.5 in Chen's book) from the perspective of language contact. There seems to be an appalling lack of research into many social aspects of loanword studies such as how social influencing factors are reflected in loanwords, how social stratification affects loanword assimilation, how loanwords, in turn, shape society and human beings in society, and how social functions of the loanword are represented and extend. The key to serious and productive research in these social aspects may ultimately lie in the application of an investigative approach in sociology to the examination of the myriad linguistic and social communities of the Han Chinese throughout recorded history and across national or geographical boundaries.

6.4 Typological studies

Typological studies of the loanword can be approached through three sub-areas: loaning types, types in terms of qualifications, and other linguistic/social types.

6.4.1 Research on loaning types

Predominant attention has thus far been paid to loaning types. A related field, namely the definitional scope of loanwords, has been heavily explored for a long time. In his *Zhongguo wenfa yaolue* 中国文法要略 (1942), Lu Shuxiang 吕叔湘, a renowned Chinese linguist, argues that lexical loaning is either semantic or phonemic and that semantic loans are classified as compound words and, strictly speaking, cannot count as loanwords because they are made by combining forms of the words or linguistic roots which are autochthonous to the borrowing language, while phonemic loans belong to the phonetically evolved type of words because their component lexical elements each constitute an inseparable integrated whole. Luo Changpei (1950) classifies lexical loaning into four types: (1) phonic conversion, which is subdivided into pure phonemic loaning, such as *shafa*; phonemic semantic loaning, such as *kekou kele*; phonemic loaning with semantic marking, such as *kache*; and phonemic pseudo-semantic loaning, such as *aimeidi* 爱美的 (for the English *amateur*); (2) new phonetic approximation with semantic cues, such as *moli* 茉莉 (jasmine, from the Sanskrit *mallika* or the Syrian *molo*) and *lu* 铝 (from *aluminum*); (3) loan translation, such as *yinyuan* 因缘 (cause); and (4) descriptive loaning, such as *hucong* 胡葱 (green onion) and *huochai* 火柴 (match which can light or ignite), as has been discussed in Section 1.2.1 in Chapter 1. Zheng Dian 郑奠 (1958) argues that descriptive loaning cannot count as a type of loanword and proposes that words borrowed from Japanese kanji should count as an additional type. Similar to Zheng's classification, Sun Changxu 孙常叙 (1957) suggests that borrowed words of foreign origin be divided into loanwords (phonemic loans and graphic loans of Japanese kanji) and translated words (namely, semantic loans, including those fully translated, half-translated, and translated with explanatory notes). However, Wang Li 王力 argues that not all translated words but truly borrowed foreign words can be considered bona fide *wailaici* and the calque, one special type of semantic loan, is close to being called a loanword (1958:516, 526). In fact, Wang does not take calques as loanwords in the narrower sense of the term; neither does he take Japanese kanji as loanwords, arguing that they are still translated words, though done by the Japanese, thus saving us the trouble (1958:528). Wang admits that words borrowed from Japanese kanji on a kun-yomi reading qualify as loanwords in a broad sense, though he insists that they're not pure ones because the sound of the source word is not borrowed in any way (1958:535). Gao Mingkai and Liu Zhengtan (1958) think that only phonemic loans, half-phonemic loans, and words borrowed from Japanese kanji qualify as loanwords. Obviously, what has long been at issue here are those words borrowed from Japanese kanji.

For a better idea of what types of lexical borrowing these Chinese scholars of linguistics think can qualify as loanwords, here is a summary table of their opinion, with "Yes" indicating that a particular type is believed to qualify as loanword, "No" indicating that it is believed to not qualify, and "?" indicating that it probably does not qualify.

	Lu Shuxiang 吕叔湘	Luo Changpei 罗常培	Zheng Dian 郑奠	Sun Changxu 孙常叙	Zhou Zumo 周祖谟	Gao Mingkai 高名凯	Wang Li 王力
Phonemic loaning	Yes	Yes	Yes	Yes	Yes	Yes	Yes
Phonemic semantic loaning	Yes	Yes	Yes	Yes	Yes	Yes	Yes
New phonetic approximation with semantic cues	Yes	Yes	Yes	Yes	Yes	Yes	Yes
Phonemic loaning with semantic marking	Yes	Yes	Yes	Yes	Yes	Yes	Yes
Hybrid	Yes	Yes	Yes	Yes	Yes	Yes	Yes
Japanese kanji on kun-yomi reading	?	?	Yes	Yes	?	Yes	≈Yes
Japanese kanji on on-yomi reading	?	?	Yes	Yes	?	Yes	No
Calque/loan translation	No	Yes	Yes	Yes	?	No	≈Yes
Semantic loaning	No	Yes	?	Yes	No	No	No
Semantic descriptive loaning	No	Yes	No	No	No	No	No

The prevailing view, represented by Gao and Liu (1958), is that phonemic or graphic/graphemic loaning constitutes the essence of a loanword. Shi (1991a) proposes that we follow the Japanese trichotomy of its lexicon into *wago* (native Japanese words, including the kun-yomi portion of *kanji* or ideograms adapted from Chinese characters in the Japanese writing system), the on-yomi portion of *kanji*, and *gairaigo* (foreign loanwords), and single out those borrowed *kanji* of Japanese origin as what might be called "quasi-loanwords."

There have been adequate discussions since the 1990s in the Hong Kong-based journal *Ciku jianshe tongxun* about where general loanwords and conceptual loanwords should belong in the national lexicon, with a general consensus that the former term is limited to phonemic or graphic/graphemic loaning, while the latter extends to a broader scope, as suggested by Zheng Dian and Sun Changxu, and that, seen from the perspective of language development, cultural exchange, and social evolution, an investigation of the latter is of more academic significance than a mere enquiry into the former.

In the early 21st century, a paper by Pan Wenguo 潘文国, a scholar with diverse research experience, takes a refreshing view toward categorizing loanwords. In his "*Wailaiyu xinlun*" 外来语新论 (2008), Pan classifies Chinese loanwords into a complex system of three different types (pure, hybrid, an self-made) in four hierarchical tiers.

6.4.2 Research on the qualifications for the loanword

Research solely dedicated to this area is rare but often combined with that of loaning types. What is more, the rare discussion of the qualifications has been greatly influenced by the conventional dualistic epistemology. In an attempt to break with this traditional mode of thinking, Shi (1991c) introduces the fuzzy concept into the discussion by assigning a total score of ten to five dimensions of the loanword (semantics, phonetics, morphemics, word form, and character form) to observe the extent to which a particular loanword is affected along the continuum by the five foreign linguistic factors. This graduation classifies lexical borrowing into 16–22 sometimes nuanced types with varying degrees of foreignness (for more details, refer to Section 3.4 in Chapter 3).

6.4.3 Other typological research

Yet to be seen are typological loanword studies in terms of functions, semantics, language community types, and contrastive research into different language types in loanword origin. At least an enquiry into functional types can be explored in combination with functional classifications of lexicon, such as general versus proper nouns or the trichotomy (terminology, everyday words, and proper nouns) so as to understand their social and cultural roles.

6.5 Lexicographic work

Lexicographic work on loanwords here not only refers to the ultimate dictionary or encyclopedia compilation but also includes such efforts as developing relevant chronological collation, corpora, resource libraries, and databases, all of which should, theoretically, at least, get started in advance of the former. It was not until 1993 that such efforts were made in earnest as scholars in Hong Kong initiated the project of developing a data bank for conceptual loanwords. Later on, similar impressive and admirable efforts were sustained by individual scholars, such as Shen Guowei in Japan and Huang Heqing in China. Institutional efforts, however, from the modern mainstream Chinese language community, are found deplorably lacking. So, in general, the institutional understanding of the loanword remains minimal in regard to the time and place of its birth as well as its first actual use.

There is a clear picture of the loanwords used in ancient China, however, thanks to the scholars dedicated to textual archaeology, standing in sharp contrast to the muddled scholarship over modern and pre-modern Chinese loanwords. This, in turn, necessarily means various failings inherent in the lexicographic work on loanwords.

Realizing the extremely comprehensive and complicated nature of lexicography, Pan Wenguo (2008) thinks that a large loanword dictionary should ideally possess six major features: a fresh start built on past achievements, synchronic focus as well as diachronic descriptions, practical orientation, substantial scope, thorough consideration, and application of corpora. In the preface to his *Xinhua wailaici cidian*, Shi Youwei (2017, 2018) also proposes that an ideal loanword dictionary should have the following ten characteristics: first, it strictly follows the criteria in loanword selection; second, it provides as broad and balanced a collection of loanwords as possible; third, it provides the accurate source word; fourth, it has further etymological information; fifth, it provides the earliest possible attestation of usage; sixth, it offers the necessary pragmatic information, including the region where it is used, user social class, frequency in use, actual pronunciation, and lexical style; seventh, it offers relevant information about the loanword in question, such as the justification for selecting it and background about the source word so as to attain a better understanding of the loanword; eighth, it has a function of associating one with other similar or opposite loanwords, if any; ninth, it provides different views or research results on the loanword to promote further research; and, lastly, it provides an interactive platform on which to dynamically add, delete, modify, or update the content of the dictionary. From what we have done so far, it is clear that there is a long way to go before such a goal can be attained. Here is a brief review of what has been achieved to date in the field of lexicography.

Arguably, the earliest loanword-related lexicographer in modern China was Ding Fubao 丁福保 (1874–1952), who, building on some Japanese dictionaries of Buddhism, compiled the multi-million-word *Foxue dacidian* 佛学大辞典 (*Dictionary of Buddhist studies.* Shanghai yixue shuju 上海医学书局, 1922), China's first loanword-related dictionary. Despite its similar subject, *A Dictionary of Chinese Buddhist Terms* (1937) by William E. Soothill (1861–1935) pales in scope in comparison to Ding's work. The *Wailaiyu cidian* 外来语词典 (Shanghai tianma shuju 上海天马书局, 1936) by Hu Xingzhi 胡行之 collects only parts of modern Chinese loanwords. Not highly acclaimed by the field, Hu's dictionary does not provide reliable word origin or source word form but is instead interspersed with a large number of place and personal names. Besides borrowed Japanese kanji, the dictionary includes semantic loans, with phonemic loans making up only a part of it.

With a total of 1,820 entries, the *Guoyu ribao wailaiyu cidian* 國語日報外來語詞典 (1981) published by *Guoyu ribao* 國語日報 (*Mandarin Daily News*) in Taiwan was arguably the very first loanword-specific dictionary in contemporary China. It mainly contains fully or partially phonemic loanwords;

common (i.e. non-proper noun) loanwords which had been discussed in that newspaper; and some few culturally loaded proper nouns, such as *Shijiamouni* 释迦牟尼 (Sakyamuni), *Xinbada* 辛巴达 (Sindbad or Sinbad, hero of *The Thousand and One Nights*), Fan'ersaigong 凡尔赛宫 (Château de Versailles), and *Xinli* 新力 (Sony Corporation, now commonly known as *Suoni* 索尼 in Chinese). With no Japanese kanji included, this dictionary provides each entry with its *Zhuyin* phonetic script, brief information about the source word, and sometimes further etymological information.

If not for divergence of opinion within the publisher or among the compilers, two more dictionaries of the kind would have come out earlier than the *Guoyu ribao wailaiyu cidian*. Despite the completion of its first draft by Gao Mingkai, Liu Zhengtan, and Mai Yongqian 麦永乾 in 1966, the *Hanyu wailaici cidian* had to wait until the end of the Cultural Revolution (1967–1976) to be published, now with the addition of Shi Youwei and a nearly complete redo, finally being published by Shanghai cishu chubanshe 上海辞书出版社 in 1984, rather than the originally scheduled publisher. With more than 10,000 total entries (variants included), the dictionary lists full or partial phonemic loans and Japanese kanji, with sufficient consideration and inclusion of those borrowed words from the languages of China's ethnic minorities. Most entries are provided with detailed etymological information and all variant forms available. In hindsight, however, there are three main drawbacks in this dictionary. Most of the entries are not provided with either documented evidence or the earliest attestation of use. Some of them, especially those of Russian origin, are collected without independent verification from Russian-Chinese dictionaries. Words of Japanese origin are insufficiently collected, and some are erroneously included because they turn out to have been made earlier in China. All those issues are in essence attributable to the inadequacy of loanword studies, reflected in the inability to provide sufficient sources to refer to and thus the failure to verify each entry at the time of compilation.

The other is the *Hanyu wailaiyu cidian* 汉语外来语词典 (Shangwu yinshuguan 商务印书馆, 1990) by Cen Qixiang 岑麒祥 (1903–1989). Most of the handwritten catalogue and note cards on this dictionary had been completed by 1977, and a draft was finished in 1981, but its publication was postponed for nine years due to content-related issues. With 4,307 entries in total, this dictionary lists phonemic loans, borrowed Japanese kanji, semantic loanwords (including phrases) translated by the Chinese, and a considerable portion of personal and place names. A great merit of this dictionary is its provision of documented evidence, though not always of the first attestation of use, for a substantial number of entries. Though the publisher suggested that most personal and place names be removed, except some ancient ones because they were not common nouns, the compiler did not take the advice. However, there are some drawbacks. The scope of the words listed in this dictionary is rather limited; many important loanwords and/or their variants are not included, while semantic words and even semantic loan phrases are. There is an obvious lack of detailed etymological information or provision of the primary source language (e.g. *miyue* 蜜月 is included without the etymological information that it originated from the Japanese *mitsugetsu*, a semantic loan of the English "honeymoon"). In all fairness, however, what a scholar in his seventies has done, single-handedly, deserves nothing short of admiration and respect.

In the early 21st century, Shangwu Yinshuguan (The Commercial Press), China's leading academic publisher, decided to compile a new dictionary of loanwords and commissioned Shi Youwei to be its editor-in-chief. Designed to build on the merits of existing dictionaries of its kind and to divide its entries into three categories—phonemic loaning including hybrids, graphic loaning (Japanese kanji), and alphabetic loaning—this *Xinhua wailaici cidian* 新华外来词词典 is intended to be medium-sized, descriptive, open, informative, and research-facilitating, with continuous supplementation and revision built into its compiling philosophy. Published in January 2019, the latest dictionary contains 20,000 entries (7,000 variants included), among which there are 6,600 loanwords of English origin, 3,000 words of Japanese origin, and 2,000 words which start with a letter. In this connection, *Yiwenhua de shizhe: wailaici* 异文化的使者—外来词 (1991) and its revised version *Wailaici: yiwenhua de shizhe* 外来词—异文化的使者 (2004), both by Shi, provide an index of loanwords and may double as small-sized dictionaries of frequently used Chinese loanwords.

Apart from these loanword-oriented dictionaries or books, loanwords are also collected in other general- or special-purpose dictionaries in China, such as *Ciyuan* 辞源, *Cihai* 辞海, *Zongjiao cidian* 宗教词典, *Xiandai hanyu cidian* 现代汉语词典, *Hanyu da cidian* 汉语大词典, and *Beifang fangyan cidian* 北方方言词典 by Chen Gang 陈刚, and various terminological glossaries or lexicons. But within these, there exist quite a few errors with regard to the loanwords listed, such as the wrong etymological and explanatory information on *sahua* 撒花 (tip or award money from the Mongol *sang*; see Section 2.4.2.3 in Chapter 2) and *bitieshi* 笔帖式 (clerk in charge of translation, documentation, and filing, from the Manchu *bithesi*, from the Mongol *bicigci*; see Section 2.4.2.4 in Chapter 2) in the revised edition of *Ciyuan*, and the citation from Japanese scholar Matajirou Takejima which was erroneously accredited to Zhang Taiyan 章太炎, who did quote him in 1902 in his *Wenxue shuoli* 文学说例 (for more details, refer to Section 1.2.2 in Chapter 1), under the entry of "wailaiyu" 外来语 in the *Hanyu da cidian*.

What are worth noting here are two works of reference on the etymology of modern Chinese neologisms: *Jinxiandai hanyu xinci yuyuan cidian* 近现代汉语新词语源词典 (2001) and *Jinxiandai ciyuan* 近现代辞源 (2010), both compiled by Huang Heqing 黄河清 and completed, for all intents and purposes, single-handedly. Both contain a large number of general loanwords and semantically translated words. What is more, Huang went to great pains to gather and collate many related words and documented sources which are either missing or neglected in the much-larger *Hanyu da cidian*.

In terms of the collection of resources for loanword studies, the only major work, to date, remains *Zhongxi wenhua jiaotong shiliao huibian* 中西文化交通史料 by Zhang Xinglang 张星烺, as discussed in Section 6.3.1 in this chapter. While Zhang's monumental work plays the role of chronologically collating the loanwords in ancient China, such efforts are yet to be seen on loanwords which appeared in pre-modern or modern China. The data bank for conceptual loanwords initiated by the Chinese Language Society of Hong Kong and led by Yao Te Hwai in 1993 has already collected several hundred entries, a considerable portion of which are loanwords in the narrow sense of the term. Each entry in the data bank normally contains five parts: index entry (usually the foreign source word), headword(s), meaning, word origin, and references; sometimes, another three parts are also included: namely, usage note, word story, and open discussion. Each entry ends with the name of its contributor(s) for transparent accountability. Each headword is edited by various scholars during different periods for revision purposes or else by a number of simultaneously invited contributors for close examination. Provided the effort is sustainable, this foundational project will be a significant milestone in the history of Chinese loanword studies.

It must be pointed out that lexicographical compilation is facing the more urgent challenge of accessing or trying to access many corpora, which might touch upon some sensitive fields or delicate subjects. It is hoped that further mind-emancipating progress will be made in this regard so that such no-go areas are open to lexicographical researchers for more reliable etymological evidence.

6.6 Normative studies

6.6.1 Loanword standardization and normative studies prior to the 1950s

Standardization has always been an important subject in loanword studies, so much so that some argue that it should be the ultimate goal of such studies. Exaggerated as this may be, its significance cannot be overestimated. The earliest contributor to Chinese loanword standardization in history was likely Xuanzang (Hsuan-tsang) 玄奘, a Buddhist monk and the greatest translator of Buddhist sutras in the 7th-century Tang dynasty, who first advocated for the famous principle of transliteration (in rendering Buddhist scriptures) from Sanskrit under the following five circumstances: (1) esoteric terms, (2) terms with a conglomeration of meanings, (3) things nonexistent in China at the time, (4) terms bearing established phonemic translations already, and (5) terms generating positive associations. In modern times, it was scientific and technical terms that first underwent explicit standardization. In his *Huaxue jianyuan* 化学鉴原 (*Mirroring the origins of chemistry*) in 1871, co-translated from *Wells's Principles and Applications of Chemistry*, Xu Shou 徐寿 (1818–1884) created the naming principle of inventing a Chinese character phonetically based on the first syllable of the Western chemical term. In his long essay *Lun Yiming* 论译名 (*On translating names and terms*), Hu Yilu (1914) proposed transliteration or phonemic loaning for ten types of words while mainly advocating for semantic loaning. In May 1909, Yan Fu was commissioned by the Ministry of Education under the imperial Qing government to compile bilingual glossaries and dictionaries of terminology. In September of that year, he was appointed the founding chief editor of the Bureau of Terminology. This was the very first official institution (and Yan the first official commissioner) dedicated to the examination of terminology in Chinese history. Unfortunately, this project was terminated before any achievements were made due to the outbreak of the Chinese Revolution of 1911–1912, which ultimately overthrew the Qing dynasty. Efforts to standardize scientific and technical terms were gradually resumed by the Medical Missionary Association, Jiangsu Provincial Education Association, and Science Society of China. A national review board for scientific and technical terms was founded in 1919. In 1928, a national board for the standardization of translated proper names was established in Shanghai, which, among other things, laid out a convention in translating foreign personal and place names, with ten concise rules governing the translation of personal names and six governing place names. Here are two such rules: if personal names in Japan, South Korea, and Vietnam are in Chinese, use the original Chinese names; if place names in Japan, South Korea, and Southeast Asia are in Chinese, use the original Chinese names. However, this rule was not well implemented, and it was not until 1932, when the National Institute for Compilation and Translation under the Ministry of Education was founded, that such national standardization was carried out in earnest. In 1933, the Institute drew up a national guideline on chemical nomenclature. By 1949, it issued around 50 such guidelines on various categories of terminology, and there were 160 collections of terminology on natural science by the institute and a few others.

6.6.2 Loanword standardization and normative studies since the 1950s

6.6.2.1 Efforts in mainland China

On normative principles and theories. The first serious effort in the latter part of the 20th century was the national symposium on the standardization of the Chinese language, convened in 1955, where general, rather than in-depth, discussions were held. The *Xiandai hanyu wailaici yanjiu* 现代汉语外来词研究 by Gao Mingkai and Liu Zhengtan introduced a focused discussion on loanword standardization and proposed two major principles thereof (1958:178–188). The first said that there should be only one phonetic shape (i.e. pronunciation) and one written form for each (monosemous) loanword. This principle is implemented in observance of six subordinate principles: general currency, phonetic correspondence between the source word and the Chinese word, simple and easy graphic form, due respect for legacy versions, semantic association, and conformity with the conventions of Chinese word formation. The second principle, which governs exceptions to the first, states that there can be two (or even more) written forms/words to convey different meanings of the same borrowed source word, such as both *mada* 马达 ("engine") and *motuo* 摩托 ("vehicle with an engine") for polysemous "motor," and there can be a new word to reflect a different style or emotional charge for the borrowed source word, even though there is already an autochthonous Chinese word with the same conceptual meaning, such as *gongping* 公平 and *feiepolai* 费尔泼赖 (presumably first used by Chinese writer Lu Xun) for the idea of "fair play." The *Wusiyilai hanyu shumianyuyan de bianqian he fazhan* 五四以来汉语书面语言的变迁和发展 (*The evolution of modern written Chinese since the May Fourth Movement*) by the Commercial Press (1959) observes that there occurred a chaotic situation between the Hundred Days of Reform in 1898 and the Chinese Revolution of 1911, such as the mixed use of Japanese kanji and Chinese self-invented words, phonemic and semantic loaning, unstable graphic forms of phonemic borrowing, and frequent variants. The post-May Fourth Movement years saw a gradual standardization toward the adoption of Japanese semantic loans and more or less unified graphic forms of phonemic loaning. Gao Mingkai (1962) expounds the theoretical inevitability of loanword existence and assimilation. Instead of inventing words for foreign borrowing on a massive scale, warns Gao, we should consider using Chinese indigenous words or indigenous lexical components in inventing words for borrowed foreign concepts; direct phonemic loans are also allowed to meet some urgent requirement for communication under the circumstances.

In about the same period, Lin Tao 林焘 (1955) also puts forward several principles in loanword standardization. Semantic loans should be universally applicable and strive for semantic accuracy. Given the Chinese characteristics of simpler syllables, with each carrying one specific meaning, we should directly calque whenever possible. Failing that, we should invent words using indigenous Chinese characters. Phonemic loanwords which have gained wide currency should be kept in use, and foreign personal or place names are still introduced through phonemic loaning. As the influence of Japanese on Chinese becomes smaller and smaller, there is no need to discuss direct borrowing from Japanese. Despite some differences, Gao and Lin have a lot in common in this area. There was no prescriptive norm laid out by China's official institutions on loanword standardization and hardly any published research on it from 1963 to the end of the Cultural Revolution. The obvious reason for this is that the social and political upheaval prevented any attempt toward the cause, which had little to do with the critical fate of the nation at the time. Another less obvious reason is that the use of scientific and technical terminology or proper nouns, which constituted the main barriers to effective communication, had already been regulated by some specific institutions at the time. Efforts in lexical standardization got back on track soon after the Cultural Revolution, though without any major breakthrough.

The research by Yao Te Hwai (1996) on loanword standardization from the perspective of the Chinese language used across the global community has broadened our horizons. Overall, there is a lack of standardization on alphabetic loanwords today. Some are obviously improperly used; some go beyond the comprehension of the general public; and many look so deceptively similar to each other that it is not easy to tell one from the other, especially those composed of three letters. Their use is often open to question, particularly their overuse in the same piece of writing. All this may call for some creative efforts on the part of the relevant regulatory departments, such as standardization into different categories or registers and the requirement to provide a word's meaning in Chinese characters upon its first alphabetic appearance so that it is through the actual use that users decide which one they prefer.

On the standardization of terminology. The establishment of an ad hoc committee on the standardization of academic words in May 1950, immediately after the founding of the People's Republic in 1949, shows the urgency and importance attached to the work, especially on terminology in natural sciences. In 1956, one year after the above-mentioned national symposium on the standardization of the Chinese language, that committee disbanded, with its work transferred to the newly established department of natural science terminology under the Chinese Academy of Sciences. The effort to standardize terminology was terminated during the Cultural Revolution and resumed in 1985, when a new national review board for the standardization of natural science terminology was established. Around the same time, a national terminology standardization committee affiliated with the International Organization for Standardization (ISO) was founded. These two bodies were charged with the administration of terminology from different angles, marking the transition from theoretical discussions to actual prescriptive decision-making, such as the choice of semantically rendered *jiguang* over phonemically loaned *laise* for "laser" in the science community. As has also been mentioned, toward the end of the 1990s, the Chinese ministry of public health explicitly stipulated the use of *aizibing* 艾滋病, pure phonemic loaning with a semantic marker, to make obsolete both the homophonic but misleading 爱滋病, literally "love-induced disease," and the near-homophonic but similarly misleading *aizhibing* 爱之病, literally "disease of love" for the simple reason that AIDS is not always caused by sexual love.

From 1949 to the time of writing this book, over 660 glossary-type collections of terminology have been prepared by the official institutions in mainland China. This huge effort can be considered an important part of general or conceptual loanword standardization because, though these resources are used exclusively for the standardization of terminology in natural sciences, most of the words therein involve phonemic and semantic borrowing.

On the standardization of proper names. In the early 1950s, the Central Compilation and Translation Bureau under the Communist Party of China stipulated several principles regarding the transliteration of personal and place names. First, phonetically, it should all be based on the Beijing dialect. Second, it should follow the convention of the originating person or place, and those long-accepted legacy transliterations should be kept, despite possible phonetic discrepancies with the source word. Third, the same transliteration should apply to the same first name and last name, and the same sound should be used for personal names. Fourth, common and easy words should be chosen over rarely used or complicated words. Since July 1956, the newly formed department in charge of standardizing translated foreign proper names under Xinhua, China's official state news agency, has carried on the work along the same principles, but with more specific operational rules, among which are: avoid using Chinese characters which contain a pejorative sense; whenever possible, prefer Chinese characters which suggest feminineness for female first names; there is no absolute phonetic correspondence with the source word, and the combination of phonetic and graphic proximity is common practice; long-held conventions may prevail over prescribed rules; and Chinese names taken by non-Chinese people should be respected and used as such.

6.6.2.2 Loanword standardization and normative studies in Taiwan

Taiwan has made its own contributions to loanword standardization. In 1980, the Central News Agency (CNA) in Taiwan published a handbook for standardized proper names in translation, and its international news department developed a plan to compile a new scheme to overhaul and standardize translated proper names. Considerably larger than the official *Waiguo diming yiming shouce* 外国地名译名手册 (*Handbook for translated foreign place names*), which had been compiled in mainland China, the 1,381-page second edition of *Waiguo diming yiming* 外國地名譯名 (*Translated foreign place names*), published in the early 1990s by the Institute for Compilation and Translation in Taiwan, provides the place name, the country where it belongs, and a Chinese translation for each entry. There exists a large discrepancy in proper name translations between Taiwan and the mainland—on average, five in every thirty would be different. Realizing this situation, the two sides have already engaged in substantive discussions and research on terminology standardization.

On the individual level, Zi Xun 子迅 (1986) re-examines the issue of the standardization of previous translations of the names for various figures of speech. In her master's dissertation on Chinese loanwords, Zhu Xiao-Yun 朱曉雲 (1986) discusses issues related to standardization. More systematic discussions are found in a monograph by Chang Ta-tsung 張達聰 (1979) and a paper by Yao Rong-Song 姚榮松 (1992). In his *Fanyi zhi yuanli yu jiaoqiao*

翻譯之原理與技巧 (*The principles and techniques of translation*), Chang advocates four principles in the phonological translation of nouns: namely, accurate phonetic correspondence, transliteration based on the original meaning, prudent use of phonetic semantic combination, and sufficient respect for legacy versions. In the fifth part of his paper "Taiwan xianxing wailaiyu de wenti" 臺灣現行外來語的問題 (Survey on the problem of contemporary loan word in the languages spoken in Taiwan), Yao exclusively discusses issues related to standardization for newly created loanwords. On the issue of the replacement of old with new translations, Yao proposes accurate expression and easy comprehensibility as the primary principle; his second principle is no indiscreet replacement of the old translation used as the base word without consideration of user/speaker preference. On the choice of phonemic versus semantic loaning, he advocates for five principles: phonemic loaning is preferred for personal or place names; calque is preferred for the compound source word to preserve the meaning of its components; semantic loaning is preferred for common words as it is easier to be assimilated and better fits the Chinese language; semantic loaning is preferred for technical or other special terms; and hybrid loaning should be minimized. As for the existing discrepancies between Taiwan and the mainland in translated proper nouns, Yao proposes two fundamental principles: being sure of the accurate pronunciation of the originating place or personal names and laying out standardized but separate general principles governing the phonetic correspondence between the recipient Chinese and the various borrowing foreign languages. In his concluding remark, Yao expresses the common aspirations of the academic community that the two sides across the Strait will strengthen their exchanges and work together for a standardized lexicon of Chinese loanwords.

Based on the 1,250 loanwords which are differently rendered across the Strait, in the 1990s, Chu Chia-ning 竺家寧, a professor of Chinese linguistics in Taiwan, headed a research team to observe trends in translating or standardizing Chinese loanwords in the two regions through an examination of their similarities and differences, with one of its purposes being to provide some tentative frame of reference for future lexical standardization and integration, general lexicon and terminology included, across the Strait. Chu's research on this was published in his paper "Liang'an wailaici de fanyi wenti" 兩岸外來詞的翻譯問題 (1996).

6.6.3 Future trends in loanword studies

Though research on future trends is usually included as part of standardization studies rather than as a separate subject for discussion, various forms of Internet-enabled new media, which have continued popping up since the early 21st century, are drastically challenging the conventional channels or modes of conceptual and lexical borrowing.

6.7 Other aspects of loanword studies

6.7.1 Statistical approaches

As an important approach, observation of linguistic statistics can offer clues to the characteristics and possible trends of a language. In terms of loanword studies, only Gao and Liu (1958) provided rudimentary statistical work prior to the relatively large amount of data presented in this book. With a total of 1,000 loanwords, their data is collected from the viewpoint of cultural exchange and arranged according to etymological information and meaning-based classification. Far from being comprehensive or even sufficient, these statistics do not include the many loanwords borrowed from major non-Han Chinese ethnic languages; therefore, their observations or conclusions are not as solidly based. Though the statistical analysis by Zhu (1986) reveals that 69.86% out of her 650 Chinese loanwords come from English, it is merely a static statistic, and it should also have provided data on their parts of speech and a contrastive data analysis of phonemic versus semantic loans.

Shen (1994) conducted a meticulous examination of the Chinese loanwords of Japanese origin which are listed in the dictionary by Liu et al. (1984), providing information on each word's part of speech, identity (i.e. Japanese-made or from Early Chinese), word formation type, and semantic category (nine in total). Regrettably, however, this research lacks an integrated analysis of the gathered statistics which would have culminated with a conclusion. With some of the research in his more recent book, published in 2010, Shen's work has laid a solid foundation for scholarship on lexical exchange between China and Japan through his continued lexical enquiry, with his tabulations of new words collected from various dictionaries and their origins.

Zhu Jingwei 朱京伟 (1993, 2003, 2005, 2006, 2007, 2009) is another remarkable scholar in this field, who, showing enormous rigor, critically re-examines not only the loanwords in the dictionary by Liu et al but also loanwords of Japanese origin in existence since the 19th century and used both by the great scholar Liang Qichao and Liang's newspaper *Qingyibao* 清議報 (*The China Discussion*) and by *Minbao* 民報 (*People's Journal*, the mouthpiece of the revolutionary coalition, *Tongmenghui*). In particular, Zhu classifies the 2- to 4-character Chinese loanwords borrowed from Japanese which appear in *Zhexue yaoling* 哲学要领—the Chinese relay translation by Cai Yuanpei 蔡元培 (Tsai Yuan-pei, 1863–1940), educator in modern China, of the Japanese version by Jiro Shimoda, of an original work by Raphael von Koeber, a notable Russian-German teacher—into four categories (those with their origin in Chinese classical texts, those without, those listed in the *Hanyu da cidian* dictionary, and those originating from Early Chinese but with a new meaning imposed by Japanese). He further sorts the 258 homomorphic words into three categories (those that appear in both Jiro's Japanese and

Cai's Chinese versions, those that appear only in the Japanese, and those that appear only in the Chinese). The research by Chang Xiaohong 常晓宏 (2009) on the loanwords of Japanese origin contained in Lu Xun's works is also impressive. The 1,335 words, a result of Chang's thorough enquiry into the literary giant's works and the concordance with those confirmed by Zhu Jingwei, Shen Guowei, and Chinese-American scholar Lydia Liu (Liu He 刘禾) to be *bona fide* loanwords of Japanese origin, are analyzed in nine academic disciplines for their characteristics in distribution. For further research, Chang suggests that etymological examination be added and distribution analysis extend to word formation and literary genres concerning those loanwords. Research by the scholars above will be very instrumental in quantitative approaches to loanword studies.

At present, dynamic linguistic analysis by means of the calculation of tokens in actual use would require more time and more collective research efforts. With great advances in IT and cloud computing, we believe that there will be breakthroughs in statistical, and especially dynamically statistical, loanword studies in the foreseeable future.

6.7.2 General theoretical research

At present, there is an obvious lack of in-depth research on the general theory of loanwords, including the causal environment, criteria for identification, hierarchical typology, patterns of assimilation and evolution, types of borrowing, impact on recipient language, culture and society, cognitive patterns, and research methodology. Both Gao and Liu (1958) and Chen Yuan (1994) have discussed the causes and conditions for the birth of loanwords; the former have also analyzed in great detail their phonetic and grammatical Sinicization. Zhang Qingyuan 张清源 (1989) has contributed his general theoretical research in several areas. Shi Youwei (1991) discusses the impact of loanwords on the means of Chinese lexical integration and, based on that, proposes a new pattern of Chinese word formation composed of unassociated characters. But, overall, general theoretical research is far from sufficient. In this regard, the observation made by Zhang Yongyan 张永言 (1982:94) is relevant here. To him, previous loanword research has been somewhat lopsided and superficial because attention was only paid to the origin and time of borrowing, with, at most, occasional investigation into the causal conditions. Necessary as this is, research should move way beyond it. For example, Zhang goes on, we should not only study when, where, why, and how a certain loanword came into being but also how it is assimilated, that is, how it subjects or adapts itself to the phonological system (e.g. syllabic formation) and syntactic structure (e.g. word formation) of the borrowing language, what semantic changes happen to it and how they take place, and what changes loanwords have helped trigger within the lexicon of the borrowing language. Only with these in-depth investigations, Zhang concludes, can loanword studies help unravel the laws governing how a language and its lexicon evolve; explain various lexical phenomena; and understand the trilateral relations among the history of individual words, of the language, and of the people involved at large.

In his seminal article *Lun xin xueyu zhi shuru* 論新學語之輸入 ("On the importation of new academic terms"), published over a century ago (1905), Chinese eminent scholar-official Wang Guowei 王国维 (Wang Kuo-wei, 1877–1927) elaborates his argument for a strategically and tactically positive approach to lexical borrowing. He first reminds his readers of the fundamental differences between China and the West: the Chinese people are characteristically pragmatic and abstraction-resistant, while Western people are characteristically thinking- and reasoning- oriented. Good at abstraction and categorization, Westerners invariably apply the dual tool of generalization and specification to the interpretation of everything in the universe, tangible or intangible, so their languages are naturally rich and diverse. In contrast, the Chinese are good at actual doing, contented with specific knowledge when it comes to theoretical aspects, and do not bother to put an exhaustive effort into conceptual categorization unless they are hard-pressed for practical needs. Wang then explains the necessity of lexical borrowing, especially from Japanese. Though everyday communication does not usually call for new exotic phrases, the pursuit of scholarship or art necessarily involves the supplementation of new terms.

> Now that Japanese scholars have already surpassed us in coining neologisms, we should simply go ahead and use theirs. What harm could there be? Therefore, except for the ones that are clearly inappropriate, we do not need to invent new terms.

What is more, he argues, Japanese neologisms are not simply coined for the nonce but become their present forms through decades of deliberation and revisions by numerous experts. Wang believes that there are at least two benefits to borrowing Japanese-made terms: less difficulty in borrowing than in inventing and no worry of barriers, thanks to the smooth academic exchange between China and Japan. With these benefits and no disadvantage whatsoever, he concludes, why should there be any qualms or hesitation about using them? Near the end of this article, he adds that the conceptual rigor is fully reflected in the fact that Japanese usually employs two characters or even four for exact expression, while Chinese is accustomed to one character.

As can be seen, Wang's views on national character, language, and lexical loaning, made more than 100 years ago, are still incisive, thought-provoking, and relevant today.

To move forward, we need to consciously enhance the methods and broaden the scope of such research by investigating how loanwords evolve in a society—in terms of application, frequency, and user community—so as to help better regulate the development of the language, loanwords included. We should be well aware that we are considerably behind the developed countries in loanword studies, and it would be impossible to have a radical transformation without sustained efforts in both theory and lexical hard work. It is our hope that more interested scholars will dedicate themselves to this ambitious goal.

6.8 Loanword studies in the early 21st century

6.8.1 Research scale

There are three main features as far as the scale of loanword studies is concerned.

First, there has been a significant increase in published works and papers on the loanword. The past two decades have seen 24 monographs exclusively on the topic and 5 related to it, along with 320 research papers. This indicates an unprecedented increase in the number of interested and dedicated researchers, with the younger generation gradually taking center stage. However, there is a lack of much-needed diversity among those papers, and some are poorly written.

Second, there are many degree-oriented dissertations on the topic. Because of their rigorous requirements, such papers are more revealing and worth more attention. Unlike in the 20th century, when virtually no dissertation on Chinese loanword studies could be found, the 21st century has seen an increasing number of young and aspiring scholars interested in studying loanwords, including some graduate students who have written excellent dissertations by exploring the area from new and enlightening perspectives. The very first of its kind in China, the PhD dissertation by Zhong Jiya 钟吉娅 (2003), for example, takes Chinese words of foreign origin as its object of inquiry and thus received much attention from the field. By 2018, there were at least 40 PhD dissertations and 213 MA theses related to loanword studies in mainland China.[1]

Third, studies on loanwords of English, Japanese, and undifferentiated origins receive the most attention.[2] New perspectives or approaches are mostly on words of English origin, including alphabetic ones. Research on loanwords of Japanese origin extends to anime and cyberspace. There are signs of resumed interest in the study of loanwords of Russian and non-Han Chinese ethnic language origin. All this seems to indicate a more comprehensive approach to loanword studies.

6.8.2 Research focus

New perspectives, alphabetic loans, and etymological investigation have become the focal points in this period.

New research perspectives. Many scholars have made new explorations into the traditional areas of loanword studies, such as the interpreting and transcription practice in the late Qing dynasty by Wang (2003); theoretical reflections by Cao (2004); alphabetic letter-word loans by He (2001), Hu (2002), Liu (2002), and Yang (2008); and loanword prefixes and suffixes by several scholars. Many have adopted new perspectives in their work, such as adaptation, Skopostheorie, memetics, reception, mass communication, translation studies, circulation, and eco-linguistics. This indicates the shift from the traditional confines of phonetic rendering, wording, and lexical make-up to a broader cross-disciplinary approach. New typological research tilts toward more practical applications, such as technical aspects (law, commodity name, agricultural machinery, weights, and measures), specific texts or platforms (dictionary, textbook, and the Internet), cross-cultural aspects, user data, semantic shift, and contrastive study. Cui (2009), for example, collects and critically re-examines the identity of those borrowed words of Japanese origin which were used in the legal system in modern China. Such new perspectives are more frequently seen in journal articles on loanwords borrowed from Western languages and those of undifferentiated origins than in more cautious and comprehensive dissertations. In this period, it is also encouraging to see quite a few papers or dissertations on semantic loans, which are traditionally not regarded as *bona fide* loanwords.

Massive entry of alphabetic letter words. The massive entry of alphabetic loans is a distinguishing mark of contemporary Chinese. Because of their instability in terms of use and uncertainty in identity, it is very difficult to have accurate data on those alphabetic loanwords which have been naturalized into the Chinese language, though there are already 104 research papers (25 degree-oriented theses and 79 non-theses) on this very topic, most of which focus on the issue of identity. The opposition to or controversy over the 239 entries of words which start with Western letters listed in the 2012 6th edition of *Xiandai hanyu cidian* indicates a lack of general cognitive consensus on or acceptance of alphabetic loanwords.[3] Social development promotes language contact, which, in turn, advances interlingual communication and language evolution, while alphabetic loaning is part of the process. The view that Chinese has to be represented with Chinese characters alone will inevitably lead to cultural and psychological resistance to the use of alphabetic loanwords, a multi-dimensional conflict we have already seen arising from the historical massive entry of graphic loanwords from Japanese.

Impressive etymological investigation. Word origin, such as source language, source word, and time of borrowing, marks the cornerstone of loanword studies, and the new century has seen an impressive amount of published research in this area, such as on loanwords from Western languages (Lin 2000), Mongolian (Fang 2001), Manchu (Ji 2004, 2005), the ethnic Zhuang language (Lan 2003), and Russian (Xu 2007; Jiang 2011). But even more work is published on semantic loans from Japanese (Peng 2000–2012; Zhu 2003, 2005, 2006, 2007, 2009, 2012a,b, 2013; He 2004, 2012a,b, 2013; Shen 2006, 2010, 2011; Chen 2007, 2019; Qiao, Xu, and Shi 2011; Gu

2012). In this period there is also a comprehensive investigation into the Chinese words for the terms used in weights and measures of the British imperial system. The study proves that some of these Chinese words are independently translated in China such as the word *ma* 码 ("yard"), which is not from Japanese as has been claimed by some but instead a semantic loan from the Chinese Min or Cantonese dialect (Shi 2008, 2016a,b). New achievements have also been made in the origin of ancient place names (Niu 2016, 2017, 2018). Etymological examination is still needed for a good number of other Chinese words which look like borrowed ones. This reminds us of not only the linguistic focus of the current scholarship but also the extreme requirement for cross-disciplinary knowledge or capabilities and the necessity for heightened attention to international research resources.

6.8.3 Cyberspace as a new driver for loanword studies

While the 1990s marked the beginning of China's Internet era, the 21st century has seen its rapid development and maturing. As a brand-new type of medium, the Internet, or cyberspace, is another vehicle for both the coming and spread of loanwords. With many accessible functions, such as the powerful search engine, cyberspace provides a platform for online discussion, exchange, blogging, and dissemination with regard to loanwords. In turn, it also contributes to loanword studies, making it a remarkable feature in contemporary scholarship.

6.8.4 Development of static and dynamic loanword resources

Apart from their obvious importance for the development of both static and dynamic loanword resources, what is in urgent need now is the latter. Roughly speaking, these loanword resources can be divided into three tiers. The first is the massive unsorted corpus, most of whose functions might, for the time being, be performed in its absence by such search engines as Baidu. The second tier is the corpus with initial screening or that of chronological lexical collation, which is also yet to be designed and developed in China. The third is the carefully chosen corpus or lexicographical works, which can be further divided into those with a specific focus and those with a general topic. The former include the *Hanyu zimuci cidian* 汉语字母词词典 (*A dictionary of Chinese alphabetic loanwords*) by Liu (2009) and 日本語から引ける中国語の外来語辞典 (*A Japanese dictionary of Chinese loanwords*) by Yoshiaki and Wang (2002), while the latter includes the *Jinxiandai ciyuan* 近现代辞源 (*An etymological dictionary of modern Chinese lexicon*) by Huang (2010) and the *Xinhua wailaici cidian* by Shi (2019), two of the largest dictionaries of their kind in recent years. Beyond the conventional prescriptive or descriptive approach to lexicography, Shi adds the informative and research functions to his dictionary.

MA and PhD dissertations in China related to loanword studies in the early 21st century (2000–2018)

Year published	PhD dissertation	MA dissertation	Total
2000	0	2	2
2001	0	4	4
2002	0	7	7
2003	3	7	10
2004	5	8	13
2005	2	8	10
2006	3	24	27
2007	5	20	25
2008	7	10	17
2009	3	6	9
2010	4	28	32
2011	3	29	32
2012	3	22	25
2013	2	10	12
2014	0	11	11
2015	0	5	5
2016	0	4	4
2017	0	4	4
2018	0	4	4
Total	40	213	253

6.9 Afterword: reflections on Chinese loanword studies

6.9.1 *The underlying cause of the complexity of Chinese loanwords*

The complexity, diversity, and various issues with regard to Chinese loanwords may in the final analysis all be attributable to the four distinguishing features of the Chinese character.

First, as the most fundamental feature, the Chinese homophonic morpheme may branch into a variety of forms, and the same homophonic morpheme may be represented with various characters. That very feature makes it possible either to retain or to neutralize the meaning of a specific Chinese character at the user's discretion, thus creating plenty of room for selecting many potential characters for the same syllable.

Second, the ideographic or semantic element which represents categories of sense constitutes another distinguishing feature of Chinese writing. This feature invariably encourages a strong tendency on the part of native speakers of Chinese toward character visualization in the hope that each character is transparent in conveying some kind of meaning or implication for semantic imagination. That is why there exists the possibility of multiple monosyllabic characters with different meanings to phonetically match the syllable of a loanword; hence, the multiple Chinese phonetic versions for the same borrowed word, such as the homophonic *liulian* 榴莲 and 榴梿, both as semantic loaning of *durian*, and the homophonic *mangguo* 芒果 and 杧果,

both as semantic loaning of *mango*. It also provides the basis for inventing hitherto non-existing character(s) so as to specifically form the phonemic loanword, such as *putao* 葡萄 (grape), *nie* 镍 (nickel), *dao* 氘 (deuterium), and *qiang* 羟 (hydroxyl).

Third, based primarily on the meaning of each component character, Chinese writing can easily associate itself with different pronunciation systems: namely, non-Chinese ones, such as the Japanese kun-yomi pronunciation scheme or various dialectal subsystems; hence, its unusual stability. Different geographic and dialectal regions of the Chinese language community can apply potentially different characters or a combination of them to loanwords, so it comes as no surprise that the same borrowed source word may be represented in various Chinese characters, such as both *haolaiwu* 好莱坞 in standard Mandarin and *helihuo* 荷里活 (pronounced /hɔːleiwu/) in Cantonese for *Hollywood*. In addition, autochthonous Japanese words written with kanji but read with Japanese kun-yomi pronunciation can easily be absorbed by Chinese. The above three features constitute the fundamental reasons for the diversity and complexity of Chinese itself, and demonstrate the powerful accommodation of the language.

Fourth, with an uninterrupted history of more than 3,000 years, the Chinese character has been a particularly important symbol of the autochthonous culture in the hearts of native Chinese speakers. With its varying degrees of semantic concentration and transparency, it has produced countless classics of literature and contributed to Chinese calligraphy and the Chinese psychology of aesthetics. Broadly considered a major source of the autochthonous Chinese culture, it stands in sharp cognitive and psychological contrast to the alphabet-based Western languages, leading to strong resistance to alphabetic loanwords. This cultural constraining mechanism means that the introduction of such loanwords should be cautious and restricted, and give speakers sufficient time to adapt.

6.9.2 The nature of and approaches to loanword studies

The formation of the self-made or autochthonous word is mostly more straightforward in that a word is created in accordance with the rules of lexical formation for actual use in order to represent a concept or something else that needs to be signified without much formative complexity. By contrast, it takes a relatively long time for a typical loanword to travel from the borrowed to the recipient language, involving various phases in the process. The phonemic loan as the bulk of the loanwords, for example, typically goes through such multiple formative steps as language contact between different ethnicities or cultures, tentative assimilation planning, translation, initial use, and constant adjustment before its ultimate acceptance. Each of the phases in this process is worth separate scholarly attention, which explains the diversity and multi-disciplinarity of loanword studies. Efforts over the past century have seen the evolution of loanword studies from the investigation of individual loanwords to collective typological research on a considerable scale and an ongoing shift from isolated descriptive approaches towards a more systemic interpretative one. Impressive published research has contributed to a multi-dimensional theoretical framework as befits an academic discipline. It can be not only a sub-field of study under general linguistics but also an area of research on the characteristics of traditional language contact based on inter-ethnic and inter-cultural communications, involving various fields of textual or documentary examination, such as human and natural history and geography as well as other sociological or cultural studies. In fact, it has already been weaning itself off being a subsidiary by-product of the above fields toward a multi-disciplinary and cross-disciplinary field of learning on its own.

Since loanword studies concerns a variety of aspects or fields of study, specific issues or problems in the process should be studied in their specific context so that different approaches may be considered. Since the loanword, a product of language contact, necessarily involves linguistic, ethnic, social, and cultural conflict and/or integration, its investigation requires lexical statistical work, comparison and contrasting, etymological tracing, intended lexical purpose served, receptive mentality, actual impact, and so on. At the same time, as a record of alien regions and peoples, it involves their histories, which, in turn, require textual and documentary "archaeology" so as to draw some reasonable inferences. What is more, as part of the lexicon, the loanword should be studied from the lexicological perspective for its formation and evolution, which includes, among other things, the choice of specific characters, internal restructuring, phono-semantic variation, functional change, and graphemic readjustment. In short, approaches to loanword studies are methodologically bound to be diverse and multi-dimensional. Instead of being confined to the conventional tunnel vision, loanword scholars should try their best to broaden their horizons so as to attain the truth.

Loanword research belongs to those who love the loanword and are dedicated to its study. We look forward to having even more young scholars join us and contribute to loanword research, a small field with great promise, with integrity, dedication, perseverance, and creativity.

As a result of this book, the author hopes to see more quality research on Chinese loanwords down the road.

Notes

1 From 2001, with the first published thesis, up to 2018, the peak occurred between 2006 and 2012, since which there has been a steady decrease. 2010 saw 16.
2 Among the 448 papers (129 degree-oriented theses and 319 journal papers) that I have collected, 150 (38 theses and 112 non-theses) are on loanwords of English origin, taking up 33.5%; 115 (33 theses and 82 non-theses) are on loanwords of

An overview of Chinese loanword studies 237

Japanese origin, taking up 25.7%; and 123 (37 theses and 86 non-theses) are on loanwords of undifferentiated origins, taking up 27.5%.

3 For example, the fierce public controversy since 2007 in Tianya 天涯社区, a popular influential Chinese-language online forum and blogging site, sparked by an article by Wang Binbin (1998) on Chinese loanwords from Japanese. The ensuing waves of emotionally charged discussions in cyberspace once again point to this multi-dimensional conflict.

Appendix

A typological table of Chinese loanwords (and their relatives)

General types	Variations	Specific subtypes	Examples/origin
A. Phonemic loaning	Phonemic loaning	(1) Pure phonemic loan	Saqima 萨其马 from Manchu *sacima*
		(2) Blend phonemic loan	Kara OK 卡拉 OK from Japanese *karaoke*
	With semantic cues or association	(3) Cohesive phonetic-cum-semantic approximation	Leida 雷达 from *radar* Pajinku 扒金库 from Japanese self-made *pachinko*
		(4) Discrete phonetic-cum-semantic approximation	Diditi 滴滴涕 from DDT
		(5) Humorous phonemic loan	Jiantouman 尖头鳗 from *gentleman*
		(6) Partial phonetic-cum-semantic approximation	Kadian 卡垫 from Tibetan *khatan* Haolaibao 好来宝 from Mongol *xolboga*
	With graphic adaptation for semantic association	(7) Special phonetic-cum-semantic approximation	Wanweiwang 万维网 from WWW
		(8) Phonemic loaning with graphic adaptation for semantic association	Qiapan 袷袢 from Uighur *tɕʰapan*

(*Continued*)

240 *Appendix*

General types	Variations	Specific subtypes	Examples/origin
B. Graphic loaning	On-yomi Japan-made kanji	(9) Phonemic loaning from Japanese kanji	Shousi 寿司 from *sushi*
		(10) Phonetic-cum-semantic approximation in Japanese kanji	Julebu 俱乐部 from *kurabu* from *club*
	Kun-yomi Chinese-made kanji	(11) Kun-yomi kanji	Shouxu 手续 from *tetzuzuki*
		(12) Kun-yomi-cum-on-yomi kanji	Shengfushou 胜负手 from *shobu-te*
	Loaned character	(13) Semantic loan from Japan-made kanji	Xian 腺 from *sen*
		(14) Non-textual symbol	卍 from Sanskrit *swastika*
		(15) Indigenous Chinese character + foreign-made Chinese character	Zinan 字喃 from Vietnamese *chu'nôm*
C. Hybrid loanword	Letter + phonemic loan	(16) Letter + phonemic loan	T xu T 恤 from *T shirt*
	Phonemic loaning + semantic marker	(17) Phonemic loan + semantic marker (post-modifier)	Kache 卡车 from *car* + *che* "vehicle"
		(18) Phonemic loan + semantic marker (pre-modifier)	Jiuba 酒吧 from *jiu* "wine" + *bar*
		(19) Phonemic loan + semantic marker (affix)	Ashe 阿蛇 from a 阿 + *sir*
		(20) Phonemic loan + semantic marker (supplement)	Shuqiu 述球 from *shoot* + *qiu* "ball"
	Graphic-cum-phonemic loaning + semantic marker	(21) Letter + semantic marker (affix)	A sir 阿 sir from a 阿 + *sir*
	Graphic loaning + semantic marker	(22) Kanji + semantic marker (post-modifier)	Xueyu 鳕鱼 from *tara* "cod" + *yu* "fish"
	Phonemic + semantic loaning	(23) Pure phonemic + semantic loan	Motuoche 摩托车 from *moto-cycle*

General types	Variations	Specific subtypes	Examples/origin
		(24) Phonemic with semantic cues + semantic loan	Miniqun 迷你裙 from *miniskirt*
D. Quasi-loanword	Letter + semantic loaning	(25) Initialism + semantic loan	TDK bei TDK 杯 from *TDK Cup*
	Graphic loaning of Chinese-character word	(26) On-yomi Japanese neologism	Guolaosi 过劳死 from *karoshi*
		(27) Return graphic loan from Japanese	Geming 革命 from *kakumei*
	Western word letter-word	(28) Full Western word	Out from English *out*
		(29) Abbreviated Western word	DIY from *do-it-yourself*
E. Semantic loaning	Self-made semantic loaning	(30) Calque	Heiban 黑板 from *blackboard*
		(31) Pure semantic loan	Moshui 墨水 from *ink*
F. Word under external influence (not generally considered *bona fide* loanword)	Self-made imitation loanword	(32) Self-made words from foreign linguistic elements	Jinlun 锦纶 influenced by *nylon*
		(33) Cohesive semantic imitation loanword	Meijiajing 美加净 from self-created *Maxam*
		(34) Discrete semantic imitation loanword	Fulimei 富力美 from self-made *Eflam*
	Self-made imitation influenced by corresponding foreign words	(35) Dual phonemic combination	Diba 迪吧 from *disco + bar*
		(36) Indigenous Chinese word + phonetic imitation	Angongzuo 安宫唑 from self-created *panazol*
		(37) Full phonetic imitation	Bosideng 波司登 imitating *Boston*
		(38) Phonemic derivative	Hongke 红客 from self-invented *honker* (hong "red" + hacker)
		(39) Combination of loaned and indigenous morphemes	Wangba 网吧 invented from *net + bar*

(Continued)

242 *Appendix*

General types	Variations	Specific subtypes	Examples/origin
		(40) Abbreviated phonemic loan + indigenous morpheme	Dige 的哥 from *dishi* phonemic loan of "tax" + *ge* "brother"
	Self-made word partially made of letters	(41) Letter + indigenous morpheme	Guowei VC 果味 VC, a drink rich in vitamin C
		(42) Letter shape + indigenous morpheme	H deng H 灯, an H-shaped lamp
		(43) Pinyin abbreviation + indigenous morpheme	GB ma GB 码, code for China's national standards
		(44) Chinese affix + letter	A Q 阿 Q from a 阿 + Q
	Self-made word fully made of pinyin abbreviation	(45) Pinyin abbreviation	HSK from *Hanyu Shuiping Kaoshi* or "Test of Chinese as a Foreign Language"
G. Chinese-made English word (not generally considered *bona fide* loanword)	Self-made abbreviated English word	(46) Self-made English initialism	CBA for Chinese Basketball Association
	Self-made English word	(47) Self-made English word	Smilence from self-created smile + silence

Notes:
1 The classification in this table is based on formal types rather than the semantic, functional, or social considerations discussed in the book. Nor does it differentiate between lexical borrowing and substrate influence. For detailed discussion, please refer to Sections 1.1.2 in Chapter 1 on lexical borrowing and substrate influence and 4.2 through 4.4 in Chapter 4 on semantic, functional, and social types of the loanword.
2 Though not generally treated as *bona fide* loanwords, semantic loans, words under external influence, and Chinese-made English words (under General Types E, F, and G in the table, respectively) are still listed here for the convenience of readers. For detailed discussion, please refer to Sections 3.4 in Chapter 3, 4.1, and 4.5 in Chapter 4.
3 Words under Specific Subtypes 33, 34, and 46 have so far not extended to the general-purpose lexicon yet but are only limited to proper names or brand names.

Bibliography of loanword studies

The shortened Bibliography of loanword studies here is selected from the original larger one in the Revised and Enlarged Chinese Edition by the author based on the the principle that all listed works must be officially published, have a considerable influence at the time, reflect the focused areas and tendency of Chinese loanword studies at the time, and represent various aspects of loanword studies. It is divided into three parts: monographs and anthologies; research papers; and dictionaries.

Monographs and anthologies

Beijing shifan xueyuan zhongwenxi hanyu jiaoyanzu (ed.) (1959) *Wu-si yilai hanyu shumian yuyan de bianqian he fazhan* [The changes and development of Chinese written language since the May Fourth Movement], Beijing: Shangwu yinshuguan.

Cao, Wei (2004) *Xiandai hanyu cihui yanjiu* [A study of modern Chinese lexicon], Beijing: Beijing daxue chubanshe.

Chang, Ta-tsung (Zhang Dacong) (1979) *Fanyi zhi yuanli yu jiqiao* [The principles and techniques of translation], Taipei: Guojia shudian.

Chang, Yingsheng (Aisin Gioro Yingsheng) (1993) *Beijing tuhua zhong de Manyu* [Manchu in the Beijing dialect], Beijing: Beijing Yanshan chubanshe.

Chen, Baoya (1993) *Yuyan wenhua lun* [On language and culture], Kunming: Yunnan daxue chubanshe.

Chen, Guanglei (ed.) (2008) *Gaige kaifang zhong hanyu cihui de fazhan* [The development of Chinese lexicon during China's Reform and Opening-up], Shanghai: Shanghai Renmin chubanshe.

Chen, Liwei (2019) *Dongwang donglai* [Mutual lexical borrowing between China and Japan], Beijing: Shehui kexue wenxian chubanshe.

Chen, Yuan (1994) *Yuyan he ren* [Language and humans], Shanghai: Shanghai jiaoyu chubanshe.

Chng, David K.Y. (Zhuang Qinyong) and Zhou Qinghai (2010) *Jidujiao chuanjiaoshi yu jinxiandai hanyu xinci* [Christian missionaries and modern Chinese neologisms], Singapore: Qingnian shuju (The Youth Book Co.).

Dong, Shouyi (1989) *Qingdai liuxue yundong shi* [A history of studying abroad in the Qing dynasty], Shenyang: Liaoning Renmin chubanshe.

Fan, Huiying (2009) *Yi hanzi wei meijie de xinci chuanbo: jindai zhongri jian cihui jiaoliu de yanjiu* [The dissemination of Chinese character-mediated neologisms: a study of lexical exchanges between China and Japan in modern history], Dalian: Liaoning shifan daxue chubanshe.

Feng, Chengjun (1934/1956–1958) *Xiyu nanhai shidi kaozheng yicong* [Collections of translated works for the study on historical geography of the Western Regions and the regions surrounding the South China Sea], Beijing: Zhonghua shuju.

—— (1980) *Xiyu diming* [Place names in the Western Regions], Beijing: Zhonghua shuju.

Feng, Tianyu (2004) *Xinyu tanyuan: Zhongxiri wenhua hudong yu jindai hanzi shuyu shengcheng* [Origins of neologisms: the interplay between Chinese, Western, and Japanese cultures and the formation of modern Chinese terminology], Beijing: Zhonghua shuju.

Gao, Mingkai and Liu Zhengtan (1958) *Xiandai hanyu wailaici yanjiu* [A study of loanwords in modern Chinese], Beijing: Wenzi gaige chubanshe.

Gu, Jiangping (2012) *Hanyu zhong de riyu jieci yanjiu* [A study of Chinese loanwords from Japanese], Shanghai: Shanghai cishu chubanshe.

He, Huazhen (2004) *Riben hanzi he hanzici yanjiu* [A study of Japanese kanji and words of kanji], Beijing: Zhongguo shehui kexue chubanshe.

He, Peizhong and Feng Jianxin (1986) *Zhongri tongxingci qianshuo* [A brief introduction to graphic loanwords between China and Japan], Beijing: Shangwu yinshuguan.

Huang, Yi (2007) *Aomen yuyan yanjiu* [A study of languages in Macao], Beijing: Shangwu yinshuguan.

Jiang, Jicheng (1991) *Jindai hanyu cihui yanjiu* [A study of modern Chinese lexicon], Changsha: Hunan jiaoyu chubanshe.

Kiyohide, Arakawa (1997) 近代日中学術用語の形成と傳播 ——地理学用語を中心に [The formation and dissemination of common academic terms in modern Japan and China] (in Japanese), Tokyo: Hakuteisha.

Lan, Qingyuan (2003) *Zhuang Han jieci tongyuanci yanjiu* [A study of loanwords and cognate words in the Zhuang and Han ethnic groups], Beijing: Zhongyang minzu daxue chubanshe.

Laufer, Berthold (Chinese trans. Lin Yunyin) (2001/2015) *Zhongguo Yilang bian* [Sino-Iranica: Chinese contributions to the history of civilization in Ancient Iran, with special reference to the history of cultivated plants and products], Beijing: Shangwu yinshuguan.

Liang, Xiaohong (1994) *Fojiao ciyu de gouzao yu hanyu cihui de fazhan* [The formation of Buddhist terms and the development of the Chinese lexicon], Beijing: Beijing yuyan xueyuan chubanshe.

Lin, Gan (ed.) (1981) *Tujue yu huihe lishi lunwen xuanji* [Selected papers on the history of ancient Turks and Uighurs], Beijing: Zhonghua shuju.

Lin, Meicun (1998) *Hantang xiyu yu zhongguo wenming* [The western regions in the Han and Tang dynasties and the Chinese civilization], Beijing: Wenwu chubanshe.

—— (2000) *Gudao xifeng: kaogu xin faxian suojian zhongxi wenhua jiaoliu* [West winds on ancient tracks: Chinese Western cultural exchanges as seen through new archaeological finds], Beijing: Sanlian shudian.

Lu, Shuxiang (1942, 1947) *Zhongguo wenfa yaolue* [Essentials of Chinese grammar], Beijing: Shangwu yinshuguan.

Luo, Changpei (1950) *Yuyan yu wenhua* [Language and culture], Beijing: Guoli Beijing daxue chuban (1989, Beijing: Yuwen chubanshe; 2011, Beijing: Beijing chubanshe).

Masini, Frederico (1993) The Formation of Modern Chinese Lexicon and Its Evolution Toward a National Language: The Period from 1840 to 1998 in Journal of Chinese Linguistics, *Monograph Series*, No. 6, Berkeley.

―――― (Chinese trans. Huang Heqing) (1997) *Xiandai hanyu cihui de xingcheng* [*The Formation of Modern Chinese Lexicon and Its Evolution Toward a National Language*], Shanghai: Hanyu dacidian chubanshe.

Matsuura, Akira, Uchida Keiichi and Shen Guowei (2006) *Xiaer guanzhen: fu tijie suoyin* [Rarities from near and far], Shanghai: Shanghai cishu chubanshe.

Ma, Zuyi (1998) *Zhongguo fanyi jianshi* [A brief history of translation in China], Beijing: Zhongguo duiwai fanyi chuban gongsi.

Niu, Ruchen (2016) *Zaoqi xiyu diceng diming tanyuan* [The origin of the substrate place names in the early period of the Western Regions in ancient China], Beijing: Zhongguo shehui chubanshe.

―――― (2017) *Xinjiang diming de jidian yu chuanyue* [A study of the place names in Xinjiang from the perspective of historical linguistics], Beijing: Zhongguo shehui chubanshe.

―――― (2018) *Zhongguo wenhua diming xue* [Chinese cultural toponymy], Beijing: Zhongguo kexue jishu chubanshe.

Pan, Yunzhong (1957) *Hanyu cihuishi gaiyao* [The introduction of the history of Chinese lexicon], Shanghai: Shanghai guji chubanshe.

Qian, Nairong (1989) *Shanghai fangyan liyu* [The dialect and slang in Shanghai], Shanghai: Shanghai shehui kexueyuan chubanshe.

Qiao, Yan, Xu Yiping and Shi Jianjun (2011) *Riyuan xinci yanjiu* [A study of new Chinese loanwords of Japanese origin], Beijing: Xueyuan chubanshe.

Schafer, Edward H. (Chinese trans. Wu Yugui) (1995) *The Golden Peaches of Samarkand: A Study of T'ang Exotics* (Orig. University of California Press, 1963), Beijing: Zhongguo shehui kexue chubanshe.

Shen, Guowei (1994/2008) 近代日中語彙交流史' [A history of modern lexical communications between Japan and China] (in Japanese), Tokyo: Kasama Shoin.

―――― (1995) 「新爾雅」とその [*Xin Erya* and its vocabulary] (in Japanese), Tokyo: Hakuteisha.

―――― (2006) *Liuhe congtan: fu tijie suoyin* [Shanghae Serial (1857–1858): with Analyses and Index] (Japanese version in 1999), Shanghai: Shanghai cishu chubanshe.

―――― (2010) *Jindai zhongri cihui jiaoliu yanjiu* [A study of modern lexical communications between China and Japan], Beijing: Zhonghua shuju.

―――― (2011) *Xin Erya: fu jieti suoyin* [*Xin Erya*: with analyses and index], Shanghai: Shanghai cishu chubanshe.

―――― (2019) *Yiming zhili xunyue chichu: Yanfu yici yanjiu* [A study of translated words by Yan Fu], Beijing: Shehui kexue wenxian chubanshe.

―――― (2019) *Hanyu jindai erzici yanjiu* [A study of the two-character words in modern China], Shanghai: Huadong shifan daxue chubanshe.

Shi, Youwei (1991) *Yiwenhua de shizhe: wailaici* [Messenger for foreign cultures: loanwords], Changchun: Jilin jiaoyu chubanshe.

―――― (2004) *Wailaici: yiwenhua de shizhe* [Loanwords: messenger for foreign cultures], Shanghai: Shanghai cishu chubanshe.

―――― (2000, 2013) *Hanyu wailaici* [Loanwords in the Chinese language], Beijing: Shangwu yinshuguan.

Sōbē, Arakawa 荒川惣兵衛 (1932) *Gairaigogaku josetsu ("modango" kenkyū)* 外來語學序說:モダン語研究 [An introduction to the study of loan-words (in modern Japanese)], Nagoya: Arakawa Sobe.

Sun, Changxu (1957) *Hanyu cihui* [Chinese lexicon], Changchun: Jilin renmin chubanshe.

Wang, Chun (2004) *Rizhong cihui de bijiao cihuilun yanjiu* [A comparative study of the theory of vocabulary in Sino-Japanese lexicon], Hangzhou: Zhejiang daxue chubanshe.

Wang, Li (1958) *Hanyu shigao* (xiace) [A history of the Chinese language (Vol. 2)], Beijing: Kexue chubanshe.

Wang, Songmao (1956) *Tantan xiandai hanyu cihui guifanhua* [On the standardization of modern Chinese lexicon], Beijing: Tongsu duwu chubanshe.

Wang, Xiaoqiu (2000) *Jindai zhongri wenhua jiaoliushi* [A modern history of Chinese-Japanese cultural exchange], Beijing: Zhonghua shuju.

Wenzi gaige weiyuanhui (1956) *Xiandai hanyu guifan xueshu huiyi wenjian huibian* [Collected papers at the national symposium on the standardization of the Chinese language], Beijing: Kexue chubanshe.

Xiong, Yuezhi (1994) *Xixuedongjian yu wanqing shehui* [The dissemination of western learning and the late Qing society], Shanghai: Shanghai renmin chubanshe.

Xu, Laidi (2007) *Han'e yuyan jiechu yanjiu* [A study of Chinese-Russian language contact], Harbin: Heilongjiang renmin chubanshe.

Yang, Xipeng (2007) *Hanyu wailaici yanjiu* [A study of Chinese loanwords], Shanghai: Shanghai renmin chubanseh.

You, Rujie (1993) *Zhongguo wenhua yuyanxue yinlun* [An introduction to Chinese cultural linguistics], Beijing: Gaodeng jiaoyu chubanshe.

Zhang, Qingchang (1990) *Hutong ji qita: shehui yuyanxue de tansuo* [The *Hutong* and others: a sociolinguistic exploration], Beijing: Beijing yuyan xueyuan chubanshe.

Zhang, Xinglang (1930; 1977, expanded by Zhu Jieqin) *Zhongxi jiaotong shiliao huibian* [Collated resources on the historical communications between China and the rest of the world], Shanghai/Beijing: Zhonghua shuju.

Zhang, Yongyan (1982) *Cihuixue jianlun* [Lexicology: a short introduction], Wuhan: Huazhong gongxueyuan chubanshe.

Zhao, Yuanren (1959/1968) *Yuyan wenti* [Issues in the Chinese language], Taipei: Shangwu yinshuguan.

Zhongguo fojiao wenhua yanjiusuo (1993) *Suyu foyuan* [The Buddhist origins of everyday terms], Shanghai: Qunzhong chubanshe.

Zhong, Jiya (2003) *Hanyu waiyuanci: jiyu yuliao de yanjiu* [Chinese words of foreign origin: a corpus-based study] (Ph.D. dissertation), Shanghai: East China Normal University.

Zhong, Shuhe (1985) *Zouxiang shijie: jindai zhongguo zhishi fenzi kaocha xifang de lishi* [Going out into the world: a history of Chinese intellectuals' investigations of the West], Beijing: Zhonghua shuju.

Zhou, Qiyu (Zhou Shangfu) (1918) *Xin mingci xunzuan* [Etymological dictionary of new words], Saoye shanfang, Shanghai 1918. Now in *Mingqing suyu cishu jicheng* [Collection of dictionaries of colloquial expressions of the Ming and Qing dynasties] (1987), Shanghai: Shanghai guji chubanshe.

Zhou, Zumo (1959) *Hanyu cihui jianghua* [On the Chinese lexicon], Beijing: Renmin jiaoyu chubanshe.

Zhou, Zhenhe and You Rujie (1986) *Fangyan yu zhongguo wenhua* [Dialects and Chinese culture], Shanghai: Shanghai renmin chubanshe.

Zhu, Jingwei (2003) 近代日中新語の創出と交流 [The creation and exchange of neologisms in modern Japan and China] (in Japanese), Tokyo: Hakuteisha.

Zhu, Xiao-Yun (1986) 中國語の外來語:日本語から借用したものを中心に [Loanwords in the Chinese language: based on those borrowed from Japanese] (MA thesis, unpublished), Taipei: Soochow University.

Research papers:

Bian, Chenglin (1992) 'Jindai hanyu wailaici de bu pinghengxing' [The imbalance in modern Chinese loanwords], *Guangxi minzu xueyuan xuebao* (zhesheban) [Journal of Guangxi University for Nationalities (Social Sciences Edition)] issue 2.

Bian, Ji (1986) '*Faxisi* yici de laiyuan' [The origin of the word *Faxisi* (Fascism)], *Ribenxue luntan* [Japanese study forum] issue 2.

Cao, Wei (2004) 'Zailun xiandai hanyu wailaici' [Rethinking loanwords in modern Chinese], *Jiangsu daxue xuebao* [Journal of Jiangsu University] issue 1.

Cai, Meibiao (1951) 'Hanyu li de menguyu' [Mongolian words in the Chinese language], *Guangming ribao* [Guangming Daily] p6, February 3.

Cen, Qixiang (1981) '*Hanyu wailaici cidian* xuyan' [Preface to the Hanyu wailaici cidian (Dictionary of Chinese loanwords)], *Zhongguo yuwen yanjiu* [Studies in Chinese Linguistics] issue 2, Hong Kong: Institute of Chinese Studies at The Chinese University of Hong Kong.

Cen, Zhongmian (1945) 'Jiechu zhonghua minzu yu tujue zhi miqie guanxi' [Unveiling the close relations between the Chinese and the Turkic people], *Dongfang zazhi* [The Eastern Miscellany] 41(5).

—— (1948) '*Modu* 冒頓 zhi yuyuan jiqi yindu' [The etymology and pronunciation of the word *Modu*冒頓], in Lin Han (ed.) (1987) *Tujue yu huihe lishi lunwen xuanji* [Selected papers on the history of ancient Turks and Uighurs], Beijing: Zhonghua shuju.

—— (1961) 'Chuci zhu yao fanan de you jishi tiao: chuci zhong de gu tujueyu' [Several inaccuracies in the *Chuci* annotations and old Turkic in *Chuci*], *Zhongshan daxue xuebao* [Journal of Sun Yat-sen University] 7(2) 53–72. Also in *Liangzhou Wenshi luncong* [Collected papers on the culture and history of China's two Zhou dynasties] (1958), Beijing: Shangwu yinshuguan and (2004) Beijing: Zhonghua shuju.

Chang, Xiaohong (2009) 'Lu Xun zuopin zhong de riyu jieci' [Japanese loanwords in Lu Xun's works], *Ribenxue yanjiu* [Japanese Studies] issue 1.

Chen, Fawei (1958) 'Hanyu jieci tantao' [Discussion on Chinese loanwords], *Hebei Tianjin shifan xueyuan xuebao* [Journal of Hebei Tianjin Teachers' College] issue 3.

Chen, Jianing and Lin Zhe (2011) 'On loanword naturalization', in *Gao Mingkai xiansheng xueshu sixiang yantaohui: jinian Gao Mingkai xiansheng danchen 100 zhounian lunwen ji* [Symposium on the academic thought of Professor Gao Mingkai: proceedings to commemorate the 100th anniversary of Professor Gao Mingkai].

Chen, Jing and Liu Xiangqing (2012) 'Shilun wangluo ciyu xieyin yinyi' [On the homophonic transliteration of netspeak], *Nanhua daxue xuebao* [Journal of Nanhua University (Social Science Edition)] issue 2.

Chen, Liwei (2007) 'Ciyu de piaoyi' [Drifting of words], *21 shiji jingji daobao* (Nanfang baoye jituan) [21st Century Economic Herald (Nanfang Media Group)] May 28, 2007.
Chen, Liu (1990) 'Hanyu wailaici yu han minzu wenhua xinli' [Chinese loanwords and the cultural psychology of the Han nationality], *Liaoning shifan daxue xuebao* [Journal of Liaoning Normal University (Social Science Edition)] issue 5.
Chen, Qiguang (2007) 'Hanyu yuanliu shexiang' [Thoughts on the sources of the Chinese language, in his *Lunyu shuowenji* [Collected papers on language], Beijing: Minzu chubanshe.
Chen, Yan (2014) 'Hanyu wailaici de fangyan biaozhu yanjiu' [Research on dialectal marking of Chinese loanwords], *Cishu yanjiu* [Lexicographical Studies] issue 3.
Chen, Yuan (1923/1927) 'Yuan xiyu ren huahua kao' [On the sinicization of people in the Western Regions in the Yuan Dynasty], in *Liyun shuwu congkan* (1934); reprint Shanghai: Shanghai guji chubanshe, 2000.
—— (1927/1928) 'Huihui jiao ru zhongguo shilue' [A brief history of the entry of Islam into China], in *Chen Yuan shixue lunzhu xuan* [Selected works of Chen Yuan on history] 1981, Shanghai: Shanghai renmin chubanshe.
Chen, Zhangtai (1996) 'Putonghua cihui guifan wenti' [Issues on the standardization of Putonghua lexicon], *Zhongguo yuwen* [Studies of the Chinese Language] issue 3.
Chen, Zhong (1963) 'Hanyu jieci yanjiu zhong de jige wenti' [Several issues in the study of Chinese loanwords], *Jianghai xuekan* [Jianghai Academic Journal] issue 1.
Cheng, Xianghui (1996) 'Chuanyi xuyao yu gangao xinci' [The need for communication and the new words from Hong Kong and Macao], *Zhongguo yuwen* [Studies of the Chinese Language] issue 3.
Chi, Ping (1961) 'Tantan hanyu zhong del wailaiyu' [On the loanwords in the Chinese language], *Renmin ribao* [People's Daily] p5, January 8.
Chu, Chia-ning (1996) 'Liang'an wailaici de fany wenti' [On the translation of loanwords across the Taiwan Straits], *Huawen shijie* [The world of Chinese language] (Taipei) (81): 1–17.
Cui, Junmin (2009) 'Jindai falu xinci dui riyu cihui de jieyong jiqi bianzheng' [On the borrowing of new Japanese legal terms], *Hebei faxue* [Hebei Law Science] issue 1.
Diming yiyin weiyuanhui (1959) 'diming fanyi yuanze caoan sizhong' [Four draft versions of the principles for the translation of geographical names], *Wenzi gaige* [Language reform] issue 19; also reprint (1960) *Waiyu jiaoxue yu fanyi* [Foreign language teaching and translation] issue 1.
Ding, Yang and Wang Baotian (2010) 'Xiandai hanyu zhong riyuan wailaici de yiyi bianyi yanjiu' [Research on the meaning variation of Modern Chinese loanwords of Japanese origin], *Chongqing jiaotong daxue xuebao* (shehui kexue ban) [Journal of Chongqing Jiaotong University (Social Science Edition)] issue 2.
Ding, Zhenglin (1977) 'Xuanshou wailaici wenti de tantao: cong wanqing zhuzuo zhong xuanshou wailaici de tihui' [On issues of loanword assimilation: a case study of the selection of loanwords from the works in the late Qing], *Anhui daxue xuebao* [Journal of Anhui University (Social Science Edition)] issue 3.
Dong, Tonghe (Tung Tung-ho) (1947) 'Lun waiguo direnming de yinyi' [On the transliteration of foreign place and personal names], *Xiandai xuebao* [Modern academic journal] Vol. 1, joint issues of 4 and 5.
Dong, Qiusi (1956) 'Fanyi gongzuo zhong de hanyu guifanhua wenti' [Issues on the standardization of Chinese in translation], in *Xiandai hanyu guifan wenti xueshu*

huiyi wenjian huibian [Collected papers at the national symposium on the standardization of the Chinese language], Beijing: Kexue chubanshe.

Fang, Linggui (1986) 'Hanyu cishu zhong de jige mengguyu jieci' [Some loanwords from Mongolian in Chinese dictionaries], *Cishu yanjiu* [Lexicographical Studies] issue 3.

Ferrand, Gabriel (1916) 'Ye-tiao, Sseu-tiao et Java', *Journal asiatique* 11(8): 521–532; also Chinese translation in Feng Chengjun (1962) *Xiyu nanhai shidi kaozheng yicong* [Collection of translated works for the study on historical geography of the Western Regions and the regions surrounding the South China Sea] Beijing: Shangwu yinshuguan.

Feng, Jiasheng (1937) 'Xiongnu minzu jiqi wenhua' [The Huns and their culture], in *Xiongnu shi lunwen xuanji* [Selected papers on the history of the Huns], Beijing: Zhonghua shuju.

Feng, Jiasheng (1987) 'Qidan minghao kaoshi' [Exploration of the titles of Khitan], in *Feng Jiasheng lunzhu jicui* [The collected works of Feng Jiasheng], Beijing: Zhonghua shuju.

Feng, Tianyu (2005) 'Zhongxiri wenhua duijiejian hanzi shuyu de liding wenti' [The issues on the determination of Chinese terminology in the exchanges between Chinese and Western or Japanese cultures], *Guangming ribao* [Guangming Daily] April 5.

Feng, Zhiwei (1994) 'Guanyu youtai minzu de yiming yongzi wenti' [On the issue of the translation of Jewish names], *Ciku jianshe tongxun* [Journal on loanword and related studies – Hong Kong] issue 5.

—— (1996) 'Guanyu shendu, tianzhu yindu de yuyuan' [On the etymology of Shendu, Tianzhu and Yindu], *Ciku jianshe tongxun* [Journal on loanword and related studies – Hong Kong] issue 10.

—— (2018) 'Guanyu fei hanyu renming he diming de zifu yiyin wenti' [On the issue of transliteration of non-Chinese names and place names], *Yuwen jianshe tongxun* [Chinese language review – Hong Kong] issue 115.

Gan, Tao (2013) 'Zhongwen meiti dui riyuan xinci de shiyong qingxiang fenxi' [Analysis of Chinese media's tendency to use Japanese-originated new words], *Yuwen jianshe tongxun* [Chinese language review – Hong Kong] issue 102.

Gao, Chun (2012) 'Cong *Ernu yingxiong zhuan* kan daoguang, xianfeng, tongzhi shiqi Beijing hua zhong qiren yu' [The imperial Manchu language in the Beijing dialect during the period of Daoguang, Xianfeng and Tongzhi seen from the late Qing novel *Ernu yingxiong zhuan*], *Xiandai yuwen xunkan* [Modern Chinese Trimonthly] issue 8.

Gao, Mingkai (1962/1990) 'Yuyan de neibu fazhan guilu yu wailaici' [The intrinsic patterns of language development and loanwords], *Guangming ribao* [Guangming Daily] July 3; also in *Gao Mingkai yuyanxue lunwen ji* [Selected essays of Gao Mingkai on linguistics Essays], Beijing: Shangwu yinshuguan.

Gao, Yu (2003) 'Hanyu wailaici yuyuan yanjiu' [Research on the etymology of Chinese loanwords], *Chugokugo Kenkyu* 中国語研究 [Studies of Chinese language] No 45, Tokyo: Hakuteisha.

Gao, Zengliang (1979) 'Ruogan jieci tanyuan' [The origins of some loanwords], *Yuyan jiaoxue yu yanjiu* [Language Teaching and Research] (Trial issue), Vol. 4.

Geng, Erling (2001) 'Wailaici de yuyi pingmian' [The semantic dimension of loanwords], *Tianjin daxue xuebao* (shehui kexue ban) [Journal of Tianjin University (Social Science Edition)] issue 4.

Gu, Jiazu (1990) 'Shilun yuyan de xishou, tonghua gongneng yu minzu xinli' [On the relations between language absorption or assimilation function and national psychology], in *Yuyan yu wenhua* [Language and culture], Shanghai: Shanghai waiyu jiaoyu chubanshe.

Guan, Yewei (1980) 'Guanyu Su Zhipo diaoshi yinjie lilun de yanjiu' [A study of Su Zhipo's theory of modal scales], *Yinyue yanjiu* [Music Research] issue 1.

Guangming ribao bianjibu [Guangming Daily Editorial Department] (1956) 'Guanyu huaxue mingci wenti de taolun' [Discussion on chemical terminology], *Guangming ribao* [Guangming Daily], p1, December 27.

Guo, Fuliang (2002) 'Cong Renmingwang ribenban kan dangdai hanyu zhong de riyu jieci' [On contemporary Chinese loanwords of Japanese origin from the Japanese edition of *People's Daily* online], *Hanyu xuexi* [Chinese language learning] issue 5.

Guo, Jianying (2003) 'Yige shiji yilai de hanyu wailaici yanjiu' [Chinese loanword studies in the past century], *Chenzhou shifan gaodeng zhuanke xuexiao xuebao* [Journal of Chenzhou Teachers Junior College] issue 2.

Guo, Lixia (2018) 'Yan Huiqing Yinghua da cidian zhong de ershi shiji chu wailaiyu' [Loanwords in Weiching Williams Yen's *English and Chinese Standard Dictionary* in the early 20th century (Parts 1 and 2)], *Yuyan wenzi zhoubao* [Language weekly] issues 1788/1789 (May 30/June 6).

Guo, Longsheng (1995) 'Guanggao zhong de wailaici' [Loanwords in advertisements], *Hanyu xuexi* [Chinese language learning] issue 5.

Guo, Moruo (1935) 'Liangzhou jinwenci daxi kaoshi' [Corpus of Inscriptions on Bronzes from the Two Zhou Dynasties], in his *Liangzhou jinwenci daxi tulu kaoshi* [Illustrated corpus of inscriptions on bronzes from the two Zhou dynasties], Beijing: Kexue chubanshe.

Guo, Xi (2005) 'Zimuci guifan shexiang' [Tentative ideas on the standardization of borrowed letterr-words], *Cishu yanjiu* [Lexicographical Studies] Issue 4.

Han, Rulin (1940) 'Tujue guanhao yanjiu' [Research on the Turkic official titles], *Zhongguo wenhua yanjiusuo jikan* [Collected papers of the Chinese Cultural Institute] Vol. 1, issue 1, Chengdu: Huaxi xiehe daxue (West China Union University).

He, Huazhen (1998) 'Ai zi tanyuan' [On the origin of the Chinese word 癌], *Cishu yanjiu* [Lexicographical Studies] issue 1.

—— (2012a) 'Zhongri jinxiandai hanzi ciyuan liuzhikao' [Research on the origins of Chinese characters in Modern China and Japan], *Yuwen jianshe tongxun* [Chinese language review – Hong Kong] issue 100.

—— (2012b) 'Minzhi chuqi de *Yiyu leiju* yu zhongri yixue hanzici yanjiu' [A study of *Igo Ruiji* (The medical vocabulary in English and Japanese) in early Meiji era and Chinese medical words used in China and Japan, *Yuwen jianshe tongxun* [Chinese language review – Hong Kong] issue 101.

—— (2013) 'Xiandai hanyu riyuan hanzici zhenbu' [Supplemented loanwords of Japanese kanji in modern Chinese], *Yuwen jianshe tongxun* [Chinese language review – Hong Kong] issue 102.

He, Wanping (2001) 'Hanyou xiwen zimu de ciyu zai cidian zhong de wweizhi' [The status of words containing Western letters in the Chinese dictionary], *Yuyan wenzi yunyong* [Applied Linguistics] issue 3.

He, Yang (1990) 'Beijing niujie diqu huiminhua zhong de jieci' [Loanwords in the Muslim community in Niujie area of Beijing], *Fangyan* [Dialect] issue 2.

Khmelevsky, Janus (1957) 'Yi *putao* yici weili lun gudai hanyu de jieci wenti' [On loanwords in Archaic Chinese: a case study of *putao*], *Beijing daxue xuebao* (renwen kexue ban) [Journal of Peking University (Humanities Edition)] issue1.

Hu, Houxuan (1934) 'Chu minzu yuanyu dongfang kao' [Examining whether Chu nationality originated from the Orient], *Shixue luncong* [Selected papers on historical studies] Vol. 1, Beijing: Beijing daxue qianshe.

Hu, Mingyang (2002) 'Guanyu waiwen zimuci he yuanzhuang waiwen suolueyu wenti' [On the issue of letter-words and foreign language abbreviations], *Yuyan wenzi yunyong* [Applied Linguistics] issue 2.

Hu, Peizhou (1991) 'Putaoyayu dui Aomen hua de yingxiang' [The influence of Portuguese on the Macau dialect], *Fangyan* [Dialect] issue 4.

Hu, Shuangbao (1989) 'Shuo *ge*' [On the word *ge*], in *Cihuixue lunwen huibian* [Collected papers on lexicology], Beijing: Shangwu yinshuguan.

Hu, Yilu (1914) 'Lun yiming' [On translating names and terms], in *Yong Bao* [Yung Pao daily] Vol. 2, issue 26/27.

Hu, Zengyi (1989) 'Manyu de *bai* zaoqi baihua zuopin *bai* de ciyi yanjiu' [A semantic study of *bai* in Manchu and *bai* in fiction written in vernacular Chinese], *Zhongguo yuwen* [Studies of the Chinese Language] issue 5.

———— (1995) 'Manyu bai tong hanyu fuci bai de jiedai guanxi' [The loan relationship between Manchu bai and Mandarin Chinese adverb bai], *Zhongguo yuyan xuebao* [Journal of Chinese Linguistics] issue 5.

Hu, Zhenhua (2015) 'Tantan *manasi* he *manasiqi* zhe liangge ci' [On the two words *manasi* and *manasiqi*], *Yuwen jianshe tongxun* [Chinese language review – Hong Kong] issue 108.

Hu, Zhengmao (2014) 'Hanyu wailaici: jieding, shiduan ji yijie tezheng' [On Classification and Characteristics of Chinese Loan Words], *Guangdong waiyu waimao daxue xuebao* [Journal of Guangdong University of Foreign Studies] issue 6.

Huang, Chunrui (2013) 'Hanyu xinci zhong eyuan wailaici benbuhua qingxiang yanjiu' [Research on the localization tendency of loanwords of Russian origin among Chinese neologisms], *Hubei jingji xueyuan xuebao* [Journal of Hubei College of Economics (Humanities and Social Sciences Edition)] issue 4.

Huang, Heqing (1989) 'Shixi wailaici zai yinghan liangzhong yuyan zhong shuliang xuanshu de yuanyin' [An analysis of the reasons for the disparity in the number of loanwords in the English and Chinese languages], *Xiandai waiyu* [Linguistics and Applied Linguistics] issue 2.

———— (1994a) 'Hanyu wailaici yanjiu zhong de ruogan wenti' [Some issues in the study of Chinese loanwords], *Ciku jianshe tongxun* [Journal on loanword and related studies – Hong Kong] issue 3.

———— (1994b) '*Luoji* yiming yuanliu kao' [Etymological research on the translation of *luoji*], *Ciku jianshe tongxun* [Journal on loanword and related studies – Hong Kong] issue 5.

———— (1994c) 'Hanyu yinyi wailaici zhong suo yunhan de yufa xianxiang' [The grammatical phenomena in Chinese phonemic loanwords], *Ciku jianshe tongxun* [Journal on loanword and related studies – Hong Kong] issue 5.

———— (1995) 'Hanyu wailai yingxiang ci' [Chinese words of foreign influence], *Ciku jianshe tongxun* [Journal on loanword and related studies – Hong Kong] issue 7.

———— (2016) '*Konglong shexingtuo* tanyuan' [On the etymological origin of *konglong* and *shexingtuo*], *Yuwen jianshe tongxun* [Chinese language review – Hong Kong] issue 111.

―― (2018a) 'Mengma kao' [On the etymological origin of *mengma*], *Yuwen jianshe tongxun* [Chinese language review – Hong Kong] issue 117.

―― (2018b) '*Kuli* shiyuan' [On the etymological origin of *kuli*], *Yuwen jianshe tongxun* [Chinese language review – Hong Kong] issue 115.

Huang, Lili (1999) 'Gangtai yuci zhi yihua jiqi yuanyin yu gangtai wailaiyu zhi bijiao' [Lexical mutations and their causes and a comparative study of loanwords in Hong Kong and Taiwan], *Zhongguo yuyan xuebao* [Journal of Chinese Linguistics] issue 9.

Huang, Shuguang (1995) 'Hanyu wenxian zhong de jige Zang Dian yuci shishi' [Interpretation of several Tibetan-Burmese words in Chinese documented resources], *Yuyan yanjiu* [Studies in Language and Linguistics] issue 1.

Huang, Xingtao (2003) 'Jindai Zhongguo xin mingci de yanjiu yu cihui chuantong de biange wenti' [Neologisms in modern China and the transformation of lexical traditions], *Ribenxue yanjiu* [Japanese Studies] issue 12.

Huang, Changzhu (1994) 'Cong mouxie waiyu zhuanming de hanyi kan haixia liangan yuyan shiyong de tong yu yi' [On the similarities and differences in language use across the Taiwan Straits from the Chinese translation of foreign proper names], *Zhongguo yuwen* [Studies of the Chinese Language] issue 6.

Ji, Xianlin (1947) '*Futu* yu *fo*' [*Futu* and Buddha], in *Zhongyin wenhua guanxishi lunwen ji* [Collected papers on the history of Sino-Indian cultural relations], Beijing: Sanlian shudian.

―― (1948) 'Lun fanwen ṭḍ de yinyi' [On the phonetic transliteration of Sanskrit ṭḍ], in *Zhongyin wenhua guanxishi lunwen ji* [Collected papers on the history of Sino-Indian cultural relations], Beijing: Sanlian shudian.

Ji, Yonghai (1985) 'Lun manyu zhong de hanyu jieci' [On Manchu loanwords from Chinese], *Manyu yanjiu* [Journal of Manchu Studies] issue 1.

―― (2004) 'Guanyu manshi hanyu' [On Manchu-style Chinese], *Minzu yuwen* [Minority Languages of China] issue 5.

―― (2004/2005) 'Cong jiechu dao ronghe: lun manyuwen de shuailuo' [From contact to integration: on the decline of the Manchu language (in two separate parts)], *Manyu yanjiu* [Journal of Manchu Studies] issue 1.

Jia, Zelin and Wang Jizhong (2010) 'Xiandai hanyu leicizhui de xingcheng jiqi yu wailaici de guanxi tanjiu' [The formation of quasi-affixes in modern Chinese and their relationship with loanwords], *Yunnan shifan daxue xuebao* (duiwai hanyu jiaoxue yu yanjiu ban) [Journal of Yunnan Normal University (Teaching and research of Chinese as a foreign language ediction)] issue 2.

Jiang, Yaming (2011) 'Yuanyu eyu de hanyu wailaici yanjiu' [A study of Chinese loanwords from Russian], *Tianjin waiguoyu daxue xuebao* [Journal of Tianjin Foreign Studies University] issue 2.

Jin, Qibin (2018) 'Modeng gujin tan: jiantan hanyu yinyi zhong de xueyi' [A study of the etymological evolution of the word modeng and Chinese humorous transliteration], *Yuwen jianshe tongxun* [Chinese language review – Hong Kong] issue 116.

Inoue, Suguru (2003) '中国的外来語の受容法' [Chinese approaches to loanword assimilation], *Nihongogaku*日本語学 [Journal of Japanese Linguistics] 22(8): 61–67.

Jiang, Kexin and Yang Hua (1995) 'Qianyi xin wailaici jiqi guifan wenti' [New loanwords and their standardization], *Yuyan wenzi yunyong* [Applied Linguistics] issue 1.

Kiyohide, Arakawa (1987) '訳語「熱帯」の起源をめぐつて--日中両語の漢字の造語力' [On the origin of the translated word 熱帯 *redai* (tropics): the word creating power of Japanese and Chinese] (in Japanese), *Nihongo Gaku*日本語学 [Journal of Japanese linguistics] 6(2):70–84, Tokyo: Meiji Shoin.

—— (1990) '中国にわたった「回帰線」' [On the the Chinese translated word回帰線 huiguixian (tropic)] (in Japanese), *Nihongo Gaku*日本語学 [Journal of Japanese linguistics] 9(2):46–62, Tokyo: Meiji Shoin.

Lai, Yan (2008) 'Hanyu jieyong yingyu wailaici de tedian ji yuyong liju' [Characteristics and pragmatic motivation of Chinese loanwords from English], *Hanyu xuexi* [Chinese language learning] issue 3.

Li, Changbao (2001) 'Yinghan wailaici duibi yanjiu' [Comparative study of English and Chinese loanwords], *Waiyu jiaoxue* [Foreign Language Education] issue 5.

Li, Jiwei (2005) 'Hanyu wailaici tongyi yiming xianxiang yanjiu' [On the translation of Chinese loanwords with the same meaning], *Yuyan wenzi yunyong* [Applied Linguistics] issue 4.

Li, Leyi (1990) 'Xiandai hanyu wailaici de tongyi wenti' [On the standardization of loanwords in modern Chinese], *Yuwen jianshe* [Language Planning] issue 2.

Li, Yan and Shi Chunhong (2007) 'Wailaici yuyi de hanyuhua jizhi ji xiangguan wenti' [Mechanisms in the lexical sinicization of loanwords and related issues], in *Diwujie quanguo yuyan wenzi yingyong xueshu yantaohui lunwen ji* [Proceedings of the fifth national symposium on the application of the Chinese language].

Li, Yanhui and Liu Xiangqing (2014) 'Muyinlun shijiao xia pinpai mingcheng hanyi zhong de yinyi yuanze tanxi' [On transliteration principles in the translation of brand names from the perspective of memetics], *Hunan diyi shifan xueyuan xuebao* [Journal of Hunan First Normal University] issue 1.

Li, Yini and Xu Jinghong (2014) 'Lun hanyu wangluo liuxingyu zhong de riyu jieci' [on Japanese loanwords in Chinese online buzzwords], *Beijing youdian daxue xuebao* (shehui kexue ban) [Journal of Beijing University of Posts and Telecommunications (Social Science Edition)] issue 4.

Li, Yunbo (2003) 'Liuru dao jindai zhongguo de riyu jieci: Liang Qichao zuopin zhong de riyu jieci' [Japanese loanwords that flowed into modern China: as study of Japanese loanwords in Liang Qichao's works], *Tianjin waiguoyu xueyuan xuebao* [Journal of Tianjin Foreign Studies University] issue 4.

Li, Yongming (1991) 'Xinjiapo chaozhouhua de waiyu jieci he teshu ciyu' [Loanword and special words in Singapore's Teochew Dialect] *Fangyan* [Dialect] issue 1.

Lian, Xiaoxia (2012) 'Zimuci de shoulu yu guifan: yi *Xiandai hanyu* cidian he *Cihai* weili' [Collection and standardization of letter-words: a case study of *Xiandai hanyu* and *Cihai*], *Yuyan jiaoxue yu yanjiu* [Language Teaching and Research] issue 2.

Liang, Xiaohong (1992) 'Fojing fanyi dui xiandai hanyu xishou wailaici de qidi' [The implication of the translation of Buddhist scriptures on the absorption of loanwords in Modern Chinese], *Yuwen jianshe* [Language Planning] issue 3.

Lin, Tao (1955) 'Guanyu hanyu guifanhua wenti' [On the issue of standardization of the Chinese language], *Zhongguo yuwen* [Studies of the Chinese Language] August issue.

Lin, Xichun (1977) 'Cong *caokulun* yici de xiefa shuoqi' [On and beyond the Chinese written forms of *caokulun*], *Guangming ribao* [Guangming Daily] p3, November 18.

Lin, Yutang (1924) 'Guanyu yiming tongyi de tiyi' [My proposal on the standardization of translated names], in his *Yuyanxue luncong* [Collected articles on linguistics], 1933, Shanghai: Kaiming shudian.

Liu, Jianmei (2002) 'Hanzi xitong zhong wailai zimu guifan qianyi' [On the standardardization of foreign letters in the Chinese script system], *Yuyan wenzi yunyong* [Applied Linguistics] issue 1.

Liu, Yongquan (2002) 'Guanyu hanyu zimuci de wenti' [On letter-words in the Chinese language], *Yuyan wenzi yunyong* [Applied Linguistics] issue 1.

Liu, Zexian (1952/1958) 'Yinyi yiyi he xingyi' [Phonemic, semantic, and graphic loaning], in *Kexue mingci he wenzi gaige* [Scientific terms and language reform], Beijing: Wenzi gaige chubanshe.

Liu, Zexian (1957) 'Hanyu buneng rongna wailaiyu ma?' [Can't Chinese accommodate foreign loanwords?], *Zhongguo yuwen* [Studies of the Chinese Language] May issue.

Liu, Zhengtan (1979) 'Guanyu bianzuan hanyu wailaici cidian de yixie wenti' [Some questions regarding compiling a dictionary of Chinese loanwords], *Cishu yanjiu* [Lexicographical Studies] issue 1.

—— (1983) 'Hanyu wailaici de lishi huigu he ciyuan kaozheng' [Historical review and etymological investigation of Chinese loanwords], *Baike zhishi* [Encyclopedic Knowledge] issue 11.

Liu, Zhongfu (2001) 'Guanyu *Xiandai hanyu cidian* shoushi wailaici de jige wenti' [Several issues concerning the collection and explanation of loanwords in the *Xiandai hanyu cidian*], *Dongyue luncong* [Dongyue Tribune] issue 4.

Lu, Yunsheng (1995) 'Neimenggu xibu diqu hanyu fangyan li de mengyu jieci' [Mongolian loanwords in Chinese dialects in western Inner Mongolia], *Minzu yuwen* [Minority Languages of China] issue 6.

Lu, Zhiwei (1953) 'Waiguoyu rendiming yiyin tongyi wenti' [On the standardization of transliteration of foreign personal and place names], *Zhongguo yuwen* [Studies of the Chinese Language] issue 8.

Lu, Shuxiang (1988) 'Nanbeichao renming yu fojiao' [Personal names and Buddhism in the Southern and Northern dynasties], *Zhongguo yuwen* [Studies of the Chinese Language] issue 4.

Luo, Qijing (1955) 'Qiantan hanyu wailaici *putao* de xingcheng jiqi yuanchu' [On the formation and origin of the Chinese loanword *putao*], *Ciku jianshe tongxun* [Journal on loanword and related studies – Hong Kong] issue 6.

Luo, Zeyu (2014) 'Liangci *pi* teshu yixiang de shengcheng yu xiaowang: cong riyu dui hanyu yingxiang de jiaodu' [The generation and extinction of the special meaning of the quantifier *pi* from the perspective of the influence of Japanese on Chinese], *Ribenxue yanjiu* [Japanese Studies] issue 23.

Meng, Weigen (1996) 'Hanyu wailaici de ciyi hanhua jiqi huiyi' [Semantic sinicization of Chinese loanwords and their back translation], *Ciku jianshe tongxun* [Journal on loanword and related studies – Hong Kong] issue 9.

Ni, Limin (1997) 'Luxun zhuzuo zhong de wailaici yanjiu' [A study of loanwords in Lu Xun's works], *Zhejiang daxue xuebao* [Journal of Hangzhou University] issue 1.

Oota, Tatsuo (1963) '清代文学に見える滿洲語' [Manchu language in Qing Dynasty literature] (in Japanese), 日本中国学会報 *Nippon-Chugoku-gakkai-ho* [Bulletin of the Sinological Society of Japan] issue 15.

Pan, Lei (2015) '中日同形語に関する一考察——中国語の"以外"と日本語の「以外」を中心に' [On Chinese and Japanese homographs: a case study of yiwai], *Ribenxue yanjiu* [Japanese Studies] issue 24.

Pan, Wenguo (2008) 'Wailaiyu xinlun: guanyu wailaiyu de zhexue sikao' [A philosophical reflection on loanword], *Zhongguo yuyanxue* [Chinese Linguistics] First Series, Jinan: Shandong jiaoyu chubanshe.

Pan, Yunzhong (1957) 'Yapian zhanzheng Yiqian hanyu zhong de jieci' [Loanwords in the Chinese language before the Opium War], *Zhongshan daxue xuebao* (shehui kexue ban) [Journal of Sun Yat-sen University (Social Science Edition)] issue 3.

Peng, Guanglu (2000–2012) 'Cong hanyu de xin ciyu kan riyu de yingxing' [The influence of Japanese on Chinese from its neologisms] (six series in total): **1)** (2000) 'Shuo ~*zu*' [On ~*zu*], in *Hanri yuyan yanjiu wenji* [Selected papers on Chinese and Japanese language studies] Vol. 3; **2)** (2000), 'Shuo ~*wu*' [On ~*wu*], in *Ribenxue yanjiu: riben guoji xueshu yantaohui lunwenji* [Japanese Studies: Proceedings of the international symposium on Japanese studies]; **3)** (2001) 'Shuo *wenti*' [On *wenti*], in *Riben wenhua luncong* [Essays on Japanese culture]; **4)** (2002) 'Shuo *xiezhen*' [On *xiezhen*], in *Riben yuyan wenhua lunji* [Collected papers on Japanese language and culture] Vol. 3; **5)** (2003a) 'Shuo *xianjin*' [On *xianjin*], in *Riben yuyan wenhua yanjiu* [Studies on Japanese language and culture] Vol. 4; **6)** (2003b) 'Shuo *zhengfa*' [On *zhengfa*], *Ribenxue yanjiu* [Japanese Studies] No 4; **7)** (2003c) 'Shuo *guolaosi*' [On *guolaosi*], *Chugokugo Kenkyu* 中国語研究 [Studies of Chinese language] issue 45; **8)** (2003d) 'Shuo *liaoli*' [On *liaoli*], in *Ribenxue yu riyu jiaoyu yanjiu* [Japanese Studies and research on Japanese language teaching]; **9)** (2012) 'Shuo *renmai* [On *renmai*], *Riyu xuexi yu yanjiu* [Journal of Japanese Language Study and Research] issue 4.

—— (2003) 'Hanyu xinci zhong de riyuan ci: yi *Xiandai hanyu cidian* (2002 nian zengbuben) wei kaocha duixiang' [Loanwords of Japanese origin in Chinese neologisms: a case study of *Xiandai hanyu cidian* (2002 Enlarged Edition)], in *Ribenyu jiaoyu yu ribenxue yanjiu luncong* (Beijing shifan daxue riwenxi bian) [Collected essays on Japanese language education and Japanese studies (ed. Beijing Normal University Japanese Department)] first series, Beijing: Minzu chubanshe.

Qian, Guanlian (1993) 'Han minzu de shenmei qingqu gei wailaiyu de ranse' [The aesthetics of the Han nationality on Chinese loanwords], in *Meixue yuyanxue* [Aesthetic Linguistics] (Shenzhen: Haitian chubanshe), also in *Ciku jianshe tongxun* [Journal on loanword and related studies – Hong Kong] issue 2.

Rong, Jie (1998) 'Zhong e kua wenhua jiaoji zhong de bianyuanyu' [Marginal language in Sino-Russian intercultural communication], *Jiefangjun waiguoyu xueyuan xuebao* [Journal of PLA University of Foreign Languages] issue 1.

Shang Youren: 1988, A bird's eye view of ethnic migration and ethnic integration in ancient Eurasia, "Northern Collection" (Changchun) issue 4.

Shao, Rongfen (1958) 'Ping *Xiandai hanyu wailaici yanjiu*' [Review: *A study of modern Chinese loanwords*], *Zhongguo yuwen* [Studies of the Chinese Language] issue 73.

Shao, Jingmin (2000) 'Xianggang fangyan wailaici bijiao yanjiu' [A comparative study of loanwords in Hong Kong dialects], *Yuyan wenzi yunyong* [Applied Linguistics] issue 3.

Shen, Guowei (1998) 'Cidian de ciyuan jishu ji ciyuan cidian' [Etymological information in the dictionary and the dictionary of etymology], *Ciku jianshe tongxun* [Journal on loanword and related studies – Hong Kong] issue 18.

—— (2000) 'Yiming *huaxue* de dansheng' [The birth of the translated word *huaxue*], *Hanzi wenhua* [Culture in Chinese written characters] issue 1.

——— (2011) 'Yanfu yu yici *kexue*' [Yan Fu and the translated word *kexue*], in *Fanyishi yanjiu* (diyiji) [Studies in Translation History 2011], Shanghai: Fudan daxue chubanshe.

Shen, Tong (1956) 'Xueshu mingci de tongyi he xueshu mingci de ladinghua' [Standardization and latinization of academic terms], *Kexue tongbao* [Science Bulletin] issue 3.

Shen, Wenfan and Pan Yiliang (2008) 'Xin shiqi riyuan jieci de yinru jiqi tedian' [The assimilation and characteristics of loanwords of Japanese origin in the new era], *Ribenxue luntan* [Japanese Studies Forum] issue 3.

Shiratori, Kurakichi (1923) 'Sur l'origine des Hiong-nou' [On the origin of the Xiong-nu], *Journal Asiatique* 11(1): 71–81.

Shi, Youwei (1991a) 'Wailaici yanjiu de shige fangmian' [Ten aspects of loanword studies], *Yuwen yanjiu* [Linguistic Research] issue 1.

——— (1991b) 'Wailaici yanjiu zhi huigu yu sikao' [Reflections and rethinking on loanword studies], *Yuwen jianshe* [Language Planning] issue 11.

——— (1991c) 'Wailaici: liangzhong yuyan wenhua de ronghe' [Loanwords: the fusion of two languages and cultures], *Hanyu xuexi* [Chinese language learning] issue 6.

——— (1995) 'Wailai de *wailaiyu* ji qita' [On the borrowed word *wailaiyu* and beyond], *Ciku jianshe tongxun* [Journal on loanword and related studies – Hong Kong] issue 7.

——— (1996) 'Wailaiyu, wailai gainian ci, wailai yingxiang ci zhi huiying' [My reflections on loanwords, conceptual loanwords and words of foreign influence], *Ciku jianshe tongxun* [Journal on loanword and related studies – Hong Kong] (8):8–13.

——— (1997) '*Langman* yuyuan xiaokao' [An etymological case study of *langman*] *Ciku jianshe tongxun* [Journal on loanword and related studies – Hong Kong] issue 11.

——— (1998) '*Ai* 癌 yi' [Etymolgogical question regarding the word *ai*癌], *Ciku jianshe tongxun* [Journal on loanword and related studies – Hong Kong] issue 17.

——— (1999) 'Lun dangdai yuyan jiechu yu wailaici' [On contemporary language contact and loanwords], 応用言語学研究』(《明海大学大学院応用言語学研究科紀要》[Selected research papers in applied language studies: Meikai roundtable in applied language studies], Meikai University, Chiba, Japan, issue 1.

——— (2007) 'Riben suoyong hanzi de hanyu zhuanxing chutan' [A preliminary study of the transformation of Chinese characters used in Japan], *Shijie hanyu jiaoxue* [Chinese Teaching in the World] issue 4.

——— (2008) 'Yingzhi duliangheng danwei yu zhongxiri jiaoliu' [The British system of weights and measures and the exchange between China and the West and Japan], in *Nanda yuyanxue* (disanbian) [Nanjing University Linguistics] Vol. 3.

——— (2014) 'Cong chuanboxue he jieshouxue shijiao kan wailaici' [Loanwords seen from the perspectives of communication studies and reception studies], *Yuyanxue yanjiu* (di shisi ji) [Linguistic studies] Vol. 14, (ed.) Beijing daxue waiguoyu xueyuan waiguo yuyanxue ji yingyong yuyanxue yanjiusuo [Institute of Foreign Linguistics and Applied Linguistics, School of Foreign Languages, Peking University].

——— (2016a) '*Xinhua wailaici cidian* bianhou lueji' [A short afterword on the compilation of *Xinhua wailaici cidian*], *Cishu yanjiu* [Lexicographical Studies] issue 1.

——— (2016b) 'Jiujie de riyuan ci' [The perplexing Japan-originated Chinese words], *Yuwen jianshe tongxun* [Chinese language review – Hong Kong] issue 111.

——— (2017) 'Wenhua fanyi shijiao xia de yiming' [Name translation from the perspective of translation as cultural act], *Nanda yuyanxue* (disanbian) [Nanjing University Linguistics] Vol. 5.

——— (2018) 'Hanyu wailaici sishi nian ji' [Forty years of Chinese loanword studies] (three series), *Yuyan wenzi zhoubao* [Language weekly] Vols. 1818, 1819, 1820.

——— (2019) 'Hanyu wailaici yanjiu qishi nian: jianyi xianqi jieci kaoyuan yanjiu' [Seventy years of Chinese loanword studies and earlier etymological research on loanwords], *Yuyan zhanlue yanjiu* [Chinese Journal of Language Policy and Planning] issue 5.

Shioyama, Masazumi (2003) 'Xican yu hanyu fanyci: guanyu *Zao yangfan shu* di er ban (1899)' [Western food and Chinese loanwords: a study of the 2nd Chinese Edition of Martha Crawford's *Zao yangfan shu* [Foreign Cookery in Chinese] (1899)], *Ribenxue yanjiu* [Japanese studies] issue 12.

Sone, Hirotaka (1987) '中国語における日本語からの借用語' [Japanese loanword in the Chinese language] (in Japanese), *Meiji gakuin ronso* [Meiji Gakuin Review] (408):15–37.

Su, Chunmei and Hu Mingzhi (2007) 'Cong Harbin fangyan zhong de eyu jieci kan eyu yu hanyu de xianghu yingxiang' [The mutual influence between Russian and Chinese: a case study of Russian loanwords in the Harbin dialect], *Heilongjiang shehui kexue* [Social Sciences in Heilongjiang] issue 1.

Su, Jinzhi (2002) 'Lun dangqian hanyu wailaici guifan de yuanze' [On the principles of the current standardization of loanwords in Chinese], *Cishu yanjiu* [Lexicographical Studies] issue 3.

Sun, Wangzhen (1995) 'Hanyu de jieci yu shuangxiang jieci' [Chinese loanwords and two-way loanwords], *Neimenggu daxue xuebao* (zheshe ban) [Journal of Inner Mongolia University (Social Science Edition) issue 2.

Su, Peicheng (2012) 'Tan hanyuwen li zimuci de shiyong he guifan' [On the use and standardization of letter-words in Chinese], *Zhongguo yuwen* [Studies of the Chinese Language] issue 6.

Tan, Haisheng (1995) 'Duiyi jieci: yue fangyan wailaiyu zhong de yizhong teshu jieci' [Translated loanwords: A special kind of loaning in the Cantonese dialect], *Guangdong jiaoyu xueyuan xuebao* [Journal of Guangdong Institute of Education (Social Sciences Edition)] issue 1.

Ueno, Keiji (1989) '中国の辞典にみる日本語' [Japanese in Chinese dictionaries], *Nihongogaku* 日本語学 [Journal of Japanese Linguistics] July issue.

Wang, Ailu and Si Fuzhen (1998) 'Wailaici de neibu xingshihua qingxiang' [The internal formalization tendency in loanwords], *Shijie hanyu jiaoxue* [Chinese Teaching in the World] issue 3.

Wang, Enxu (1987) 'Yuanyu eyu de hanyu wailaici' [On Chinese loanwords originated from Russian], *Dongbei shifan daxue xuebao* [Journal of Northeast Normal University] issue 5.

Wang, Binbin (1998) 'Ge zai zhongxi zhijian de riben: xiandai hanyu zhong de riyu wailaici wenti' [Japan between China and the West: Japanese loanwords in modern Chinese], *Shanghai wenxue* [Shanghai literature] issue 8.

Wang, Guowei (1905) 'Lun xin xueyu zhi shuru' [On the importation of new academic terms, in (1997) *Wang Guowei wenji* [Collected Works of Wang Guowei] Vol. 3, Beijing: Zhongguo wenshi chubanshe.

Wang, Jihui (1999) 'Zimu ciyu de wailai ciyu xingzhi fenxi' [Analysis of the nature of letter-words as loanwords], *Hanyu xuexi* [Chinese language learning] issue 5.

Wang, Jiajun (1948) 'Tianjin liuxingyu zhong zhi wailaiyu shiyi' [Loanwords in Tianjin buzzwords explained], *Tianjin wenhua* [Tianjin Culture] issue 2.

Wang, Jie (2009) *'Shelisun* suyuan' [On the etymology of *shelisun*], *Yuwen jianshe tongxun* [Chinese language review – Hong Kong] issue 91.

Wang, Jue (1992) 'Hanyu zhong riyu jieci sanlun' [On Chinese loanwords of Japanese origin], in *Hanyu yanjiu lunji* (di yi ji) [Collected essays on the Chinese language] Vol. 1, (ed.) Xuezhou shifan xueyuan zhongwenxi [Chinese Department of Xuzhou Teachers' College], Beijing: Yuwen chubanshe.

—— (1993) 'Hanyu dui wailaici de yuyin xunhua' [Phonetic domestication of loanwords in Chinese], *Jiefangjun waiyu xueyuan xuebao* [Journal of PLA University of Foreign Languages] issues 1/2/5.

—— (1996) 'Wailaici wenhua xunhua mianmian guan' [Aspects of the cultural domestication of loanword], *Nantong shizhuan xuebao* [Journal of Nantong Teachers Junior College (Social Sciences Edition)] issue 1.

Wang, Li (1954) 'Lun hanyu biaozhunyu' [On the standard Chinese language], *Zhongguo yuwen* [Studies of the Chinese Language] June issue.

Wang, Lida (1958a) 'Xiandai hanyu zhong cong riyu jielai de cihui' [Modern Chinese lexicon borrowed from Japanese], *Zhongguo yuwen* [Studies of the Chinese Language] issue 2.

—— (1958b) 'Cong goucifa shang bianbie buliao riyu jieci' [It is impossible to tell loanwords of Japanese origin by means of word formation], *Zhongguo yuwen* [Studies of the Chinese Language] issue 9.

Wang, Liaoyi (1939) 'Lun hanyi diming renming de biaozhun' [On the standards for translating geographical and personal names], *Jinri pinglun* [Commentary today] Vol.1, issue 11.

Wang, Riwei (1981) 'Dingling minzu kao' [The origin of the ancient Dingling Nationality], in *Tujue yu huihe lishi lunwen xuanji* [Selected papers on the history of Turks and Hui], Beijing: Zhonghua shuju.

Wang, Shasha (2013) 'Hanyu wangluo liuxingyu zhong riyuanci chutan' [A preliminary study of Japanese loanwords in Chinese online buzzwords], *Hubei guangbo dianshi daxue xuebao* [Journal of Hubei Radio and TV University] issue 3.

Wang, Shuhuai (1969) 'Qingmo fanyi mingci tongyi wenti' [Issues in the standardization of translated nouns in the late Qing Dynasty], *Jindaishi yanjiusuo jikan* [Collected papers by the Institute of Modern History] Vol. 1.

Wang, Tiekun王铁昆 (1991) 'Shinian lai de hanyu xin ciyu yanjiu' [A study of new Chinese words for the past decade], *Yuwen jianshe* [Language Planning] issue 4.

Wang Tiekun王铁琨 (1993) 'Hanyu xin wailaiyu de wenhua xinli toushi' [Cultural and psychological aspects of new loanwords in Chinese], *Hanyu xuexi* [Chinese language learning] issue 1.

Wang, Xiao (2009) 'Cong yuyan jiechu de jiaodu fenxi dangdai hanyu zhong de riyu jieci' [A study of Japanese loanwords in contemporary Chinese from the perspective of language contact], *Riyu xuexi yu yanjiu* [Journal of Japanese Language Study and Research], issue 4.

Wang, Yangzong (2003) 'Guanyu Qing mo kouyi yu bishu yixie fa de chubu tantao' [A preliminary discussion on the interpretation and dictation methods in the late Qing dynasty], *Ribenxue yanjiu* [Japanese Studies] issue 12.

Wang, Zhongliang (1995) 'Harbin diqu shiyong de zhong'e yangjingbang' [Pidgin Russian used in Harbin], *Ciku jianshe tongxun* [Journal on loanword and related studies – Hong Kong] issue 6.

Wang, Zongyan (1950) 'Yinyi he yiyi' [Phonemic translation and semantic loaning], *Fanyi tongbao* [Translation Bulletin] Vol. 1, issue 5.
Wei, Huiping (2002) 'Hanyu wailai cisu chutan' [A preliminary study of foreign morphemes in the Chinese language], *Hanyu xuexi* [Chinese language learning] issue 1.
Wen, You (1980) 'Yuyuan congkao: *ya ou wu* sanci cidi kao' [Etymology: A sequential study of the three Chinese words *ya*, *ou*, and *wu*], *Zhonghua wenshi luncong* [Journal of Chinese Literature and History] issue 4.
Wen, You and Shi Youwei (1987) 'Huayi yiyu' [Chinese-foreign translated glossaries], in *Zhongguo da baike quanshu – minzu juan* [Chinese Encyclopedia | Ethnicities Volume], Beijing: Zhongguo da baike quanshu chubanshe.
—— (1988) 'Huayi yiyu' [Chinese-foreign translated glossaries], in *Zhongguo da baike quanshu – yuyan wenzi* [Chinese Encyclopedia | Languages], Beijing: Zhongguo da baike quanshu chubanshe.
Wu, Huizhen (2011) 'Jiyu yuanxing fanchou lilun de wailaiyu yuyi pianli xianxiang tanxi' [An analysis of the semantic deviation of loanwords based on the prototype category theory], *Anhui gongye daxue xuebao* [Journal of Anhui University of Technology (Social Science Edition)] issue 5.
Wu, Liquan (1994) 'Hanyu wailaici yinyi de tedian jiqi wenhua xintai tanjiu' [Research on the characteristics and cultural mentality of Chinese phonemic loanwords], *Fudan xuebao* [Journal of Fudan University (Social Science Edition)] issue 3.
—— (1996) 'Xieyi: hanyu wailaici yinyi de yizhong dute xingtai' [homophonic transliteration: a unique type of Chinese phonemic loanwords], *Changchun daxue xuebao* [Journal of Changchun University] issue 1.
Wu, Shixiong (1997) 'Zailun hanyu wailaici de fenlei he dingyi wenti' [Rethinking the classification and definition of Chinese loanwords], *Ciku jianshe tongxun* [Journal on loanword and related studies – Hong Kong] issue 11.
Wu, Sicong (2003) 'Hanyu wailaici dui hanyu cihui xitong de yingxiang' [The Influence of Chinese loanwords on the Chinese lexical system], *Yunnan shifan daxue xuebao* (zhexue shehui kexue ban) [Journal of Yunnan Normal University (Philosophy and Social Sciences Edition)] issue 1.
Wu, Tieping (1991) 'Jieci de ciyi' [The semantics of loanwords], in his *Lun bijiao he yuyan jiechuxue* [On comparison and language contact studies], also in *Qian kexue* [ ] issue 6, and reprinted in *Ciku jianshe tongxun* [Journal on loanword and related studies – Hong Kong] 1993(1).
Xian, Wenhan (1979) 'Youguan xiandai hanyu guifanhua de jige wenti' [Several questions about the standardization of modern Chinese], *Zhongguo yuwen* [Studies of the Chinese Language] issue 1.
Xing, Gongwan (1991) 'Guanyu Hanyu Nandaoyu de fashengxue guanxi wenti' [On the issue over the origin of Chinese and Austronesian], *Minzu yuwen* [Minority Languages of China] issue 3.
Xiong, Yuezhi (1994) '1842 nian zhi 1860 nian xixue zai zhongguo de chuanbo' [The spread of Western learning in China from 1842 to 1860], *Lishi yanjiu* [Historical Research] issue 230.
Xiu, Dejian (1995) 'Guanyu zhongri lianguo yuyan xishou wailaiyu de duibi yanjiu' [Contrastive study of the absorption of loanwords in China and Japan], *Jiefangjun waiguoyu xueyuan xuebao* [Journal of the PLA University of Foreign Languages] issue 1.

Xu, Fu (1945) 'Yanshi duyin kao' [A phonetic examination of the family name Yan], in *Xiongnu shi lunwen xuanji* [Anthology of papers on the history of the Xiongnu], Beijing: Zhonghua shuju.

Xu, Wenkan (1993) 'Hanyu wailaici de yuyuan kaozheng he cidian bianzuan' [Philological Research on the Etymology of Loanwords in Sinitic and Dictionary Compilation], in *Sino-Platonic Papers* Philadelphia: University of Pennsylvania, (36):1–13.

—— (1996) 'Guanyu *shendu, tianzhu, yindu* dengci de yuyuan' [On the etymology of the Chinese words *shendu*身毒, *tianzhu*天竺, and *yindu*印度], *Ciku jianshe tongxun* [Journal on loanword and related studies – Hong Kong] issue 10.

Xu, Guimei (2012) 'Luxun xiaoshuo yuyan zhong de riyu yuansu jiexi' [The Japanese elements in the language of Lu Xun's novels], *Luxun yanjiu yuekan* [Lu Xun Research Monthly] issue 3.

Xu, Lihua (1991) 'Maodun xiaoshuo zhong wailaici de guifan yunyong' [On the standard use of loanwords in Mao Dun's novels], *Yuwen yuekan* [Chinese language monthly] issue 5.

Xu, Shuzhen (1994) 'Mins yuyuan yu wailaici de hanhua' [Folk etymology and sinicization of loanwords], *Sichuan waiyu xueyuan xuebao* [Journal of Sichuan International Studies University] issue 1.

Xu, Haoguang and Liu Yanxin (1996) 'Hanyu zhong de manyu jieci gaishu' [An overview of Chinese loanwords from Manchu], *Manzu yanjiu* [Manchu Minority Research] issue 1.

Xue, Wenbo (1980) 'Huihui xingshi kao (I)' [An etymological study of the surnames of Chinese Muslims], *Ningxia daxue xuebao* [Journal of Ningxia University] issue 4.

Yan, Xuewen (1994) 'Zhongri liangguo wailaici jieyong fangshi de bijiao' [Comparison of the means of lexical borrowing in loanwords between China and Japan], *Jinzhou shifan xueyuan xuebao* [Journal of Jinzhou Teachers College] issue 1.

Yang, Fuquan (2008) '*Minzu* kaoyuan' [An etymological study of the Chinese word *minzu* (democracy)], *Yuwen jianshe tongxun* [Chinese language review – Hong Kong] issue 90.

Yang, Hua and Jiang Kexin (1995) 'Qianyi xin wailaici jiqi guifan wenti' [A study of new loanwords and their standardization], *Yuyan wenzi yunyong* [Applied Linguistics] issue 1.

Yang, Ting (1995) 'Xiandai hanyu wailaiyu yunyong zhong de yige xin tedian' [A new feature in the use of loanwords in modern Chinese], *Yuwen yuekan* [Chinese language monthly] issue 5.

Yang, Wenzhi (2016) 'Ruhe tongyi yu guifan waiguo renming diming de fanyi' [How to unify and standardize the translation of foreign personal and place names], *Yuwen jianshe tongxun* [Chinese language review – Hong Kong] issue 111.

Yang, Xipeng (2008) 'Jiexingci yu zimuci' [Graphic loanwords and alphabetic letter-words], in *Nanda yuyanxue* (disanbian) [Nanjing University Linguistics] Vol. 3.

Yang, Xinru (2016) 'Tantan *le*叻, *keke* 岢岢, *niangre*娘惹' [A study of the loanwords *le*叻, *keke* 岢岢, *niangre*娘惹], *Yuwen jianshe tongxun* [Chinese language review – Hong Kong] issue 112.

Yao, Rong-Song (1992) 'Taiwan xianxing wailaiyu de wenti' [Survey on the problem of contemporary loan word in the languages spoken in Taiwan], *Taiwan shifan daxue xuebao* [Bulletin of National Taiwan Normal University], (37):329–362.

Yao, Te Hwai (1994) 'Yetan *youtai*' [Rethinking the origin of the word *youtai* (Jew)], *Ciku jianshe tongxun* [Journal on loanword and related studies – Hong Kong] issue 5.

——— (1996) 'Huayu cihui de zhengli he guifan' [The organization and standardization of the Chinese lexicon], *Ciku jianshe tongxun* [Journal on loanword and related studies – Hong Kong] issue 9.

——— (1997) 'Shangdi ye fengkuang: zhongwen shengjing yiyici xuankan' [God may also be crazy: variously translated words in the Chinese version of the Bible], *Ciku jianshe tongxun* [Journal on loanword and related studies – Hong Kong] issue 11.

——— (2009) 'Mingzi de waiyizhong he zhongyiwai' [Translation of names into and from Chinese], *Yuwen jianshe tongxun* [Chinese language review – Hong Kong] issue 92.

Xiao, Hui and Tao Yukang (2000) 'Dengxiao yuanze shijiao xia de shangbiao fanyu wenhua lianxiang' [Trademark translation and cultural association from the perspective of the principle of equivalence], *Waiyu yu waiyu jiaoxue* [Foreign Languages and Their Teaching] issue 11.

Ye, Xuyi (2017) '日中同形語字形類化度の統計—自然言語処理における漢字分割法の利用を中心に' [Statistics on the similarity of Japanese and Chinese homomorphic words with the focus on Chinese character division method in natural language processing], *Ribenxue yanjiu* [Japanese Studies] (27):74–89.

Yu, Yousun (1935) 'Riyi xueshu mingci yange' [Evolution of academic terms translated from Japanese], *Wenhua jiaoyu xunkan* [Cultural education weekly], Vol. 1, issue 69.

——— (1936) 'Tan riyi xueshu mingci' [On academic terms translated from Japanese], *Wenzhe yuekan* [Literary and philosophical monthly] Vol. 1, issue 7."

Yu, Zhongxin (1996) 'Huiguici lun' [On return loanwords], *Ciku jianshe tongxun* [Journal on loanword and related studies – Hong Kong] issue 10.

Yu, Pin and Zhu Jifang (2003) 'Yuanxing jieci: xiandai hanyu xishou wailaiyu de xin fazhan' [Graphicl loanwords: the new development of modern Chinese in absorbing borrowed words], *Zhongguo yuwen* [Studies of the Chinese Language] issue 6.

Yuan, Hanqing (1987) 'Woguo heshi kaishi shiyong *huaxue* yici' [When did China begin to use the word *huaxue* (chemistry)?], in *Zhongguo keji shiliao* [China Historical Materials of Science and Technology] Vol. 3.

Yuan, Senlin and Huang Jianna (2016) 'Qianxi ershiyi shiji yilai hanyu zhong riyu wailaici zhuru xingshi' [An analysis of the forms of entry of Chinese loanwords from Japanese since the 21st century], *Hainan guangbo dianshi daxue xuebao* [Journal of Hainan Radio and TV University] issue 1.

Yuan, Xinmei (2005) 'Zimuci de shouru yu zhuyin wenti' [On the entry listing and phonetic marking of letter-words], *Cishu yanjiu* [Lexicographical Studies] issue 4.

Yuchi, Zhiping (1995) '*Feng* zhimi he yiyu zoulang' [The mystery of the word *feng* (wind) and ancient foreign languages], *Yuyan yanjiu* [Studies in Language and Linguistics] issue 2.

Zeng, Zhaocong, Zhang Jingwen, Yang Yumeng, and Han Ye (2009) '*Xin mingci xunzuan* zhong de riyuan wailaici yanjiu' [A study of loanwords of Japanese origin in the dictionary *Xin mingci xunzuan*] in *Yuwen jianshe tongxun* [Chinese language review – Hong Kong] issue 92.

Zhai, Dongna (2000) 'Qianxi hanri tongxingci de baobian secai he shehui wenhua yinsu' [An analysis of the positive/negative tone and social cultural factors in

Chinese and Japanese common homographs], *Riyu xuexi yu yanjiu* [Journal of Japanese Language Study and Research] issue 2.

Zhang, Dexin 'Disanci langchao: wailaiyu yinjin he guifan chuyi' [The third wave: on the absorption and standardization of loanwords], *Yuyan wenzi yunyong* [Applied Linguistics] issue 3.

Zhang, Husheng (1989) 'Xizang minjian fojiao yishu de jingpin: *chacha* kao' [A gem in the folk fine art of Tibetan Buddhism: the etymology of *tsha-tsha*], *Xizang yishu yanjiu* [Tibetan Art Studies] issue 4.

Zhang, Jiading (1989) 'Beijing xiancun manyu zaji' [Miscellaneous notes of the existing Manchu words in Beijing], *Manyu yanjiu* [Journal of Manchu Studies] issue 2.

Zhang, Jinwen (2003) 'Guanyu hanyu jieci de fenlei wenti' [On the classification of Chinese loanwords, *Cishu yanjiu* [Lexicographical Studies] issue 3.

Zhang, Miao and Gao Miaomiao (2011) '*Fengtian tongzhi* zhong dongbei fangyan de manyu jieci kaozheng' [Textual research on the loanwords from Manchu in China's Northeast Dialect in *Fengtian tongzhi*] *Manyu yanjiu* [Journal of Manchu Studies] issue 2.

Zhang, Qingchang (1978) 'Mantan hanyu zhong de many jieci' [A study of Mongolian loanwords in the Chinese language], *Zhongguo yuwen* [Studies of the Chinese Language] issue 3.

────── (1991) 'Yizhong wujie beijie de ci yuanyi xianxiang' [On the the original meaning of the mistaken loanswords], *Yuyan jiaoxue yu yanjiu* [Language Teaching and Research] issue 4.

Zhang, Qingyuan (1989) 'Cong xiandai hanyu wailaiyu chubu fenxi zhong dedao de jidian renshi' [Some observations gained from the preliminary analysis of loanwords in modern Chinese], in *Cihuixue lunwen huibian* [Collected essays on lexicology], Beijing: Shangwu yinshuguan.

Zhang, Shuangfu (1994) '*Huayi yiyu* yanjiu' [A study of *Huayi yiyu* (Chinese-foreign translated glossaries)], *Neimenggu shehui kexue* [Social Sciences in Inner Mongolia] issue 6.

Zhang, Xizeng (1970) 'Guoyu li wailaiyu de yanjiu' [A study of loanwords in the Chinese language] (print-out version, Taipei).

Zhang, Yingde (1958) 'Xiandai hanyu zhong nengyou zhemeduo riyu jieci ma?' [Can there be so many loanwords from Japanese in modern Chinese?], *Zhongguo yuwen* [Studies of the Chinese Language] June issue.

Zhang, Yingde and Gao Zirong (1958) 'Yiyici shi wailaici ma?' [Are semantic loans loanwords?], *Yuwen xuexi* [Chinese language learning] issue 3.

Zhang, Yongyan (1992a) '*Qinglu* he *wuyu*' [*Qinglu*轻昌and *wuyu*乌育], Yuyan yanjiu [Studies in Language and Linguistics] issue 5; also in his *Yuwenxue lunji* (1992), Beijing: Yuwen chubanshe.

────── (1992b) 'Yuyuan tansuo sanli' [Three case studies of etymology], *Zhongguo yuyan xuebao* [Journal of Chinese Linguistics] issue 3; also in his *Yuwenxue lunji* (1992), Beijing: Yuwen chubanshe.

────── (1992c) 'Hanyu wailaici zatan' [A miscellaneous study of Chinese loanwords], *Yuyan jiaoxue yu yanjiu* [Language Teaching and Research] issue 2; also in his *Yuwenxue lunji* (1992), Beijing: Yuwen chubanshe.

Zhang, Zhenmin (1915) 'Yiming' [On translating names], *Jiayin* [The Tiger] Vol. 1, issue 6.

Zhao, Futang (1983) 'Guanyu zhongri tongxingci de bijiao yanjiu' [A comparative study of common Chinese and Japanese homographs], *Riyu xuexi yu yanjiu* [Journal of Japanese Language Study and Research] issue 4.

Zhao, Jie (1993) 'Beijinghua zhong manhan ronghe ci tanwei' [A probe into the Manchu-Han integrated words in the Beijing Dialect], *Zhongguo yuwen* [Studies of the Chinese Language] issue 4.

Zhao, Yuanren (1970), 'Jieyu juli' [Interlingual and Inter-dialectal Borrowings in Chinese], in *Zhongguo xiandai yuyanxue de kaituo yu fazhan: Zhao Yuanren yuyanxue lunwen xuan* [Exploitation and development of modern Chinese linguistics: selected works of Zhao Yuanren on linguistics], 1992, Beijing: Qinghua daxue chubanshe.

Zhaonasitu (Junast) (1991) 'Lun hanyu zhong de mengguoyu jieci *hutong*' [On the Mongolian loanword *hutong* in Chinese], *Minzu yuwen* [Minority Languages of China] issue 6.

Zheng, Dian (1958) 'Tan xiandai hanyu zhong de riyu cihui' [On the Japanese lexicon in modern Chinese], *Zhongguo yuwen* [Studies of the Chinese Language] issue 2.

Zheng, Wuxi (2009) 'Shilun yuyan jiechu yinfa de Qiangyu dui dangdi hanyu de ganrao' [On the language contact-induced interference of the Qiang language with the local Chinese language], *Aba shifan gaodeng zhuanke xuexiao xuebao* [Journal of Aba Teachers College] issue 4.

Zhengzhang, Shangfang (2018) '*Zhina* (China) zuichu de laiyuan' [The origin of *Zhina* (China)], *Yuwen jianshe tongxun* [Chinese language review – Hong Kong] issue 115.

Zhong, Zhaohu (1953) 'Wailai xueshu mingci yinggai zai shenme yuanze shang tongyi qilai' [On what principle should borrowed academic terms be standardized], *Zhongguo yuwen* [Studies of the Chinese Language] issue 8.

Zhong, Shaohua (2016) 'Jindai minzu gainian chuanru zhongguo de youlai ji *minzu* yici de ciyuan' [The origin of the borrowing of the concept of "nation" in modern China and the etymology of the word *minzu* (nation)], *Yuwen jianshe tongxun* [Chinese language review – Hong Kong] issue 111.

Zhou, Dingguo (1994) 'Tan hanyu yinyi wailaici guifanhua' [On the standardization of phonemic loanwords in Chinese], *Yuwen jianshe* [Language Planning] issue 10.

Zhou, Dingyi (1962) 'Yinyici he yiyici de xiaozhang' [The rise and decline of the phonemic loaning and semantic loaning], *Zhongguo yuwen* [Studies of the Chinese Language] issue 10.

Zhou, Fagao (Chou Fa-kao) (1955) 'Zhongguoyu de jiezi' [Loanwords in the Chinese language], in his *Zhongguo yuwen yanjiu* [A study of the Chinese language], Taipei: Zhonghua wenhua chuban shiye weiyuanhui.

Zhou, Gang and Wu Yue (2003) 'Ershi nian lai xin liuxing de riyuan wailaici' [The new popular loanwords of Japanese origin in the past 20 years], *Hanyu xuexi* [Chinese language learning] issue 5.

Zhou, Huasong (1951) 'Tongyi yiming he ladinghua' [Standardization in translated names and Latinization], *Fanyi tongbao* [Translation bulletin] Vol. 2 issue 2.

Zhou, Hongbo (1995) 'Wailaici yiyin chengfen de yusuhua' [Morphemeization of transliterated elements in loanwords], *Yuyan wenzi yunyong* [Applied Linguistics] issue 4.

Zhou, Yimin and Zhu Jiansong (1994) 'Guanyu beijinghua zhong de manyu ci' [On the Manchu words in the Beijing Dialect], *Zhongguo yuwen* [Studies of the Chinese Language] issue 3.

Zhou, Youguang (1982) 'Diming guoji biaozhunhua de duyin wenti' [On the pronunciation of the internationally standardizd place names], in his *Xin yuwen de jianshe* [Language planning for the new language and script] 1992, Beijing: Yuwen chubanshe.

Zhu, Jingwei (1993) 'Xiandai hanyu zhong riyu jieci de bianbie he zhengli' [Determination and organization of Japanese loanwords in modern Chinese], *Ribenxue yanjiu* [Japanese studies] issue 1.

―― (2003) '19世紀以降の中日語彙交流と借用語の研究—研究の資料と方法をめぐって' [Research on Chinese-Japanese lexical communication and borrowing since the 19th century: resources and methodology], *Ribenxue yanjiu* [Japanese studies] issue 12.

―― (2005) '蔡元培の日本語翻訳に初期の哲学用語の移入' [The borrowing of early philosophical terminology from Cai Yuanpei's Japanese language translation], *Ribenxue yanjiu* [Japanese studies] issue 15.

―― (2006) '社会主義用語の形成に見られる特徴――語構成と語誌記述の視点から' [The characteristics of the formation of socialist terminology: from the perspective of word formation and lexical records], *Ribenxue yanjiu* [Japanese studies] issue 16.

―― (2007) 'Liang Qichao yu riyu jieci' [Liang Qichao and Japanese loanwords], *Ribenxue yanjiu* [Japanese studies] issue 17.

―― (2009) '*Minbao* (1905–1908) zhong de riyu jieci' [Japanese loanwords in *Minbao* (1905–1908)], *Ribenxue yanjiu* [Japanese studies] issue 19.

―― (2012a), '*Shiwubao* (1896–98) zhong de riyu jieci: wenben fenxi yu erziyu bufen' [Japanese loanwords in *Shiwubao* (1896–98): textual analysis and two-character words], *Riyu xuexi yu yanjiu* [Journal of Japanese Language Study and Research] (3):19–28.

―― (2012b) '*Shiwubao* (1896–98) zhong de riyu jieci: sanzici yu sizici bufen' [Japanese loanwords in *Shiwubao* (1896–98): three-character and four-character words], *Ribenxue yanjiu* [Japanese studies] (22):94–105.

―― (2013) 'Qingyibao (1898–1901) zhong de erzi riyu jieci' [The two-character Japanese loanwords in *The China Discussion* (1898–1901)] (23):25–40.

Zhu, Qingzhi (1994) 'Hanyu wailaici erze' [Two loanwords in Chinese], *Yuyan jiaoxue yu yanjiu* [Language Teaching and Research] issue 1.

Zhu, Yongkai (1995) 'Xianggang yueyu li de wailaici' [Loanwords in the Hong Kong Cantonese], *Yuwen yanjiu* [Linguistic Research] issue 2.

Zi, Xun (1986) 'Cong mouxie xiuci jiu yiming tan yuyan de biange he guifan' [On language evolution and standardization as seen from the translation of some rhetorical terms], *Yuwen jianshe tongxun* [Chinese language review – Hong Kong] (19):22–23.

Zou, Guotong (1956) 'Guanyu renming yiyin wenti de shangque' [Discussion on the transliteration of personal names], *Zhongguo yuwen* [Studies of the Chinese Language] issue 4.

Zou, Jiachan (2003) 'Dangdai hanyu xinci de duoyuanhua quxiang he diqu jingzheng' [The diversification of contemporary Chinese neologisms and regional competition], *Yuyan jiaoxue yu yanjiu* [Language Teaching and Research] issue 2.

Zou, Yuhua (2014) '*Xiandai hanyu cidian* shoulu xiwen zimu kaitou de ciyu zhi weifa yufou de falu fenxi' [On the legality of listing acronyms and word beginning with

Greek or Latin letters in *Xiandai hanyu cidian*], *Yuyan jiaoxue yu yanjiu* [Language Teaching and Research] issue 4.

Zou, Yuhua, Ma Guangbin, Liu Hong, and Han Zhixiang (2005) 'Guanyu hanyu zong shiyong zimuci de yuyan taidu de diaocha' [A survey on the language attitude towards using letter-words in Chinese], *Yuyan jiaoxue yu yanjiu* [Language Teaching and Research] issue 4.

Zou, Yuhua, Ma Guangbin, Ma Shujun, Liu Zhe, and Ma Yujing (2006) 'Zimuci zhixiaodu de diaocha baogao' [A survey eport on the cognitive awareness of letter-words], *Yuyan wenzi yunyong* [Applied Linguistics] issue 2.

Dictionaries:

Cen, Qixiang (1990) '*Hanyu wailaiyu cidian*' [A dictionary of Chinese loanwords], Beijing: Shangwu yinshuguan.

Fang, Linggui (2001) '*Gudian xiqu wailaiyu kaoshi cidian*' [An annotated dictionary of the loanwords in classical dramas of China], Shanghai: Hanyu da cidian chubanshe.

Fukuzawa, Yukichi (trans. and revised) (1860) '増訂華英通語*Zotei kaei tsugo*' [Expanded *Huaying Tongyu*", Edo (Tokyo): Kaido Zohan.

Guoyu ribao chubanbu bianyizu (1980) '*Guoyu ribao wailaiyu cidian*' [A dictionary of loanwords by *Mandarin Daily News*], Taipei: Guoyu ribaoshe.

Hu, Xingzhi (1936) '*Wailaiyu cidian*' [A dictionary of loanwords], Shanghai: Tianma shudian.

Huang, Heqing, Xu Wenkan, and Yao Te Hwai (2001) '*Jin xiandai hanyu xinci ciyuan cidian*' [An etymological glossary of selected modern Chinese words], Shanghai: Hanyu da cidian chubanshe.

Huang, Heqing (2010) '*Jin xiandai ciyuan*' [An etymological dictionary of modern Chinese lexicon], Shanghai: Shanghai cishu chubanshe.

―――― (2020) '*Jin xiandai hanyu ciyuan* (shangxia ce)' [An etymological dictionary of modern Chinese lexicon (2 volumes)], Shanghai: Shanghai cishu chubanshe.

Jin, Zhe, Yao Yongkang, and Chen Xiejun (eds.) (1988) '*Dangdai xin shuyu*' [New contemporary technical terms], Shanghai: Shanghai renmin chubanshe.

Li, Yuming (ed.) (2016) '*Quanqiu huayu da cidian*' [21st Century Contemporary Chinese Dictionary], Beijing: Shangwu yinshuguan.

Liu, Yongquan (2009) '*Hanyu zimuci cidian*' [A dictionary of Chinese alphabetic loanwords], Beijing: Waiyu jiaoxue yu jianjiu chubanshe.

Liu, Zhengtuo, Gao Mingkai, Mai Yongqian, and Shi Youwei (1984) '*Hanyu wailaici cidian*' [A dictionary of loan words and hybrid words in Chinese], Shanghai: Shanghai cishu chubanshe.

Lobscheid, Wilhelm (1897) '*Xin zeng yinghua zidian*' [A Dictionary of the English and Chinese languages, with the Merchant and Mandarin Pronunciation] (revised by Kingsell Fung), Yokohama: Kingsell & Co.

Luo, Zhufeng (ed.) (1993) '*Hanyu da cidian*' [An unabridged Chinese dictionary on historical principles], Beijing: Hanyu da cidian chubanshe.

Morrison, Robert (1815–1823) *A Dictionary of the Chinese Language* (six volumes in three parts), Macao: The Honorable East India Co.'s Press.

Shen, Mengying (2002) '*Shiyong zimuci cidian*' [A practical dictionary of alphabetic letter-words], Shanghai: Hanyu da cidian chubanshe.

Shi, Youwei (ed.) (2019) '*Xinhua wailaici cidian*' [Xinhua dictionary of Chinese loanwords], Beijing: Shangwu yinshuguan.

Suzuki, Yoshiaki, and Wang Wen (2002) '日本語から引ける・中国語の外来語辞典' [A Japanese dictionary of Chinese loanwords], Tokyo: Tokyodo.
Wang, Xiangrong and Ye Lan (1903) '*Xin Erya*' [A dictionary of neologisms], Shanghai: Mingquanshe.
Wang, Jianyi and Wang Yanliang (1995) '*Rihan tongxingci bianyi cidian*' [A differentiating dictionary of Japanese and Chinese homographs], Beijing: Shangwu yinshuguan.
Williams, Samuel Wells (1874) '*Hanying yunfu*' [A Syllabic Dictionary of the Chinese Language], Shanghai: American Presbyterian Mission Press.
Yu, Genyuan (ed.) (1994) '*Xiandai hanyu xinci xinyu cidian*' [A dictionary of new Chinese words and expressions], Beijing: Zhongguo qingnian chubanshe.
Zhang, Yifan and Tsukagoshi Toshihiko (1999) '最新中日外来語辞典' [The Newest Dictionary of Chinese Japanese loanwords], Tokyo: Japan China Communication.
Zhongguo shehui kexue yuan Yuyan yanjiusuo Cidian bianjishi [Lexicographical Section of Institute of Linguistics, Chinese Academy of Social Sciences] (1978; 1996; 2002; 2012) '*Xiandai hanyu cidian*' [The Contemporary Chinese Dictionary] (6th Edition), Beijing: Shangwu yinshuguan.
Zhou, Hongbo (ed.) (2003) '*Xinhua xin ciyu cidian*' [Xinhua dictionary of neologisms], Beijing: Shangwu yinshuguan.
Zou, Jiayan (Benjamin K. Tsou) and You Rujie (2007) '*Ershiyi shiji huayu xin ciyu cidian*' [A 21st century dictionary of Chinese neologisms], Shanghai: Fudan daxue chubanshe.

Index

affix-type semantic marker 139
archetypal loanword 144, 145, 148, 149, 177
autochthonous word 8, 10, 12, 18, 23, 29, 97, 130, 195, 224, 235–236

calque (loan translation) 3, 9, 14
cohesive type 130–131, 134
conceptual loanword 23–24, 30–31, 163–165, 212, 217–218, 222
cultural conflict 117–124
cultural integration 4, 49–50, 107–117

descriptive loaning 9–10, 216
discrete word formation 130–131, 134

graphic loaning 2, 16, 67–68, 140–143
graphic loanword 16–18, 67–68, 72–74
graphic remolding for semantic association 116–117
graphic transcription 200–201
guyouci 固有词 12

homophonic proximity 113, 137–138
humorous phonemic loaning 113–114, 137–138
hybrid (word) 1, 14–15, 141–142

imitation loanword 128–131
indigenous word 2–3, 12, 23, 27, 39, 110, 121–122, 224

Japan-made Chinese word 14–15, 18, 24, 98–101, 128, 142, 158, 170–180
jieci 借词 1, 9–10, 13, 15–16, 29
jieruyu 借入语 9, 29
jieyongyu 借用语 9, 13, 29
jieyu 借语 9–10

jieyuci 借语词 9–10
Kyowa-go (Xieheyu) 184–185

linguistic and cultural dual nature 125–128
linguistic and cultural integration 107–117
linguistic mixture (language mixing) 182–184
loanword of Japanese origin 5, 98–101, 128, 142, 158, 170–180

meta-culture 107, 134

phonemic loaning 2, 137–140
phonemic loanword 20, 23, 91–98, 120, 180
phonetic approximation with semantic cues 125, 191
phonetic readjustment 201
phonetic-cum-semantic approximation 137–138, 161
Pidgin English 180–184
post-modifier semantic marker 139
pre-modifier semantic marker 139
pseudo-loanword 147

quasi-affix 97–98, 129–130
quasi-autochthonous 12, 177
quasi-indigenous Chinese word 3
quasi-indigenous word 18
quasi-loanword 2–3, 16–18, 22, 101, 177, 217

return loan(word) 5, 29, 67, 89, 176

semantic loaning 2, 16, 74, 113
semantic marker 1–2, 10, 14, 65, 114, 139, 140, 196

structural borrowing 27
substrate (loan)word 3–4, 16, 39–40, 48–50, 61–62, 242
supplement-type semantic marker 140

variant 31, 132, 187–189, 204–205

waiguoyu 外国语 7, 13, 29
wailaici 外来词 1, 8–10, 14–17, 24, 29–30
wailaiyu 外来语 8–12, 14–16, 31
waiyuanci 外源词 9
wasei kango 和製漢語 99, 143

word of foreign influence 25, 31
word with borrowed morpheme(s) 3

xieyin 谐音 113, 137–138
xingsheng 形声 116, 141

Yangjingbang (*Yangkingpang*) 洋泾浜 180–182
yici 译词 7
yiming 译名 7, 29
yiyu 译语 7

zimuci 字母词 2, 16–22, 101–104, 140
ziyuanci 自源词 12